D1522290

THE ORIGINS
OF THE
PLATONIC ACADEMY
OF FLORENCE

THE
ORIGINS
OF THE
PLATONIC
ACADEMY OF
FLORENCE

ARTHUR FIELD

PRINCETON UNIVERSITY
PRESS
Princeton, New Jersey

COPYRIGHT © 1988 BY PRINCETON UNIVERSITY PRESS
PUBLISHED BY PRINCETON UNIVERSITY PRESS,
41 WILLIAM STREET,
PRINCETON, NEW JERSEY 08540
IN THE UNITED KINGDOM:
PRINCETON UNIVERSITY PRESS,
GUILDFORD, SURREY

LIBRARY OF CONGRESS
CATALOGING-IN-PUBLICATION DATA
FIELD, ARTHUR M., 1948–
THE ORIGINS OF THE PLATONIC ACADEMY OF FLORENCE
BY ARTHUR FIELD.
P. CM.
BIBLIOGRAPHY: P.
INCLUDES INDEXES.
ISBN 0-691-05533-5 (ALK. PAPER)
1. ACCADEMIA PLATONICA (FLORENCE, ITALY)
2. FLORENCE (ITALY)—INTELLECTUAL LIFE.
3. FLORENCE (ITALY)—HISTORY—1421–1737.
I. TITLE.
DG735.6.F47 1988
945'.5105—DC19   88-9952

THIS BOOK HAS BEEN COMPOSED IN GALLIARD

CLOTHBOUND EDITIONS
OF PRINCETON UNIVERSITY PRESS BOOKS
ARE PRINTED ON ACID-FREE PAPER,
AND BINDING MATERIALS ARE CHOSEN
FOR STRENGTH AND DURABILITY.
PAPERBACKS, ALTHOUGH SATISFACTORY
FOR PERSONAL COLLECTIONS,
ARE NOT USUALLY SUITABLE
FOR LIBRARY REBINDING

PRINTED IN THE UNITED STATES OF AMERICA
BY PRINCETON UNIVERSITY PRESS,
PRINCETON, NEW JERSEY

TO RUTH AND ART

CONTENTS

PREFACE

FOR the modern world the "problem of the Renaissance" is largely a problem of genius. Even if we strain our norms of relativism to where we can sniff at the humanists and sneer at the philosophers, we still have to move with leaden feet through the several great rooms of the galleries; or if we race through these rooms, it is only because we know them too well, want to study the forgotten pieces, or feel more comfortable around intellects closer to our own. Even those economic and social historians who in their studies have ignored the intellectual and artistic worlds altogether have been moved, for the most part, not simply by the richness of the archives but by the knowledge that "genius" cannot arise by accident.

Textbooks still refer to the period of Lorenzo de' Medici as the "flowering of the Renaissance." If the label is impressionistic, it is at least based on impressions gained by works all can see and most can appreciate, the great works of art and literature. Students of poetry and the fine arts have by and large looked kindly on the Lorenzo period. Students of philosophy and science have found there the first expressions of those systems that truly "belong" to the Renaissance—that is, the Neoplatonic and Hermetic philosophies. Historians, on the other hand, have not been especially generous toward Medicean Florence. Here we do not have to read far to discover what went wrong: With the Medici ascendancy over Florence, the heroic individuality of Petrarch, the civic ideals of Leonardo Bruni, the "activist" universality of Leon Battista Alberti were pushed aside as the "Medici intellectuals" began to speculate on the eternal verities in the villa and court.

If I look on the philosophical humanists more positively than is the current fashion, I should like to think that my approach is not based on idolatry, simply, but on the belief that these humanists served an important intellectual function for an emerging political and social class, a class that held power, to be sure, but was ideologically unsophisticated. In this study I thus attempt to answer the old charge, found so often in the secondary literature, that the philosophical humanists of the Platonic Academy were creating an isolated, elite, villa- or court-centered culture, that these intellectuals were esoteric philosophers or "schoolmen" whose "external world" was measured by Medici patronage.

These humanists did indeed educate many Florentine laymen into a speculative philosophical culture. Their success in this can be seen in contemporary testimony from the bounds of our period. At the time of the Peace of Lodi of 1454 no one in Florence, it was said, knew any philosophy except some ethics. A decade later Donato Acciaiuoli would boast that all Florentines, it seemed, had been brought up in the Academy. And Cristoforo Landino, lecturing in Italian on Petrarch (ca. 1465), would describe for the Florentines the political and social dangers of having a citizenry that was philosophically illiterate.

In this book I attempt to look afresh at the role of humanist intellectuals in Florence during the first decade after the Peace of Lodi of 1454, a period that ends with the founding of the Platonic Academy and the Medici patronage of Marsilio Ficino in 1462 and 1463. Many years ago I proposed a study of the early Platonic Academy as a dissertation topic, and I was told by a prominent Renaissance historian that I would be wiser to choose a subject less thoroughly studied. As I began to look at the texts, however, I started to have an opposite concern: I wondered how many of the sources for the early philosophical renaissance had even been *read* by modern scholars. I do not see how any reading of the notebooks of John Argyropoulos's lectures on Aristotle can yield the conclusion, repeated so often in the secondary literature, that he was actually a Platonist (or Plotinian) and not an Aristotelian, or how any reading, even a superficial one, of Donato Acciaiuoli's commentaries on Aristotle can support the widely held hypothesis that he was repelled by Platonic metaphysics. There have been a few studies of Marsilio Ficino's teacher of Aristotle, Niccolò Tignosi; but none has yet brought to light the one interesting autobiographical statement appearing in *all three* of his commentaries on Aristotle, that he had been a student of Paul of Venice. That Cristoforo Landino began to take a philosophical approach toward the Latin poets only from the Lorenzo period, that is, from the 1470s, appears in almost every detailed study of the literature of the Academy; but new manuscripts of his early lectures indicate that he was a Platonic allegorizer certainly in the 1460s, and probably even earlier.

To others this work owes much. I feel privileged to have studied under Frederick Krantz (now at Concordia University, Montreal) and Hanna H. Gray and Karl J. Weintraub (University of Chicago). For my method and some fundamental ideas I owe them a great deal. Paul Oskar Kristeller has been bountiful, as is his custom, with his time and advice; he also criticized carefully an earlier form of Chapters IV–IX. Ralph G. Williams gave me many good suggestions about the same chapters, and Charles Trinkaus scrutinized them also. Thomas N. Tentler kindly read and criticized an earlier form of Chapter II. Chapter IV owes much to anonymous reviewers for *History of Universities* (University of London), and Chapter V to John Monfasani. James Hankins read the manuscript as a whole and provided a detailed and extremely useful critique. My colleague Anthony Grafton went over the text in page proofs and rescued it and me from several dozen small errors and more than a few major ones. The staffs of many libraries have been generous and helpful. I mention in particular those of three Florentine libraries: the Archivio di Stato, Biblioteca Medicea Laurenziana, and Biblioteca Nazionale Centrale. This study, finally, would not have been possible without generous fellowships from the American Academy in Rome, the American Council of Learned Societies, the Fulbright Commission, and the Harvard University Center for Italian Renaissance Studies (Villa I Tatti).

NOTE ON THE TEXT

I N the main text and the notes, all dates, unless otherwise indicated, are in the modern style.

The letters of Poggio Bracciolini will be cited by book and letter number, followed by the volume and page number of T. Tonelli's edition (Florence 1832) in parentheses. All are reprinted in Poggio's *Opera omnia*, ed. R. Fubini, vol. 3 (Turin, 1963). The letters I cite are not yet covered in the new edition being prepared by Helene Harth.

In Latin quotations, I often list two sources together, either two manuscripts or a manuscript and an edition, and these are sometimes listed consecutively, divided by a semicolon and then followed by a colon and then the Latin. In such cases I choose what I consider to be the better readings and do not always indicate variants. When the second source, whether a manuscript or an edition, is preceded by "cf." it means that I am following the first, but the second includes all or part of the corresponding passage. Where "cf." is followed by a printed edition, the reader should not assume that I consider the edition defective.

Several of the humanist works cited have good English translations. Where I indicate that I have used but altered a translation, in nearly every instance the adaptation has been made solely to make the terms and style conform to those I use elsewhere.

Unless otherwise indicated, text divisions and translations from the classics are taken from the Loeb editions.

For manuscript references, the shortened shelf-mark citations may be found in the list of abbreviations. In citations such as "fol. 47," the *recto* of the leaf is to be assumed.

ABBREVIATIONS

Ambros.: manuscript, Milan, Biblioteca Ambrosiana, main collection.

Casanatense: manuscript, Rome, Biblioteca Casanatense, main collection.

Cons. e Prat.: manuscript volume, Florence, Archivio di Stato, Repubblica, Consulte e Pratiche.

DBI: *Dizionario biografico degli italiani*. Rome, 1960–.

Ep.: Epistula.

Gino Capponi: manuscript, Florence, Biblioteca Nazionale Centrale, fondo Gino Capponi.

GW: *Gesamtkatalog der Wiegendrucke*. Leipzig, 1925–.

Laur.: manuscript, Florence, Biblioteca Medicea Laurenziana, main collection (or minor fondo if not followed directly by a number).

Magl.: manuscript, Florence, Biblioteca Nazionale Centrale, fondo Magliabechiano.

MAP: filza or manuscript volume, Florence, Archivio di Stato, Archivio Mediceo avanti il Principato.

Monte Comune: manuscript volume, Florence, Archivio di Stato, Monte Comune.

Naz.: manuscript, Florence, Biblioteca Nazionale Centrale, fondo Nazionale or main collection.

Not. Antec.: manuscript volume, Florence, Archivio di Stato, Notarile Antecosimiano.

Ricc.: manuscript, Florence, Biblioteca Riccardiana, main collection.

Vat.: manuscript, Vatican City, Biblioteca Apostolica Vaticana (with fondo defined by further abbreviation after "Vat.").

PART ONE

THE PHILOSOPHICAL
RENAISSANCE
AND THE ROLE
OF INTELLECTUALS

I

INTRODUCTION

IN 1462 or 1463 the aged Cosimo de' Medici (1389–1464) gave to Marsilio Ficino, the son of his physician, both the annual profits from a farm near the Medici villa at Careggi and a Greek text of Plato.[1] Ficino was supposed to translate the Platonic dialogues and thereby make them available for the first time to a Latin audience. Ficino immediately began to draft translations, and in his lectures, commentaries, treatises, and letters, he explained Plato to the Florentine public. A circle of acquaintances interested in these studies called itself the Academy.

According to Ficino, late in life Cosimo began to question commonly accepted worldly values, those that had helped make him the wealthiest and most powerful figure in contemporary Florence.[2] Spiritually troubled and in poor health, he looked to Ficino's words and music for comfort. Come to me quickly, he wrote Ficino, and explain to me Plato's *On the Highest Good* (that is, the *Philebus*)—and do not forget to bring your Orphic lyre.[3] Ficino was delayed in coming and so outlined, in

1. The traditional date for the Academy's founding is 1462, when Cosimo is said to have endowed Ficino with a villa at Careggi, which then became the site of the Platonic Academy. But the situation is complex: see Chapter VII, n. 96, below.

2. For Cosimo's "introspective" phase, see Vespasiano da Bisticci, *Le vite*, ed. A. Greco (Florence, 1970–1976), II, 210; Bartolomeo Scala, *Dialogus de consolatione* (Laur. 54, 10, fols. 104–22v); and C. S. Gutkind, *Cosimo de' Medici, Pater Patriae, 1389–1464* (Oxford, 1938), pp. 215–16, 242ff.

3. In Ficino's collected letters, in *Opera omnia* (Basel, 1576; rept. Turin, 1959), p. 608; cf. *The Letters of Marsilio Ficino*, trans. Language Dept., School of Economic Science, London (London, 1975–81), I, 32: "Contuli heri me in agrum Charegium, non agri, sed animi colendi gratia. Veni ad nos Marsili quamprimum. Fer tecum Platonis in nostri librum De summo bono, quem te isthic arbitror iam e Graeca lingua in Latinum, ut

3

writing, the substance of Plato's dialogue: great possessions and great
virtues are useless, they can even be harmful, if they are not accompanied by wisdom.[4] Later that year, as Cosimo lay dying, Ficino explained another Platonic work, the *Axiochus*, or *On Death*. Through this
work, Ficino wrote just after Cosimo's death, "Cosimo began to deplore
the misery of this life, and he so inveighed against the errors of mortals
that he called death a gain, and, since he aspired already to celestial be-
atitude, he said acutely and elegantly many things in contempt of life."[5]

Aristotle as well as Plato stimulated the aged Cosimo. Through Cosimo's efforts and especially those of his son, Piero, the Byzantine philosopher John Argyropoulos had been hired in the mid–1450s to teach
Aristotle at the University of Florence. Cosimo provided Argyropoulos
with a house near his own in Florence and met now and then with the
Byzantine and his circle.[6] One of Argyropoulos's students, Donato Acciaiuoli, took his careful notes from lectures on the *Nicomachean Ethics*,
made some substantive changes, gave them literary polish, and turned
them into his own commentary. As he finished each fascicle, in 1463 or
1464, he sent a copy to Cosimo, at the latter's request, who was said to
have listened eagerly as his secretary, Bartolomeo Scala, read the sections to him.[7]

Cosimo was only one among a great number of businessmen, politicians, humanists, poets, lawyers, students, and dilettantes who turned,
rather abruptly, to Platonic and other philosophical studies in the first
decade after the Peace of Lodi of 1454. The precepts of classical moral
philosophy, to be sure, had always enjoyed wide currency in Renaissance Florence, and the humanists had incorporated some Aristotle,
Cicero, and Seneca into their program of studies. In the first half of the
Quattrocento, moreover, Leonardo Bruni and others translated some
Plato.[8] But after the Peace of Lodi philosophical studies intensified, and,

---

promiseras, transtulisse. Nihil enim ardentius cupio quam quae via commodius ad felicitatem ducat cognoscere. Vale, et veni non absque Orphica lyra." As A. Della Torre
(*Storia dell'Accademia platonica di Firenze* [1902; rept. Turin, 1968], p. 559n.) and others
have noted, the letter was surely composed or rewritten by Ficino himself.

4.   *Opera omnia*, p. 608.

5.   Preface to his translation, to Piero de' Medici, in *Opera omnia*, p. 1965: "Die . . . vi-
gesima antequam corporis vinculis purus eius spiritus solveretur, sole iam occidente coe-
pit huius vitae miseriam deplorare, atque ita in errores mortalium invehi ut lucrum
quoddam diceret esse mortem, ubi permulta et acute et copiose de huius vitae con-
temptu disseruit, utpote qui iam ad supernam beatitudinem adspiraret."

6.   G. Cammelli, *Giovanni Argiropulo* (Florence, 1941), p. 120. For the Medici role in the
appointment of Argyropoulos, see Chapter IV, below.

7.   See Chapter VIII, n. 24, below.

8.   See the survey by E. Garin, "Ricerche sulle traduzioni di Platone nella prima metà

within nonprofessional circles, their focus shifted from an earlier eclectic use and an emphasis on ethics toward an attempt to comprehend systematically moral, natural, and metaphysical philosophy. Contemporaries noted the suddenness of the shift. Alamanno Rinuccini would write that before his generation (that is, before the 1450s), no one seeking a general education would do more than take a "little sip" from the vessel of philosophy: all thought they had done more than enough if they knew some ethics. Doctors and theologians alone, he argued, took up natural philosophy and metaphysics.[9] Also, in a short treatise on education written for his son, Rinuccini explained that to be an educated Florentine one *now* had to move beyond ethics to natural and speculative philosophy.[10] Rinuccini's friend Donato Acciaiuoli gives similar testimony. At the time of the Peace of Lodi, Acciaiuoli complained that learning in even the liberal arts seemed to be dead in Florence. Just one decade later he would write that the study of letters "never before so flourished in Florence" and that "many are so trained in the Aristotelian and Platonic teachings that they seem to have been brought up in the Academy."[11]

That a dramatic expansion in Florentine humanist culture took place after the Peace of Lodi cannot be doubted, and any endeavor at trotting out examples of an earlier interest in speculative philosophy will not cancel this fact. As is apparent even from the citations above, the humanists themselves were aware that major intellectual changes were taking place.

In this study my object is to describe, as carefully as possible, this birth of a philosophical culture in Renaissance Florence; more ambitiously, I intend to offer hypotheses concerning the causes and origins of the Neoplatonic movement. I shall be analyzing in particular what may be called a new ideology. To begin, and to provide an outline of sorts for the rest of this study, I will take up one after another some

---

del sec. XV," in *Medioevo e Rinascimento: Studi in onore di Bruno Nardi* (Florence, 1955), I, 339–74.

9. Letter to Roberto Salviati, 1489, in *Lettere ed orazioni*, ed. V. R. Giustiniani (Florence, 1953), pp. 188–89.

10. Dated 1474, ibid., p. 97.

11. Letter (composed for Vespasiano da Bisticci) to Alfonso de Palencia, 24 Sept. 1463, ed. in F. Fossi, *Monumenta ad Alamanni Rinuccini vitam contexendam* (Florence, 1791), pp. 61–62: "Primum litterarum studia numquam magis in hac urbe viguerunt, multique hic adolescentes, multique iuvenes reperiuntur eruditi litteris graecis atque latinis, plerique etiam ita Aristotelicis Platonicisque disciplinis instructi, ut in Academia educati videantur." For the text, see Chapter V, n. 1, below. For Acciaiuoli's earlier, negative assessment of learning in Florence, see Chapter IV, below.

currently held hypotheses about the beginnings of Florentine Platonism.

Textbooks, especially, account for the revival of Plato with the fall of Constantinople. When the Turks took Constantinople in 1453, many Greek scholars fled to the Latin West, and they took their manuscripts and ideas with them. Ficino would write that the "spirit of Plato," dead in the Latin West since antiquity, had dwelt in Byzantium until his own time, when it "flew to Italy."[12] For the "Byzantine hypothesis" the role of John Argyropoulos is crucial. He came to Florence in the summer of 1454, was offered a job at the University of Florence teaching Greek language, literature, and philosophy in 1455, and finally accepted a university appointment in early 1457. Eugenio Garin has argued that Argyropoulos was a thorough Platonist: he wove Platonic doctrines into his lectures on Aristotle, lectured on Platonic texts privately, and would have lectured on Plato publicly had university rules permitted it.[13] According to Garin, Argyropoulos was the real founder of Florentine Neoplatonism, and Marsilio Ficino and his followers in bad faith attempted to claim for themselves the credit for a movement that was already well underway when they began their philosophizing. As they overemphasized their own roles, so too they sought to praise their patrons, the Medici, as the true founders of the Academy.[14]

Garin's hypotheses have a paradoxical, or, perhaps we should say, an ambiguous edge, for although he gives great credit to Argyropoulos as the founder of Florentine Platonism, he yet attempts to divorce Argyropoulos and his followers from the speculative and metaphysical interests of the Ficino group. In fact, for Garin, Argyropoulos and those of his circle are anti-Medicean civic humanists: they are committed to the study of moral philosophy and the "active" study of rhetoric, and they disdain the metaphysical speculation characteristic of Ficino and his Academy.[15]

Many of those who became part of the Platonic Academy or were influenced by it got their first introduction to speculative philosophy through the lectures of John Argyropoulos. The Byzantine's role is important, though I shall argue that Garin exaggerates its importance and misunderstands the force of Argyropoulos's teaching. But since Garin's

12. See below, Chapter V, n. 3.

13. For Garin's arguments, see the sources cited below, Chapter V, nn. 5 and 6.

14. See the sources cited below, Chapter V, n. 8.

15. See especially Garin's summary in his "Donato Acciaiuoli cittadino fiorentino," in his *Medioevo e Rinascimento*, 4th ed. (Bari, 1973), pp. 202–3.

theses are both complex and widely accepted, I shall attempt, in later chapters, to take them up in some detail.

A safer explanation for the philosophical revival, which appears now and then in the secondary literature, is simply that humanist culture itself had become ripe for Platonic influence, that Platonism, in other words, was "due." By the mid-Quattrocento, humanists were learning Greek earlier and better, a large number of classical and Christian Greek works had been translated, and earlier favorites among Latin texts had now been mastered. Rhetorical and other prose texts, for instance, continued to be studied, but they no longer proved a challenge to the humanist teacher's genius—more difficult texts in Latin poetry were now preferred by the humanist lecturer.[16] Much of the humanist movement seems to have had an inner momentum, and fashions changed as familiar texts were assimilated and new ones approached. The revival of Greek studies in the Latin West was an Italian-wide phenomenon, and we can be reasonably certain that if Florence had gone into a deep sleep after the Peace of Lodi, other cities and other cultures would have had their Platonic translations and commentaries. Since late antiquity, moreover, many educated Christians believed that Platonism was the ancient philosophy most in harmony with their revealed religion. In its form developed by Marsilio Ficino, Neoplatonism permitted Florentines and others to study and enjoy pagan philosophy without religious fears. That Platonism was "due" is correct, and the observation has proved useful in refuting strained theorems of causality.[17] But even those who have presented this hypothesis, as valid as it is, have for the most part recognized that the new texts of Plato contributed little to the substance of the new ideas. Platonism through Ficino had been thriving some twenty-five to thirty years before the first complete Latin translation of Plato's dialogues saw the light of day (the translation was published in 1482 and printed in 1484).[18] The form of the Platonic revival, especially in the earlier period, depended far less on individual scholarly critiques of the Platonic texts than on the types of scholastic Platonizing

16.   For educational fashion, see the general remarks of A. Grafton, *Joseph Scaliger: A Study in the History of Classical Scholarship*, vol. 1 (Oxford, 1983), p. 15, and now Grafton and L. Jardine, *From Humanism to the Humanities: Education and the Liberal Arts in Fifteenth- and Sixteenth-Century Europe* (Cambridge, Mass., 1986), pp. 83ff.

17.   P. O. Kristeller, "The Platonic Academy of Florence," now in his *Renaissance Thought and the Arts* (Princeton, 1980), pp. 89–90.

18.   P. O. Kristeller, "The First Printed Edition of Plato's Works and the Date of Its Publication (1484)," in *Science and History: Studies in Honor of Edward Rosen*, Studia Copernicana, 16 (Wrocław, 1978), pp. 25–35.

carried out both in the university and in monastic circles, cultures in which Ficino himself was nurtured.

While usually not neglecting the Byzantine influence, a theory that is chronologically ideal, and while sometimes acknowledging that Platonism was "due," historians have tended to seize on one central hypothesis to explain the revival of Plato. The Medici took the humanists outside the city and placed them in villas, where these intellectuals could reflect on the eternal verities with a closed circle of special associates. With the transformation of Florence from a republic to a princely state, the thesis goes, humanism underwent a transformation from a civic-humanist or worldly culture to a Platonic or courtly one.[19]

Rightly or wrongly, the historical portrayal of the Medici role in the transformation of Florentine culture is largely a reflection of a Platonic world realized in the golden age of Lorenzo the Magnificent (first citizen of Florence from 1469 to 1492). During the early Lorenzo period Ficino's major philosophical works were being published, including his first commentaries on Plato (1469) and the *Theologia Platonica* (1474).[20] Here too Cristoforo Landino, in his *Disputationes Camaldulenses* of the early 1470s, described a philosophical discussion at the convent of Camaldoli, where Leon Battista Alberti donned a Platonic robe and expounded on the virtues of the contemplative life, the Platonic theory of the highest good, and the allegorical journeys of Aeneas toward wisdom.[21] And here also the young ruler of Florence, Lorenzo de' Medici, wrote Platonic poetry and fulfilled each of Plato's alternative recipes for a happy republic—one where philosophers rule or rulers philosophize.[22]

But if we wish to examine the Medici as agents of the intellectual changes, we shall need to look at the period some ten to fifteen years before Lorenzo came to power. With new discoveries and a new appreciation of Ficino's early works, and new evidence relating to Landino's early career, we now know that at the founding of the Platonic Academy by Cosimo in 1462 or 1463 many of Marsilio Ficino's central ideas were already well developed, and we can be reasonably certain also that Cris-

---

19. The thesis has been forcefully presented by E. Garin in several publications: see especially "I cancellieri umanisti della repubblica fiorentina da Coluccio Salutati a Bartolomeo Scala," in his *La cultura filosofica del Rinascimento italiano* (Florence, 1961), pp. 3–27; *L'Umanesimo italiano*, 8th ed. (Bari, 1975), pp. 94ff.; and "Donato Acciaiuoli cittadino," pp. 199–267.

20. The commentaries were on the *Philebus* and the *Symposium*: for editions, see Chapter II, n. 21, and Chapter VII, n. 80, below.

21. Ed. P. Lohe (Florence, 1980).

22. A. Buck, *Der Platonismus in den Dichtungen Lorenzo de' Medicis* (Berlin, 1936); P. O. Kristeller, "Lorenzo de' Medici platonico," in his *Studies in Renaissance Thought and Letters* (1956; rept. Rome, 1969), pp. 213–19.

toforo Landino had for several years been giving philosophical, Platonizing lectures on both Latin poets and Dante.[23]

Since Platonism as a movement really began to take off during the last decade of the life of Cosimo de' Medici (d. 1464), new questions must necessarily arise regarding the Medici role. It is far easier to speculate on a Medicean philosophical "court" during the 1470s and 1480s, where we can picture Lorenzo de' Medici reciting his Platonic verse to his courtiers and protégés. It is much more difficult to imagine a Cosimo intellectually suited to shape a philosophical movement or politically able or willing to do the same. What must be explored also is whether the ideology itself of Neoplatonism called for political passivity under princely rule, for the literal withdrawal of intellectuals and others from the active political and social life to a world of contemplative and speculative isolation.

But let us set aside, for now, this question of Platonic ideology, as we confront one startling fact regarding the timing of the rebirth of speculative philosophical studies in Florence. In the 1450s Florence and the Medici were in no position whatsoever to create any sort of villa-centered culture of isolated intellectuals enjoying the *Pax Medicea*. Rather, the first great burst in philosophical studies took place at a time of Medici party collapse, when Florence seemed to be characterized not by the Medici peace but by the *tumultus popularis*. This striking phenomenon, almost universally overlooked in intellectual histories of the period, forces us both to reexamine the entire question of the relation of the intellectuals to the Medici party and to reconsider the social function and meaning of the Neoplatonic movement itself.

23.   See below, Chapters VII and IX.

II

HUMANIST INTELLECTUALS
AND THE
MEDICI PARTY

I N the Age of Lorenzo one may happily and readily find the philosophical expressions and intellectual settings that invite hypotheses
about a new speculative culture. Set now in the villa, now in the
court, this fashionable Neoplatonism honored its new Florentine
prince. Whether such a depiction of the Golden Age of Lorenzo is true
or false is not our subject here. In this chapter, instead, we shall look at
the intellectuals and the Medici rather more broadly; at the same time
we shall focus on that period when Florentine Neoplatonism first flourished, the decade from the Peace of Lodi (1454) to the death of Cosimo
de' Medici (1464). We shall begin with Cosimo, the founder and first
patron of the Academy, and look first at some of the limits of his personal ability to shape the philosophical renaissance. We shall then turn
to Cosimo's party.

While Lorenzo de' Medici was a humanistic and philosophical poet,
Cosimo's learning came from the book of life.[1] He did, of course, ini-

---

1. I have seen no study of Cosimo's level of literacy. Vespasiano da Bisticci remarked
on his "bonissima peritia delle lettere latine" (*Vite*, II, 168, cf. 169), but Vespasiano was
not especially learned himself, and, like the modern scholar with his curriculum vitae, his
heroes often acquire one more language than they actually have. Much of the evidence
for Cosimo's learning is late and seems forced. In a preface to Cosimo of December 1463,
Alamanno Rinuccini recalled a meeting where Cosimo quoted from Cicero's *Dream of
Scipio* as if he were reading it (*Lettere ed orazioni*, p. 62); and Bartolomeo Scala, in January 1464, described for Lorenzo de' Medici Cosimo's wide learning in all areas of the
classics (see A. M. Brown, "The Humanist Portrait of Cosimo de' Medici, Pater Patriae," *Journal of the Warburg and Courtauld Institutes* 24 [1961], 199–200). But the casual
remark of Niccolò Machiavelli, that Cosimo was "without learning, . . . but filled with a
natural prudence" (see below, p. 14), is probably closer to the mark. For a recent, positive assessment of Cosimo's intellectual role in the philosophical renaissance, see

tially endow the Academy and hence had a major role in the philosophical renaissance. But it is doubtful that Cosimo could have recognized subtle intellectual changes beyond their dimmest outlines, and he certainly could not have determined formally in any thinker their particular direction. He may have had something of a humanist education under Roberto de' Rossi, but this is not certain, and such training left no clear mark.[2] He wrote little or nothing in Latin (nor, indeed, anything of literary or philosophical note even in Italian). His hand is found in the margin of no classical text, and the letters he himself composed, probably all in Italian, are bare of classical references.[3] Cosimo evidently claimed that he had read all "thirty-seven" books of Gregory the Great's *Moralia* in "only" six months, and Vespasiano da Bisticci recorded this as a illustration of Cosimo's great learning.[4] The work is not short, and it would have taken a good scholar more than a week, I suppose, to get through it. Cosimo had a copy of it in his study: whether he was plodding through the original or an Italian translation is not known.[5] His private library also contained much Italian popular and devotional literature. The classical authors represented are for the most part trophies of his book hunting or, perhaps, relics from his earlier studies under Rossi.[6] Cosimo was an exceptionally intelligent businessman and political craftsman. He was clever and had a remarkably shrewd sense of timing. Humanists called him wise, but they really meant he was astute—and that he supported the humanities. Had there been one Platonic idea in Cosimo's brain we can be sure the humanists would have seized on it.[7]

But Cosimo learned from the humanists how to be decorously un-

---

A. M. Brown, "Platonism in Fifteenth-Century Florence and Its Contribution to Early Modern Political Thought," *Journal of Modern History* 58 (1986), 383–413 at 389ff.

2.   Vespasiano, *Vite*, II, 168; Gutkind, *Cosimo*, pp. 4–5, 207n.

3.   Some of the letters are edited in A. Fabroni, *Magni Cosmi Medicei vita*, vol. 2 (Pisa, 1788).

4.   Vespasiano, *Vite*, II, 195.

5.   F. Pintor, "Per la storia della libreria medicea nel Rinascimento," *Italia medioevale e umanistica* 3 (1960), 198 ("Morali di San Ghirigoro in III volumi lettera antica").

6.   See the list of books, ibid., pp. 197–99. For a good summary description of the contents, see also Gutkind, *Cosimo*, p. 227.

7.   To be sure, humanists and philosophers did argue that Cosimo's mind was *objectively* Platonic and that he himself fulfilled a Platonic ideal: see especially Niccolò Tignosi's description, pp. 150–52, below. Also, Cosimo seems to have had some considered appreciation of the notion that the artist as a creator gave form through his activity to higher ideals resting in his brain (see Gutkind, *Cosimo*, p. 234): some might call this Platonic rather than Aristotelian or even commonsense, and the Platonists certainly used the image often. Alison Brown has recently attempted to show that Cosimo was attracted to some Platonic opinions: "Platonism in Fifteenth-Century Florence," esp. pp. 389ff.

learned. He used to call Franco Sacchetti the "kidney," since Sacchetti
had no learning but liked to have intellectuals around him, the kidney
being a lean organ surrounded by fat.[8] Then and now, Cosimo's wisdom
appears attractive. He spoke with aphorisms and disjunctive statements,
and he won fame as a careful spectator of the human condition.[9] Not
long after the Medici palace on the Via Larga was finished, his most
promising son, Giovanni, died, and Cosimo remarked, "This is too big
a house for so small a family."[10] We can imagine an analogous but light-
hearted statement from Cosimo when the priest Lorenzo Pisano wanted
to dedicate to Cosimo his commentary on the *Song of Songs*. With the
commentary still unfinished after eighteen books, Lorenzo seems to
have approached Cosimo as a patron. "This is too long a commentary
for so short a work!"—what else could have evoked Ficino's jocular letter to Cosimo?

> Lorenzo Pisano, the priest, is expounding for you Solomon's
> *Song of Songs*. He has so far written eighteen books, if I remember
> aright, to explain one small book. If you are surprised, Cosimo,
> that Lorenzo wrote so lengthily when Solomon was so brief, I
> reply that Lorenzo was obliged to be lengthy because Solomon
> was so brief. The more intricate the knot which Solomon tied, the
> more devices were necessary to unravel it.
> . . . But farewell, lest I become prolix myself while excusing pro-
> lixity.[11]

What was Cosimo's contribution to the new learning? Ficino stated
that Cosimo was inspired by speeches of Gemistus Pletho to found the
Platonic Academy. Here we have no other literary evidence and must
speak of possibilities.[12] The Byzantines at the Council of Florence had
made a striking impression on the Florentines. Vespasiano da Bisticci
remarked that the Greeks were dressed in the same "serious and digni-

8.   Angelo Poliziano, *Detti piacevoli*, ed. T. Zanato (Rome, 1983), p. 46, no. 16; Poliziano, *Tagebuch*, ed. A. Wesselski (Jena, 1929), p. 12, no. 16. Zanato's edition is based on
more manuscripts and is more complete; but the older edition has copious notes—*and*
an index. That these sayings and witticisms are to be attributed to Politian is questionable.

9.   Gutkind, *Cosimo*, p. 240.

10.   Niccolò Machiavelli, *History of Florence*, VII, 6, in *The Chief Works and Others*, trans.
A. Gilbert, vol. 3 (Durham, N.C., 1965), p. 1345.

11.   *Letters*, I, 48–49 (trans. altered very slightly); cf. *Opera omnia*, p. 615.

12.   The useful recent study by C. M. Woodhouse, *George Gemistos Plethon, the Last of
the Hellenes* (Oxford, 1986), contains no new information linking Pletho, Cosimo, and
the young Ficino.

fied" way that they had been for some "fifteen hundred" years or more![13] With their full beards the Greeks physically resembled the Magi in paintings of the Adoration, and vice versa: this gave them an aura of wisdom and mystery even before they spoke.[14] The only idea of Pletho yet discovered that may have influenced the early development of Florentine Platonism is the notion of the unity of ancient philosophical systems. With Cosimo's commonsense approach toward learning and his cleverness in penetrating human nature, it is not wholly implausible that the theory that Plato and his student Aristotle were not as different as the schoolmen claimed had its appeal. Cosimo, too, like many merchant-humanists such as Alberti, Manetti, and Palmieri, seems to have been genuinely interested in bringing teachings reserved for professionals into the public forum. He, after all, created Florence's first public library, and he underwrote the book-hunting efforts of such figures as Poggio Bracciolini and Niccolò Niccoli.[15] Cosimo could have been moved to found the Academy simply by a sense of duty. Pletho was a respected and renowned Platonist, Platonism was the fairest flower of ancient Greek philosophy, enjoying a special affinity with Christianity, and Florence was the new Athens. It was probably a combination of historical vision as to Florence's role in Western culture and pride with regard to his role as *primus inter pares* that led Cosimo to support the revival of the Platonic Academy. Not dissimilar was his earlier patronage of Ambrogio Traversari's Latin translations of pseudo-Dionysius and the Greek Church Fathers.[16]

As to Cosimo's interactions with the world of ideas, little can be said. He was certainly involved in learned discussions, and the roles given him in humanist dialogues do not appear wholly unnatural. In his introduction to his collection of eulogies of Cosimo, the *Collectiones Cosmianae*, Bartolomeo Scala claimed that Cosimo was well read in ancient philosophy.[17] But Scala, as editor of the pieces, faced the wretched requirement of having to surpass his contemporaries in their praise, and his arguments appear strained indeed. Another philosophical humanist

13. See below, Chapter V, n. 10.

14. See below, Chapter V, nn. 10, 12.

15. B. L. Ullman and P. A. Stadter, *The Public Library of Renaissance Florence: Niccolò Niccoli, Cosimo de' Medici and the Library of San Marco* (Padua, 1972), pp. 3–27; R. Sabbadini, *Le scoperte dei codici latini e greci ne' secoli XIV and XV* (1905; rept. Florence, 1967, with the author's additions and corrections ed. by E. Garin), esp. I, 72–92.

16. For Traversari, see C. L. Stinger, *Humanism and the Church Fathers: Ambrogio Traversari (1386–1439) and Christian Antiquity in the Italian Renaissance* (Albany, N.Y., 1977).

17. Cited by A. Brown, "Platonism in Fifteenth-Century Florence," p. 392.

and Medici protégé, Marsilio Ficino, also labored to find in Cosimo every intellectual virtue. But his praise, fulsome as it is, rings far truer. While Plato showed us what virtues are, Ficino wrote, "Cosimo put them into practice every day."[18] Humanists did indeed find in Cosimo the embodiment of Platonic virtue. But the object of this sort of praise has the air of the unlearned good man, the one who, led solely by his instincts and practical knowledge of the world and of man, seizes on truths by his natural cunning. Niccolò Machiavelli, who had no especial reason to find praise or blame in this prince of an earlier era, remarked in passing that Cosimo was "senza dottrina, ma eloquentissimo e ripieno d'una naturale prudenza."[19] His judgment rings far truer than do those of Cosimo's contemporaries, determined to discover a sage as well as a statesman. To be sure, Cosimo had a degree of direct contact with Ficino's philosophizing. He was evidently consoled by Ficino's "philosophical" music from his lyre. In Ficino's one letter to Cosimo that has philosophical content, the summary of the *Philebus*, mentioned earlier, he underscored Cosimo's great material and moral virtues, and he stated that we attain happiness through wisdom, which permits us to make "right use" of our gifts.[20] The letter is neither philosophically imaginative nor groundbreaking. One might suppose that if Cosimo had been up-to-date with the wider range of Ficino's Platonism, he might have viewed the letter's emphasis on his "possessions" as somewhat indiscreet. A year or so later Ficino would describe the dialogue in terms much more abstract, as dealing with hierarchical relations between relative and absolute goods, between intelligence and will, and between beauty and truth.[21]

18. *Letters*, I, 108; *Opera omnia*, p. 649 (letter to Lorenzo de' Medici entitled "Imitatio potior est quam lectio").

19. *Istorie fiorentine*, VI, 6, ed. F. Gaeta (Milan, 1962), p. 461; cf. *History of Florence*, in *Chief Works*, III, 1344.

20. *Letters*, I, 32–34; *Opera omnia*, p. 608. See p. 191, below.

21. *Argumentum* to translation of the *Philebus*, 1464, ed. M. J. B. Allen, in Ficino, *The Philebus Commentary* (Berkeley, 1975), pp. 485–87. As Cosimo was approaching death, Ficino read to or paraphrased for him his translation of the ps.-Xenocrates, *De morte*. According to marginal notes in some manuscripts (see P. O. Kristeller, *Supplementum Ficinianum* [1937; rept. Florence, 1973], I, cxxxvi–vii), at one point Cosimo exclaimed, "Oh, how true is this utterance!" (*O quam vera sententia!*). The passage (at Ficino, *Opera omnia*, p. 1965, lines 35–36) is the conclusion of a section on the misery of the human condition, where the Platonic author goes through the various stages of a person's life to show that each is characterized by grief. The section prompting Cosimo's exclamation ("Demum senectus ipsa clam serpit, in quam omne naturae sordidum et insanabile malum confluit") describes the physical sufferings of old age. Cosimo's reaction has less the smell of a Platonic philosopher than that of an old man suffering from gout. The statement is typically Cosmian in that, amid a philosophical discussion, he seizes on a

Cosimo's contacts with the Aristotelian school led by John Argyropoulos are no more striking. Vespasiano da Bisticci recounts a debate
between the jurist Otto Niccolini and John Argyropoulos on whether
law was part of moral philosophy or subservient to it. Cosimo was present and, according to Vespasiano, knew the answer (Argyropoulos's position, that law was subservient to ethics), but "for the sake of hearing
the two debate" he pretended not to know.[22] Cosimo's reticence may
have been Vespasiano's flattery. Even if Vespasiano's account is accurate, it reveals only that Cosimo knew some Aristotelian ethics or that
he was abreast of recent developments in legal humanism, which emphasized the positive, functional nature of law rather than its participation in a divine and transcendental truth. These developments, owed
largely to the brilliant critique of law by Poggio Bracciolini, were significant in laying the theoretical groundwork for the Medici regime.[23]
In old age, as we stated earlier, Cosimo heard Bartolomeo Scala read or
explain to him Donato Acciaiuoli's commentary on the *Nicomachean
Ethics*, based largely on Argyropoulos's lectures. Cosimo's interest in the
text was probably genuine, but it should be remembered also that late
in life Cosimo was preoccupied with dying well, which, as he learned
from the humanists, meant also appearing to die well. This required him
to have learned from his life that knowledge was more important than
things and to approach death with Socratic good humor. Cosimo's wife

commonsense passage he could relate to. If indeed he made the statement, I imagine that
it provoked hearty and good-natured laughter from those present.

22.   *Vite*, II, 203–4.

23.   See F. Krantz, "Florentine Humanist Legal Thought, 1375–1450" (Ph.D. diss., Cor-
nell University, 1971), esp. pp. 206ff., and now also his "Between Bruni and Machiavelli:
History, Law and Historicism in Poggio Bracciolini," in *Politics and Culture in Early
Modern Europe: Essays in Honor of H. G. Koenigsberger*, ed. P. Mack and M. C. Jacob
(Cambridge, 1987), pp. 119–51 (hereafter "Poggio"). We will later look briefly at Poggio's
theory of law. For the debate on law between Cosimo, Niccolini, and Argyropoulos, cf.
A. Brown, "Platonism in Fifteenth-Century Florence," pp. 390–91. Brown notes correctly that Cosimo wanted to make law subject to moral philosophy, and she states that
"here Cosimo is disassociated from Niccolini's attempt to free law from moral constraints." Hence Cosimo here would want law "subject to the moral restraints imposed
by the church and customary law." But at the same time Brown wants Cosimo to be part
of a more modern approach, and she emphasizes his interest in the idea of "law as an
aspect of truth to be discovered freely by the philosopher ruler." I think, however, that
her discussion of Cosimo in the debate is somewhat confused. Law as *scientia* was a
more conservative position, defended by those jurists who held it to be part of a superior
truth. Humanists such as Bruni and especially Poggio wrested law from science and
made it part of moral philosophy. That is, they said that good men holding power
should use law as they see fit, and they should not let it be subject to "scientific," juridical
formulas. That law was subject to moral philosophy, in other words, did not mean that
it was subject to "the moral restraints imposed by the church and customary law" (as
Brown argues) but that it was closer to what she describes as "an aspect of truth to be
discovered freely by the philosopher ruler."

asked him not long before he died why he was spending such long periods of time with his eyes closed. Cosimo told her he was doing that "to get them used to it."[24] If the testimony that he really had to be convinced that his soul was immortal is genuine, then his Socratic good humor either depended on his mood or was based more on form than content. Late in life Cosimo could take comfort in knowing that his words to his wife would be repeated after his death, that humanist eulogies would emphasize his dedication to wisdom, and that humanists and historians would not only measure Cosimo's deeds and declare him the greatest private citizen in the history of the world but would also pronounce him a "harmonious personality," one whose life would have served as a model even if fortune had not smiled.[25] This is not to argue that his late interests were wholly or even partially insincere, but that, like other Renaissance men, Cosimo took great care for his external appearance, and he sought fame.

Even if Cosimo was actively involved in the new studies, we would still be forced to conclude that his personal role has been exaggerated. Cosimo's close relations with Ficino date from a period *after* the latter's ideas were fairly well developed and *after* they had enjoyed a fairly wide Florentine circulation. Only in 1462 do we first have evidence of Cosimo's sustained interest in Marsilio Ficino.[26] Ficino's earliest known patron was Piero de' Pazzi, whom he taught logic in 1451 and to whom he dedicated his translation of (pseudo-) Plato's *Minos* more than a decade later. The Canigiani family appear as patrons in the later 1450s: Ficino dedicated two short philosophical tracts to Antonio Canigiani and was in close contact with Antonio's father, Giovanni. The Agli and Capponi families may also have been early patrons. Ficino's philosophical letter to Pellegrino degli Agli, *De divino furore*, is dated December 1457 (it circulated early also in an anonymous Italian translation). To Francesco Capponi Ficino dedicated, in 1458, another short but significant philosophical work, *Di dio et anima*. This Italian work also circulated widely. Only in 1462 does Cosimo de' Medici appear as a patron, receiving from Ficino a translation of some Orphic hymns. Then, in April 1463 Marsilio Ficino dedicated to Cosimo his Latin translation of the Greek text of that part of the *Corpus Hermeticum* then known as the *Pimander*. Perhaps as a result (on April 18) Cosimo formally endowed Ficino with the

24. Cited by Niccolò Machiavelli, *History of Florence*, VII, 6, in *Chief Works*, III, 1344. In another version, Cosimo told his wife that his eyes were closed because she was "in his line of vision"! (Gutkind, *Cosimo*, p. 208n).

25. For the humanists' praise of Cosimo for his virtues, as opposed to his "deeds," see Brown, "Humanist Portrait of Cosimo."

26. For the following early works of Ficino, see Chapter VII, below.

annual profits from one of his farms at Careggi.[27] By September of that year Tommaso Benci turned Ficino's version of the *Pimander* into Italian so that unlettered businessmen (as Benci stated in the preface) could know its contents.[28] Both the Latin and the Italian versions of the *Pimander* were extremely popular: it is only with these that we should measure popularity in part according to norms set by Medici fashion.[29]

Not only is there striking evidence of Ficino's popularity before the Medici officially "endorsed" his Platonic efforts in 1462 or 1463, but there is a remarkable degree of contact between Ficino and those who became Medici opponents. The Pazzi tie has been mentioned, though we should heed historians' warnings about assuming that an individual's political disposition was necessarily shared by his family.[30] But Ficino was closely associated with Iacopo Bracciolini and Francesco Salviati, each of whom was executed for his role in the Pazzi conspiracy of 1478. These contacts remained close up to the time of the conspiracy.[31] Some of Ficino's political associations, in fact, became highly embarrassing to him and his friends later, forcing him to cancel letters and rewrite dedications, and causing him to win opprobrious remarks from generations of liberal historians since.[32]

But might not the intellectual changes have taken place on a more subtle level, so that even if the Medici did not actually drill certain ideas into the humanists' heads, they at least shaped a new social and political world that the humanist ideas reflected? If indeed the substance of the new philosophical teaching was that the active life should be abandoned and the speculative life pursued, and that the life of the mind was best exercised in the villa and court, removed and isolated from the ring of the florin and the smell of the crowd, might we not then argue that, in

27.   According to the document discussed in *Marsilio Ficino e il ritorno di Platone: Mostra di manoscritti, stampe e documenti, 17 maggio–16 giugno 1984*, catalog ed. S. Gentile, S. Niccoli, and P. Viti (Florence, 1984), pp. 175–76, no. 140; see also Chapter VII, n. 96, below.

28.   Preface ed. in Kristeller, *Supplementum Ficinianum*, I, 98–101.

29.   For the diffusion of the versions of the *Pimander*, see the works cited below, Chapter VII, n. 7.

30.   See, e.g., R. Goldthwaite, *Private Wealth in Renaissance Florence* (Princeton, 1968), esp. pp. 259ff.

31.   For Ficino and Iacopo Bracciolini, see the letters in Ficino, *Opera omnia*, pp. 657–58, 741, 780–81; for Salviati, ibid., pp. 649, 667, 743. Riccardo Fubini has recently argued that Ficino may have actually been on the conspirators' side: "Ficino e i Medici all'avvento di Lorenzo il Magnifico," *Rinascimento*, 2d ser., 14 (1984), 3–52.

32.   Ficino was not, however, as meticulous in making those changes as some scholars have suggested. For the rewritten dedications and canceled letters, see Kristeller's introductory guide to his *Supplementum Ficinianum*, vol. I, and now Fubini, "Ficino e i Medici," esp. p. 48.

the long view, the Medici had removed intellectuals from the city so that
they could speculate on the eternal verities in their splendid solitude? In
later chapters we shall, of course, scrutinize this conception of the new
philosophical culture. Nearly all scholars have assumed an affinity between the "Medici" and the Academy, based on something more than
patronage. Certainly in the Age of Lorenzo there was a literal affinity.

But if we wish to juxtapose Platonic ideas and those that should belong to "Medicean" Florence—and we will return to this problem—we
should have a clear idea, or at least a clearly defined idea, of what is
meant by the "Medici." When we speak of the Medici, are we referring
to a family, faction, party, or class? To clarify the question, and here we
will be able only to touch on it, we would have to know a great deal
about an extremely complex and elusive subject, the interactions of social and political relations in Quattrocento Florence. Traditionally, for
the early fifteenth century, the difference between the Medici supporters
and their opponents has been described according to somewhat intui-
tively derived labels: the former are called a party and the latter a faction,
the former are called more popular and the latter more oligarchic. Occasionally even these distinctions are suppressed, as implied by the sub-
title of *The Rise of the Medici* by Dale Kent: *Faction in Florence*, it reads.[33]
In summarizing her arguments, Kent has emphasized the "factional"
theme: "Our examination of the personal associations of those exiled in
1434 reveals a pattern similar to that discernible in the Miceans, the
same preponderance of connections with one another, and the same
comparative absence of many important relationships with the opposing party."[34]

But in her concrete descriptions of how the "factions" developed and
functioned, Kent makes distinctions. The Medici "faction" was made
up of those who, in the early Quattrocento, were anxious to increase
their status in the Florentine government; their opponents' faction
wished to preserve the status quo.[35] Most Medici partisans were major
guildsmen; they tended on the whole to be people on the economic rise;
many of them were *gente nuova*, those who immigrated to Florence in
the Trecento.[36] Their opponents were more aristocratic, from older, established families; they were often magnates who had passed the peak
of their prosperity (the final Medici victory resulted in the "virtual liq-

33. Oxford, 1978.
34. P. 185.
35. Pp. 24–25.
36. Pp. 67, 104ff., 116f., 140, 211ff.

uidation of the magnates as a genuine social category").[37] The Medici "faction" showed greater interest in mind-affected affairs: they were disproportionately strong in the *pratiche*, or nonelected government advisory councils, and they attracted people "more amenable to direction." Their opponents "lacked political consciousness."[38] Kent concludes that "fundamental class interests" were not in opposition but that "subtle differences in social and political background" significantly affected the "structure and organization" of the opposing "factions" and "reflected their differing attitudes."[39]

In late medieval and early modern urban economies, however, class lines are never carefully drawn, and the Italian cities are especially complex. In all periods the thoughts and allegiances of individuals do not depend precisely on their class statuses; in the Renaissance city strong kinship ties confuse economic and political relations. But based solely on Kent's analysis we can only conclude that class interests were at the heart of the struggles.[40] Neither the Mediceans nor their opponents were ideologically sophisticated, though the Mediceans were conscious of ideological factors. The anti-Mediceans had a strong political definition—with political power they dominated or wanted to dominate the rest of the population, and hence they were indeed a faction. Those adhering to the Medici represented a class on the social and economic rise, anxious to gain a share of political power in proportion to their economic power. The "Medici" then were not a faction. Nor were they a class, since their programs appealed to various classes, or at least attempted to do so, and their members only roughly approximated the class of those on the economic rise.[41] The "Medici" were not a family, faction, or class, but what they for centuries have been called, a *party*. They formed a party in the modern sense—a group having a program that attempts to appeal to all segments of the population—even if objectively its appeal was narrowed by its benefits to a certain class.[42] Their

---

37.   Pp. 148–49, 211–13, 220, 346–47. See also Giuliano Ugolini in *Un'altra Firenze: L'epoca di Cosimo il Vecchio*, ed. anon., with a "relazione generale" of Piero Ugolini (Florence, 1971), pp. 306–7; cf. pp. 341–42.

38.   *Rise of the Medici*, pp. 134–35, 149–50, 348–49.

39.   P. 348.

40.   Some of the above general comments about the Kent thesis have been made also by S. K. Cohn, Jr., review in *Renaissance Quarterly* 33 (1980), 70–72.

41.   Curt Gutkind has pointed to middle- and lower-middle-class participation in the Medici party (*Cosimo*, pp. 110ff.), but the question still needs much study.

42.   Max Weber has defined a *party* as an "association" whose membership rests on "formally free recruitment" and whose goal is "ideal or material advantages" for its members: *Economy and Society*, tr. vv., ed. G. Roth and C. Wittich (New York, 1968), p. 284.

opponents have rightly been called a *faction*, a closed circle looking out
after its own interests.

How, then, do we define the role of the Medici family—Cosimo,
Piero, and Lorenzo de' Medici—within the Medici party? Generalizations about the family as a whole, at least for now, cannot be drawn.
According to Curt Gutkind, the biographer of Cosimo, a major shift
took place after the putsch against Piero de' Medici in 1466: from then
dates the beginning of the House of the Medici.[43] Since this study does
not go beyond the 1460s, we need not attempt to inquire about the later
developments. For the earlier period Gutkind's description of the Medici role is excellent. Cosimo

> had to be content that trustworthy people should hold office, for
> he could not influence the normal course of administrative busi-
> ness. This did not prevent debates on specially important ques-
> tions being held in his house or in his villa at Careggi, or his ap-
> pearing occasionally at the Palazzo [della Signoria] and conferring
> there, so that he might give the authorities some indication of the
> lines on which they were to work. But when a modern historian
> [that is, F. T. Perrens] exclaims emphatically that Cosimo is re-
> sponsible for all and everything, he wildly overshoots the mark.
> The fundamental conception is wrong. In particular he was not
> responsible whenever judicial authorities passed civil or penal sen-
> tences. Cosimo was not the Prime Minister of a parliamentary
> country, often to be held guilty for the real or alleged failings of
> others. If Cosimo "ruled," he did it through his "party."[44]

As Nicolai Rubinstein has shown, the Medici party attempted to control the government both by acquiring now and then exceptional powers (by creating plenipotentiary commissions, or *balìe*) and by limiting
those eligible for regular public office (through electoral officers called
the *Accoppiatori*). Through the Accoppiatori, especially, the Medici
sought to ensure a preponderance of Medici partisans in the highest
levels of government and to distribute rather widely the government
offices among the party members.[45]

The limits of Cosimo's control over his party is illustrated by the records of the *pratiche*, the regular sessions of leading citizens called to ad-

43. *Cosimo*, p. 139.

44. Ibid., p. 119.

45. *The Government of Florence Under the Medici (1434 to 1494)* (Oxford, 1966), pp. 1–67
passim.

vise the Florentine government.[46] Medici partisans continued to dominate these advisory groups even when the party lost control of the Florentine government (after Cosimo returned from exile in 1434, this loss of power was from 1455 to 1458 only). For the period in which I have examined these debates, 1454–63, party leaders referred to Cosimo only four times. They urged that Cosimo be consulted (1) to give instructions to órators sent to Rome to negotiate peace (4 October 1453); (2) to examine a draft of the peace treaty (10 July 1454); (3) to advise on the calling of a *parlamento* and hence on retaking the government by force (1 August 1458); and (4) to advise on removing the University of Florence to Pisa, or at least moving the nonhumanistic chairs there, and whether it was better to have learned men in Florence or greater stability in Pisa (19 January 1460).[47] Hence for this period party leaders in their official discussions turned to Cosimo for advice only during diplomatic difficulties, in questions that could greatly affect Florentine humanists, and, most importantly, in times of severe political crisis.

For complex reasons, some of which I will discuss later, from 1455 to 1458 the Medici party lost control of the Florentine government. They retook it with a "revolution from above" in the Parlamento of 1458. It only *appears* to be odd that the leaders of that coup were also leaders of the "del Poggio" putsch of 1466 directed against Piero de' Medici.[48] For

---

46.   Although the *pratiche* are the major source for entire monographs on Florentine political history, little attention has been given to their internal makeup. Their records are preserved in the Archivio di Stato, Florence, under Repubblica, Consulte e Pratiche, collected in volumes (hereafter "Cons. e Prat."). At times the secondary literature treats the *pratiche*'s members as those chosen by the Signoria and at times as if they resulted from meetings within Florentine wards. Gutkind also identifies an organization called the *consulta* as made up of the Signoria and one of the two other executive branches, the Colleges (*Cosimo*, p. 294). Certainly within the sessions, recorded in the *Consulte e Pratiche*, debates are held over whether to *call* a *pratica*; however, in most secondary literature any meeting recorded in these records tends to be treated *as a pratica*. It is curious that historians of Florentine politics have allowed these sources, so essential to Florentine political history, to remain so enigmatic. The only general discussions I know, none completely satisfactory, follow: G. Rezasco, *Dizionario del linguaggio italiano storico ed amministrativo* (1881; rept. Bologna, 1966), s.v. "Pratica," no. 16; F. Gilbert, "Florentine Political Assumptions in the Period of Savonarola and Soderini," *Journal of the Warburg and Courtauld Institutes* 20 (1957), esp. pp. 187–95; Gilbert, *Machiavelli and Guicciardini: Politics and History in Sixteenth-Century Florence* (Princeton, 1965), pp. 65–66. For the year 1401 there is now a good, detailed discussion of the variety of the sessions in *Le "Consulte" e "Pratiche" della Repubblica fiorentina nel Quattrocento*, ed. E. Conti, vol. 1 (Pisa, 1981), pp. ix–liv.

47.   Cons. e Prat. 53, fols. 41–42, 97–99; 55, fols. 61v–68; 56, fols. 34v–38v. The last of these sections, the debate over the university, has been edited by G. Brucker, "A Civic Debate on Florentine Higher Education (1460)," *Renaissance Quarterly* 34 (1981), 517–31.

48.   For example, Agnolo Acciaiuoli and Dietisalvi Neroni: see N. Rubinstein, *Government*, pp. 165–66. See also A. Municchi, *La fazione antimedicea detta "del Poggio"* (Florence, 1911) [printed but not published: on its curious history see G. Pampaloni, "Fer-

if our earlier description of the "Medici rule" is correct, we may then
define the 1466 putsch principally as a party revolt, an attempt to replace
its weak leadership. We are certain that two of the rebels, Agnolo Acciaiuoli and Dietisalvi Neroni, had wanted to become party leaders as
Cosimo's health was failing in the 1460s, and on Cosimo's death began
planning to remove Piero as party head.[49] Ultimately, of course, they
failed. The Pazzi conspiracy of 1478 has also something of the nature of
a party revolt, but by now political circumstances had changed: whether
the antityrannical nature of the conspiracy was only formal need not be
addressed here. What is important for this study is that humanists' dedications and letters to, and client relations with, "Medici opponents," at
least for the earlier period, represent an adherence only to certain figures
who happened at some point to join conspiracies against rulers of the
Medici party: they will not, that is, prohibit us from examining links
between the humanists and the party itself.

Cosimo's shrewdness in building and leading the Medici party has
made him an attractive figure to students of politics from Machiavelli to
the present. He created the Medici party, and he prevented it from becoming simply another faction. He was superbly gifted both in choosing the right men to carry out policy and in honoring and manipulating
those who might be political threats. He wisely seized on those elements
of political ideology that should be promoted. He was also a master of
dissimulation. When in the 1430s the war to subject Lucca, which he
had strongly supported, failed, blame for its failure managed to fall on
his rivals, the Albizzi faction.[50] When Cosimo found that the popular
reform of the *catasto* would pass in early 1458, he pretended to support
it, even as it caused several party leaders to begin planning their "revolution from above," which resulted in the antipopular constitutional re-
forms after the Parlamento that August.[51] Whether his grain distribution
to the poor was founded on simulation, the pursuit of good works, or
genuine sympathy—or all of these—is not known. There must be some
truth to the old notion that Cosimo was "loved" by the people—or at
least by those whose houses were not destroyed by Medici building
projects.[52]

menti di riforme democratiche nella Firenze medicea del Quattrocento," *Archivio storico
italiano* 119 (1961), p. 14n.; a copy of Municchi's work is in the Biblioteca Nazionale Centrale, Florence].

49. Rubinstein, *Government*, pp. 134, 136.

50. See Gutkind, *Cosimo*, pp. 68–72.

51. Rubinstein, *Government*, p. 89.

52. For the "popular" Cosimo, see Gutkind, *Cosimo*, esp. pp. 110ff., 134f. For a vivid

The Medici bank was central to Cosimo's party leadership. It had, for one thing, a diplomatic function. The bank gave the Medici family wide-ranging and important contacts in many cities and governments throughout Europe.[53] Some indeed have argued that the promotion of a single figure as apparent head of the Florentine government was the result of the republic's growing need to conduct foreign policy more forthrightly than was possible with the ever-changing officials selected by lot.[54] The Medici bank also made the family the richest in Florence. Many of Cosimo's clients were simply people who owed him money. Often powerful Medici partisans controlled tax assessments in each *gon-falone*, and Medici loans could and did rescue those in tax arrears.[55] One had to be debt-free to hold office, and this form of "patronage" was extremely important in broadening and strengthening the party.[56]

Patronage in a more traditional sense distinguished Cosimo from other political leaders. Cosimo saw to it that entire groups of artists, philosophers, and humanists would remain more or less loyal to the Medici family. Of course patronage relationships with Renaissance humanists were not wholly one-sided—it was not simply the rich paying to have certain ideas produced or to see themselves praised in dedications. Even where the humanists appear to be fulsome in their praise of patrons, when they began writing the gushing orations and poems more typical of the princely courts, their portraits had an obverse side. If an indecorous patron was praised for his decorum, the praise could either shape the patron's behavior or present to his friends or his court a nice contrast between the ideal and the reality. Italian humanists themselves would criticize their natural patrons only if their pride was not honored or their pockets not lined. When just after Cosimo's death the humanists pronounced Cosimo the greatest private citizen in the history of the world, underscored several times the *pater patriae*'s liberality, and then presented their laudations to Piero de' Medici, they made sure that Piero got the point by affixing a preface stating that Cosimo's image surely,

---

description of popular reaction to Cosimo's palace building, see Giovanni Cavalcanti, *Istorie fiorentine* (Florence, 1838–39), II, 210–12 (reference owed to Dale Kent).

53. For the breadth of the activities, see R. de Roover, *The Rise and Decline of the Medici Bank, 1397–1494* (Cambridge, Mass., 1963). See also the remarks of A. Molho, "Cosimo de' Medici: *Pater Patriae* or *Padrino*," *Stanford Italian Review* 1 (1979), pp. 19ff., 28ff.

54. See, e.g., Kent, *Rise of the Medici*, p. 349.

55. Molho, "Cosimo de' Medici," pp. 21ff.

56. That the Medici bank could to a degree aid the Medici party as a whole was only possible because Cosimo was not disposed to use his political power to achieve economic domination (hence his bank was not a commercial enterprise in the modern sense). See the acute remarks of R. A. Goldthwaite, "The Medici Bank and the World of Florentine Capitalism," *Past and Present* 114 (1987), 3–31.

naturally, and necessarily thrived in his son.[57] From the autumn of 1464 until the failure of the revolt in 1466, Piero was under intense pressure not only from the party leaders but also from the party intellectuals. But the intellectuals apparently remained loyal. Patronage was an extra force gluing humanist intellectuals, regardless of political ideas, to the Medici party. Cosimo served the party with loans and patronage: he extended its membership, affirmed its members' loyalty, and endorsed an ideology, simultaneously creating personal clients and personal loyalty. As Machiavelli noted, the party leader Neri Capponi (d. 1457) helped people out through public means, and he had many friends, while Cosimo used both public and private means, and he had both friends and partisans.[58]

    We can now turn to the problem of Medici party ideology, and, our central concern, the contribution of humanist ideas to this ideology. Before we look specifically at the humanists in the late Cosimo period, let us consider more generally humanist ideology and the Medici party. Here of course we must be careful. Attempts to describe humanism in any one period as an ideology invite reductionism and one-sidedness, just as do attempts to define "humanist ideas" for the Renaissance as a whole. And in the first half of the Quattrocento, values that one might take to be "Medicean" seem often to be simply values common to the Renaissance. Moreover, humanists were educators and secretaries, and much of their work was merely functional.
    As educators they taught future businessmen, professionals, and humanists how to read and write. With their texts they gave the future ruling class at least a taste of classical culture, with its positive emphasis on man's political and social nature, the value of the arts, and the pursuit of worldly fame. The extent, though, to which the merchants learned these values through the study of the humanities remains a question. Values were learned by experience and formalized by humanists; values formalized by humanists were diffused in various ways. Most businessmen wanted the humanists simply to teach them to read and write; for many some mathematical training added to this would make them sufficiently well-rounded.[59]
    As secretaries and chancellors, humanists argued Florence's cause in

57.   For the literature praising Cosimo, see Brown, "Humanist Portrait of Cosimo."

58.   *History of Florence*, VII, 2, in *Chief Works*, III, 1338.

59.   For the limits of humanist education in shaping the "Renaissance man," see now A. T. Grafton and L. Jardine, "Humanism and the School of Guarino: A Problem of Evaluation," *Past and Present* 96 (1982), 51–80, and their *From Humanism to the Humanities*, pp. 1–28.

an international forum. At the beginning of the Quattrocento what Hans Baron has called "civic humanism" became for a time a dominant element in humanist thought. Florentine apologists linked the city's economic and cultural greatness to its political institutions, which diffused power widely among those "fitted" to rule. The arguments were directed both to Florentine citizens and to the political, business, and educated classes in opposing states.[60]

Some of these and other values promoted by the humanists served specifically to create a "counter-hegemony" to the ideology promoted in religious circles. The humanists argued effectively for the superiority of the active life of the citizen to the contemplative life of the monks; they also argued for the superiority of the contemplative life by stealing the term from the monks and giving it a classicizing definition, emphasizing a dedication to intellectual pursuits and man's potential in discovering and shaping his own destiny. In consolatory letters to friends they developed new, secularizing norms for assuaging grief. They also demystified money, took over Aristotle's conception of money as a commodity and his conception of wealth as accumulated labor, and then developed a theoretical justification for the taking of profit.[61]

Humanists in Florence also promoted values that seem more particularly linked with the Medici regime. Poggio Bracciolini described the Florentine nobles as those from good families, with great wealth, and eligible for public office.[62] He argued that the Florentine nobility was a nobility of virtue: for him a nobility of blood was a foreign concept. He showed how the Venetian nobility differed from that of the Florentines: the former were a consortium of families rigidly defined—a "faction," he called it.[63] The mixed nobility was precisely what the Medici party represented.

Another Poggian idea that seems closely related to the political values of the Medici regime is a new critique of law. In a proto-Machiavellian fashion, Poggio described the historicity of law, divorced human law both from natural and divine law, and showed how traditional "links" of human and divine law were schemes of lawgivers to attach a numinous authority to their positive law. Laws, he said, are tools by which the stronger impose their authority upon the weaker. Laws are like spi-

---

60. *The Crisis of the Early Italian Renaissance*, 2d ed. (Princeton, 1966).

61. See Leon Battista Alberti, *Della famiglia*, ed. C. Grayson, in Alberti, *Opere volgari*, vol. 1 (Bari, 1960), pp. 141ff.; Matteo Palmieri, *Della vita civile*, ed. G. Belloni (Florence, 1982), pp. 173ff.; Poggio Bracciolini, *De avaritia*, in *Opera omnia*, ed. R. Fubini, 4 vols. (Turin, 1963–69), I, 1–31.

62. *De nobilitate*, in *Opera omnia*, I, 68.

63. Ibid., pp. 64–83; for Venice, ibid., pp. 67–68.

der webs (citing the ancient Anacharsis): they hold in the weaker and are broken by the stronger. In short, laws are a function of power.[64] Poggio's point was that if good men held power they should not be restrained in their promulgation of positive law by juridical formulas or lawyers' hypotheses. Nor should the apparatus of government block the implementation of good policy. These ideas of Poggio were ideally suited to the Medici regime—as long as they were not diffused too widely.

   Programs and values directed toward a mercantile elite characterized Florentine humanism in the first half of the Quattrocento. But we should remember that if these humanist ideas had been merely a reflection of ideas of "merchants," we should expect their earliest and brightest flowering to have been in Venice, which had a highly developed and rigidly defined merchant nobility.[65] Florentine humanism depended on a mercantile elite, but a "mercantile elite" continually in a state of flux. For many merchants, more "noble," "aristocratic," or "feudal" ideas had their role. In their marriages they often spurned the wealthier for the better families. Frequently their attitude toward an economic rival was not that of a businessman scrutinizing his account books but that of a knight riding forth. Florentine humanism, moreover, was formally the product of many figures from obscure or "traditional intellectual" back-

64.   For Poggio's legal theory see the superb analysis by F. Krantz, "Poggio," pp. 119–51. I shall look at Poggio's conception of law again when I take up Ficino's scholastic mentor, Niccolò Tignosi, Chapter VI, below. For links between new legal theories and the Medici regime, see now Brown, "Platonism in Fifteenth-Century Florence." Brown, however, leaps from the jurists' theories to Medicean Platonic doctrines without mentioning the necessary intervening step, the development of legal humanism.

65.   I owe this observation to Richard Goldthwaite. I have not seen the question discussed in print. My point here is that the leaven for the new ideas ought not to be viewed as experience simply but experience formed by social relations. Whatever the merits of the approach of M. Baxandall, *Painting and Experience in Fifteenth Century Italy* (Oxford, 1972), his attempts to trace common Renaissance forms of observation, based on individuals' practical experience, cannot account, it seems, for the uniqueness of the Florentine Renaissance.

   Unfortunately, historians of Renaissance Florence have not studied the interrelation between the intellectual and social worlds with the degree of subtlety of historians of other cultures. Here we can not blame simply the intellectual historians, for the social world of Renaissance Florence has by and large escaped careful definition. As intellectual histories tend too often to be descriptive and impressionistic, so social histories are too often anecdotal. Unfortunately, for now, the best analyses of the intellectual phenomena have treated the ideas apart from social relations, just as some of the better social studies have ignored the world of ideas. When attempts are made to join the worlds together, conclusions tend to devolve around "civic liberty" versus "Medicean tyranny" or around such things as Alberti's view of the merchant-qua-artist. Even if one is not so cynical as to think that historians' enthusiasm for Alberti is because much of his work is in Italian, not Latin, one must still conclude that Alberti was, and should be considered, a humanist of second rank—a great and original thinker, to be sure, but not a great classicist and not one who epitomized Quattrocento humanist thought.

grounds.[66] Most humanists came from a scholarly world dedicated to religion and law. Some came from aristocratic families in decline. Many came from towns subject to Florence. A great number were from rising petty-bourgeois families, bitterly disappointing their fathers by not improving their station through a legal career. Nearly every humanist, especially in the earlier period—Petrarch, Salutati, Bruni, Alberti, Valla, Poggio, Landino—was a law school dropout. The social contradiction now and then had a curious result. Guarino of Verona, one of the most famous humanists of the early Quattrocento, applauded his own son when he quit his humanistic studies and went out and made a success of himself.[67] Moreover, the humanists often relied on "traditional" arguments. They saw their studies as more ennobling than those of lawyers dedicated to gain. When tested by humanist rivals they dropped all bourgeois pretensions: they put on their armor, mounted their steeds, and did battle. Only in pitched battle did their humanism take over, with its pursuit of eloquence, free use of the classics, and abrogation of all laws human and divine.

Before examining the political and social ideas of the humanists in the late Cosimo period, we must briefly survey the status of the Medici party itself. After Cosimo returned from exile in 1434, the leading Medici opponents were banished and the Accoppiatori determined who among those remaining would be eligible for the highest offices in Flor-

66.   In his notebook "Appunti e note sparse per un gruppo di saggi sulla storia degli intellettuali" (1932), in his *Quaderni del carcere* (Turin, 1975), III, 1511ff., Antonio Gramsci discussed the question of whether intellectuals constituted an autonomous social group or were part of one or another social class. He argued that each emerging social class has created for itself a group of "organic" intellectuals trained in a technical sense and also able to express social and political ideas. In a capitalist society these may be described as capitalist managers. But besides these intellectuals there are "traditional" intellectuals, emerging from preceding economic structures, who represent social and intellectual continuity with a preceding age. These tend to be educators, lawyers, and, especially, clerics. These traditional intellectuals tend not to arise from the emerging social class—the typical sort, in Gramsci's day, would be the aspiring priest or lawyer from the countryside. Many of these educators, ecclesiastics, and jurists remained tied to their "traditional" pursuits, but as some of them became spokesmen for other classes (e.g., the capitalist or proletarian class), their traditional training and awareness of continuity with an earlier age tended to make them more skilled and effective than the "organic" intellectuals of the classes themselves. According to Gramsci, that the "traditional" intellectuals tended not to come from the capitalist class did not in itself predispose them to oppose capitalism. Each social group seeking to become dominant struggles to assimilate and conquer the "traditional" intellectuals to its own cause.
   In the course of this and later chapters I shall use here and there Gramsci's categories. They at least can help us understand why Poggio Bracciolini, Marsilio Ficino, and Cristoforo Landino were better intellectuals for the Medici party than Alessandro degli Alessandri, Antonio Canigiani, or Donato Acciaiuoli.

67.   Guarino, letter to his son Girolamo, in his *Epistolario*, ed. R. Sabbadini, vol. 2 (Venice, 1916), pp. 436–43, no. 785.

ence. For a time, after 1434, the Medici party directed its major efforts
toward consolidating its rule and penalizing members of the opposing
faction. It did not attempt to alter the constitutional structure of Florence. Some of Cosimo's support came from the middle classes, and the
great Councils of the Commune and of the People gained an ever
stronger middle- and lower-middle-class voice.[68] For the first decade of
Cosimo's rule the lower classes did little to oppose the designs of the
new *dirigenti*, who suppressed the oligarchs, endorsed an expanding
Florentine economy, and represented the party of peace. Then in the
mid-1440s Florence went to war: the necessities of war created various
balìe, groups of Medici adherents having a special authority to impose
law, an authority granted by the higher officials of the government
(those selected for the Signoria and the Colleges) and approved by the
more popular Councils of the People and of the Commune.

Florence's participation in the Italian wars of the 1440s and early 1450s
forced the city to generate great sums of money and impose huge tax
burdens, and from this arose the first major signs of political revolt by
the enfranchised lower classes. By the late 1440s the laws creating electoral controls through the Accoppiatori were approved in the popular
councils by only slight margins. With peace in 1454 the argument that
the Accoppiatori were required to protect the commune from foreign
enemies had to be abandoned, and with the loss of electoral controls the
Medici party started to collapse. In 1455 the party gave up electoral controls over the Signoria and began to have great difficulties getting tax
bills passed in the councils. In 1456 the highest offices in the city, the
Signoria and the Colleges, began to lose their Medici character and to
reflect broader segments of the Florentine population, and the pro-
Medici chancellor Poggio Bracciolini was thrown out of office. In 1457
the Medici-Signoria schism widened, and many feared a popular take-
over of the government. In 1458 the leading citizens were punished with
major reassessments of taxes urged by popular elements, and a complete
loss of power seemed imminent.[69] A plague marked the summer of 1457,
and throughout this period, and even until 1460, economic recession
fed popular resentment toward the ruling class.[70]

How did the Medici party lose power in the 1450s? For one thing
pressures from the lower classes forced changes in the composition of

68. Gutkind, *Cosimo*, pp. 110–14.

69. Rubinstein, *Government*, pp. 88ff.; Cons. e Prat., vols. 53–55.

70. S. Cohn states, without citing an authority, that recovery began in late 1458 ("The
Character of Protest in Mid-Quattrocento," in *Il tumulto dei Ciompi: Un momento di storia fiorentina e europea* [Florence, 1981], p. 204). From the records of the Consulte e Pratiche, however, it seems that recovery was not *felt* until November 1460 (see the speeches
of 5 November 1460, Cons. e Prat. 56, fols. 110v *seqq.*, where a spontaneous celebration of
sorts breaks out in the advisory session).

the government. But when the Medici party leaders discussed causes they blamed not simply the arrogance and impudence of the lower classes, although these were constant themes. Cristoforo Landino seems to have reproduced a commonplace when he argued in a lecture that the *popolani* were "by nature lethargic," adding at once that they were often "incited." When stirred to revolt, he knew, they were led by the politically ambitious better-born.[71] During the political crisis, in 1456, the Medici partisan Alessandro degli Alessandri declared that "we have no enemies but our very own selves."[72] According to Machiavelli, after the Peace of Lodi members of the Medici party, jealous of Cosimo's power within the party, sought to abate that power by inviting into the government other political forces. Machiavelli observed: "Cosimo, to check this dissension, could use either of two methods: he could reorganize the government by force with the partisans who were left to him and oppose all the others; or he could let things go and with time make his friends realize that they were taking power and reputation not from him but from themselves."[73]

Cosimo chose the second method, and Machiavelli's description of its effect was true. Indeed it appears that with popular pressures after the Peace of Lodi large segments of the Medici party were in revolt. Whether this was due to a desire to replace the Medici party leadership, a resurgence of Florentine democracy, or individual acts of bravura, remains a question. As early as January 1455 Medici loyalists in the *pratiche* were complaining about the lack of unity. On the failure of a tax bill, Giovannozzo Pitti noted that "if we were united, the provision would be able to pass. . . . There are as many opinions as there are men."[74] Unity in giving counsel, of course, was an ancient theme. But other laments were more pointed. Apparently, large segments of the Medici party sought to do what a Medici loyalist, Bernardo Gherardi, complained about early in 1455, that is, "to win favor with the *popolo*."[75] Illegal voting blocks formed, leading one Medici loyalist to conclude that the failure of a certain tax bill was not due to the spontaneous will of the

71. In a *praelectio* to his course on Petrarch, ca. 1465–67: see below, p. 267.

72. 15 Sept. 1456 (Cons. e Prat. 54, fol. 34): "Non habemus inimicos nisi nosmet ipsos qui implicamus nos et sumus in confusione [confusiones *ms.?*]" (!).

73. Machiavelli, *History of Florence*, VII, 2, in *Chief Works*, III, 1338. A contemporary to the events, Marco Parenti, used similar terms to describe the party revolt. See M. Phillips, *The Memoir of Marco Parenti: A Life in Medici Florence* (Princeton, 1987), pp. 234–35.

74. 17 Jan. 1455 (Cons. e Prat. 53, fol. 150): "Omnis modus tributorum difficultatem habet. Sed si uniti essemus optineri posset. Tamen tempus, indigentia requirit ut provideatur. Quot homines sunt tot sententie." Cf. Cicero, *De finibus*, 1.5.15, etc.

75. 17 Jan. 1455 (Cons. e Prat. 53, fol. 151): "Omnis gubernatio que sit casu male se habet. Sunt qui volentes placere populo finem infelicem habuerunt."

voting bodies but to "another secret cause."[76] Accompanying voting
blocks were conspiracies. In November 1457 one revolutionary conspiracy involving Piero Ricci, Carlo Bardi, and Antonio Battista was discovered. According to the confession exacted from them, these conspirators had argued that with fewer than fifty well-to-do Florentines they
could incite the starving *popolo minuto*, and then, after taking the government, they would get rid of Cosimo and "squeeze the many who
have sucked this land in the time of war."[77] This statement, coming three
years after the war's end, ought not to be viewed as a vague lament
against the "rich": the object of the conspirators' wrath, those who held
power "in the time of war," can only be the Medici partisans. In 1458
another conspiracy was detected, this time led by Girolamo Machiavelli.[78] When in 1458 the ruling class was punished by new tax assessments, the party members finally learned that Cosimo was right: as Cosimo lost power, so did they.

Finally, in August 1458—assisted by troops supplied by the Milanese
signore Francesco Sforza—Cosimo, Luca Pitti, and the Medici party retook the government by force. They held a Parlamento, assumed plenipotentiary powers, and exiled some party rebels and other opponents.
In the words of Sforza's agent in Florence, the party "punished the
young tom-cats in order to frighten the lions," and the latter "were
trembling with anxiety and assert that they will behave like good children."[79] Niccolò Machiavelli later wrote of a rule of "terror" that for the
next eight years was "unbearable and violent."[80] But at least until the
death of Cosimo, businessmen rejoiced, orators applauded, and the
party was at peace.

In the 1450s, therefore, the Medici party for a time lost power through
a popular revolt from below coupled with an aristocratic revolt within
the Medici party itself. Both the lower and upper classes, in short, contributed to the party's temporary demise.

The nature of lower-class political expression changed radically from
the Tre- to the Quattrocento. Samuel Cohn has shown that demo-
graphic changes in the Quattrocento, induced by palace building and
laws regulating movement and association within the city, increasingly

76. Domenico Martelli, 30 May 1458 (Cons. e Prat. 55, fol. 19).

77. Cohn, "Character of Protest," pp. 205–7; cf. Cons. e Prat. 54, fols. 152ff. See also n.
87, below.

78. Apparently he was doing nothing more than creating a voting bloc; he was exiled
and arrested again in 1460 for plotting against the regime (Rubinstein, *Government*, pp.
103, 109, 121).

79. Gutkind, *Cosimo*, p. 137, citing a letter of Nicodemo Tranchedino of 18 Aug. 1458.

80. *History of Florence*, VII, 3, 4, in *Chief Works*, III, 1340.

forced the working classes into social relations centered in the parish.[81] More difficult now was working-class political action embracing the city as a whole: the working classes could no longer function as one of several competing groups within the city, as had been possible in the Trecento. Anthony Molho has argued that in the Quattrocento political and social contacts between the upper and lower classes became restricted. Anecdotes about Cosimo's relations, for instance, with the lower classes are always about him and the peasants, never him and the urban poor.[82] Other scholars, however, have pointed to close relations between several leading citizens and *popolani*. Cosimo himself seems to have had within the middle and lower classes loyal political operatives who helped broaden the party and attempted to enforce the party line in voting councils.[83] Other important families also had close ties with groups from the lower classes; documents mentioning these retainers suggest that they were what might today be called "the boys" or "thugs."[84] Silence about the latter associations in popular literature suggests that they were not "socially normative" or real political relations. When the Medici party leaders found consciously formed political alliances between the upper and lower classes, they spoke of conspiracies and worried about the loss of their own power. Classes did converge in many of the confraternities. When this resulted in conspiratorial or political relations there were campaigns to have the companies suppressed.[85] But there is evidence that many confraternities were not centers of friendly interchange between members of different classes but places more purely devotional and where social intercourse was highly formalized.[86]

The record is almost silent on the political and social ideas of the lower class.[87] With the growing stratification of Florentine society,

81. *The Laboring Classes in Renaissance Florence* (New York, 1980), pp. 115–28; "Character of Protest," pp. 199–220.

82. Molho, "Cosimo de' Medici," esp. pp. 5–18.

83. Gutkind, *Cosimo*, pp. 110ff.

84. For the "close ties," see D. V. and F. W. Kent, "Two Vignettes of Florentine Society in the Fifteenth Century," *Rinascimento*, 2d ser., 23 (1983), esp. pp. 252–60.

85. R. F. E. Weissman, *Ritual Brotherhood in Renaissance Florence* (New York, 1982), esp. pp. 116–18, 163ff.

86. See J. Henderson, "Piety and Charity in Late Medieval Florence: Religious Confraternities from the Middle of the Thirteenth Century to the Late Fifteenth Century" (Ph.D. diss., University of London, 1983), chaps. 2–3.

87. For the problem of lower-class political expression, see Cohn, "Character of Protest," pp. 199–220, which is based largely on crime records from 1454 to 1466. While I generally agree with Cohn's conclusions, I think he could have defined even more narrowly the types of revolts according to the general political situation in Florence: that is,

chroniclers and storytellers of the Quattrocento kept them hidden.[88] They do, however, appear in court records. In July 1458, when the Medici party was contemplating its complete loss of power, a thief was led to his execution. As he approached the Piazza della Signoria, his mother began to wail. At once a disturbance began, the armed guard for the thief was assaulted, and he got free. He made his way to the church of Santa Croce, where he hid in the roof. The Florentine judiciary officials, the Otto di Guardia, followed him there—on the way a crowd gathered and pelted them with rocks. The Otto and their agents found the thief and took him back to the Piazza della Signoria, where he was beheaded in front of a piazza "full of people." Communal officials investigating the incident discovered that the mother's wail was a signal for revolt, that the resulting tumult had been organized. Nineteen conspirators, all, as far as we know, from the lower classes, were exiled.[89]

This little tumult of July 1458 may be regarded as a symbol, or manifestation, of the growing unity and power of the lower classes. On the streets, as we shall see, these classes were subjecting their betters to ridicule, and in the government the lower and middle classes were steadily and effectively taking control.

---

it seems from his evidence that the character of protest from 1454 to 1458 differed significantly from that of 1459 to 1461, and that perhaps even a third sort could be defined for the years leading up to the "del Poggio" putsch of 1466. Cohn refers to a conspiracy of November 1457 that had "little ideological basis"; but the conspirator's statement, quoted earlier, that he wanted to "squeeze the many who have sucked this land in time of war," to block these same from participating in government offices, and to kill or exile Cosimo, suggests at least a considered political strategy (pp. 205–7). The conspirator's alleged confession took place three years after the end of the general Italian wars, and during these three years economic conditions had not improved. However, only the wartime government was specifically recognized to be "Cosimo's government"; afterward, as some Medici partisans lamented, things began to unravel. That the conspirator also wanted to enrich himself by 100,000 florins may be true—but then, this was an exacted confession. The examples of "revolt" cited from 1460 and 1461—the isolated poisonings, stabbings, and barn burnings—say little, since these came just after the "government of terror" (to use Machiavelli's description) following the Parlamento of 1458, when the Signoria used its own judiciary, the Otto di Guardia, in a plethora of instances to handle, in Cohn's apt words, the "social tensions and potential threats to the Signoria's domination" (p. 205). In the early 1460s we should indeed expect those revolts that occurred to be "atomized," for the more general popular revolt of the mid-1450s, which manifested itself both in the streets and in the government, had, simply, been put down. I shall refer later to the remark of the Medici party member Francesco Ventura in 1458, when "advisers" to the hostile government were contemplating taking it by force: it would be, Ventura stated, the "worst sort of example to the *popolo*, who could do the same thing very often."

88.   Related to this stratification is the development of humanist historiography: see M. Becker, "Florentine Politics and the Diffusion of Heresy in the Trecento: A Socioeconomic Inquiry," *Speculum* 34 (1959), 74–75. As Cohn has argued, some of the "silence" is due simply to the changing nature of court records ("Character of Protest," pp. 199–200).

89.   Cohn, "Character of Protest," pp. 213–14.

But the Medici party also lost power though the behavior of members of the upper classes. In response to the resurgence of the lower classes, did they seek a unity of their own? Perhaps they did achieve unity of a sort. But one searches in vain for examples of the class solidarity and personal sacrifice manifested in the small but popular tumult of July 1458. To be sure, those of the upper classes risked their necks in vendettas and quite often became involved in conspiracies. But no one would risk death for his fellow man, and certainly no one would die for Florence. One may note the extraordinary indifference of the upper-class Florentines to any cause whatsoever. Tragedy could never develop in Renaissance Italy (as it did in other cultures) because no one could have a tragic flaw: nothing could lead a person from the upper classes to follow a certain course regardless of circumstance. Ancient tragedy gave the humanists figures of speech and historical memorabilia, not ideas. In comedy the Florentines excelled. In Machiavelli's *Mandragola* the characters are either stupid or bright. If they are bright they are shrewd and calculating.[90]

One may speculate that when the ruling classes learned from the humanists the definition of friendship—that it was the union of all things human and divine—they could find little of its reality in their own class: its ritualized, formal, and perhaps even real expression could be found in religious circles, but it manifested itself most strongly in the lower classes.

Even if—and this is purely speculative—the working classes provided a leaven for the growing aristocratic conception of the importance of friendship, in considered opinions the upper classes spoke of the lower only with scorn, or, rather, scorn mixed with fear. In part the dread centered on plague, for the lower classes, it was held, were its seedbed.[91]

The Florentine aristocracy sought not only physical isolation but self-definition. Like aristocracies of all periods, it did this in part through rites of exclusion. Aristocrats' dress and manners were different. Like the ancients who trained horses and took up athletics, the Renaissance

90.   The reasons for the failure of Italian Renaissance tragedy is an old, complex subject: see, e.g., J. Burckhardt, *The Civilization of the Renaissance in Italy*, trans. S. G. C. Middlemore, rev. and ed. I. Gordon (New York, 1960), pp. 231ff. While I have been told by friends in Italian literature that my conclusion is too sweeping, I have decided not to modify it. My observation derives from remarks made in lectures by Professor Oscar Büdel. He compared the Italian situation to "bullfights" in Gascony. In these fights cows are used instead of bulls. The cows never put their heads down and charge blindly (as bulls would) but smartly keep them up to find the easiest point of attack. Likewise, in the *Mandragola*, Lucrezia was not at all blinded by the spot she found herself in. She "looked around," relativized the absolute, and then like the duchess of Malfi reached the conclusion: "If you're all for this world, why not I?"

91.   See now A. G. Carmichael, *Plague and the Poor in Renaissance Florence* (Cambridge, 1986).

aristocrats had their own useless activities, such as jousts and hunts, which in their very "uselessness" distinguished aristocrats from the lower classes. For some of the elite the pursuit of classical culture was little more than a symbol of aristocratic refinement. In politics the upper classes haughtily refused to admit that the lower classes could organize much of anything. They did, however, believe the lower classes to be quite capable of being led into revolt by others. Whether the lower classes in mid-Quattrocento Florence were indeed revolutionary, the Medici leaders and others from the upper class feared them greatly, and they freely articulated these fears.[92]

Let us look briefly at a few of these opinions as they appear during the party crisis in the records of the *pratiche*, the advisory sessions of the government, which still remained under Medici control even as the government itself was slipping away. By the summer of 1456 Medici party leaders were complaining that their advice was being so consistently ignored by the Signoria and Colleges that their advisory sessions were becoming meaningless.[93] Leading citizens suffered public humiliation. According to Machiavelli, they found that they "had become equal to those whom they were accustomed to hold far inferior, and those who were wont to be their equals had become their superiors. They were not respected or honored, rather they were many times mocked and derided, and there was talk about them and about the republic along the streets and in the squares without any caution."[94] The Medici party spokesman Guglielmo Tanaglia's lament in November 1457 underscores Machiavelli's conclusion: "Once we told others what to do, now others tell us."[95] Some of the ridicule was Italian-wide. An elite, after all, was supposed to rule "naturally." We hear a Medici partisan complain: "I know what they are saying about us"—his *they* had no antecedent![96] As

92. See the remarks of Molho, "Cosimo de' Medici," esp. pp. 5–18.

93. For example, Neri Capponi, 3 July 1456 (Cons. e Prat. 54, fol. 15v): "Nichil actum est. Civitas manen⟨s⟩ [manenda *ms.*?] sic male se habet. Practica incipit venire in tedium, et si videbitur modum [*sic*] ab illa procedere, non acceptabitur." And Giovannozzo Pitti, 8 July 1456 (ibid., fol. 17), recorded in *oratio obliqua*: "Visum est sibi quod quotiens domini voluerunt consilium a practica semper habuerunt cum conclusione, quod nihilominus et plus et minus quod dominis et collegiis placet id capiatur." Marco Parenti also noted that the Priors were now beginning to act "on their own accord, without first asking those whom they were accustomed to regard as the chief citizens" (noted by M. Phillips, *The Memoir of Marco Parenti*, p. 234).

94. *History of Florence*, VII, 2, in *Chief Works*, III, 1339. In a chronicle for 1458 Benedetto Dei remarked also on the "pride and arrogance" of many citizens opposed to the Medici regime (noted by R.F.E. Weissman, *Ritual Brotherhood*, p. 168n).

95. 22 November 1457 (Cons. e Prat. 54, fol. 167): "Olim admonebamus alios, nunc alii nos monent."

96. Bernardo Giugni, 22 Nov. 1457 (Cons. e Prat. 54, fol. 167): "Amisimus auctoritatem et famam. Et scio que de nobis obloquantur."

the Medici partisans were planning on retaking the government by force, Agnolo Acciaiuoli, a leader of the coup, worried that with it "we will make all of Italy talk about us."[97]

The party leaders knew precisely when they had lost power: with the loss of electoral controls after the Peace of Lodi in 1454. Carlo Pandolfini expressed it well: "After the peace was made, the city began to rot."[98] That many feared the Florentine *popolo* is strikingly revealed in Francesco Ventura's arguments to his Medici party companions against retaking the government by force. If the attempt is dangerous, he said, it is bad to counsel it; if it is not dangerous, "it is the worst sort of example to the *popolo*, who could do the same thing very often"![99]

Let us turn, finally, to our main subjects, the humanists' response to the crisis of the Medici party and the degree to which their ideologies may be viewed as belonging either to the Medici party or to the ruling class. We shall look first at how they responded to the party crisis; we shall then turn to the problem of their ideology. The humanists' approaches seem to be roughly a function of their social backgrounds and social and political statuses.

Some humanists, to borrow an expression from Antonio Gramsci, may be called "organic intellectuals" of the ruling class—that is, those who were from the great aristocratic, mercantile families, who were eligible for public office, and whose livelihoods did not depend on their humanistic activity.[100] Donato Acciaiuoli and Alamanno Rinuccini were such figures, anxious in the early and mid-1450s to expand their culture by taking up Greek literature and philosophy; they later became part of the circle of John Argyropoulos. From each there are few letters during the crisis, and their precise opinions are difficult to trace. Neither had

97. Letter to Francesco Sforza, 4 Aug. 1458, Ambros. Z 247 sup., fasc. IX, fol. 315: "Quanto m'è suto possibile mi sono ingegnato che al male vivere d'alcuni et alle cose nostre disordinate et al governo nostro di qui non molto honesto si provega et ponga rimedio senza scandolo et rumore, et idio me ne sia testimone che . . . non si è potuto vincere questa loro bestialità, di che ho molestia assai considerato che di noi faremo parlare tutta Italia."

98. 31 July 1458 (Cons. e Prat. 55, fol. 56): "Post pacem factam tabescit civitas."

99. 1 Aug. 1458 (Cons. e Prat. 55, fol. 64): "Nam si periculum est, non est prudens consilium illud velle. . . . Si vero non est periculum, rem esse apud populum peximi exempli, qui idem sepius facere posset." The statement is certainly sincere: after the Parlamento Ventura took important posts in the Medici government (Rubinstein, *Government*, pp. 113 and n., 134). Ventura may have been recalling a remark attributed to Cosimo about the Parlamento of 1433, which sent Cosimo into exile and was followed the next year by the pro-Medici Parlamento of 1434. The one of 1433 was the first in many years. According to Cosimo, "they taught us how to do it to them" (Poliziano, *Detti piacevoli*, p. 69, no. 164; *Tagebuch*, p. 78, no. 162).

100. See n. 66, above.

early, strong Medici ties. The Medici foe Palla Strozzi, in fact, was Donato Acciaiuoli's maternal grandfather. In 1448 Acciaiuoli complained
that the Florentine leadership was constantly engaged in wars and de-
luded the populace with false hopes of peace. Apparently he was in part
blaming the Medici.[101] But this complaint was by no means based on
any popular feeling. The next year, in a notebook, he discussed the remedies for plague. In these difficult times, he wrote, rebellions customarily occur: we have wisely armed the castles and placed foot soldiers in
the city.[102] Then in 1453 Acciaiuoli criticized those in Florence who opposed Cosimo's controversial alliance with Sforza.[103] Other letters cele-
brate the peace of 1454 and express optimism and hope for economic
recovery.[104]

By the summer of 1455, however, when the Medici party began to lose
its hold on the government, Acciaiuoli's tone turns angry. On 12 June
1455, after announcing that his business interests had survived the winter, he described the political situation in Florence:

> You asked me to write to you regularly about urban affairs: I
> would prefer that you were kept in ignorance. For what good do
> we have here to uplift your spirits? Grain is extremely expensive,
> money is quite scarce, and everything is greatly lacking. There is
> too much stupidity, too little wisdom; without the latter, no re-
> public has ever been able to last long. If republics are happy, as
> Plato, the greatest philosopher, believed, when wise men rule,
> those must be miserable when fools govern rashly. The country is
> unhappy. In the greatest peace all Italy has ever known it suffers
> more grievously than ever before in our time. Imagine what dan-
> ger we would be in if that mighty and most fierce war yet contin-
> ued![105]

101. Ed. in part in Della Torre, *Storia*, pp. 336–37.

102. Magl. VIII 1390, fol. 22–22v.

103. Letter to Banco da Casavecchia, Magl. VIII 1390, fols. 83v–84v.

104. Letters to Iacopo Ammannati, 25 Oct. 1454, Magl. VIII 1390, fol. 90–90v; to Giannozzo Manetti, 20 Jan. 1455, ibid., fol. 93.

105. Letter to Agnolo Baldesi, Magl. VIII 1390, fol. 19–19v (autograph and with many
corrections, which will not be noted): "Res urbanas quas ut ad te scribam singulis litteris
a me petis tibi ignotas esse vellem. Quid enim boni est quod animum tuum delectare
possit? Summa frumenti caritas, summa pecuniarum inopia, omnium rerum summa pen-
uria. Plurimum stultitie [stultie *cod.*], sapientie parum, sine qua nulla res p. potuit
umquam esse diuturna. Nam si beate sunt res publice, ut placet Platoni maximo philosophorum, quas sapientes viri regunt, misere sint ille oportet quas stulti sua temeritate
gubernant. Patria infelix que in amplissima totius Italie pace gravius vehementiusque la-
borat quam umquam antea nostra etate laboravit. Vide quanto in periculo versaremur, si

Acciaiuoli left few other letters before the 1460s. But in this one early letter, the agony over the suffering republic, the call for rule by the wiser, and the bitterness toward fools running things "at whim" are precisely the opinions of the Medici counselors in the government.

In the early 1460s, in his preface to a translation of Plutarch's life of Demetrius, dedicated to Piero de' Medici, Acciaiuoli applauded Cosimo's "restoration" of the republic in the late 1450s.[106] At this same time he assisted Vespasiano da Bisticci in helping Cosimo arrange the library Cosimo was providing for the Augustinian canons at the Badia of Fiesole.[107] Probably in 1463 Cosimo directly intervened with the Accoppiatori to make Donato Acciaiuoli eligible to become Gonfaloniere di Giustizia, the city's most prestigious political office.[108] Then, as we said earlier, Donato dedicated to Cosimo his commentary on the *Nicomachean Ethics*.[109] After Cosimo's death in 1464 Acciaiuoli was chosen to compose the decree naming him *pater patriae*.[110] Afterward he not only remained close to the Medici but blasted those critical of Medici power. "Many prominent citizens," he wrote to a friend in 1470, "seem to have persuaded themselves that too little authority in running the republic is in the hands of individual citizens." For some reason they are always seeking novelties which they think are better. But Lorenzo de' Medici is virtuous, and he is directing the republic to a tranquil and safe harbor.[111]

Acciaiuoli's fellow humanist Alamanno Rinuccini also left few early

---

ad hunc diem maximum illud ac ardentissimum bellum esset deductum!" A shorter, revised form of this letter, dated 14 June 1455, appears on fol. 19v.

106. For this work, and its date, see Chapter VIII, n. 62, below.

107. A. C. de la Mare, "New Research on Humanistic Scribes in Florence," in A. Garzelli, ed., *Miniatura fiorentina del Rinascimento, 1440–1525: Un primo censimento* (Scandicci [Florence], 1985), I, 443.

108. According to Vespasiano da Bisticci, *Vite*, II, 28.

109. For the dating, see Chapter VIII, n. 24, below.

110. Acciaiuoli's autograph of the decree is in Naz. II II 10, fols. 23–24. See also V. R. Giustiniani, *Alamanno Rinuccini, 1426–1499: Materialien und Forschungen zur Geschichte des florentinischen Humanismus* (Cologne, 1965), pp. 166–69.

111. Letter to Domenico Pandolfini, 23 Oct. 1470, Magl. VIII 1390, fol. 55: "Nam plerique cives magne existimationis sibi persuasisse videntur parum auctoritatis esse in privatis rei publicae ad hanc civitatem regendam, atque ex eo maiorem a populo in eligendo presertim summo magistratu impetrandum censent. Utinam sibi et huic rei publicae consulant, que suis civibus cure debent ut in aliquo tandem portu quieto tranquilloque consistat. Quod ego exoptare magis quam sperare possum, quamquam Lau(rentii) adolescentis mirifica indoles virtutis multum me recreat et reficit, quem ad tranquillitatem rei publicae totum conversum video." During this period, evidently, Lorenzo de' Medici was uncertain about Acciaiuoli's loyalty: Gentile Becchi attempted to reassure him of it in a letter of 2 March 1471 (cited by A. M. Brown, *Bartolomeo Scala, 1430–1497, Chancellor of Florence: The Humanist as Bureaucrat* [Princeton, 1979], p. 12n.). For the debate over the Florentine constitution at this time, see Rubinstein, *Government*, pp. 178ff.

letters. In a dedication to a translation of some Plutarch, published just after the Medici retook the government in 1458, Rinuccini congratulated Cosimo for bringing internal peace to the commonwealth.[112] Later, on 11 August 1462, Rinuccini was chosen to deliver a speech commemorating the fourth anniversary of the coup ("This is a day the Lord hath made, let us rejoice and be glad in it").[113] He remained strongly loyal to the Medici until the 1470s, when he had a falling out with Lorenzo. Anticipating in the late 1470s a collapse of the Medici regime, he prepared a tract, *De libertate*, which accused the Lorenzo government of having become a tyranny. But the government did not fall, and Rinuccini's brief fling with republican rhetoric came to a sudden halt. His treatise on liberty was not published.[114] Certainly for our period both Acciaiuoli and Rinuccini were loyal Medici partisans, and they were selected for and appointed to the most prestigious internal and external offices of the republic.

From a background completely different from the "organic" humanist intellectuals of the ruling class, led by Acciaiuoli and Rinuccini, were, again using a Gramscian term, the "traditional" intellectuals. These were traditional in the sense that they were professionally bound to their intellectual activities: from the "traditional" intellectual backgrounds of religion, law, teaching, and medicine, those who became humanists had to use the humanities to support themselves. These men were typically of modest social background, and few were native Florentines. At the beginning of the philosophical renaissance, the most spectacular of this group was perhaps the greatest humanist of the Quattrocento, Poggio Bracciolini.

Born in 1380 in Terranova, a small town near Arezzo, Poggio was from a family not well-to-do, and in his youth he sought to raise himself by becoming a notary. His career was typical of that of many early humanists in that he abandoned law for the humanities; it was atypical in that he used his intellectual skills and his consequent political connections to his great economic advantage. By the 1450s, after a long and successful career as a papal secretary, many investments in land, and cap-

---

112. *Lettere ed orazioni*, pp. 222–24; for the date, see Giustiniani, *Alamanno Rinuccini*, pp. 128ff.

113. *Lettere ed orazioni*, pp. 191–93.

114. For Rinuccini and the Medici regime, see now the brief but excellent survey by M. Martelli, "Profilo ideologico di Alamanno Rinuccini," in *Culture et société en Italie du moyen-âge à la Renaissance: Hommage à André Rochon* (Paris, 1985), pp. 131–43. See also F. Adorno, "La crisi dell'Umanesimo civile fiorentino da Alamanno Rinuccini al Machiavelli," *Rivista critica di storia della filosofia* 7 (1952), 19–40, and Giustiniani, *Alamanno Rinuccini*, pp. 243–48. For Rinuccini's loyalty to the Medici during the time of the "del Poggio" conspiracy of 1466, see Pampaloni, "Fermenti di riforme," pp. 18–19.

ital acquired through investments in the Medici bank, he had become quite wealthy.[115] After Cosimo returned from exile in 1434, Poggio's position as a Medici partisan, leading Florentine intellectual, and important political contact in Rome, resulted in a special exemption for him from Florentine taxes.[116] Not inappropriately was he called Poggius Florentinus.[117] In 1453 he appeared to be an ideal successor to Carlo Marsuppini as chancellor of Florence.

For Poggio, unlike Acciaiuoli and Rinuccini, we have the letters and documents that permit us to trace his response to the crisis of the Medici party. For July and August 1455 he was chosen a lord of the Signoria in the last *a mano* election by the Medici-controlled Accoppiatori. From this time his personal difficulties began: his election to the prestigious position, he wrote, was greeted with considerable jealousy on the part of the *popolo*.[118] Soon of course the chancellor would find himself working for an increasingly popular government. He absented himself more and more from the Chancery, was forcibly carried by a petty guard into the Palazzo della Signoria late in 1455 (he filed a protest), and was betrayed by the government in the selection of a friend to an appointed office.[119] Of public affairs, he mentioned in a letter of 1456, he could not write, for the "mind shrinks back in horror."[120] In August 1456 appears the last official letter from the Chancery bearing Poggio's signature.[121] Soon, in an extraordinary, shocking move, the popular Florentine government refused to reappoint Poggio as chancellor. Medici partisans desperately tried to reform the Chancery, to bring in notaries and humanist assistants so that Poggio could nominally remain in office. The

115. See the documents published by E. Walser, *Poggius Florentinus, Leben und Werke* (Leipzig, 1914), pp. 325–427, rept. (that is, this section) in Poggio, *Opera omnia*, IV, 327–431; the sketch in L. Martines, *The Social World of the Florentine Humanists, 1390–1460* (London, 1963), pp. 123–27; and now *"Contratti di compre di beni" di Poggio Bracciolini: il Ms. Horne n. 2805*, ed. R. Ristori (Florence, 1983).

116. Walser, *Poggius*, pp. 349–51.

117. See the remarks of F. Krantz, who surveys the Florentine connections ("Poggio," pp. 119–20n.)

118. Ep. XIII, 9 (Tonelli III, 195–96), rept. in Poggio, *Opera omnia*, vol. 3.

119. For the absence from the chancery, see N. Rubinstein, "Poggio Bracciolini cancelliere e storico di Firenze," *Atti e memorie della Accademia Petrarca di Lettere, Arti e Scienze*, n.s., 37 (1958–64 [1965]), 215–39, esp. pp. 217ff., and Walser, *Poggius*, p. 286n.; for the incident at the palazzo, see the document in Walser, *Poggius*, pp. 396–97; and for the betrayal, Vespasiano, *Vite*, I, 547. See now also R. Black, *Benedetto Accolti and the Florentine Renaissance* (Cambridge, 1985), pp. 91ff.

120. Ep. XIII, 18 (Tonelli III, 216–17).

121. Walser, *Poggius*, p. 286n. The last is 7 Aug. 1456 (Florence, Archivio di Stato, Signori, Carteggi, Missive, Prima Cancelleria, vol. 40, fols. 209v–210 [new foliation]).

reform failed, and Poggio was removed from the government.[122] To add injury to insult, the government took away the tax exemption that Poggio had enjoyed for decades.[123] As far as we know, Poggio returned to the government only once more, when, in 1458, at the age of seventy-eight, he participated in a *pratica* of some 220 persons that July: the meeting was, in effect, a Medici show of force, a huge party rally creating the momentum that led to the Medici coup the next month.[124]

In late 1456 or early 1457, just after being thrown out of office and losing his tax exemption, Poggio answered Florence by writing and circulating an invective, *Contra fidei violatores*, against the popular government.[125] Ostensibly, the work, in which Poggio opposed human law to natural law, runs counter to those tendencies in his thought that scholars have regarded as "characteristic"—his emphasis on the concreteness of "things" and the radical relativity of law and justice.[126] Poggio began

122. So shocking is the dismissal of Poggio that, even if they have acknowledged that Poggio had some difficulties in Florence, scholars have tended to conclude that his retirement was due largely to personal, not political, causes. In "*Studium Florentinum* Controversy, 1455," *History of Universities* 3 (1983), 43, I suggested that Poggio might have officially abandoned the Chancery as early as 1457—before the appointment of Benedetto Accolti as chancellor in 1458. As far as I know, only in a recent monograph (1985) by Robert Black has the evidence been published to show that Poggio's term as chancellor expired on 31 Aug. 1456 and that he was not reappointed (*Benedetto Accolti*, pp. 92ff.). 92ff.).

123. Black, *Benedetto Accolti*, p. 98.

124. Cons. e Prat. 55, fol. 27v, noted in my "*Studium Florentinum* Controversy," p. 57, n. 72. Poggio had heavy investments in the Medici bank (see the documents cited above, n. 115); also, early in 1457, both Cosimo and his sons Giovanni and Piero appear as witnesses in the emancipation of one of Poggio's sons (document edited in Walser, *Poggius*, pp. 407–8). But one still sees in secondary literature the hypothesis that Poggio in his last years became estranged from Florence because he was repelled by a Medicean hegemony (e.g., R. Fubini, following Walser, in Poggio, *Opera omnia*, II, 889). For this there is no evidence whatsoever and a great deal of counterevidence. That the supporters of Poggio were Medici partisans has now been clearly demonstrated by Black, *Benedetto Accolti*, pp. 91–98.

125. Ed. R. Fubini, in Poggio, *Opera omnia*, II, 891–902. I found incorrect readings and lacunae in Fubini's edition, and, where the Latin is quoted, I shall cite the manuscript: Laur. 90 sup., 7, fols. 94v–101. Poggio also wrote a laudation of Venice that may be dated to this period (*Opera omnia*, II, 925–937); if so, his praise of Venice for having a government where good people rule was intended as an attack on the popular Florentine government of the mid- to late 1450s. The dating, however, is controversial, and I shall not discuss it.

126. These tendencies have been carefully and thoughtfully described by Krantz, "Poggio," pp. 119–51, upon whose analyses many of the following arguments depend. He, however, largely ignores this invective, lumping it with Poggio's "orations and more formal works," which adopt "an essentially static perspective" (pp. 137–38). N. S. Struever has analyzed the invective as an "ethical treatise" in an approach quite different from the one I am taking here (*The Language of History in the Renaissance* [Princeton, 1970], pp. 144–99, esp. p. 163).

the invective by arguing that the violation of *fides*—that is, promises and agreements—should be condemned in both private and public affairs: military alliances, commercial credit, marriages, even speech (that is, words expressing the mind), all depend on good faith.[127] But *fides* is especially important when confirmed by public decrees. If a violation of good faith is shameful and unworthy of a free man, so much more should it be condemned when it characterizes public offices and those who represent the republic.[128]

But as Poggio began to discuss more concretely the function of *fides* in the city, he moved away from humanist generalizations toward a model of sorts for the proper relations between classes and the proper function of each class and toward an analysis of the causes of public corruption. The *popolani*, he said, are ignorant and tend spontaneously to act with deceit. Customarily the prudence of the magistrates corrects their errors. What is happening now in Florence, he said, is that those who hold even the highest offices are following the customs of the people, are moved by ignorance rather than prudence, envy rather than reason. When this happens the city becomes a "conspiracy of the breakers of faith," a "perverse faction," and thus the "republic ought to be called a tyranny."[129]

Poggio concluded the treatise with an old theme: a law not conforming to justice is no law at all. The distinction between a "natural law" and a "human law," the validity of the latter depending on its conformability to the former, Poggio had seemingly repudiated some seven years before in his *Secunda disceptatio convivalis*, in which he viewed law as a function of power. Indeed humanists had always tended toward "historicizing" law, seeing law in terms of its concrete historical circumstances rather than in its relationship with natural reason.[130] But Poggio in his invective juggled terms significantly while maintaining the distinctions: better people are not bound by positive law.

> Justice can be abolished by no popular consent, injustice can be permitted by no law. Nor, in the view of the wise, ought one to obey statutes of this kind. This perversity is the mark of a tyranny, which does not consult the public good but the private one, which having forgotten the common good refers all things to its own

127. *Opera omnia*, II, 892–901.

128. Ibid., p. 891.

129. Ibid., pp. 895–99.

130. For the *Secunda disceptatio convivalis*, part 2 of Poggio's *Historia tripartita*, and its relation to earlier tendencies of legal humanism, see Krantz, "Poggio," esp. pp. 143–51. I return later to some of the questions raised here.

profit. But let the abuses of laws of this sort be absent from republics. For good faith, rights, equity, and justice shrink back from
the very name and dignity of such laws. Let those things prevail
which see to it that a city deserves its name, that it be called a *res
publica* and not a tyranny. Those things are to be abolished which
bring abomination, disgrace, and shame to the city; those who are
manifestly the promoters of such things are destructive citizens
and are to be thrown out of cities, for they destroy what is necessary to a city's existence.[131]

Poggio thus turned an abstract notion—the distinction between "real
law" conforming to justice and that law promulgated by men—into the
concrete proposal that the authors of the bad law be exiled. The distinction then was between the bad law enacted by the magistrates and the
real *iustitia* known to the wiser. His earlier theory of law, the proto-
Machiavellian notion of law as a function of power, was reinforced with
a rhetorical use of an old abstraction—natural justice versus human
law—and applied to the political situation in Florence, the *sapientes* of
the Medici party opposing the magistrates running the government.
One can hardly imagine a more effective pro-Medicean argument or a
better theoretical instrument to use in retaking power.[132]

Poggio died in 1459. Particularly in style but also in substance the new
generation of humanists went in a direction of its own. When Poggio
himself spoke of the "new generation" of humanists he meant the school
of Lorenzo Valla, the philologists and rhetoricians who, in Poggio's
terms, could only appreciate the "force of words," not the style of lan-

131.   Laur. 90 sup., 7, fol. 101 (cf. *Opera omnia*, IV, 902): "Nullo enim populi consensu
iustitia aboleri, nulla lege iniuria permitti potest, neque similibus statutis parendum sapientes volunt. Tyrannidis ista perversitas, quae non publicae sed privatae consulit utili-
tati, quae omnia ad suum quaestum refert communis utilitatis oblita. A rebus vero publicis eiusmodi legum abusiones absint. Abhorrent e⟨n⟩im ab earum nomine et dignitate
fides, iura, aequitas, iustitia. Valeant quae efficiunt ut iure civitas appellari queat, ne potius tyrannis quam res p. nominetur. Abolenda siquidem sunt quae infa⟨nd⟩um dedecus
obprobrium afferunt civitati, quorum qui se auctores praebent, pestiferi sunt cives et ex
urbibus eiiciendi, cum ea tollant sine quibus nulla unquam civitas fuit."

132.   Poggio's terms in his invective are not unlike many expressions common to the
pratica debates whenever the advisers attempted to become more "theoretical." Compare, for example, Alessandro degli Alessandri's lament on the failure of a tax bill, 20
January 1456 (Cons. e Prat. 53, fol. 207): "Dicam fideliter et consulam ut potero in tanta
re rei publice nostre. Et sequar bonum comune [comunem *ms.*] et non particulare. Sine
iustitia res publice deserte et sectis[?] habitate censeri[?] possunt. Ideo hortor omnes ut
secundum iustitiam vivant quod scio omnes esse facturos." This Alessandro, a strong
Medici partisan, had some training in the humanities, was the dedicatee of Matteo Palmieri's *Della vita civile*, and, late in 1456, participated in the *pratiche* referred to earlier
that attempted to protect Poggio's position in the Chancery. For a sketch, see Martines,
Social World, pp. 329–30; and Pampaloni, in *DBI*, vol. 2 (1960), 161–62.

guage or the substance of ideas.[133] For our period and for a considerable time afterward the voice of this new humanism is virtually silent in Florence. This is but one debt, if we may call it that, of the young humanists to Poggio. Where they differed so strikingly was in their dedication to philosophy. In a letter to Poggio in the mid-1450s, a young Florentine scholar told the aged chancellor that he wished to take up philosophy. Poggio encouraged him, but warned him to approach the Greek sources first-hand, not to rely on translations—Landino would give Ficino similar advice in 1456. Poggio's confession in the letter is revealing: *philosophiae ars a me deest*. He did not imply that he was worse for not having taken up philosophy, or that it was useless, or that he did not like it; he merely stated that it was not part of his learning.[134] As we noted earlier, within a decade and a half Alamanno Rinuccini would state that philosophy was necessary for *everyone*'s learning. But Poggio's little confession, *philosophiae ars a me deest*, suggests the smoothness of the intellectual transition to a philosophical culture. There was not—and we shall take up this point later—the anxiety and fears that philosophy would replace rhetoric that some modern scholars would wish to find.

Poggio's position as a humanist and intellectual in the Medici party was unique. He had been nurtured in the party for decades and had become one of its leaders. Unlike most leaders, he had assimilated broad humanistic traditions, and not just Florentine ones, which helped make his political and moral thought in the 1450s highly creative and rhetorically effective.

If Poggio was a "traditional intellectual" who became a party intellectual, what were his humanist heirs? Alamanno Rinuccini and Donato Acciaiuoli were party intellectuals of a different sort, organic members of the ruling class. Rinuccini praised Poggio more than once, but only in general terms and as one in a list of famous humanists.[135] Donato Acciaiuoli, by contrast, met Poggio in 1455, declared him an indispensable leader for his own humanistic studies, and then late in the decade asked the old man to check over his translation of some Plutarch.[136] But a clearer intellectual debt to Poggio, as we shall argue in later chap-

---

133. For an excellent summary description of Poggio's position, see R. Sabbadini, *Storia del Ciceronianismo e di altre questioni letterarie nell'età della Rinascenza* (Turin, 1885), pp. 19ff. I return to the question in another context in Chapter IV.

134. Poggio, Ep. XII, 31 (Tonelli III, 174–75). The scholar Poggio addresses is Johannes Bartholomaeus, perhaps to be identified with Giovanni di Bartolomeo Guidi: see Chapter IX, n. 25, below.

135. *Lettere ed orazioni*, pp. 87, 94, 108.

136. See Donato Acciaiuoli's letter to Poggio, 8 March 1455, ed. Fossi, *Monumenta*, pp. 107–8; see also Chapter VIII, n. 62, below.

ters, was owed by two other "traditional intellectuals," Marsilio Ficino and Cristoforo Landino. Marsilio Ficino's teacher of philosophy, Niccolò Tignosi, was a close friend of Poggio and became the interlocutor who expressed Poggio's critique of law in the *Secunda disceptatio convivalis*. Some time in the 1450s Ficino came to know Poggio directly, serving as a witness for him in a legal matter.[137] Landino may have worked for Poggio in the Chancery and was highly devoted to him: he owed in part to Poggio his first salaried appointment at the University of Florence.[138]

Unlike the "self-made" Poggio, Landino and Ficino had to support themselves as teachers and scribes. Each depended on patronage. Because of their social status, neither could hold those political offices filled by lot, and thus neither needed to comment directly on political affairs. Ficino strove consciously to project the image that he was completely oblivious to politics. By 1457 and 1458 three Medici partisan families, the Agli, Capponi, and Canigiani, were probably his patrons. Cosimo's son Giovanni may have been something of a patron from the 1450s; by 1462 or 1463, of course, Cosimo was his leading patron. Cristoforo Landino was less conscientious in avoiding politics, in part, perhaps, because he worked for the Chancery, sought to rise in it, and aspired also to academic positions in the public Studio. In early 1458, Landino dedicated to Giovanni Canigiani a poetic eulogy of Neri Capponi, one of the most powerful leaders of the Medici party, who, in the government, had attempted to strong-arm party members into some degree of unity against the resurgent *popolani* of the great councils. Landino praised Capponi's political prudence and grieved that his death had come at such a "difficult time" for the Florentines.[139] At about this time Landino wrote a long poem in praise of Poggio Bracciolini, in which he blasted the popular government for having failed to honor properly its aged chancellor. Landino dedicated the poem to his principal patron, Piero de' Medici.[140]

I have argued that the intellectuals most intimately connected with the philosophical renaissance—both the "organic" intellectuals of the

137. The document has been cited in several studies. See now the description in *Marsilio Ficino e il ritorno: Mostra*, p. 174 no. 138.

138. See Chapter IV, below.

139. *Carmina omnia*, ed. A. Perosa (Florence, 1939), pp. 156–58: "Ah, quanta in dubiis velox prudentia rebus / pectoris, impendens vaticinantis erat, / quamque graves casus, quam multa pericula quondam / effugit monitis curia nostra suis!" (lines 9–12); "Tempore nam duro tali privatur alumno / publica res, qualem saecula rara ferunt" (lines 65–66).

140. Ibid., pp. 123–29. See also R. Black, *Benedetto Accolti*, pp. 105–7.

ruling class and the "traditional" intellectuals or professional humanists—had their fortunes bound to a greater or lesser extent with those
of the Medici party or family. Either by their occasional political statements or their status as clients they may be described, at least broadly,
as "Mediceans." The essential question we must now address is this:
apart from the occasional direct statement on Florentine politics, in
what way may the ideologies of the humanists be viewed as the "ideology of the Medici party"? Do we conclude that as the Medici hoped to
rule Florence unimpeded, an ideology of the contemplative life assuredly followed, and as the humanists embraced the notion they became party ideologists?

The relation between the intellectuals and the party is more complex.
Too one-sided are arguments that the intellectuals were used or manip-
ulated by the ruling class. The simple hypothesis that the intellectuals
"shared in" the ideas of the ruling class obscures the simpler truth that
the relation between the two was dialectical. Instead of scrutinizing the
intellectuals for a "Medicean" ideology we may just as easily use a different set of assumptions and scrutinize the party elite for the ideas of
the intellectuals. Is it improper to suppose that ideas that are patronized,
translated into more popular languages, repeated in various contexts,
copied, and glossed in wide circles of the literary and economic elite are
our ruling class ideas? If so, manuscript catalogs and inventories will not
be dismissed, as some historians would want, as relics of antiquarian
history but treated as valuable sources for the study of the social prolif-
eration of ideas.[141]

Humanists and philosophers took familiar texts and common forms
of thinking and transformed them into new types of truths—they attempted, in other words, to create a new ideology. This transformation
needs to be studied in its particulars, in its details. The highest and most
systematic expression of moral philosophy was in Aristotle's *Nicomachean Ethics*, translated by Leonardo Bruni into an eloquent Latin and
then adapted and turned into Italian through such works as Leon Bat-

141. Discussions of the "social audience" of humanism have tended to focus on the
content of the humanist ideas rather than their forms of expression. For a rare discussion
of Ficino's early works according to the social classes of their audience, see P. O. Kristeller, "Marsilio Ficino as a Man of Letters," pp. 14ff. For a good example of the light
that manuscript studies can throw on the development of an ideology, see J. Soudek,
"Leonardo Bruni and His Public: A Statistical and Interpretative Study of His Annotated Latin Version of the (Pseudo-) Aristotelian *Economics*," *Studies in Medieval and
Renaissance History*, vol. 5 (London, 1968), pp. 51–136, and his "A Fifteenth-Century Humanist Bestseller: The Manuscript Diffusion of Leonardo Bruni's Annotated Latin Version of the (Pseudo-) Aristotelian *Economics*," in E. P. Mahoney, ed., *Philosophy and Humanism: Essays in Honor of Paul Oskar Kristeller* (London, 1976), pp. 129–43.

tista Alberti's *Della famiglia* and especially Matteo Palmieri's *Della vita civile*. As scholars have shown, new secularized ideas of moral philosophy permeated the discussions and the consciousness of the Florentine political class.[142] Donato Acciaiuoli took these familiar ethical precepts and insisted that their real message was not what it appeared to be, that Aristotle's true teaching was that one should pursue the contemplative life. Cristoforo Landino took Virgil, the hero of the Latin language (*"our* Homer"), the sometime moralist (through medieval allegorizing), and Italian patriot (the poet of the Roman Empire), and turned him into a Platonic philosopher, one who led men toward the world of contemplation. More boldly, Dante's Hell, Purgatory, and Heaven were stripped of any commonsense meaning: Dante became a pagan philosopher, and the journey through the three realms became Everyman's struggle through the vices toward virtues, and through the active virtues toward the contemplative ones.[143] Marsilio Ficino was boldest of all: he turned Christian theology into a philosophy and Platonic philosophy into a theology. Inspired of course by teachings of classical Neoplatonists, Ficino at last was able to rob Christ of his individuality and fit him into a Platonic cosmos. The chief teaching of Christianity, the love of God, became man's separation from his body and the spiritual ascent of the individuated soul toward unity with God.

Can these leaders of the philosophical renaissance not be said to be creating an ideology, in their attempts to alter common patterns of thinking to create new forms? We know that Ficino did not think he was paganizing Christianity but rather explaining its true teachings. Landino knew he was finally opening up the "true minds" of Virgil and Dante.[144] While his interpretation of Virgil was no worse, and certainly more skilled and more interesting, than that of the Christian moralists, his interpretation of Dante was the most distorted and ahistorical that had ever been. But he was convincing: no Florentine would attempt another interpretation of Dante until the mid-sixteenth century.[145]

Even if the most fruitful way of studying the thought of Marsilio

---

142. See, e.g., G. Brucker, *The Civic World of Early Renaissance Florence* (Princeton, 1977), pp. 283–318.

143. Landino's commentary on Dante is dated 1481, outside our time period, and I shall not discuss it in the chapter on Landino. For Landino's early approach toward Dante, see my "C. L.'s First Lectures on Dante," *Renaissance Quarterly* 39 (1986), 16–48. For Landino's paganizing of Dante, the best analysis I have seen is F. J. Fata, "Landino on Dante" (Ph.D. diss., Johns Hopkins University, 1966).

144. At times, however, Landino discussed Virgil's Platonism as if it may not have been the poet's considered opinion: see Chapter IX, below.

145. M. Barbi, *Della fortuna di Dante nel secolo XVI* (Pisa, 1890), p. 178.

Ficino is to study it apart from its political and social context—and this I do not deny—it seems highly probable that even some of the more speculative ideas of Ficino were informed by the political and social world of Quattrocento Florence. To paraphrase Antonio Gramsci's remark on Croce, Plato, and Agnelli, Marsilio Ficino may have felt himself more closely tied to Hermes Trismegistus than to Giovanni Canigiani, but this should not keep us from studying the significance of the latter relation.[146] Ficino and Landino were indeed Gramsci's "traditional" intellectuals who became intellectuals for a political and social elite. They held this role not by fleeing to the villa or by insisting on contemplative withdrawal; rather, they spread their ideas in the heart of Florence and to as many as would hear them. Theirs was no ideology produced for them by the Medici party, where they would become disseminators of ready-made truths; rather, striking chords and hitting on predisposed spirits, to be sure, they themselves, in large part, created the ideology of the Medici party.

This approach toward the philosophical renaissance will differ greatly from those that have customarily treated humanist thought as an ideology. Most who view Platonism as the official or unofficial ideology of the Medici party (or of Lorenzo the Magnificent's Florence) give the Medici far too great a role, and they tend to minimize or ignore the creativity of the professional intellectuals themselves. We shall not attempt to imagine what a merchant in the early 1460s "should be" thinking; we shall be interested in what he did think, which lectures he thought worth attending or sending his sons to, and which works he thought worth translating and studying. The assumption, therefore, that humanism is an ideology will not determine the analysis of its formal expression. But it will require us to consider constantly our humanists' and philosophers' audience. Many social historians, and some intellectual historians, have viewed humanist thought in the Medici period as a function of Medici power, as if the rubric "ruling class men make ruling class ideas" were the recipe for understanding the phenomena of intellectual and cultural change. In a curious twist of leftist methodologies humanist thought thus becomes "necessitated" as the nature of the ruling class becomes "free."

We do find a striking harmony between ideas formalized by intellectuals in the philosophical renaissance and the desiderata expressed by Medici party loyalists in the government advisory councils. Classical erudition in meetings of the *pratiche* is rare, but one quotation from Sallust became the political maxim of the late 1450s and the 1460s: "With

---

146.   Gramsci, notebook 12 (1932), *Quaderni del carcere*, III, 1515.

harmony small states (or things) increase, with disharmony the greatest fall apart" (*concordiâ parvae res crescunt, discordiâ maximae dilabuntur* [*Jugurtha* 10.6]).[147] To a degree new forms of unity had always been part of the Medici party program.[148] But when the party actually and spontaneously began to crumble, in the crisis of the 1450s, the theme of unity, harmony, and even love took on a new urgency. Alamanno Rinuccini used the Sallustian maxim in a speech of January 1457 welcoming a youth into a confraternity.[149] Later, in 1462, on the fourth anniversary of the Medici coup, Rinuccini delivered a speech in Italian again reproducing the Sallustian theme but this time giving it much deeper philosophical content. We shared food in a feast today, he stated, and this sharing is like the Christian mass, for it unites the many of us into one. Referring to the banners proclaiming *libertas*, after the new name for the Signoria (the *priores artium* were now the *priores libertatis*), Rinuccini emphasized themes of harmony and love:

> I shall say nothing of the fact that through this day is confirmed, renewed, and made stable the liberty of this illustrious and glorious people. Just as they carry about publicly the name of liberty written and inscribed, likewise they are able by their activity and its results to possess and enjoy it. Nor shall I speak of the fact that through this same day are corroborated and enlivened your holy and inviolable laws, in the observance of which consists all good and civil life. Nor shall I speak of the fact that through this same day are reunited and reconciled the souls of your citizens and in them have been created a firm and stable union and harmony, which are so necessary not only in public but also in private life. Each person is so aware of this that there is no need to repeat it. I shall only recall to your memory that most weighty teaching of Sallust, that "concordia parvae res crescunt, discordia maximae dilabuntur." Since all these things have come to this city through the celebrated act of four years' ago—the image of it is displayed here—it seems to me that one can through these your servants, individually and in the name of the whole Florentine people, sing

147.   In Sallust the *res* evidently means *res publicae*. Seneca quotes it in a letter (*Ep.* 94, 46), and the *res* seems to lose its political significance and mean "things." The expression appears also in Saint Jerome's gloss on the "house divided" of Matt. 12:25–26 (*Commentaire sur S. Matthieu*, ed. E. Bonnard [Paris, 1977], I, pp. 224-26). In the quotation from Rinuccini that follows, the *res* is translated *cose*, as it had been earlier in Matteo Palmieri's *Della vita civile*, p. 164.

148.   See, e.g., the remarks of Kent, *Rise of the Medici*, p. 349, and now C. Finzi, *Matteo Palmieri: Dalla "Vita civile" alla "Città di vita"* (Varese, 1984), esp. pp. 170ff.

149.   *Lettere ed orazioni*, p. 22.

together with the Psalmist that verse which reads, "Haec dies quam fecit Dominus; exultemus et laetemur in ea." Because truly God, who is the origin and giver of every good, has made this day so that we may rejoice and be glad in it.[150]

A year and a half earlier, in January 1461, Piero de' Medici became Gonfaloniere di Giustizia and was required to make a speech before the new Signoria, Colleges, and counselors in the *pratica*. He too quoted (or rather misquoted) the expression from Sallust. Two things, he said, are necessary for maintaining the good status of the republic, that the citizens preserve justice and that they

> have harmony and be of one mind, so that in running the republic they can avoid those divisions which ruin the land, but wisely act and think with unanimous mind and will all the things which they adjudge to be related to the safety of the fatherland, its citizens, and the seemliness of the commonwealth. By so doing not only shall the present happiness be preserved but also the resources and glory of the republic shall increase with ever greater intensity. For experience itself [!] teaches that with harmony small states increase, with disharmony, however, they are destroyed in the greatest way [!]. Thus all ought to take pains to see that these so many goods not be lost through dissensions of citizens, to their shame and ruin. For all citizens are at the same time brothers: though they are born of different parents, they still have the same fatherland and place of abode and hence they all ought to think of themselves as comrades and brothers, constituted so by nature itself and by laws. Thus they will preserve the republic as a common parent with all their strength, zeal, and endeavor.[151]

---

150. Ibid., pp. 191–92. The second of Rinuccini's Latin quotations is Ps. 117:24.

151. 5 Jan. 1461 (Cons. e Prat. 56, fol. 123v): Petrus ait "existimare dominos duo imprimis agenda esse, ut cives quesito bono in perpetuum frui possint, iustitiam scilicet observare ac ministrare, quoniam ea neglecta nulle res p. nulla imperia beata vel diuturna esse possunt, que si recte atque ordine administretur, gratissimum deo ipsi opus civitati ac civibus cunctis saluberrimum exercetur; deinde ut cives ipsi concordiam et unanimes animos habeant, neque in regenda re p. cum pernitie patrie dissideant, sed omnia concordi voto atque animo sapienter agant et cogitent, que ad salutem patrie ac singulorum civium ad decorem rei p. spectare arbitrabuntur. Sic enim agendo non solum que nunc adest felicitas conservabitur, sed etiam rei p. opes ac gloria continuo magis ac magis augebuntur. Experientiam enim satis docere concordia parvas res crescere, discordia vero maxime [*sic!*] labefactari. Itaque omnes adniti debere ne per illorum dissensiones tot bona cum dedecore ac danno maximo amictantur; esse enim cives omnes insimul fratres; quamquam enim e diversis parentibus nati sint, tamen cum eandem habeant patriam et domicilii sedem debere omnes censere se velut socios ac fratres a natura ipsa et legibus constitutos, ut rem p. velut communem parentem viribus cunctis omni studio atque in-

In their commentaries on the *Nicomachean Ethics* of the early 1460s, both
Niccolò Tignosi and Donato Acciaiuoli would gloss Aristotle's statement that when men are friends there is no need of justice between them
(*Eth. Nic.* 8.1.4/1155a) by reproducing the Sallustian maxim as well.[152]
Then in the early 1470s Cristoforo Landino, chancellor of the Parte
Guelfa, used the maxim to defend the society from the charge that, since
they were a *parte*, or a "part of the whole," they were necessarily "divi-
sive." The Guelfs stand for division, he argued, the division of the soul
from its earthly prison; in seeking this division the Guelfs promote harmony and concord.[153] And what about Marsilio Ficino? Did he also adhere to the Sallustian truth? Perhaps, but he never, as far as we know,
quoted it. What he found instead—and this is typical of his thinking—
was a similar truth expressed in a less political and more "speculative"
form. From his scholastic and religious studies he seized on a teaching
of Empedocles: all things that stand firm, all things that move, friendship (*amicitia*) draws together but disharmony (*discordia*) scatters.[154]

In the 1450s and 1460s the Ficino circle discussed the unity of the
ruling class through bonds of Platonic love, the necessity of common
action toward the common good, the indignity of seeking personal
goals outside of this common endeavor. These themes will be explored
later. Unfortunately, we shall not be able to examine in any depth the
dialectical relationship between the formal development of the ideas
themselves and political and social relations in Florence. Our time period is so brief that statements of precise relationships would be misleading if not false. Many of the ideas seem to have an inner momentum,
or they seem to be purely the result of study of a new text. A description
of how or why any idea originates can only be approximate in the best
of circumstances; but for even an approximate description, we would
need to know much more than we do about the intellectual and psychological development of the humanists in question. Though some dispute this, Quattrocento humanists did not tend to be highly introspec-

---

dustria tueantur." In direct discourse without diphthongs the *maxime* in the Sallust quotation is correct, and the error here may be the scribe's.

152.   Tignosi, in Laur. 76, 49, fol. 145; Acciaiuoli, in Magl. XXI 137, fol. 124v (cf. ed.
1478, sig. [D]D1). For these commentaries, and their manuscripts, see Chapter VI, n. 44,
and Chapter VIII, n. 24, below.

153.   Edited in M. Lentzen, *Studien zur Dante-Exegese Cristoforo Landinos, mit einem
Anhang bisher unveröffentlichter Briefe und Reden* (Cologne and Vienna, 1971), pp. 260ff.

154.   From his *Summa philosophiae* to Michele Mercati, ca. 1455, ed. in P. O. Kristeller,
Studies, p. 74. For a nearly identical reference, see Ficino's *Di dio et anima* (1458), ed. in
Kristeller, *Supplementum Ficinianum*, II, 130. Ficino may have been led to the passages by
a religious mentor, Lorenzo Pisano. See p. 184, below.

tive.[155] To account for the appearance of any idea, we would need to know much more also about the thought of both popular preachers and ecclesiastical scholastics, the more elite counselors to the Florentine government and those in more popular offices, storytellers, dramatists, and artists, and, finally, lawyers with their legal *consilia*. We shall examine ideas as they arise without attempting to account, except in general or hypothetical terms, for why they appeared when they did. Instances of their popularity will be treated as mere phenomena. Here I hope to avoid what so often happens in Renaissance intellectual historiography: origins are confused with causes, expression is confused with motive, and the spirit of the age generates its own spirit.

155. For the limits of introspection in the Italian Renaissance, see the general remarks of K. J. Weintraub, *The Value of the Individual; Self and Circumstance in Autobiography* (Chicago, 1978), chaps. 5–7.

PART TWO

THE
FLORENTINE
LYCEUM

III

THE STUDENTS OF
JOHN ARGYROPOULOS

I N the last chapter we looked at several strata of Florentine intellectuals in the mid-Quattrocento. There were those from the ruling
class, for many of whom public intellectual activity meant simply giving political advice. Some of these, of aristocratic background, had political ambitions independent of the Medici family. Then there were
those from "traditional intellectual" backgrounds: many—schoolmen,
lawyers, and clerics—followed "traditional" pursuits. Some of these and
others turned to the humanities and would use their humanistic training
to support themselves. Those most responsible for the popular expression of the ideas of the philosophical renaissance either were from the
ruling class or were their clients. In this and the next two chapters we
shall look especially at the better born themselves, their educational
goals and how these goals were realized. In Quattrocento Florence the
behavior of this merchant-nobility was largely dictated by fashion, and
the aristocratic youth required the best schooling. At the dawn of the
philosophical renaissance, John Argyropoulos and his Lyceum were the
rage.

Supported actively by Donato Acciaiuoli and his friends and nominally, at least, by the Medici family, John Argyropoulos in 1455 was offered a lectureship at the Florentine University in Greek language, literature, and philosophy. He waited until the winter of 1456–57 to accept
a position, and he began to lecture on Aristotle's logic, dialectics, and
ethics. By the autumn of 1458 he had moved on to Aristotle's natural
philosophy, first the *Physics*, then the *De anima* and the *Meteorologica*.
Later he lectured on Aristotle's *Metaphysics*. Florence paid him a large
salary (four hundred florins per year, equivalent to the highest human-

istic salaries in the Quattrocento) and, after he had taught for almost a decade, honored him with citizenship and a tax exemption.[1] Figures as famous as Lorenzo de' Medici and Angelo Poliziano were his early students.[2] Another humanist of some note, Bartolomeo Fonzio, adorned his notebooks of classical and humanist notabilia with excerpts from Argyropoulos's lectures and translations.[3] Foreign scholars passing through Florence visited the learned Byzantine so that they could tell their friends back home that they had tapped the wisdom of Florence's most famous humanist-philosopher.[4]

For those humanists in Florence who were accustomed to the study of Latin eloquence alone, the culture of Argyropoulos, like that of the other Byzantines, offered great enrichment.[5] He was born in Constan-

1.   A. Gherardi, ed., *Statuti della Università e Studio fiorentino dell'anno 1387, seguiti da un'appendice di documenti dal 1320 al 1472* (1881; rept. Bologna, 1973), pp. 489–92.

2.   A. Rochon, *La jeunesse de Laurent de Médicis (1449–1478)* (Paris, 1963), pp. 37–39; I. Maïer, *Ange Politien: La formation d'un poète humaniste (1469–1480)* (Geneva, 1966), pp. 24–28. In the colophon of a manuscript of Leonardo Bruni's translation of the *Nicomachean Ethics*, copied in May 1457, Benedetto Colucci da Pistoia mentioned that he was a student of Argyropoulos (Bologna, Bibl. Universitaria, cod. 2703, fol. 126): "Ethicorum Aristotelis libri expliciunt nuper a Leonardo viro nostre tempestatis doctissimo traducti ac scripti per me Benedictum Colucci scribam Pistoriensem anno salutifere incarnationis MCCCCLVII die XVII Madii cum Florentie in domo Mariotti de Bartholinis vitam ducerem ac disciplina fruerer Iohannis Argilopoli [*sic*] viri doctissimi quem [?] deus [?] omnipotens me sequi ac imitari dignetur concedere. Amen." See also L. Frati's description of the manuscript in *Studi italiani di filologia classica* 17 (1909), 93 (under no. 1425), and A. Frugoni, ed., *Scritti inediti di Benedetto Colucci da Pistoia* (Florence, 1939), p. vii (desc. evidently taken from Frati).

3.   S. Caroti and S. Zamponi, *Lo scrittoio di Bartolomeo Fonzio, umanista fiorentino* (Milan, 1974), pp. 44, 49, 60.

4.   Vespasiano, *Vite*, I, 329, 330, 418; II, 205.

5.   For Argyropoulos, the works most relevant to this study include Gherardi, ed., *Statuti*, pp. 271, 467, 489–92; Vespasiano, *Vite*; Zippel, "Per la biografia dell'A." (1896), now in his *Storia e cultura del Rinascimento* (Padua, 1979), pp. 179–97; Della Torre, *Storia*, pp. 366–401 *passim*; S. P. Lampros, *Argyropouleia* (Athens, 1910); Cammelli, *Argiropulo*; Garin, "Donato Acciaiuoli cittadino"; Garin, "Platonici bizantini e platonici italiani: 1. Nuove indagini sul Pletone," in his *Studi sul Platonismo medievale* (Florence, 1958), pp. 155–90; E. Bigi, "G. A.," *DBI*, vol. 4 (1962), 129–31; J. Seigel, "The Teaching of Argyropulos and the Rhetoric of the First Humanists," in T. K. Rabb and J. E. Seigel, eds., *Action and Conviction in Early Modern Europe: Essays in Memory of E. H. Harbison* (Princeton, 1969), pp. 237–60; V. Brown, "Giovanni Argiropulo on the Agent Intellect: An Edition of Ms. Magliabecchi V 42 (ff. 224–228v)," in J. R. O'Donnell, ed., *Essays in Honour of Anton Charles Pegis* (Toronto, 1974), pp. 160–75; D. J. Geanakoplos, "The Italian Renaissance and Byzantium: The Career of the Greek Humanist-Professor John Argyropoulos in Florence and Rome (1415–1487)," *Conspectus of History* 1 (1974), 12–28; J. Monfasani, *George of Trebizond: A Biography and Study of His Rhetoric and Logic* (Leiden, 1976), pp. 375–78. *If* the attribution is correct, P. Canivet and N. Oikonomidès, "[Jean Argyropoulos], La comédie de Katablattas: Invective byzantine du XVe s.," *Diptycha* 3 (1982–83), 5–97 and plates 1–2, throws new light on Argyropoulos's early career. But the attribution is questionable: it would require that Argyropoulos be born ca. 1393-94 and at

tinople about 1410. After early training in Greek rhetoric and philosophy, he may have joined (the evidence is confusing) other Byzantine
intellectuals at the Council of Florence in the late 1430s. From 1441 to
1444 he lived in Padua at the house of the Florentine exile Palla Strozzi.
There he taught Greek rhetoric and philosophy privately to some Pad-
uan nobles and polished his Latin through conversation and instruction
at the University of Padua. He may have lectured on Greek literature
and language at the University, in the arts faculty; his studies were in
the arts, including Latin—that is, scholastic—philosophy. By 1448 he
was back in Constantinople in a prestigious position teaching at the
Museum of the Xenon. He fled when Constantinople fell to the Turks
in 1453, made his way to Venice and then Padua, and spent part of the
summer of 1454 in Florence, where he became acquainted with a group
of young Florentine aristocrats and intellectuals led by Donato Acciaiuoli and Alamanno Rinuccini.

Not long after his short stay in Florence, Argyropoulos probably returned to Greece, to the court of Thomas Palaeologus, who held an area
in the Peloponnesus not yet conquered by the Turks. Soon future students and Medici patrons in Florence won for him the aforementioned
university position. He remained in Florence some fifteen years, took
up teaching in Rome in the early 1470s, returned briefly to Florence
toward the end of the decade, and then went back to Rome, where he
died in 1487.

Many students of John Argyropoulos would also become members
of the Platonic Academy—if, that is, one may describe as "members"
those in that loose association of scholars, merchants, and politicians
attracted to Platonic teachings as interpreted by Marsilio Ficino. To understand the origins of the Platonic Academy we must analyze why the
followers of Argyropoulos turned from Aristotelian to Platonic studies.
Or did they? Many seemed to move freely between the Lyceum and the
Academy. But in describing the "transition" from Aristotle to Plato,
from John Argyropoulos to Marsilio Ficino, most scholars have followed the radical interpretation of the philosophical renaissance offered
by Eugenio Garin. According to Garin, John Argyropoulos was a Platonist: he taught his preferred Platonic doctrines in his lectures on Aristotle, and, privately to those of his circle, he lectured on the Platonic

---

some time have become a priest (on this "ecclesiastical career," see the confusing testimony noted by Lampros, pp. XVI–XVII [in Greek pagination]). For Argyropoulos's
later career, see A. Verde, *Lo Studio fiorentino, 1473–1503*, 4 vols. (Florence, 1973; Pistoia,
1977; Florence, 1986): vol. 1 contains an annotated bibliography to the secondary works,
for which the notes of vol. 2, p. 321, provide an index of sorts. See also Verde's "G. A. e
Lorenzo Buonincontri professori nello Studio fiorentino," *Rinascimento*, 2d. ser., 14
(1974), 279–87.

dialogues themselves. A form of Platonism, the theory goes, was already fashionable before Ficino and the Medici founded their Academy.[6]

Marsilio Ficino himself, to be sure, recognized an important Byzantine role in the revival of Plato. In Byzantium, Ficino wrote in 1464, the "spirit of Plato" had dwelt since antiquity, and it had now "flown to Italy."[7] Much later he argued that the Byzantine Gemistus Pletho's discourses on Plato during the Council of Florence, in the late 1430s, had first inspired Cosimo de' Medici to found the Platonic Academy.[8] But wherever the "spirit of Plato" had dwelt before his own time, for Ficino it now resided in his Academy. In 1464 Ficino knew the historical importance of his translations of Plato, and at least since 1458 he had been aware of the uniqueness and originality of his interpretation of the Platonic corpus.[9]

Modern scholars, however, have been less generous toward Ficino than Ficino was toward himself. For many the "spirit of Plato" did not fly to Italy with the Greek text of Plato (as Ficino claimed) but was borne to Florence by John Argyropoulos when he left the Greek world for Italy after the Turks took Constantinople. Some contemporary testimony lends support to this hypothesis. In 1463, for instance, Donato Acciaiuoli wrote that Platonic and Aristotelian studies were so flourishing in Florence that the Athenian Academy, it seemed, had been brought back to life. He credited John Argyropoulos with the revival.[10] Decades later another student, Alamanno Rinuccini, would also discuss the philosophical renaissance, and once again the revival was due to Argyropoulos, with no mention whatsoever of Marsilio Ficino or his Platonic circle.[11] Such testimony as this has led Eugenio Garin to argue that political and ideological reasons prevented Ficino's followers and the Medicean Platonic Academy from acknowledging their debt to the Byzantine: the "tacit use of citations," Garin notes, "is no modern invention."[12]

Were the students of Argyropoulos a special lot? In some older studies, in which the Quattrocento Academy is seen as the prototype of the

6. See the sources cited below, Chapter V, nn. 5–8.

7. See below, Chapter V, n. 3.

8. See Kristeller, "Byzantine and Western Platonism in the Fifteenth Century," in his *Renaissance Thought and Its Sources* (New York, 1975), p. 161.

9. See Chapter VII, below.

10. Letter (for Vespasiano da Bisticci) to Alfonso de Palencia, 24 Sept. 1463, ed. in Fossi, *Monumenta*, pp. 60–63.

11. Letter to Roberto Salviati, 1489, in *Lettere ed orazioni*, pp. 188–89.

12. "La rinascita di Plotino," in his *Rinascite e rivoluzioni: Movimenti culturali dal XIV al XVIII secolo* (Bari, 1976), pp. 96–97; cf. "Donato Acciaiuoli cittadino," p. 265.

Early Modern one, the students of Argyropoulos and those of Ficino
are in a happy harmony, dedicated to the scientific pursuit of truth. Certainly many young Florentines moved freely in both circles.[13] But Kristeller has noted the "coolness" and "lateness" of relations between Marsilio Ficino and Donato Acciaiuoli, and the "complete silence" between
Ficino and Alamanno Rinuccini.[14] Even while arguing that Argyropoulos was the founder of Florentine Neoplatonism, Garin goes further
than Kristeller in emphasizing the separateness of the two schools.
Garin, instead, finds ideological differences and has the two schools do
battle. Students of Argyropoulos, committed to logic, rhetoric, and
moral philosophy, upheld older, republican ideas of the active life of the
citizen in the world. The Ficino circle believed in flight from the world
and speculative studies carried out in contemplative withdrawal, where
"civic duties" were turned over to their Medici patrons.[15]

The "Argyropoulos circle," as we said, was led by Donato Acciaiuoli,
who, with Alamanno Rinuccini, had persuaded the Medici and other
leading Florentines to give a public appointment to Argyropoulos in
the Florentine Studio. Acciaiuoli was Argyropoulos's most diligent student. During the first half-decade of Argyropoulos's residence in Florence, Acciaiuoli recorded his teacher's lectures verbatim, or nearly so.
Thereafter, he attended lectures when public duties permitted it.[16] According to Vespasiano da Bisticci, when plague closed the Florentine
university, Acciaiuoli took his teacher with him to a villa in the country,
where he, his brother Piero, and others continued their studies in Greek

13.   See the summary remarks of Della Torre, *Storia*, p. 562.

14.   "L'état présent des études sur Marsile Ficin," in *Platon et Aristote à la Renaissance*
(Paris, 1976), p. 68. See below, Chapter V, n. 60, Chapter VIII, n. 86, and pp. 241–43. I
wonder if some of Ficino's letters of 1457–58, during the first year of Argyropoulos's public appointment, contain veiled references to the Byzantine's popular lectures. On 1 Nov.
1457 he urged Antonio Serafico to cultivate philosophy "with his whole heart" while
others do so "merely with their tongues" (ed. in Kristeller, *Supplementum Ficinianum*, II,
82). At about this same time, he urged Piero de' Pazzi to take some time off from that
"public philosophy," which in these years he was "especially cultivating," to read, at least
in passing, the "private" philosophical letter of his client: "Obsecro te propter humanita-
tem tuam vir optime, ut publice philosophie quam his temporibus precipue colis paulum
surripias temporis, quo hanc tui clientis epistolam vel per transennam ut dicitur legas"
(ed. ibid., II, 84; for the date, see Kristeller, *Studies*, p. 49). Donato Acciaiuoli, by contrast, seems to refer to Cosimo's Platonic Academy very soon after it was founded. On 9
July 1462 he wrote to Banco da Casavecchia as follows: "Si me tantum amas, quantum
Vespasiano persuasum est se a nova achademia diligi, surripe, queso, aliquid tempus ad
scribendum" (ed. in Della Torre, *Storia*, p. 410). These statements, of course, merely affirm Kristeller's statement regarding the mutual "coolness."

15.   See the sources cited above, n. 12, and Chapter I, n. 19.

16.   See Chapter VIII, below.

language and philosophy.[17] Again according to Vespasiano, another Florentine noble, Franco Sacchetti, invited Argyropoulos into his house also for private lessons and conversation. Here the whole Acciaiuoli circle gathered: Donato and Piero Acciaiuoli, Alamanno Rinuccini, Marco Parenti, Carlo d'Antonio di Salvestro, Banco da Casavecchia, and several members of the Pandolfini family. Sacchetti also brought grain and wine to Argyropoulos's house and "saw after his every need."[18]

What links these students and disciples, except that they nearly all were from the best and oldest families in Florence and hence were among the citizen-heroes of Vespasiano da Bisticci's biographies? Garin has emphasized their "commitment" to the traditional humanist studies and the values of the active life. Certainly they were committed to the *reality* of the active life, for these merchant-aristocrats were sufficiently well-to-do to be eligible for public office. But I would argue that no "activist" ideology, either of their own or of their teacher Argyropoulos, explains the attraction of the Byzantine's lectures. Rather, that the students of Argyropoulos *were* from the best and oldest families may explain the appeal of his program of studies.

Let us begin by considering Vespasiano da Bisticci's portrait of Argyropoulos's most diligent student, Donato Acciaiuoli. As if by way of introduction Vespasiano felt he had to describe at length Acciaiuoli's grandfather, Donato di Iacopo. This elder Donato, Vespasiano wrote, was a

> tall, fair, well-proportioned man of benign and striking presence, so that one who might know nothing of him would say, on seeing him, that he was born to command. He wore over his vest a long gown interwoven with gold which reached the ground and was furnished with buttons of silver gilt, worked to look like thread; these buttons reached from the top to the bottom. Over this gown he wore a cloak of crimson damask brocaded with gold and lined with silk and open on the right side. On his head he wore a gray beaver hat with hood under. He kept a fine establishment of horses and servants.[19]

Our Donato, Donato di Neri, was likewise "physically very attractive," wrote Vespasiano, "of white skin and pink complexion." His manner

---

17. *Vite*, II, 12–13; Rinuccini, *Lettere ed orazioni*, pp. 33–34; Giustiniani, *Alamanno Rinuccini*, pp. 120–24.

18. *Vite*, II, 215–17.

19. Vespasiano, *Vite*, II, 8–9. For this passage I have taken the translation (adapting it slightly) from W. George and E. Waters: Vespasiano da Bisticci, *Renaissance Princes, Popes, and Prelates* (New York, 1963), p. 272.

was serious but graceful. He and his brother Piero "always went about Florence together, and all looked upon them in admiration, due to the nobility of their family, the distinction of their habits, and their physical beauty as well."[20]

Shining in this aristocratic light, our modern historians' hero of the *vita attiva e civile*, when he came of age (the early 1460s), did indeed fulfill those public offices for which every male Florentine from a better family and not in political trouble or tax arrears was eligible. And his eloquence and grace made him a favorite choice for elective embassies.[21] According to Vespasiano, Donato learned in foreign courts that when a visiting ambassador removed his hat, the host did the same; when a visitor awaited a prince in an anteroom the host should enter the anteroom, take the guest's hand, and lead him into his own apartment. These courtly practices had not been followed in Florence until the 1470s, Vespasiano noted, when Donato Acciaiuoli became Gonfaloniere di Giustizia and ordered them done.[22]

Vespasiano da Bisticci wrote that Donato "was like a mirror before all, both to the young and to others."[23] This theme marks Cristoforo Landino's funeral oration on Donato in 1478: Strive to your utmost, Landino urged the young Florentines, and we will have here many Donato Acciaiuolis![24] How different an ideal in the 1450s was Landino himself! In his *catasto* report of 1458, he had to declare that he had no house and that his sole possessions were his horse and a modest university salary.[25] Marsilio Ficino, who came to lead the Platonic Academy, was only slightly better off financially.[26] While Acciaiuoli found cousins who were knights and ancestors who were nobles, it took Ficino years to figure out how to spell his surname.[27] Ficino served as a model for almost no one. He supported himself by tutoring the elite, he was mel-

---

20.   Vespasiano, *Vite*, II, 9–10.

21.   For a list of Acciaiuoli's regular and special offices, see Ganz, "Humanist as Citizen," pp. 290–91.

22.   Vespasiano, *Vite*, II, 36–37.

23.   Ibid., II, 21–22.

24.   *Reden Cristoforo Landinos*, ed. M. Lentzen (Munich, 1974), p. 76.

25.   Ed. in A. M. Bandini, *Specimen literaturae Florentinae saeculi XV . . .* (Florence, 1747–51), I, 174–75 (Bandini's date is s.f.).

26.   For Ficino's social and financial status, see the documents cited by P. O. Kristeller, "M. F. and His Work after Five Hundred Years," in *Marsilio Ficino e il ritorno di Platone: Studi e documenti*, ed. G. C. Garfagnini (Florence, 1986), I, 171–80, and P. Viti, "Documenti ignoti per la biografia di M. F.," ibid., I, 251–83.

27.   For Ficino's surname, see Della Torre, *Storia*, p. 479n.; see also the several autograph corrections in *Marsilio Ficino e il ritorno: Mostra*, pp. 1ff.

ancholic, he lisped, and he looked rather peculiar. When he walked about Florence his shoulders were hunched and his arms too long.[28]

The Florentine ruling class was defined in part by its wealth, in part by its participation in public life. It was also defined by its manner, the style of elegance that Vespasiano da Bisticci would so happily describe in Donato Acciaiuoli and his ancestors. The ruling class was also defined by its style of education. This education was shaped both by professional requirements and by fashion. All from the ruling class had to know how to read and write; most also needed to know enough mathematics to keep or at least scrutinize the family books. Almost all held public office, and to give counsel effectively they had to know how to speak, and here the humanists especially could be of assistance. Services of this sort were generally recognized as valuable. When in 1460, for instance, advisers to the Florentine government proposed to transfer the Studio to Pisa, it was suggested that the humanistic chairs remain in Florence, and this was the solution adopted a dozen years later when the move was finally approved.[29] Many of the young and better born, however, went beyond the minimal, "necessary" studies, and at different periods in the Quattrocento wider humanistic studies of a particular sort or under a particular figure became, simply, "fashionable." In the early Quattrocento, for instance, the best Florentines studied under Roberto de' Rossi: that these studies were in fashion lends weight to the meager evidence that Giovanni di Bicci de' Medici put his son, Cosimo, under Roberto's tutelage.[30] Then in the early 1430s Francesco Filelfo held a position in the Florentine Studio: according to Vespasiano da Bisticci, "all the sons of the well-to-do men" in Florence attended his lessons.[31]

28.   See G. Corsi's biographical sketch, ed. in R. Marcel, *Marsile Ficin (1433–1499)* (Paris, 1958), pp. 685–86, and trans. in Ficino, *Letters*, III, 143. For Ficino's physical appearance, see also Kristeller, "L'état présent des études," p. 76, n. 71, the plates in *Il lume del sole: Marsilio Ficino medico dell'anima*, eds. P. Castelli et al. (Florence, 1984), and the plates in Kristeller, "Marsilio Ficino and His Work."

29.   Ed. Brucker, "Civic Debate on Florentine Higher Education (1460)," p. 531. Brucker argues that the debate points to the Florentines' indifference toward the sort of learning praised by Leonardo Bruni—that is, the humanities. Indeed, one of the debaters suggested that Florence could get along perfectly well without the *studia bonarum artium*: but in a university context this term covered a much wider area than the humanities proper, and the "economic question" of the university largely hinged on funding for the *professional* disciplines.

30.   Della Torre, *Storia*, pp. 196–200; cf. Vespasiano, *Vite*, II, 168: "Furono nella età di Cosimo molti uomini di conditione, che studiorono sotto la disciplina di Ruberto." For Cosimo, see Gutkind, *Cosimo*, pp. 4–5, 207n.

31.   Vespasiano, *Vite*, II, 54: "Venuto a Firenze, sendo di prestantissimo ingegno, ebbe tutti i figliuoli degli uomini da bene alle sua letioni."

At the height of his popularity Filelfo would boast of four hundred students ("or perhaps even more").[32]

For a good example of the expanding humanistic conception of an aristocratic style in the earlier Quattrocento, we may repeat the famous account of the conversion of Piero de' Pazzi to the humanities. The story originates with Vespasiano da Bisticci. Piero de' Pazzi, Vespasiano stated, was from an "ancient and noble" Florentine family. Physically very beautiful (*di bellissimo aspetto*), he spent his youth in worldly pleasures. His father, a noble but illiterate merchant, did not worry about his son getting a humanistic education. One day Niccolò Niccoli approached Piero and asked him whose son he was. He said, "Andrea." Then Niccolò asked him what his occupation was. He said, "I have a good time." Then Niccolò said to him: you are from a noble family and are good-looking; it is shameful that you do not devote your time to learning Latin, which "would be for you a great ornament." If you do not learn it, you will be reckoned nothing when the flower of youth passes. Deeply ashamed, Piero de' Pazzi went out looking for a suitable *praeceptor*, and afterward, in his pursuit of learning, he never lost an hour of time.[33]

While Latin culture sufficed as an ornament for Piero de' Pazzi, in the first half of the Quattrocento the humanistic program itself expanded and, for many humanists, came to include Greek. Whether taken up by professional humanists or the educated merchant class, the thrust behind the new Greek studies was almost wholly aristocratic. There was a desire, to be sure, to disclose a "better" Aristotle through a better translation, but even here this desire was founded in part on aristocratic rivalry, an attempt, specifically, to embarrass the scholastics. Greek also allowed the humanists to compete with one another, and even with ancient Latins, in preparing translations of selected texts. When Donato Acciaiuoli drafted a Latin translation of some lives of Plutarch, he submitted his text to Poggio Bracciolini for comment. Poggio found the translation comparable in quality to the translations of Leonardo Bruni—for Poggio this was an extremely laudatory comparison, for he shamelessly regarded any work of a Florentine chancellor as the epitome of eloquence.[34] More commonly, within the ruling class, the knowledge of Greek was described as a great "ornament" (as, in fact, Vespasiano da

32. Letter to Giovanni Aurispa, 31 July 1429, in *Epistolae familiares* (Venice, 1502), fol. 9–9v. Vespasiano da Bisticci, however, stated that there were "two hundred or more" (*Vite*, II, 54).

33. Vespasiano, *Vite*, II, 309–10. Recounted by Burckhardt, *Civilization of the Renaissance in Italy*, p. 170.

34. Vespasiano, *Vite*, II, 26.

Bisticci described Piero de' Pazzi's Latin)—a largely "useless" study be-
fitting an aristocrat. In the mid-Quattrocento, for Donato Acciaiuoli
and members of his circle, the knowledge and use of Greek seems to be
almost a rite of passage, and in their letters they display, often indeco-
rously, their expanded culture. In a letter congratulating Manetti for his
funeral oration on Leonardo Bruni (1444), for instance, Niccolò della
Luna in the space of about a page managed to include four instances of
his Greek learning ("ut Greco utar proverbio," "Socraticum illud . . .
exemplum," "non . . . ut Aristarchus," and "ut Grece loquar").[35] Acciaiuoli likewise began to insert Greek phrases into his Latin letters and
encounter the same in letters he received. The prize catch of course was
to receive a letter written entirely in Greek from a famous humanist,
such as Filelfo. In response to one Greek letter, from Lianoro Lianori,
Acciaiuoli in 1454 praised Greek language as the "decor" and "light" of
the world: I, however, he said, must for now write in Latin, since I have
only just begun Greek. Alamanno Rinuccini will answer you in Greek:
he is ἑλλινικότερος [sic!] than I.[36]

Even more useless than Greek was speculative philosophy. It was so
useless, in fact, that the humanists remarked on its "uselessness" in attacking or avoiding it. They excluded it from the *studia humanitatis* and
deemed it rather an appropriate subject for the doctor or theologian.
Yet from about the middle of the Quattrocento, before the founding of
the Platonic Academy, many younger humanists and lay intellectuals
were turning to speculative philosophy. As Alamanno Rinuccini would
later note, before his generation—that is, before the 1450s—no one in
Florence, except doctors and theologians, took up natural philosophy
or metaphysics; but this is now, he said, part of every Florentine's education.[37] That a "useless" study should become fashionable in an aristocratic culture, however, does not explain the particular form of the "uselessness." Perhaps we can better understand the origins of the new,
speculative interests by looking at how their flowering was viewed in
one individual, Giannozzo Manetti.

When he described the "limits" of the humanists of the previous generation, Alamanno Rinuccini offered the name of Manetti as the sole
exception. Among the humanists of the earlier Quattrocento, almost no
one except Manetti had mastered natural philosophy and metaphysics.[38]
Vespasiano da Bisticci, who knew Manetti well, was also struck by this

35. Ricc. 1166, fols. 13v–14.
36. Dated 1 Oct. 1454, Magl. VIII 1390, fol. 89v.
37. *Lettere ed orazioni*, pp. 188–89.
38. Ibid.

peculiar dedication to speculative philosophy.[39] And he was so impressed by Manetti's range of knowledge and activity that he gave the Manetti biography more space than any other.[40] For the Acciaiuoli circle, Manetti was a figure born too soon: he burst upon the early Quattrocento and became the model for a whole group of Florentine humanists. Since we are more concerned about his "image" than his reality, we shall look at some length at that portrait of Manetti drawn by his close friend and a steadfast adherent of the Acciaiuoli circle, the book dealer Vespasiano da Bisticci.

According to Vespasiano, Manetti's father, Bernardo, wanted to turn Giannozzo (1396–1459) into a good merchant and saw to it that he got early training in reading and writing. Then Giannozzo took up mathematics, and he became so good at it that by the age of ten or eleven he handled cash receipts and expenditures for the family bank.[41] Manetti would later compare the evening tally to God's reckoning of a man's life at the hour of death. God gave man time as a merchant turns over money to the cashier: when the cash is counted at the end of the day, if the total does not equal the amount recorded, it is a disgrace.[42] Manetti's life is characteristically serious and intense. He decided that he was suited to become something more than a mere merchant and, after taking up Latin grammar, began studying logic, philosophy, and theology under the monks Girolamo da Napoli and Evangelista da Pisa, who taught at the convent of Santo Spirito, near Manetti's house in Florence's Oltrarno. For nine years, according to Vespasiano, Manetti studied without interruption, never in that period taking time to cross the Arno![43] Manetti even rested intensely, never giving himself more than five hours of sleep a night.[44] In his famous treatise on the dignity of man, Manetti would later write that man by nature could understand (*intelligere*), act (*agere*), and laugh (*ridere*). Man *should*, however, spend his time on the first two.[45] Again we learn from Vespasiano that the

39. In his *Breve descriptione* summarizing his *Vite*, Vespasiano da Bisticci went through the early humanists and remarked that Manetti "fu de' primi che, in quella età de' secolari, desse opera a filosofia, et che entrasse in una scienzia tanto ardua et tanto difficile" (*Vite*, II, 506).

40. Vespasiano wrote both a *Vita* of Manetti (*Vite*, I, 485–538) and a *Comentario della vita* (ibid., II, 515–622).

41. *Vite*, II, 519.

42. Ibid., II, 586–87.

43. Ibid., I, 487; II, 520–22.

44. Ibid., I, 487; II, 520.

45. *De dignitate et excellentia hominis*, ed. E. R. Leonard (Padua, 1975), pp. 91–92.

teaching was followed. Manetti "never engaged in any diversion, in order never to lose time."[46]

As a humanist from a good, old family, Manetti seems similar to Leon Battista Alberti, who also believed in the rational use of time. Alberti believed that God gave man three things to use and develop or throw away: certain faculties of the mind, the body, and time.[47] Like Manetti, Alberti believed in the intensive use of the mind in thinking and doing. Was this, as some maintain, a "bourgeois" ethic? Surely the mercantile activity of Manetti and Alberti shaped their thought. But this "work ethic" (as Max Weber has noted) differed greatly from that later developed by the Protestants.[48] For the Italian merchant-humanists the rational use of time glorified not God but man. It was used as in the cashbox analogy: it is stored up in the ever more cultivated and complete individual; then it is paid out in exemplary activity. There is an individualistic, "selfish" aspect to the Alberti and Manetti ethic, promoting the development of what Burckhardt called the extraordinary, unusual type of Renaissance figure, the "universal man."[49]

Manetti, however, was the more typical Burckhardtian "Renaissance man," the "many-sided man": unlike the *uomo universale* Alberti, Manetti could not write treaties on painting, was no architect, and could not jump over horses from a standing position.[50] According to Vespasiano, Manetti became so good in Latin that he could deliver an extemporaneous oration better than Carlo Marsuppini could deliver a prepared one.[51] His Greek was excellent, and his knowledge of Hebrew allowed him to debate theological questions with Jewish scholars.[52] Manetti moved most freely in Latin scholastic circles. He mastered natural philosophy, metaphysics, and Christian theology, and often participated in scholastic debates, stunning everyone with the range and depth of his thought. To Vespasiano da Bisticci's wonderment, Manetti could even debate really "knotty" questions like the nature of the Trinity.[53]

Among those enterprises appropriate for his class, Manetti also seemed to strive toward universality in the active life. He married, raised

---

46. *Vite*, II, 586.

47. *Della famiglia*, pp. 168–69.

48. M. Weber, *The Protestant Ethic and the Spirit of Capitalism*, trans. Talcott Parsons (New York, 1930), chap. 2, pp. 194–98, n. 12.

49. *Civilization of the Renaissance in Italy*, pp. 124ff.

50. For the "many-sided" man, see ibid.

51. *Vite*, I, 518–520; II, 578–79.

52. Ibid., I, 486, 504; II, 524–25, 557–58.

53. Ibid., I, 492–93; II, 537–38, 544–45, 603.

children, and ran the family business. He held regular and prestigious public offices in Florence and its subject territories. His greatest fame was as an ambassador: Florence chose Manetti for its most formal and dignified missions. In 1445, for instance, he represented the Florentine government at Naples for the marriage of a son of Alfonso of Aragon. At a procession welcoming the ambassadors, according to Vespasiano, all the Neapolitans came out hoping to catch a glimpse of this famed Florentine humanist. They came with boards, paper, and pens to take down the oration in writing. And when Manetti delivered his speech, all stood so attentively that when a fly landed on the king's face, no one moved to brush it away.[54]

Manetti was also exemplary in religious activity. He carefully learned holy scriptures, he fasted, he gave alms, he heard Mass. He also went to confession, but one wonders what he had to confess: he never lied, he never spoke badly of anyone, he accepted adversity in good spirit, he never laughed, and he never lost an hour of time.[55]

For a Vespasiano nature smiled on such men as Manetti. He was from "laudable ancestors." His body was "wonderfully organized," with no defect—neither liver disease, rheumatism, gout, stones, "nor any type of infirmity." He never had a stomachache, never a headache. His physical appearance was perfect, due to his moderation in eating, drinking, and sleeping. Nature also gave him an unheard of memory, fitting him with a head so large that his hats had to be made to order. He was of good stature, neither too large nor too small, neither thin nor fat.[56]

In Vespasiano's biography we indeed find the perfect Renaissance man. Intellectually Manetti moved outward to embrace nearly all areas of knowledge; actively he followed every worthy pursuit. "Ours are the mountains, ours are the hills, ours are the valleys," . . . "ours are the arts, ours are the sciences"—so reads for several pages Manetti's list, in his famous treatise on the dignity of man.[57] Man's potential was almost without limit: God made man (he wrote in the same treatise) "very beautiful, very talented, very wise, very rich, and very powerful."[58] Such a man could not leave theological disputations to the Jew and the scholastic, and he could not leave religious good works to the monk. God

54. Ibid., II, 542–43. Pius II also made note of this Neapolitan fly (cited by Gutkind, *Cosimo*, pp. 225–26).

55. *Vite*, I, 488, 490, 495; II, 521, 523–24, 586, 612, 620.

56. Ibid., I, 485; II, 615–16.

57. *De dignitate et excellentia hominis*, pp. 77–82.

58. Ibid., p. 71: "Primum itaque deus hoc tam dignum ac tam prestans eius opificium tanti fecisse et existimasse videtur, ut hominem formosissimum, ingeniosissimum, sapientissimum, opulentissimum, ac denique potentissimum efficeret."

had given man noble condition and time and would render account at
the end. For such a man, pursuing perfection, never losing an hour, the
entry into paradise would be a short step indeed.

   To a follower of Manetti, born fitted to rule and dominate, might we
also want to say, "Ours are the republics, ours are the women"? For the
Manettian compromise was difficult. The desire to rule and dominate
forced the follower of Manetti to extremes. When we view the political
careers of the Acciaiuoli circle, we find men intensely loyal to the Medici
but also straining under the desire to rule. From the oldest and best
families, many were tied to an old anti-Medici established aristocracy;
the sons of the exiled Strozzi are prominent in Vespasiano's biographies.
Donato Acciaiuoli's mother, Maddalena, was Palla Strozzi's daughter.
Donato's older cousin, Agnolo Acciaiuoli, constantly pined for political
power, rivaled Cosimo de' Medici for party leadership, and finally
helped lead the putsch against Piero de' Medici in 1466. Donato's
brother-in-law, Renato di Piero de' Pazzi, was hanged for his alleged
part in the Pazzi conspiracy of 1478. But by all outward appearances,
most in the Acciaiuoli circle were intensely loyal to the Medici. When
revolts occur—the putsch of 1466 or the conspiracy of 1478—certain of
them suddenly emerge as conspirators. Historians have attempted to
explain these conspiracies as if they were survivals from the early fifteenth century—the ideas of Leonardo Bruni and the early Quattrocento bursting forth, the perennial Florentine bud that would blossom
gloriously with Niccolò Machiavelli. To be sure, these revolts have an
antiquarian tinge, and we may speculate that the conspirators looked
back on the good old days of factional politics, when Florence had not
only its Medici but also its Albizzi and its Strozzi. Many of these aristocrats hoped to "Venetianize" Florentine politics, to create a fixed merchant-nobility. Some rebels apparently wanted to do no more than compete with Cosimo and Piero for party leadership. Like Ficino's patrons,
the Acciaiuoli circle was composed of the rich and powerful, and from
these we should not be surprised to find leaders of revolt.

   In their sexual relations the Acciaiuoli circle also tended to extremes:
those who did not dominate others' bodies dominated their own. Manetti counseled continence, though he apparently fulfilled the duties of
the marriage bed. In his *Dialogus in symposio* to Donato Acciaiuoli, dated
1448, one of the subjects proposed was which animal is most useful to
man. All, it turns out, are equally useful, for God has placed his creation
at man's disposal ("ours are the foxes, ours are the wolves, ours are the
water-snakes"[59]). But Manetti devoted more words to bees than any

59.   I am quoting from the *De dignitate et excellentia hominis*, p. 81.

other animal. Bees never lose an hour of time. And they certainly do not waste time in sexual intercourse, preferring to devote themselves wholly to feeding and caring for their little ones (*catuli* is the Latin word Manetti chose for "little bees"[60]). For Manetti's followers, sexuality could only mean promiscuity or abstinence. Niccolò della Luna, a prominent member of the Manetti circle, would complain in letters of the womanizing of his young friends, a vice from which, Della Torre has observed, Niccolò himself was not immune.[61] Cristoforo Landino, not part of the Acciaiuoli circle, yet attempted to bail out one of its members, Francesco Filarete, caught in a sex scandal: he has one fault only, Landino wrote to Lorenzo de' Medici in the early 1460s, and that is what the Greeks call "philogynia idest el troppo amare le femmine."[62] Donato Acciaiuoli followed the norms of Manetti's good bees. He entered his marriage bed a virgin (according to his prenuptial confessor, so struck and startled that he passed the word about) and afterward remained continent.[63] On a diplomatic mission to Milan, Duke Galeazzo decided to test this famous continence and sent a beautiful girl to Acciaiuoli's room one evening; Donato immediately had her led away, to the utter amazement of the Milanese court. For Vespasiano also the behavior was "strange and unaccustomed." After all, "in Donato were all the qualities of those prone to lust": he was rich, noble, and "physically more beautiful than all those of his age."[64]

For a Manetti, who believed that man could strive toward and attain perfection, on his own, relations with the forthcoming generation of merchants, scholars, and nobles offered particular challenges. With a single model of a perfect individual, the humanist's son had to be perfect. By nature the son's higher faculties depended solely on the father (the mother provided at most some physical or sensitive characteristics), and the father could not claim that nature had cheated him. According to Vespasiano, there was in Manetti's son, Agnolo, "all of the hope of his father." From his father and others Agnolo had learned, by the age of twelve, Latin, Greek, and Hebrew, and when he was only thirteen his

60. Laur. 90 sup., 29, fol. 20v; cf. Aristotle, *De generatione animalium* 3.9–10/759a–61a.

61. See Della Torre, *Storia*, pp. 295–99. But Vespasiano da Bisticci wrote that Niccolò "non tolse mai donna per potere meglio vacare alle lettere" (*Vite*, II, 371).

62. Ed. in Landino, *Reden*, p. 93.

63. Vespasiano, *Vite*, II, 32.

64. Ibid., II, 32. The story of the untouched maiden was an old one, applied to more than one saint and celibate before Acciaiuoli's time, and its association with Acciaiuoli may well be fanciful. But then again, the tale's ubiquity may have provoked the duke's experiment.

father took him on diplomatic missions.[65] If the son fell short of the ideal, the father's response was severe. Another of Manetti's sons, Bernardo, was not disposed toward the humanities. Manetti injected him into his *Dialogus in symposio*, set in Venice in 1448 and dedicated to the adolescent Donato Acciaiuoli. In the dialogue, Manetti, on a diplomatic embassy, joins distinguished Florentine friends at a dinner, where they hope to take their minds off a major outbreak of plague. So as not to "waste their time eating, drinking, and worrying," they decide to have a disputation.[66] Manetti's son Bernardo is asked to propose a topic. Bernardo states that his father's library is full of Latin, Greek, and Hebrew codices, but Bernardo confesses that he hasn't read any of them! He does know Italian, however, and so proposes a subject from Boccaccio's *Decameron*.[67]

For a Manetti, a son was weighed by a single model of perfection: he either approached that model or subjected himself to ridicule. Created in the image and likeness of the father, the son provided the perfect occasion for the father's immortality. There was a third type of son, the one who died. According to Vespasiano, Manetti had developed a theory, which he stated publicly, that his fellow Florentines who did not lead a conscientious, upright life were punished by God with the deaths of their sons. When a well-known Florentine lost a son to plague and then did not reform, Manetti remarked that God would take another son. Soon thereafter, a second son died.[68] What happened to the theory when, finally, Manetti's own son Antonino died of plague? Vespasiano does not say. We see, however, in Manetti's dialogue on the death of his son that he was inconsolable. Refusing to follow the Stoic arguments of one of the interlocutors, Donato Acciaiuoli's cousin Agnolo Acciaiuoli, that grief was "customary" and not "natural," Manetti trotted out countless examples of ancients and moderns to prove that all do indeed mourn the loss of a son.[69] Acknowledging that it was perhaps selfish to grieve one's loss and that his son had indeed gone to a better world, Manetti yet had to suffer over one thing: he had overseen the cultural development of his son and could not bring it to completion.[70] As for

65. Ibid., II, 353–55.

66. Laur. 90 sup., 29, fols. 1–3v.

67. Ibid., fol. 4v.

68. *Vite*, I, 489–90; II, 618–19.

69. *Dialogus consolatorius*, ed. A. de Petris (Rome, 1983), pp. 68–126. *All* mourn, that is, except the plebeians (pp. 124–26).

70. Ibid., p. 58: "Hec egritudo nostra, fateor, mea, non defuncti filii spectat incommoda. . . . Et ita mea incommoda spectat, ut etsi ego non nullas ex susceptione, educatione ac dilectione eius voluptates perceperim, maiores tamen, si longior vita fuisset, ca-

the notion that God punished the father by taking the son, Manetti remained silent or, rather, twisted the theory slightly and turned it on its head. Death was an evil and did extend through generations, but the death of the son was an evil borne by the father in the feeling of grief.[71] In the dialogue, Manetti did not attempt to account for God's selection.[72]

The world of Manetti—that of noble merchants devoted to learning—was one of models and exemplary lives. It is little wonder that Manetti "put all his hope" in his son Agnolo, reacted nastily when his son Bernardo fell short, and went into a moral panic when a third son died. At the end of every day each son had to explain to his father what he had done with his time during the day, and each had to produce a description of what was intended for the next.[73] With the death of his son, the one thing for which Manetti could not be consoled was that he would never be able to see the finished result of his son's intellectual and cultural training. When Manetti was thirteen he knew how to balance the family books; when his son Agnolo was thirteen, he was trained in Latin, Greek, and Hebrew, and, accompanying his father on embassies, he was becoming habituated to the diplomatic life.[74]

Like their counterparts both ancient and modern, the young Florentine aristocrat strained to follow models and overcome rivals. As if to give Donato Acciaiuoli his highest praise, Cristoforo Landino concluded his funeral oration on him, as we noted earlier, by urging Flor-

---

pere sperabam. Quibus per mortem me privatum cernens, ⟨non⟩ mediocriter angor." See also pp. 214–18.

71. Ibid., pp. 144ff.

72. Only in the Italian version of the dialogue did Manetti come close to repeating the opinion that Vespasiano said was associated with him: that God punished the father by taking the son. He stated (through an interlocutor) that "Idio . . . puniva le grav(i) sceleratezze degli uomini per la morte de' figliuoli né più né meno come se quella fosse la maggiore pena che in questo mondo si potesse dare alla umana natura" (p. 203). He then said he would give two examples, one from the Old Testament and one from the New. The first is God taking the sons of the Egyptians by plague. The second is the Massacre of the Innocents. For the second, however, Manetti did not mention the guilt of the Innocents' fathers; rather, he showed how God was so revolted by the massacre that he took vengeance on Herod (pp. 203–5). Indeed, the entire argument, absent in the Latin version, is part of a long section of examples of the grief felt by saintly Hebrews and Christians due to the deaths of their sons (pp. 142ff.). The grief, an evil, is general, due to man's sinful nature.

73. Vespasiano, *Vite*, II, 616.

74. In other families the ideals of perfection were inverted: in Quattrocento processions and festivals, Trexler has argued, sons represented the perfected images of flawed fathers ("Ritual in Florence: Adolescence and Salvation in the Renaissance," in C. Trinkaus and H. Oberman, eds., *The Pursuit of Holiness in Late Medieval and Renaissance Religion* [Leiden, 1974], pp. 200–264, esp. pp. 223–32).

ence's youth to model themselves on their late humanist diplomat.[75] The
pursuit of the exemplar, indeed, characterizes the Renaissance, from Petrarch, who worried about what model to choose, to Benvenuto Cellini,
who saw each contemporary as a competitor and a threat.[76] But for the
Acciaiuoli circle the model had to be made flesh. In his biography of
Charlemagne, written in 1461, Donato Acciaiuoli noted that he wanted
to create a model of virtue—not a "feigned" model, as Xenophon had
done with Cyrus, but a real man produced by nature.[77] Acciaiuoli himself came close to the Manettian ideal: he was a good family man, served
the republic in various offices, and mastered the humanistic disciplines,
including Greek, as well as natural philosophy, mathematics, and metaphysics. But he reached this ideal only after a long period of study and
activity.

Early in life Acciaiuoli complemented his studies in the humanities
with serious attention to moral and religious practice. Vespasiano da
Bisticci wrote:

> His life and customs were the very best example to all: he went to
> confession every month, he took communion three or four times
> a year, he fasted regularly on the required vigils and throughout
> Lent. In his youth, to avoid young men of bad customs, Piero
> [Donato's brother] and Donato and their teacher [Iacopo Am-
> mannati] entered a confraternity of young men who lived by a
> very strict rule and who did everything to make good customs a
> habit. Later, when he became older, he entered into the nocturnal
> confraternity of San Girolamo, and he went there every Saturday
> he was in Florence, and he spent the night there sleeping on a
> sack.[78]

Acciaiuoli had the class status to win public offices and yet the wealth
and cultural background to avoid the more mundane duties of the active
life. A follower of Manetti, he could seek perfection in both spheres and

75. *Reden*, p. 76.
76. See Weintraub, *Value of the Individual*, chaps. 5–6.
77. See the Italian and Latin versions of the preface, ed. in D. Gatti, *La Vita Caroli di Donato Acciaiuoli* (Bologna, 1981), pp. 79–82, 99–101.
78. *Vite*, II, 23: "La sua vita e costumi erano di grandissimo esempro, non passava mese ch'egli non si confesassi, e l'anno tre o quatro volte si comunicava, digiunava tutte le vigilie comandate e tutta la quaresima, che mai non lasciava. Nella sua pueritia per fugire i giovani alieni da buoni costumi, entrò Piero et Donato e 'l suo precettore in una compagnia di giovani, dove si viveva con grandissima oservanza di costumi e tutto fe' per fermare bene l'abito de' costumi. Di poi, venendo in più età, entrò in una compagnia di notte, si chiama di sancto Girolamo, e andavavi ogni sabato, quand'era in Firenze, che non mancava, e albergavavi la notte, et dormivavi in sur uno sacone."

pretend that his choice was perfectly free. Apparently attempting to begin a friendly disputation, Acciaiuoli put the question of the two types of life to Marco Parenti in 1455:

> I have gone over in my mind many times the problem of which sort of life is better and more worthy of praise: to serve the republic and to fulfill the duties of a good and wise man by taking part actively in it, or to choose a life removed from all public and private activity, a life yet laborious in the diligent pursuit and investigation of the highest things. We have learned that Pythagoras, Plato, Democritus, and many other great philosophers followed this latter course: having despised private and public actions they applied their talent to the pursuit of truth. This course our theologians have also followed, who labor to explain and bring to light the truth they have discovered, while living a life as far removed as possible from all public matters. Since many arguments can be made for either side, I have decided to put the question before you.[79]

In the 1440s, still a teenager, Donato already seemed anxious to pursue the life of the mind, to move, like Manetti, away from a mere "mercantile" culture. Iacopo Ammannati, the future secretary to Pope Pius II, became his tutor and brought his Latin rhetorical skills to perfection.[80] At the age of about fifteen Donato Acciaiuoli delivered an elegant Latin oration before the Florentine Studio.[81] Later, as the Italian wars intensified in the late 1440s and Florentine taxes increased, Donato was forced to work for the family business under his older cousin Agnolo Acciaiuoli. Donato would declare haughtily that these were years wasted, with studies interrupted, when he was held prisoner in what he called sometimes the "mechanical arts," sometimes the "mercenary

---

79. Magl. VIII 1390, fol. 95 (cf. Della Torre, *Storia*, pp. 363–64, whose version follows some of Acciaiuoli's later superscripts): "Sepe versavi animo et mecum cogitavi quenam sit melior ac laudabilior vivendi ratio, an ad rem p. se conferre in eaque gerenda boni et sapientis hominis prestare officium, an eligere vitam ab omni publica et privata actione remotam, laboriosam tamen continuoque [continuo) assidue *superscr.*] versantem in studio ac investigatione maximarum rerum, ut Pythagoram, Platonem, Democritum aliosque multos et magnos philosophos fecisse [vixisse *superscr.*] accepimus, qui contemptis privatis et publicis actionibus quicquid habuerunt ingenii ad inquirende veritatis studium contulerunt, vel etiam, ut theologi nostri fecerunt, qui veritate inventa in ea illustranda et in lucem deducenda elaborarunt vixeruntque ab omni re p. remotissimi. Cum in utramque partem multa occurrant, que possunt adduci in medium, statui hanc questionem ad te deferre." For Marco Parenti, see now M. Phillips, *The Memoir of Marco Parenti*.

80. Della Torre, *Storia*, pp. 331–32.

81. Vespasiano, *Vite*, II, 24–25.

arts"—terms he used interchangeably and apparently confused.[82] The
Peace of Lodi in 1454 restored his freedom of choice.

But Acciaiuoli's letterbook and notebooks for the late 1440s and early
1450s prove that the period of "captivity" was not time wholly lost. His
letters contain many drafts and corrections, attempts to work and re-
work his letters into an eloquent, publishable form.[83] Some letters deal
with books he wanted copied.[84] Many deal with politics. He also engaged in literary exercises. In one he described a particularly gruesome
crime.[85] In another (as we noted earlier) he discussed political dangers
during plague. In such times, he stated, internal revolts are likely to occur: Florence has wisely stationed foot soldiers throughout the city and
armed and provisioned the castles in the countryside.[86]

Acciaiuoli's culture had an early philosophical direction also. In the
1440s, after learning to speak and read Latin, he followed Manetti's example in turning to logic and dialectics. After some study at the University of Florence, Donato, like Manetti, went to the clergy, to a Domin-
ican friar lecturing at San Marco, one Agnolo da Lecco, who taught the
logical texts of Paul of Venice.[87] In 1455 Donato wrote Agnolo as follows:

> When I had hardly reached the early years of adolescence a won-
> derful desire of learning philosophy seized me, and as I grew older
> the desire became so vehement that I turned all my thoughts to
> the understanding and pursuit of wisdom, and I thought nothing
> in life was worth pursuing unless it was joined with the knowledge
> and doctrine of the highest things. The greatest opportunity to

82.   Letters to Iacopo Ammannati, 1453, Magl. VIII 1390, fol. 82–82v, and to Agnolo (da
Lecco), 27 Feb. 1455, ibid., fol. 94–94v. For confusion over *res mechanicae* and *res mercenariae*, see the autograph corrections, fols. 91, 94v (two on latter page).

83.   Magl. VIII 1390.

84.   There is a good summary of these in E. Garin, "Donato Acciaiuoli cittadino," pp.
207–8n. (the source he cites should be corrected from Magl. VIII 1439 to Magl. VIII
1390).

85.   Magl. VIII 1390, fols. 24–25.

86.   Dated 6 July 1449, ibid., fol. 22–22v.

87.   Della Torre, *Storia*, p. 334. These lectures of Agnolo da Lecco may well be the same
as those attended by Marsilio Ficino's friend Antonio Serafico in 1451–52. See the document dated 2 Oct. 1451, ed. M. T. Sillano in *Le ricordanze di Giovanni Chellini da San
Miniato, medico, mercante e umanista (1425–1457)* (Milan, 1984), p. 182. In his edition of
Vespasiano da Bisticci's *Vite* (II, 10–11n.), A. Greco states that this Agnolo is listed in a
document of the Florentine Studio (citing Gherardi, ed., *Statuti*, pp. 461–62). This is
incorrect. Greco has evidently taken his reference from an early form of E. Garin's article
on Acciaiuoli (in *Rinascimento* I [1950], 53, 54n.), where, due presumably to an error in
typesetting, many of the footnotes are one place removed from where they should be.

satisfy my desire came with your arrival in this city, when I was by divine favor allotted you as my teacher—nor could I have wished for any teacher more learned, pleasant, or agreeable. Joined by some of my friends, as you know, I turned my attention, even more zealously than my age would seem to call for, to dialectics and philosophy.[88]

The first known product of Acciaiuoli's study in logical method appears in 1450, when he exchanged letters and arguments with Manetti on a scholastic question, that of the problem of original sin and the condemnation of unbaptized infants.[89]

Although Acciaiuoli could learn his Latin from Iacopo Ammannati, his Greek from Francesco da Castiglione, and some philosophy from Agnolo da Lecco, he still continually sounded a theme which he would repeat often in the 1450s: for the Florentine youths to be properly educated they must have a leader for their studies. Carlo Marsuppini would have played the role admirably, and Acciaiuoli wrote in 1451 that he would put off his studies in dialectics if Marsuppini could be persuaded to accept a university position in the humanities.[90] But then Marsuppini died in 1453. After Marsuppini's death Acciaiuoli would work desperately, and unsuccessfully, to get Manetti to return to Florence.[91] As early as 1448 Acciaiuoli had likened Manetti to a "father."[92] Now in the 1450s he would begin referring to Poggio and Filelfo as his "leader" or "exemplar."[93] Of his several models only Filelfo was suitable or possible as a real pedagogue: he was probably Acciaiuoli's first choice to replace

88. Dated 27 Feb. 1455, Magl. VIII 1390, fol. 94 (with draft notes on fols. 8, 10): "Vix e ludo pueritie emersus primos adolescentie annos attigeram, cum me philosophie mirum desiderium cepit et crescente etate ita vehementer desiderium crevit ut omnes cogitationes meas ad cognitionem sapientie studiumque converterem. Nihil in vita expetendum putarem nisi quod esset cum maximarum rerum doctrina scientiaque coniunctum. Huic mee cupiditati summa occasio oblata est, cum te in hanc urbem venientem divino beneficio sum magistrum sortitus, quo nec doctiorem quemquam, neque gratiorem, neque iocundiorem mihi in mentem venisset optare. Itaque cepi dialectice, ut scis, una cum nonnullis equalibus meis et philosophie etiam studiosius operam dare quam etas mea postulare videretur."

89. Acciaiuoli to Manetti, 20 Sept. 1450, Magl. VIII 1390, fols. 33v–34v. Manetti's response, dated 8 Oct. 1450, is in Naz. II IV 109, fols. 82–83. See also Manetti's letter to Vespasiano da Bisticci of the same date, ed. in G. M. Cagni, *Vespasiano da Bisticci e il suo epistolario* (Rome, 1969), pp. 125–28, no. 7.

90. See Acciaiuoli's letter cited below, Chapter IV, n. 7.

91. See Acciaiuoli's letters to Manetti of 12 Sept. 1454, 20, 24 Jan. 1455 (Magl. VIII 1390, fols. 89, 93, 93–93v).

92. 4 Dec. 1448, Magl. VIII 1390, fol. 101.

93. For Poggio, see the letter cited above, Chapter II, n. 136; for Filelfo, see below, Chapter IV.

Marsuppini in the Studio, as we shall see. John Argyropoulos, however, was eventually hired. Argyropoulos, at any rate, seemed to know what the Acciaiuoli circle wanted. Aristotle taught, Argyropoulos stated in his first oration at Florence, that man was born imperfect but was able to become perfect through knowledge. Argyropoulos then outlined for his students a multiyear program of studies in logic, dialectics, ethics, natural philosophy, and metaphysics, at the end of which universal knowledge and human perfection would be reached.[94] Acciaiuoli began eagerly and listened attentively: as Vespasiano da Bisticci correctly observed, Acciaiuoli "took down in writing everything that Argyropoulos said in voice."[95]

Full of confidence after the Peace of Lodi, Donato Acciaiuoli and others of his circle began mapping for themselves a road to true wisdom. But almost at once they found opposition from other strata of intellectuals, and they discovered also that they would be dealing with a peculiar institution, the University of Florence.

94.   Oration before lectures on the *Nicomachean Ethics*, 4 February 1457, in K. Müllner, ed., *Reden und Briefe italienischer Humanisten* (1899; rept. Munich, 1970, with indexes and bibliographical addenda by B. Gerl), pp. 3–18. See also Chapter v, below.

95.   *Vite*, II, 25. For the accuracy of Vespasiano's observation, see pp. 207–208, below.

IV

THE STUDIO
CONTROVERSY,
1455

FLORENCE will never have a university as strong or as popular as Perugia's, "joked" a jurist in the fifteenth century, as long as the wool in Florence is properly spun.[1] The Studio in fifteenth-century Italy was indeed a communal investment. Students seeking careers in law and medicine went where the housing was cheap and the professors expensive, and Florence rarely offered either. Founded in 1321, the University of Florence suffered from frequent closings and near closings—it was not that war was disruptive but that the Florentines often discovered that they had better ways to spend their money. At least in the Quattrocento, moreover, even in the best of times the university was poorly funded.

All things considered, the humanities at the Florentine Studio fared rather well. Even if not all Florentines believed that teaching the humanities promoted good customs, they at least realized that the human-

This chapter is based largely on my article, "The *Studium Florentinum* Controversy, 1455," *History of Universities* 3 (1983), 31–59. The article reproduces a few Latin quotations omitted here and provides additional information on some minor points. In the latter instances my notes will refer to the article. This chapter, however, contains some information not included in the earlier version.

1. The epigram is reproduced by Otto Niccolini in a *pratica* debate on the status of the University of Florence, ed. Brucker, "Civic Debate on Florentine Higher Education (1460)," p. 531.

For the Florentine Studio, see G. Prezziner, *Storia del pubblico Studio e delle società scientifiche e letterarie di Firenze*, vol. 1 (1810; rept. Bologna, 1975); Gherardi, ed., *Statuti*; G. Brucker, "Florence and Its University, 1348–1434," in Rabb and Seigel, eds., *Action and Conviction*, pp. 220–36; Brucker, "A Civic Debate"; Verde, *Lo Studio fiorentino*, vols. 1–4; and K. Park, "Readers at the Florentine Studio according to Communal Fiscal Records (1357–1380, 1413–1446)," *Rinascimento*, 2d. ser., 20 (1980 [1981]), 249–310.

ists could teach them how to read and write. The humanities were val-
ued so highly that when the university, for economic reasons, was
moved to Pisa in 1473, the more important humanistic chairs remained
in Florence. And while most salaries at the university were low, humanists occasionally joined select doctors and lawyers in winning lucrative
positions. Among the humanists, Carlo Marsuppini held one such position in the mid-Quattrocento, as did Francesco Filelfo earlier in the
century and John Argyropoulos, Cristoforo Landino, and Politian later.
While these humanistic "chairs" were rarely defined apart from the lecturers who occupied them, in 1455 the Acciaiuoli circle of young Florentines worked to see the Marsuppini position "restored" (*illa exedra
recreata*) through hiring a worthy successor.[2] Hence arose one of the
most puzzling, and confusing, episodes of Florentine intellectual history.

While the particular events surrounding the controversy have been
described in various ways, scholars have agreed on one fact. Early in 1455
Cristoforo Landino—the humanist, poet, and friend of Marsilio Ficino—and John Argyropoulos—the Byzantine philosopher—competed
for a university position, and Argyropoulos was the immediate winner.
Scholars have taken their start from this in interpreting the philosophical renaissance. Some have the competition as but one chapter of an
international Plato-Aristotle controversy: Landino and Plato oppose
Argyropoulos and Aristotle. Others would have Landino uphold older,
rhetorical values and Argyropoulos represent the new, philosophical interests. Still others turn this argument on its head: Argyropoulos continues an older tradition with its emphasis on ethics and the *vita activa*,
while Landino joins Ficino and other Medici protégés in a commitment
to the higher value of the contemplative life.[3] While these sorts of ques-

2.   In a letter to Andrea Alamanni, dated 15 Apr. 1455, Donato Acciaiuoli noted that
many Florentines "ascendere exhedram illam auderent, quam nuper Caroli Aretini et
multorum ante doctissimorum hominum voce decoratam atque ornatam vidimus"
(Magl. VIII 1390, fol. 97: cf. Fossi, *Monumenta*, p. 82, who corrects *exhedram* to *cathe-
dram*). Cf. Acciaiuoli's letter to Domenico Sabino, quoted in my "*Studium Florentinum
Controversy,*" pp. 53–54, n. 39.

3.   While not analyzing the controversy per se, G. Voigt offered penetrating insights
into the Florentine Studio and the status of several humanistic chairs: *Die Wiederbele-
bung des classischen Alterthums* (1893; rept. Berlin, 1960), I, 365–67. For the Studio controversy, see especially V. Rossi, *Il Quattrocento* (Milan, 1898), pp. 51–53 (and many later editions); Della Torre, *Storia,* pp. 364ff.; Cammelli, *Argiropulo,* pp. 43ff.; Garin, "Donato
Acciaiuoli cittadino," pp. 199–267 *passim*; Marcel, *Marsile Ficin,* pp. 189–197; Seigel,
"Teaching of Argyropulos," pp. 241ff.; and Cardini, *La critica del Landino* (Florence,
1973), pp. 66–84. The occasionally cited nuptial opusculum by C. Marchesi, *Carlo Marsuppini d'Arezzo e Donato Acciajoli: Uno scandolo nello Studio fiorentino* (1899), now reprinted in his *Scritti minori di filologia e di letteratura* (Florence, 1978), I, 11–16, is merely
an edition, without comment or notes, of three of Acciaiuoli's letters.

tions are central to our study, in this chapter we are more concerned with their very basis. We shall argue, in fact, that Landino and Argyropoulos never competed for a chair at the University of Florence. Further, we shall suggest that each had good reason to look favorably on the academic aspirations of the other.

How would liberal studies in Florence be revived after the midcentury wars? The question preoccupied those Florentines involved in the Studio controversy. By the middle of the Quattrocento, intellectual life in Florence had fallen to a low level indeed. Death by now had taken many heroes of the early humanist movement, such figures as Ambrogio Traversari, Niccolò Niccoli, and Leonardo Bruni. Florentine politics had driven out the great patron of the arts, Palla Strozzi, and Padua became the seat of Strozzi's thriving circle of literati. The Medici party had also exiled Francesco Filelfo, who later became a court humanist for the Visconti in Milan. Embassies for the wartime Florentine government kept Giannozzo Manetti busy in several Italian capitals. Negotiations went more smoothly for Florence than they did for Manetti: finally considered unpatriotic or anti-Medici, or both, Manetti was hit with tax assessments so high that residence in the Arno republic became impossible for him. Then there were those not driven from Florence but drawn to Rome. Patronage of the first humanist pope, Nicholas V (1447–55), far outstripped any endowments from the war-weary Florentines. Florence's leading patron, Cosimo de' Medici, stayed busy running the family business and guiding the state. To be sure, considering the times his patronage was exceptional, but until peace was won his initiatives, especially in literary and philosophical matters, were few.

But one great light remained in Florence: Carlo Marsuppini.[4] As a chancellor (from 1444) he was considered the equal of Leonardo Bruni.[5] As a humanist he was second to none, and contemporaries could cheerfully overlook what moderns will not, that he had a dismal record of scholarly publication.[6] Young Florentines viewed Marsuppini as a teacher of first rank, and older ones saw to it that he was paid 350 florins yearly as a lecturer, an extraordinary sum for a teacher in the humani-

4.   For Marsuppini, the only general monograph is the short study by Zippel, "Carlo Marsuppini" (1897), now in his *Storia e cultura*, pp. 198–213. For further bibliography, see P. G. Ricci's introduction to his "Una consolatoria inedita del Marsuppini," *Rinascita* 3 (1940), 384–89, and the notes that follow. More information may be found in Brown, *Bartolomeo Scala*.

5.   For Marsuppini's public career, see D. Marzi, *La Cancelleria della Repubblica fiorentina* (Rocca S. Casciano, 1910), and now R. Black, *Benedetto Accolti*.

6.   See A. Moschetti, "Una lettera inedita di Carlo Marsuppini," *Giornale storico della letteratura italiana* 26 (1895), 377–83.

ties.[7] Marsuppini was one of the few Florentines in the Quattrocento to acquire a "universal" humanist chair at the Studio: he lectured on Greek and Latin literature, rhetoric, poetry, and moral philosophy, and possibly on the speculative branches of philosophy as well.[8]

The continuity or revival of the "universal" humanistic chair after the death of Carlo Marsuppini—not the ideologies or political affiliations of Cristoforo Landino and John Argyropoulos—is the central theme in the Studio controversy of 1455.[9] As I argued in the last chapter, Gian-

7.   A law of August 1451 provided 350 florins for rhetoric and poetry, and, for that provision, granted a special exemption from the law that no professor was to receive more than 150 florins annually (Gherardi, ed., *Statuti*, pp. 260–62). For the choice of Marsuppini, see Acciaiuoli's letter to Iacopo Ammannati, 10 Oct. 1451, ed. in Marchesi, *Scritti minori*, pp. 11–12 (cf. Della Torre, *Storia*, pp. 351–52), and Brown, *Bartolomeo Scala*, p. 11, n. 35. Marsuppini is also mentioned in a note dated 30 July 1452 from the *ricordi* of Giovanni Chellini (Milan, Università Commerciale Luigi Bocconi, Istituto di Storia e Economia, ms. 2 [perhaps a provisional shelf mark]), p. 173a: "Ricordo che a dì 30 di luglio prestai il mio libro de vita et moribus filosophorum [i.e., Diogenes Laertius or Walter Burley] in carte bambagine in coverte [?] di carta di pecora legato a Filippo di Giovanni Corbizi studiante in cose sotili [?] sotto messer Carlo d'Arezzo." I was led to this manuscript by the summary description in the typescript of P. O. Kristeller's forthcoming volumes of the *Iter Italicum*, seen at the Warburg Institute, London, June 1980. The *ricordi* have now been edited by M. T. Sillano: *Le ricordanze di Giovanni Chellini da San Miniato*, cited (her edition of this passage, at p. 188, differs slightly).

8.   A list of Studio lecturers *in artibus* from 1431 names Marsuppini "ad legendum Poesiam, Rethoricam, Phylosofiam, Grecum et Eticam[!]" (Gherardi, ed., *Statuti*, p. 414; cf. Park, "Readers at the Florentine Studio," pp. 288, 291). Confusing titles for humanistic chairs covering more than one discipline are not uncommon. For Marsuppini as a philosopher see Cristoforo Landino, *De anima* (for editions see Chapter IX, n. 30, below), and the eulogy in his *Carmina*, pp. 103–13; Vespasiano, *Vite*, I, 591; J. Monfasani, *George of Trebizond* (Leiden, 1976), pp. 41–43; and n. 7, above. For the evolution of the humanistic chair in the fourteenth and fifteenth centuries, see the general remarks by Kristeller, *Studies*, pp. 572–73. Marsuppini also lectured on law: Brown, *Bartolomeo Scala*, pp. 10–11.

9.   The following sketch of the Acciaiuoli group depends heavily on the lengthy second chapter of Della Torre, *Storia*, pp. 239–425. See also Ganz, "Humanist as Citizen," and her "Donato Acciaiuoli and the Medici: A Strategy for Survival in '400 Florence," *Rinascimento*, 2d. ser., 22 (1982), 33–48. For lively portraits of many of the group's members, see the *Vite* of Vespasiano da Bisticci. One error, originating with Fossi's *Monumenta*, pp. 73–76, repeated by Della Torre, *Storia*, pp. 361–64, and in nearly all studies of the period since, needs to be corrected. A letter from Donato Acciaiuoli's autograph letterbook (Magl. VIII 1390, fol. 91–91v), dated 21 Dec. 1454 (actually "VIIII Kal. Januarii idest XXI Decembris" [!]), has been interpreted as a letter, written anonymously, from an amicus—that is, Donato Acciaiuoli—to Marco Parenti, Alamanno Rinuccini, and Antonio Rossi, asking to be admitted to their circle. The letter is curious, for while one may note from other sources Acciaiuoli's "insecurity" about his own level of culture, one also cannot fail to recognize that he was already playing a leadership role in the group he was presumably about to enter! Albinia de la Mare has shown that the address of the letter, correctly transcribed, reveals it to be indeed from an amicus but that it is addressed to Donato Acciaiuoli as well as the other three figures: the letter must, therefore, be a composition of Donato Acciaiuoli *gratia exercitationis*. A similar correction to the address in reply, 18 Jan. 1455 (Magl. VIII 1390, fols. 92v–93), shows it to be from all four members of the circle (A. C. de la Mare, "Vespasiano da Bisticci" [Ph.D. diss., University of Lon-

nozzo Manetti had epitomized the goal of universality, with his free movement in the worlds of the active and contemplative lives and his ability to communicate with all strata of intellectuals. For the young the goal required a tutelage, an initiation.

The aristocratic intellectuals of the Acciaiuoli circle were apparently grouped in the 1440s around a rather obscure figure, Niccolò della Luna. They had close ties with Palla Strozzi and the branch of his family in Florence that had not been exiled by the Medici. They also maintained close ties with Francesco Filelfo in Milan. With war taxes (especially from 1448), plague (from 1449), and finally Niccolò della Luna's abandonment of the world for the monastic life (ca. 1450), this aristocratic group of scholars was left stranded and fragmented. Donato Acciaiuoli later wrote that the *magna rerum perturbatio* of this period required him to defer serious studies in the humanities to "another time." He and others had to see after their families' business interests, necessary if only because of heavy wartime taxes.[10] While not abandoning his studies altogether, Acciaiuoli shared with others the desire for greater leisure and more systematic studies. He emphasized always, for reasons I mentioned earlier, the need for scholarly leadership. His first great opportunity came in the autumn of 1451, when the University of Florence reopened (it was closed by plague in 1449), and Carlo Marsuppini was persuaded to accept a lectureship in the humanities, with a salary of 350 florins. Soon Florence's alliance with Milan prompted peace negotiations, which in turn promised the leisure for a full devotion to humanistic studies. Then suddenly in April 1453 Carlo Marsuppini died. Donato Acciaiuoli knew the proper metaphor: we, he wrote, are untrained soldiers in search of a general.[11]

How soon the more aristocratic of Marsuppini's students—the remnants, that is, of the della Luna or Acciaiuoli circle—began to meet after the chancellor's death is not known. The lack of a suitable teacher plus the wartime pursuit of the florin may have left studies suspended. Meetings and common studies had surely begun not long after the general Italian peace was concluded at Lodi in the summer of 1454.[12] What sort

---

don, 1965], II, 315). For a recent edition of the letters (but retaining the erroneous addresses), see Giustiniani, *Alamanno Rinuccini*, pp. 84–86.

10.   Della Torre, *Storia*, pp. 319–20, 335–38.

11.   Letter to Iacopo Ammannati, n.d., ed. Fossi, *Monumenta*, pp. 48–49n., and C. Marchesi, *Scritti minori*, pp. 12–13. The letter was written soon after Marsuppini's death, since it falls in Acciaiuoli's letterbook (Magl. VIII 1390, fol. 82–82v) before a letter dated 6 July 1453. For the relevant excerpt, see pp. 86–87, below. From 1453 to 1455, Acciaiuoli repeated the metaphor many times.

12.   The important correction, first made by A. C. de la Mare (see n. 9, above), would suggest that conscientious studies began earlier than most scholars have assumed.

of studies were these? Evidence from Acciaiuoli's letters suggests "typical" humanist activity: a common reading and explication of a classical
text, disputations on questions presented directly or indirectly by the
text, and literary activity *gratia exercitationis*.[13] By the autumn of 1454 the
group met regularly at a designated hour at the home of Alamanno Rinuccini.[14]

   Besides a general and permanent peace, what most members of the
Acciaiuoli group expressly wanted was a teacher whose skill and fame
would make him a worthy replacement for Carlo Marsuppini. The only
resident scholar equal in fame was Poggio Bracciolini. Acciaiuoli sought
out his company and was overwhelmed: of all learned men, he wrote
the chancellor, I choose you as my leader and model.[15] But Poggio surely
would not and probably could not assume any active role. Never a
teacher by profession, he was occupied with his scholarly activities and
his duties as chancellor. Another figure, Giannozzo Manetti, was equally
famous and, as we have stated, had long and close ties to Acciaiuoli and
other members of his circle. Acciaiuoli tried, and failed, to convince the
leaders of the republic to remit the penalizing tax assessments on Manetti. In consequence, the latter's return to Florence became difficult if
not impossible. Like Poggio, Manetti was an elderly and respected orator and secretary, not a professional teacher of the humanities.[16] A third
figure, the Byzantine John Argyropoulos, while less famous than the
others, made an immediate and striking impression on the young scholars when he first arrived in Florence in 1454. A teacher by profession, he
was, with the fall of Constantinople to the Turks in 1453, sorely in need
of employment. Soon after their first meeting in 1454, Acciaiuoli wrote
him that he was working "night and day" to get him honorable employment.[17]

   We know that Acciaiuoli and others of his group, after a long struggle, succeeded in winning a university appointment for Argyropoulos.
Must we also assume that Argyropoulos was the primary figure the

---

13.   Della Torre, *Storia*, pp. 358ff.

14.   Ibid., pp. 355–58.

15.   Letter of 8 Mar. 1455, ed. Fossi, *Monumenta*, pp. 107–8.

16.   See Acciaiuoli's letters to Manetti, 20, 24 Jan. 1455, Magl. VIII 1390, fol. 93–93v. On
Manetti during wartime, a balanced account is Gutkind, *Cosimo*, pp. 131–33. See also Vespasiano, *Vite*, I, 524ff. I have seen no notice that Manetti taught professionally, although
he apparently, at some point, lectured informally on some of Aristotle's moral philosophy to some of his well-to-do friends (ibid., II, 525–26).

17.   Magl. VIII 1390, fols. 85v–86 (cf. eds.: Fossi, *Monumenta*, p. 59; Zippel, "Per la biografia dell'Argiropulo" [1896], p. 181; Lampros, *Argyropouleia*, p. 222): "Mihi . . . tu tuaque omnia non solum memorie sunt, sed etiam tante cure, ut die noctuque cogitare non
desinam, nisi quonam pacto te virum doctissimum meique amantissimum ornare dignitate et beneficiis afficere possim."

group had in mind when they spoke of the need to replace Marsuppini?
Previous accounts of the Studio controversy have included this premise.
Argyropoulos was certainly well suited to take up several areas of Marsuppini's "universal" position, namely Greek language, literature, and
philosophy. But there is little evidence that Argyropoulos had either the
talent or the temperament to teach Latin eloquence. Never in his academic career in Italy, whether at Padua, Florence, or Rome, is he known
to have lectured publicly in rhetoric, and, a zealous defender of the philosophical discipline, he more than once spoke of oratory with disdain.
To be sure, Argyropoulos had no doubt mastered the basic principles of
Byzantine rhetorical theory; some Florentines may even have entertained hopes that he would explain these, in Latin, at the university
before he began his courses in philosophy.[18] But unless we assume that
Argyropoulos tried to come to Florence under wholly false pretenses,
or that he had teaching interests which both he and his students declined to mention publicly, we should attempt to discover elsewhere the
candidate considered worthy of the Marsuppini chair. There is strong
evidence, indeed, that Acciaiuoli, Rinuccini, and others were primarily
interested not in Argyropoulos but in Francesco Filelfo, the scourge of
the Medici.

Filelfo (1398–1481) had lectured in Florence as early as 1429.[19] From

18.   In his inaugural orations at Florence, Argyropoulos pointedly refused to adorn his
speeches with the usual humanistic excursuses: see pp. 241–43, below. For Argyropoulos's negative attitude toward rhetoric, see also the evidence gathered by Seigel, "Teaching of Argyropulos." Argyropoulos consistently described all rhetorical studies as "pre-
paratory" or "preliminary." Serious, "advanced" studies start with logic and dialectics,
which likewise serve as a groundwork for studies in philosophy proper, which begin
with ethics. For his *ordo scientiarum*, see Chapter v, below.
   Argyropoulos's own training, however, was in Byzantine rhetoric as well as philosophy. See J. Monfasani, "The Byzantine Rhetorical Tradition and the Renaissance," in
Renaissance Eloquence, ed. J. J. Murphy (Los Angeles, 1983), pp. 180–81. In his first public
appointment in 1455, according to a letter from Alamanno Rinuccini, Argyropoulos was
selected to teach "oratoriae facultatis ac philosophiae praecepta" (*Lettere ed orazioni*, p.
13). But the first statutory evidence, dated 5 Oct. 1458 (reconfirming an appointment
from the autumn of 1456), gives Argyropoulos the title "totius philosophiae professor"
(Gherardi, ed., *Statuti*, p. 467), a title he retained thereafter. While the earlier title could
well point to some lectures in rhetoric, nonprofessional and humanistic titles were noto-
riously vague, and, without other evidence, I do not think we should presume that many
Florentines looked on Argyropoulos as the new master of Latin eloquence. Indeed,
whatever title he may have held as a "rhetorician" was probably owed to some instruction he gave on occasion on the Greek language. I have seen no evidence that any such
lectures were public (see Vespasiano, *Vite*, II, 11–12). Pierfilippo Pandolfini refers to some
lectures of Argyropoulos on Sophocles, in a letter to Xanthus Viriatus dated about 1460
(Magl. VI 166, fols. 111–12v at fol. 112; for this manuscript, see Chapter v, n. 53, below).

19.   The following sketch of Filelfo in the 1430s is based on Vespasiano, *Vite*, II, 53ff.;
G. Zippel, *Storia e cultura*, pp. 216–53; Gutkind, *Cosimo*, pp. 73ff. (for a lively and sympathetic portrayal of Cosimo's role); R. G. Adam, "Francesco Filelfo at the Court of

the beginning his lectures were a huge success, and his salary was large (350 florins per year in the early 1430s). Cosimo de' Medici and such humanists as Niccolò Niccoli, Bruni, and probably Ambrogio Traversari were his early supporters. But for a variety of reasons Filelfo alienated some of them, including Cosimo, with the result that his status in Florence became closely bound with that of the anti-Medici Strozzi and Albizzi factions. Not long after Cosimo returned to power in 1434 (he had been exiled in 1433), Filelfo was banished. Filelfo's *Commentationes Florentinae de exilio*, a slanderous dialogue attacking Cosimo and his humanist supporters, soon followed. Filelfo never finished the work, but he did circulate some excerpts and threaten to publish more. He stayed several years in exile at the University of Siena and then became a resident humanist at the Visconti court in Milan. Carlo Marsuppini, meanwhile, emerged as the leading humanist lecturer in the Florentine Studio.

By the late 1440s international politics and personal considerations caused Filelfo to seek some accommodation with Medicean Florence. The death of Filippo Maria Visconti in 1447 left Milan without a ruler and Filelfo without a patron. When Francesco Sforza took power in 1450, Cosimo de' Medici reversed Florence's traditional policy toward Milan and courted the new Milanese *signore*; in August 1451 Florence and Sforza entered into a formal alliance against Venice. Hoping that the Sforza would continue with the sort of support that he had enjoyed under the Visconti, Filelfo quickly composed an epic, the *Sforziad*, to honor his new patrons.[20] But the consequent patronage was not what he expected. From the early 1450s, if not earlier, it seems, Filelfo actively campaigned to return to Florence as either a secretary or an academic.[21]

Filelfo began to correspond regularly with Andrea Alamanni, a Florentine political and intellectual leader, a former member of the della Luna circle, and a man influential with the Ufficiali dello Studio, the group in charge of university appointments.[22] In December 1450 Filelfo

Milan" (Ph.D. diss., Oxford University, 1974, now being published by the Deutsches Historisches Institut, Rome), I, 122ff.; and Park, "Readers at the Florentine Studio." Vito R. Giustiniani is preparing a critical edition of some of Filelfo's letters.

20. Adam, "Filelfo," I, 27.

21. Returning to Florence required more than an academic appointment: Filelfo first had to get his banishment revoked. Vespasiano da Bisticci, who knew Filelfo, wrote that the latter "cercò con grandissima istantia di ritornare a Firenze" (*Vite*, II, 55). Filelfo's efforts to return to Florence have been noted by Voigt and Della Torre and explored in some detail by Adam, "Filelfo," I, 24–47, 122–38. For some "late" (1460–61) allusions to the attempted return, see pp. 100–101, below.

22. The letters to Andrea Alamanni were in both Greek and Latin. See Filelfo, *Epistolae*, fols. 53ff.; *Cent-dix lettres grecques de François Filelfe publiées intégralement pour la pre-*

wrote Andrea that he was overjoyed to learn that an old enemy, Carlo Marsuppini, sought a reconciliation; but early the next year he expressed his regret that his impression was mistaken.[23] Meanwhile he appealed to the Medici. In a carefully worded *volgare* letter to Giovanni de' Medici, Cosimo's son, Filelfo claimed that, appearances to the contrary, he had never felt ill-will toward the Medici family.[24] Marsuppini's death in 1453 removed one obstacle to Filelfo's return, but he could hardly have been cheered by Poggio's election to the Chancery. Filelfo's polemics with Poggio in the 1430s and 1440s had been vicious and well publicized. As the Studio controversy was looming, in January 1455, Filelfo again wooed the Medici by dedicating to Piero de' Medici, one of the Ufficiali dello Studio that year, an emended version of his *Sforziad*. He concluded the letter of dedication with his best wishes to Cosimo and to the "most eloquent" Poggio.[25] Neither Cosimo nor Poggio responded.[26]

While the death of Carlo Marsuppini brought Poggio to Florence, it also left the university without a leading teacher in the humanities. If the Florentines wanted to replace Marsuppini, to choose a lecturer of international fame who was able to lecture in "poetry, rhetoric, philosophy, and Greek," they could have found no one as conspicuously well suited as Filelfo. He himself claimed to have mastered *all* the works of the ancients, both Greek and Latin.[27] And in his academic career he lectured on, or promised to lecture on, the orations, letters, and rhetorical and philosophical works of Cicero, on Terence and Livy, on Homer, Thucydides, and Xenophon, on Aristotle's *Nicomachean Ethics*, and finally on Dante and Petrarch.[28]

---

mière fois d'après le Codex Trivulzianus 873, *avec traduction, notes et commentaires*, ed. E. Legrand (Paris, 1892), pp. 54ff.; and T. Klette, *Die griechischen Briefe des Franciskus Philelphus*, vol. 3 of his *Beiträge zur Geschichte und Literatur der italienischen Gelehrtenrenaissance* (Greifswald, 1890), pp. 117ff. For Andrea Alamanni, see n. 45, below.

23.   See the letters dated 2 Dec. 1450 and 18 Feb. 1451, in *Epistolae*, fols. 53, 63.

24.   See the letter dated 12 Feb. 1451, ed. G. Benadduci, "Prose e poesie volgari di Francesco Filelfo," *Atti e memorie della R. Deputazione di storia patria per le province delle Marche* 5 (1901), 259–60; cf. V. Rossi, "L'indole e gli studi di Giovanni di Cosimo de' Medici," *Rendiconti della Accademia Nazionale dei Lincei, Classe di scienze morali, storiche, critiche e filologiche*, 5th ser., 2 (1893), 52.

25.   Ed. in Della Torre, *Storia*, pp. 367–68n.

26.   For Cosimo and Filelfo in the 1450s, see the anecdote attributed to Politian, pp. 101–102, below, and Brown, *Bartolomeo Scala*, p. 18. In the autumn of 1453, long after their disputes had cooled, Poggio still managed to insert into a letter a gratuitous slap at Filelfo, comparing him—horrors!—to Lorenzo Valla (Ep. XI, 15 [Tonelli III, 74–77]).

27.   E. F. Rice, Jr., *The Renaissance Idea of Wisdom* (Cambridge, Mass., 1958), p. 50.

28.   For Filelfo's lecture subjects, see L. A. Sheppard, "A Fifteenth-Century Humanist,

Donato Acciaiuoli had begun writing Filelfo in 1451, if not earlier.[29] He no doubt met Filelfo in 1452 when he accompanied, unofficially, Dietisalvi Neroni on a diplomatic mission to Milan.[30] After returning from that mission he corresponded with Filelfo frequently. Letters from Acciaiuoli in July or August 1454 included a commendation for Bartolomeo Scala and a request for a copy of Filelfo's commentary on Petrarch's *Trionfi*. Filelfo answered warmly.[31] In another letter, dated 5 September 1454, Acciaiuoli thanked Filelfo for praising his eloquence and that of other young scholars: but such praise, he suggested, was premature. "We," he wrote,

> can only be learned and skillful in the way that raw recruits can serve as soldiers in an excellent, difficult, and most laborious training when they do not have a general. For when you were here, when the studies of letters were flourishing, it was not possible, on account of my age, to choose you or one like you (something rare indeed) as a general, whom I could follow and imitate, and from whom I could learn the precepts of speaking and writing.

Then, without alluding to Filelfo's return, Acciaiuoli suggested that Filelfo could expect to receive much support in Florence: his older cousin, Agnolo Acciaiuoli, and Agnolo's friends were anxious to see Filelfo situated in a dignified public position (*honoratus*) with a large salary (*fortunatus*).[32]

Acciaiuoli betrayed his concern over Marsuppini's replacement very soon after the chancellor's death in April 1453. A practical consideration overshadowed his grief: Where in Florence, he wrote Iacopo Ammannati in the early summer of 1453, can be found another Carlo Marsuppini?

Francesco Filelfo," *Library*, 4th ser., 16 (1935), 3–4; Gherardi, ed., *Statuti*, p. 424; Vespasiano, *Vite*, II, 53–58; Müllner, ed., *Reden und Briefe*, pp. 146–62.

29. See Filelfo's letter to Acciaiuoli, 13 June 1451, in *Epistolae*, fol. 65v.

30. Vespasiano, *Vite*, II, 27 and n. ("Sendo a Milano multi uomini dotti, ispesso si truovava a disputare ora d'una scientia ora d'una altra"); cf. Della Torre, *Storia*, p. 408 and n.

31. See the two letters of Acciaiuoli bearing the date 6 Aug. 1454, ed. in Della Torre, *Storia*, p. 372, nn. 1–2; cf. Magl. VIII 1390, fol. 86–86v. Filelfo's "response" to one of these is dated 4 Aug. 1454 (!), *Epistolae*, fols. 86v–87. Scholars have tended to trust the dating of Acciaiuoli's letters, since his letterbook is an autograph (Magl. VIII 1390). The dating of his letters, however, presents numerous difficulties. I tend to question the dating of *all* the letters and would suggest that many of the dates indicate when Acciaiuoli copied the letters into his letterbook, often with revisions and often two or three weeks after they were first drafted. See my "*Studium Florentinum* Controversy," p. 55, n. 47.

32. Magl. VIII 1390, fol. 88–88v.

You write that the death of Carlo of Arezzo weighs heavily upon you: I well believe it. . . . How much Latin literature and all the liberal arts have lost through his death is, as you write, easily understood. For the long-slumbering Latin language was awakened by Carlo and called forth to light: now he is dead, and one must think that it not only went back to sleep but almost died with him. I do not see what the young and studious can now hope for. Our general is now dead, and there is no one left who can instruct those who would continue in his program of training, no one left who can properly lead the troops. For who among our men can even begin to approach Carlo in expounding orators or explaining poets? Who has his sharpness of intellect, his depth of memory, or his great breadth of knowledge?[33]

The question in the letter—who among our men?—deserves to be underscored: the entire Studio controversy turned on whether any native Florentine was capable of holding Marsuppini's position. The question became a matter of public debate in 1455; whether it was discussed openly before the Peace of Lodi in the summer of 1454 is not known. By the autumn of 1454, at any rate, the question threatened to tear the Acciaiuoli group apart.

From Acciaiuoli's perspective, one of the group, Antonio Rossi, helped betray it. From a noble but not wealthy family, Rossi was a humanist of second rank, learned in both Greek and Latin, somewhat older than most members of the Acciaiuoli circle, and a tutor to noble families. Through private lectures he had gained many loyal students and several influential patrons, including Matteo Palmieri, Franco Sacchetti, and Dietisalvi Neroni. In December 1454 Rossi quit the Acciaiuoli circle and began a campaign to win an appointment to a humanist chair at the university. Acciaiuoli accused him of arrogance: he was too proud for his friends, unwilling to acknowledge deficiencies in his own learning, and presumptuous to compare himself to Carlo Marsuppini. A heated exchange of letters followed. By January Rossi's credentials were being discussed in the Florentine government.[34]

33. Magl. VIII 1390, fol. 82; Fossi, *Monumenta*, pp. 48–49n.; Marchesi, *Scritti minori*, pp. 12–13.

34. For Rossi, see Matteo Palmieri's letter of support to Piero de' Medici, 1 June 1455, ed. A. Messeri, "Matteo Palmieri cittadino di Firenze del secolo XV," *Archivio storico italiano*, 5th ser., 13 (1894), 334–35 (Della Torre has identified the "Francho" of the letter as Franco Sacchetti [*Storia*, p. 376], who happened to be one of the *Ufficiali dello Studio* [Giustiniani, *Alamanno Rinuccini*, p. 92; Verde, *Lo Studio fiorentino*, I, 272]); Black, *Benedetto Accolti*, p. 170n.; Acciaiuoli's letters to Rossi, dated 25 Dec. 1454, 1, 4, and 30 Jan., 16 Feb., 23 Mar., and 15 May 1455 (Magl. VIII 1390, fols. 18, 91v–92, 93v–94, 95v; the fourth,

For the Acciaiuoli circle the blow fell the next month. On 25 and 26 February 1455 the Councils of the People and of the Commune in Florence approved a bill that allowed the Signoria and Colleges to choose two lecturers in rhetoric and poetry for the University of Florence, who together were to receive, in funds provided by the communal *monte*, up to 250 florins per year.[35] Four Florentine humanists offered themselves for the posts: Cristoforo Landino, Antonio Rossi, Francesco da Castiglione, and Bernardo Nuti.[36] Another Florentine, the philosopher and Augustinian hermit Guglielmo Becchi,[37] a non-Florentine humanist, Domenico Sabino,[38] and perhaps an obscure lecturer in logic, Agnolo da Lecco,[39] were minor candidates; at some point Bartolomeo Scala also

---

ed. Della Torre, *Storia*, pp. 377–78; the sixth, ed. Fossi, *Monumenta*, p. 77); Acciaiuoli's letter to Andrea Alamanni, 15 Apr. 1455 (see n. 47, below); Garin, "Donato Acciaiuoli cittadino," pp. 218–19; Martines, *Social World*, pp. 344–45; Giustiniani, *Alamanno Rinuccini*, pp. 141–42n. (Giustiniani reproduces a birth register giving 1409 as the date of birth of an Antonio Rossi, who may indeed be our Rossi, but one Antonio di Antonio Rossi appears in another register, Florence, Archivio di Stato, Tratte 443bis, fol. 3r, born 16 Jan. 1415). See also n. 77, below.

35.   Gherardi, ed., *Statuti*, pp. 264–65. The oft-repeated notion that the law stipulated that the appointee be a Florentine is incorrect.

36.   These are the four figures referred to in the polished form of Acciaiuoli's letter to Andrea Alamanni, 15 Apr. 1455, which I will discuss shortly. Poggio also referred to "at least" four ("habet enim haec civitas saltem quatuor"), without naming them, in his letter also to Andrea Alamanni, 27 June 1455 (see below). Landino we shall look at later. For Rossi, see n. 34, above.
       Francesco da Castiglione won fame primarily as a teacher of Greek, numbering Donato Acciaiuoli and Marsilio Ficino among his students. For his academic career, see Della Torre, *Storia*, pp. 348–51 and nn., 771. (The date of the letter Della Torre quotes on p. 350, n. 3, from Francesco da Castiglione to Giovanni di Cosimo de' Medici, should be corrected to 4 Dec. 1462: see Kristeller, *Studies*, p. 200, n. 39. The letter's current shelfmark is MAP VIII, 438.) See also Kristeller, *Supplementum Ficinianum*, II, 340–41; S. Pecori, in *Dictionnaire d'histoire et de géographie ecclésiastiques* (Paris, 1977), XVIII, 710–12; and Brown, *Bartolomeo Scala*, p. 275n. During the Studio controversy, Francesco was presumably delivering Lenten sermons (26 Feb.–6 Apr. 1455) at the church of Santa Croce, Florence (see letter from Poggian Chancery, 15 Feb. 1455, requesting the sermons: Florence, Arch. di Stato, Signori, Carteggi, Missive, Prima Cancelleria, vol. 40, fol. 109–109v). Adam, "Filelfo," II, 279, n. 30, mistakenly has Acciaiuoli's reference to "Franciscus" in his letter of 15 Apr. 1455 to be to Filelfo instead of Castiglione.
       Of Bernardo di Francesco Nuti (Nutius, Nuzi, Nuzzi) little is known before the late 1460s, when he had a role in Ficino's commentary on Plato's *Symposium*. For his later career, see Kristeller, *Supplementum Ficinianum*, II, 348. For his earlier scholarly activity see Landino, *Carmina*, pp. 38–40; C. Marchesi, *Bartolomeo della Fonte (Bartholomaeus Fontius): Contributo alla storia degli studi classici in Firenze nella seconda metà del Quattrocento* (Catania, 1900), pp. 15–20; and (for a description of notebooks kept by one of his students) Caroti and Zamponi, *Lo scrittoio di Bartolomeo Fonzio*, pp. 43, 53.

37.   For the new evidence concerning Becchi, see my "*Studium Florentinum* Controversy," pp. 38, 53, n. 38.

38.   Ibid., pp. 38, 53–54, n. 39.

39.   Donato Acciaiuoli strongly praised Agnolo da Lecco's talents as a teacher in a let-

became a candidate.[40] While several Florentines supported one or another figure, the real controversy began with a protest by members of the Acciaiuoli circle: they were enraged by the entire proposal. While Carlo Marsuppini had lectured in Florence on Greek and Latin literature, rhetoric, poetry, and philosophy, the proposed chair was in rhetoric and poetry alone. Furthermore, the salary would not attract a top scholar: a Marsuppini, for instance, had been paid nearly three times the mean salary, 125 florins, of the proposal. In 1451, in fact, Marsuppini's salary had absorbed all funds assigned to rhetoric and poetry in the Studio.[41] The larger salary, the sort a Marsuppini could expect, followed naturally from the fame of the teacher, which depended on his eloquence, originality, and breadth of knowledge, as well as such factors as the status of his friends and patrons. The supporters of Landino, the leading candidate, vigorously defended his academic credentials. They pointed to his two years of public lectures, which may indeed have been popular. But the mean proposed salary, 125 florins, was the most Landino in these years could have expected.[42] His skill as a lecturer, after all, had hardly been tested, and his fame as a poet and Platonist had not yet been won. Just as important, he was unable to lecture on Greek literature or on philosophy based on Greek sources.[43]

The debate over the proposal took place both inside and outside the Florentine government. Within the government, while the several candidates competed, Acciaiuoli campaigned to block the election of anyone to the Studio post (and hence to annul the bill approved by the popular councils). His position was difficult, and he won the reputation of a troublemaker and an upstart—or so his cousin, Agnolo, who now

---

ter to him dated 27 Feb. 1455 (quoted in part, pp. 74–75, above), immediately after, that is, Acciaiuoli's insistence before the Florentine government that no one in Florence was suitable for the chair in rhetoric and poetry. As in Acciaiuoli's letter to Domenico Sabino (see my "*Studium Florentinum* Controversy," pp. 53–54, n. 39), this letter may have been a polite refusal to support Agnolo's candidacy for a Studio position.

40.   Scala was a candidate by the end of 1456: see p. 99, below.

41.   See n. 7, above. Landino himself may have been an unsalaried lecturer during Marsuppini's tenure: see Chapter IX, below.

42.   Landino's credentials are described in Acciaiuoli's letter on the Studio controversy, 15 Apr. 1455, which I will discuss shortly. Landino was paid 45 florins per year in 1456–57, probably for lectures on Dante (see my "Cristoforo Landino's First Lectures on Dante," pp. 32–34); when he finally won the position in rhetoric and poetry, he was paid 100 florins per year (Gherardi, ed., *Statuti*, p. 467).

43.   There is considerable confusion about Landino's teaching career before 1458, which I described but did little to dispel in my earlier version of this chapter, "The *Studium Florentinum* Controversy," p. 54, n. 43. For new evidence concerning his early career, see now my "Cristoforo Landino's First Lectures on Dante" (where I also discuss briefly Landino's knowledge of Greek) and Chapter IX, below.

publicly supported Landino, warned him.[44] Outside the government
the debate consisted of letters to two figures influential with the university's governors, Andrea Alamanni and Piero de' Medici.[45]

Acciaiuoli wrote first, in late March (but the letter is finally dated 15
April 1455), to his close friend Andrea Alamanni, who was outside of
Florence (and probably with Filelfo in Milan) at the time of the controversy.[46] Donato most likely never sent this letter, and, even if he showed
it to some close friends, he surely did not allow it to circulate.[47] But the
letter is our best source for the Acciaiuoli group's position. The out-
raged Donato focused his attack on the greedy leaders of the republic
and on the supporters of Landino, the leading candidate. What audac-
ity, he wrote, that the candidates should attempt to take for themselves
that money assigned to the faculty of rhetoric![48] What arrogance, that
the candidates should compare themselves to Carlo Marsuppini! What
ignorance such lecturers would bring to Florence! Donato expressed
shock, moreover, that when the issue was brought before the Colleges

44.   See Acciaiuoli's letters to Alamanno Rinuccini, 22 Mar. 1455 (ed. in Giustiniani,
Alamanno Rinuccini, pp. 86–87), and to Andrea Alamanni, 15 Apr. 1455 (ed. Fossi, *Monumenta*, p. 80, and Marchesi, *Scritti minori*, pp. 14–15).

45.   For Andrea Alamanni's position in Florence, see Della Torre, *Storia*, pp. 315–17,
358–71, 382–83n.; Giustiniani, *Alamanno Rinuccini*, pp. 90–92; and the brief sketch by
A. Perosa in *DBI*, vol. 1 (1960), 564. Donato Acciaiuoli called Andrea the "defensor et
quasi patronus studiorum et nostrae academiae princeps" in letter to him, 15 Apr. 1455
(ed. Fossi, *Monumenta*, p. 79) and "patronus . . . huius nostri gymnasii" in a rough draft
of the same (Magl. VIII 1390, fol. 16). He had influence with the Ufficiali dello Studio:
Rinuccini addressed him as one who "cum gratia, tum fide et auctoritate plurimum va-
lea[t] apud eos qui gymnasio instaurando praefecti sunt" (31 May 1455, *Lettere ed orazioni*,
p. 11). Outside of Florence at the time of the controversy, Andrea Alamanni had the polemics addressed to him (e.g., the letters of Acciaiuoli, Rinuccini, and Poggio, discussed
below). Many earlier letters of Filelfo were surely tacit appeals for support; there are
none during the height of the controversy, probably because Alamanni was with Filelfo
in Milan. For Guglielmo Becchi's possible appeal to Alamanni, see my "*Studium Florentinum* Controversy," p. 53, n. 38.
    Piero de' Medici was one of the Ufficiali dello Studio and actual recommendations
went to him. From Naples Matteo Palmieri recommended Antonio Rossi (see n. 34,
above). Filelfo's overtures, and a dedication of Becchi (see my "*Studium Florentinum*
Controversy," p. 53, n. 38), seem relevant to Piero's special status with the university.
John Argyropoulos dedicated many of his translations to Piero (Cammelli, *Argiropulo*,
pp. 183–84, lists five). Both Argyropoulos and Landino later gave Piero credit for their
appointments (the evidence is discussed in nn. 93 and 94 below).

46.   Giustiniani presents strong but indirect evidence that Andrea Alamanni was in
Milan (*Alamanno Rinuccini*, p. 91).

47.   Ed. Fossi, *Monumenta*, pp. 79–82, and Marchesi, *Scritti minori*, pp. 13–16. For this
letter, see my "*Studium Florentinum* Controversy," pp. 39, 55, n. 47.

48.   That is, the money assigned to the chair of rhetoric, preserved intact for one figure,
Marsuppini, in 1451 (see n. 7, above), was now being (greedily) divided up by the several
candidates.

so few would speak in opposition. No one, it seemed, wanted a lecturer of first rank; most seemed satisfied if young Florentines got some training in rhetoric and poetry—a mere "mercantile" education—and the salary offered the candidates was unworthy "even of a small town like Prato." Shameful it would be, he argued, if, in the greatest peace Italy had ever known, two should be chosen with such a small salary to teach poetry and the precepts of rhetoric. Donato announced his campaign: all of the faculties of the arts would have to be provided for or the selection of any one candidate would be blocked.[49]

In late May Alamanno Rinuccini wrote Andrea Alamanni a more "publishable" letter, with many of the same points presented in a less acerb tone. He emphasized the earlier intellectual greatness at Florence—the marvelous skill of the two Aretines, Bruni and Marsuppini; the learned disputations of Giannozzo Manetti, who was "brilliant in early branch of learning"; and those of George of Trebizond, "an expert second to none in the field of rhetoric."[50]

Meanwhile Filelfo made another overture to Piero de' Medici. In a letter he promised another installment of his emended *Sforziad* as well as a tract on government, each of which, he said, would glorify Florence and the Medici family. Showing considerable cheek, he dared to ask Piero to send money for his daughter's dowry! But he also lamented his exile from Florence, blaming not the Medici but bad luck and his own stupidity. He noted: Here in Milan "I seem to have neither a suitable public position nor an adequate salary."[51]

By late June, Florence's most respected humanist, Poggio Bracciolini, entered the controversy with yet another letter to Andrea Alamanni. Formally an answer to the letter from Rinuccini, Poggio's letter began by praising Rinuccini's eloquence and dedication to the humanities. But I see that he wants, Poggio wrote, an orator brought in from outside of Florence, without whom, he believes, the pursuit of eloquence is not possible. He is right that there are too few learned men in our age. But the blame is his own: eloquence is the result of continuous practice and work; it cannot be taught. The great lights of our age—Petrarch, Salutati, Bruni, Roberto de'Rossi, Niccolò Niccoli, Carlo Marsuppini, Am-

---

49. Ed. Fossi, *Monumenta*, pp. 79–82, and Marchesi, *Scritti minori*, pp. 13–16.

50. *Lettere ed orazioni*, pp. 10–12; cf. Giustiniani, *Alamanno Rinuccini*, pp. 90–93.

51. Dated 17 May 1455, ed. G. Benadduci, "Prose e poesie volgari di Francesco Filelfo," pp. 132–33: "Tre cose mi paiono comunemente in questa nostra vita civile et activa desiderarse: onore, utile e piacere. Le quali, per malvagità di fortuna e forse ancora per mia imprudenza, non avendo io potuto conseguire presso di voi in Firenze, arei carissimo ottenere in Milano presso questo illustrissimo Signore . . . . E per non tediarve in lungo parlare, a me non pare avere qui né onor conveniente, né utilitate necessaria."

brogio Traversari, and Giannozzo Manetti—all became eloquent through assiduous reading, not through hearing lectures on eloquence. If someone should teach rhetoric all he could do is to expound on the ready-made precepts of Cicero and Quintilian: this is simple enough, and we have in Florence at least four men who can do this as well as those outsiders Rinuccini wants. We know that men become eloquent through the reading of orators, poets, historians, and philosophers, and by continuous practice. We know that elegance of style cannot be taught; sophisticated disputations on the minor points of rhetoric (*in triviis*) have no use for us.[52]

Scholars have interpreted Poggio's letter in various ways: as an educational treatise espousing autodidacticism, as an expression of Florentine state chauvinism, as a statement of intellectual conservatism in an era of educational and philosophical innovation, and as the broadside of a jealous old man fearful of being upstaged. Yet these personal and political considerations should not obscure the more theoretical elements of the letter. In arguing that eloquence cannot be learned through formal instruction, Poggio was clearly interpreting the debate in terms of the theory of rhetoric, and he was using arguments he had perfected earlier in his famous polemics with Lorenzo Valla.

I shall not review the dispute with Valla in its entirety here, noting only that, contrary to some recent interpretations, Poggio did take an identifiable position in the controversy, and this should not be reduced to what has been called his philological conservatism or his theological scruples. While Valla's position has been not only studied in depth but defended in recent studies, Poggio has been reduced to a few phrases and defensive arguments. Against recent conclusions that Valla, unlike Poggio, appreciated the historicity of language and saw Latin as a "living language," one should weigh the earlier consideration of the outstanding classicist Remigio Sabbadini, that Poggio's style "ci fa rivivere in tutto il suo splendore una lingua morta," or Vittorio Rossi's judgment that Poggio's Latin preserved "un amabile sapore di lingua viva," or Walser's argument that Poggio's Latin was "eine wahrheft lebende Sprache."[53]

52. Ep. XIII, 3 (27 June [1455]) [Tonelli III, 183–88].

53. Students of the Poggio-Valla polemics have tended to take up Valla's arguments sympathetically and in detail while dismissing Poggio's "conservatism." But if Poggio's approach toward language proves his conservatism and "antihistoricity," why does this backwardness not appear in his other works? For a more "historistic" Poggio, see Krantz, "Poggio," pp. 119–51.

For Valla and the "lingua viva," see S. I. Camporeale, *Lorenzo Valla, Umanesimo e teologia* (Florence, 1972), p. 191. The quotations on Poggio's style are from Sabbadini, *Storia del Ciceronianismo*, p. 19; Rossi, *Il Quattrocento*, p. 81; and Walser, *Poggio*, p. 272. Walser's

The Valla-Poggio polemics began in December 1451 when Poggio happened on an edition of his letters annotated (that is, emended) by a person he took to be a student of Lorenzo Valla.[54] Poggio's first thought, according to George of Trebizond, was to send an assassin after Valla; instead he prepared an invective, which he published in February 1452.[55] He accused Valla of impiety toward both pagans and Christians: Valla was attempting to subject all authors, living and dead, to a rigid, super-rational grammatical scheme, which was purely a product of Valla's own set of rhetorical criteria. Valla attacks not only the grammarians (Priscian, Servius, Donatus) but also the philosophers (Aristotle, Boethius), historians (Livy, Sallust), orators (Cicero), and Christian writers (Jerome, Augustine). He spares only Quintilian.[56] Valla answered Poggio with three invectives he called *antidota* or *apologi*, in which he emphasized Poggio's wretched Latinity, his stupidity, his vulgarity (the *Facetiae*), and several lapses in his private life; generally he attempted to make Poggio into a silly old fool.[57] Poggio answered with a second invective, perhaps his most famous and certainly his most vulgar: he accused Valla of crimes ranging from pederasty to heresy.[58] He followed with a third, a fantastically and, in the opinion of Walser, delightfully imaginative description of Valla before the gates of Hell, demanding that the Devil construct a statue in his honor and enlisting evil spirits in his campaign to degrade ancient and modern authors.[59] In a fourth invective, Poggio played perhaps his strongest card: he dug up and quoted verses Valla had written to illustrate points of grammar, verses so bad that that utterly destroyed Valla's claim to be the arbiter of poetic eloquence.[60] Valla answered with another antidote, which por-

---

account of the dispute is lively and not as sympathetic to Poggio as one would expect. Sabbadini is excellent. Camporeale's study of Valla is the most detailed work on the controversy, and it should be consulted for dating and bibliography; but it is a study of Valla, and his treatment of Poggio lacks depth. His argument that theological issues were central to Poggio is, in my opinion, misleading. When the polemics got especially vicious (that is, after Valla published the name and address of Poggio's mistress and starving illegitimate children in Rome!) Poggio indeed emphasized Valla's "heresy," but generally he seemed as offended by Valla's "impiety" in "attacking" Cicero as he was by his critique of Jerome. For the controversy, see now also Ari Wesseling's introduction to Lorenzo Valla, *Antidotum primum* (Assen, 1978).

54. Walser, *Poggio*, p. 273; Camporeale, *Lorenzo Valla*, p. 33; Wesseling, ed., *Antidotum primum*, pp. 26–27.

55. Walser, *Poggio*, p. 273; *Oratio I*, in *Opera omnia*, I, pp. 188–205.

56. *Oratio I*, in *Opera Omnia*, I, p. 189.

57. I am following closely Walser, *Poggio*, pp. 273–74.

58. Ibid., p. 274; *Oratio II*, in *Opera omnia*, I, pp. 206–34.

59. Walser, *Poggio*, p. 275; *Oratio III*, in *Opera omnia*, I, pp. 234–42.

60. Walser, *Poggio*, pp. 275–76; *Oratio IV*, ed. R. Fubini, in *Opera omnia*, II, pp. 865–85.

trayed scenes in a schoolroom where students of Guarino vainly attempt
to teach the semiliterate Poggio rules of grammar.[61] After one last invective by Poggio, the dispute finally ended, in early 1453, little more than
a year after it had begun, with each figure proclaiming himself the victor.[62] Both Poggio and Valla recklessly and perhaps often in bad faith
quoted words of support they said famous contemporaries had spoken.
This necessitated denials and retractions and resulted in much nastiness.[63] The dispute spread over all Italy; patronized by states and princes
in a war yet fully raging, humanists had to balance several loyalties. In
an age when humanists were orators and orators were diplomats, both
Poggio and Valla left themselves open to the charge that their dispute,
coming at a time when Italians should unite against the Turks, was an
exercise in extreme vanity.[64]

   Valla's conception of language was radical in one sense and conservative in another. On one level he could understand that the Latin of a
Jerome failed to express the Greek of a Saint Paul, and he could criticize
the former in terms of what he knew of the latter. This required a historical, critical understanding of how Latin developed in relation to
Greek. In terms of understanding the historicity of language, how the
usage of a language reflected the state of a culture, Valla was second to
none. His language theory has philosophical significance as well. In his
Dialectical Disputations Valla attempted to reduce Aristotle's philosophical categories to grammatical ones, so that "substance" and "accident,"
for instance, could devolve into "noun" and "adjective." These notions
reflect his distrust of philosophical systems per se. Finally, Valla hoped
to establish with greater accuracy the rules of Latin. He wanted to
show how the best classical usage was reached with Quintilian and
how his rules and usage could be revived. He showed that grammatical corruption from this best usage represented also a corruption in
thought, how truth (*res*) was affected by language (*verba*). While many
humanists, including Poggio, saw the historicity of language in terms
of words reflecting reality, so that language must change as reality
changes, Valla gave equal stress to the inverse of the relationship: the
structure of any language itself (*verba*) affected how reality as a whole
was conceived (*res*). His emphasis on usage, therefore, became in effect

61.   Walser, *Poggio*, pp. 276–77.
62.   Ibid., p. 277; *Oratio V*, in *Opera omnia*, I, pp. 242–51.
63.   Walser, *Poggio*, p. 277; and especially Camporeale, *Lorenzo Valla*, pp. 336ff., 376–387.
64.   This was the emphasis of Filelfo, "ein wahrlich seltsamer Friedensengel" (Walser, *Poggio*, p. 277), in his "attempt" to conciliate his two former enemies.

a moral and even religious campaign. His most influential work of the Quattrocento, the *Elegantiae linguae latinae*, reflects this emphasis.[65]

Part of Valla's appeal is precisely his historical consciousness. Yet his critical method, his "radicalism," has another edge. According to modern standards of exegesis Valla seems conservative indeed. Few today would criticize Jerome's Latinity. Even those who insist that classical Latin reached its height with Cicero or Sallust would not criticize the several styles according to a single standard. When Poggio "conversed with the dead" he seems truly to have enjoyed the variety of styles and personalities he confronted. He saw Valla as a stone-faced, nitpicking critic, attacking the dead, who could not answer in defense, and as taking both himself and his classical authors far too seriously. For Valla Latin was a living language in that it matured and then decayed in the past and could be made alive again through restoration; for Poggio it was living in that its forms could be adapted with some degree of freedom according to one's experience, mood, or personal preference. If one tests the notion of a "living" language according to practice, Poggio would have to be declared the victor. His Latin style, as he himself knew, was far livelier and hence superior to Valla's. Poggio compared Valla and his campaign for Latin elegance to a certain man who promised his fellow citizens he could fly. All day long they waited while he stood atop a high tower, often flapping his arms as if he were about to take off. Finally, as the sun was setting and the townsfolk were getting restless, he lowered his pants and "mooned" the people below.[66]

In his invectives, Poggio emphasized that Latinity was established historically, not according to its "reason" but by its "authority." It was not the Latin language but the Romans who dominated peoples, and the Romans, by *usus* and *auctoritas*, saw that the Latin language ruled. "Men dominate, not language." The "teacher of speaking in the Latin manner was always *usus*," Poggio wrote in the first invective, and "this *usus* is found in the books and writings of the ancient authors." By subjecting all modern and ancient authors to a definable system, Valla must spend his time in petty, grammatical subjects, disputations carried out

---

65. See Camporeale, *Lorenzo Valla*, pp. 31–208 *passim*.

66. *Oratio I*, in *Opera omnia*, I, p. 195: "Persimilis est Valla noster homini ridiculo, qui cum aliquando se ex quadam turri volaturum certo die profiteretur, ac populus ad id spectaculum convenisset, homines suspensos variis alarum ostentationibus usque ad noctem detinuit. Deinde omnibus volatum cupide expectantibus, populo culum ostendit." The same story appears in Poggio's *Facetiae* (*Opera omnia*, I, p. 435), where we find out that the location is Bologna, and where the incident is used to illustrate Gregory XII's promises, and performance, in ending the Great Schism in the 1410s.

in triviis. Hence, Valla, your writings become a tired song, *sine sale, sine sapore.*[67]

While Poggio's precise feelings on the Studio controversy cannot now be known, we can be sure that his arguments were directed against a specialist in Latin rhetoric. He stated that he opposed the candidate or the type of candidate that Rinuccini had in mind, and here we can only imagine a Filelfo, a Valla or his disciple, or perhaps a more recent enemy, George of Trebizond.[68] Whoever he was, this person would at-

---

67.   *Oratio I*, in *Opera omnia*, i, p. 194: "At illud infantissimum opus [*sc.* Libri elegantiarum], non solum nulla elegantia, sed summa absurditate, summa impudentia, summa barbarie est refertum. Totus est sermo de vi verborum, et disputantiunculae cuiusdam paedagoguli stulti, aut grammaticuli in triviis de quaestiunculis puerilibus atque inanibus disputantis, ut qui stultissimus fieri, et linguae latinae omnino ignarus cupiat, libros eos memoriae commendet. At fatuus ille loquax, ut verba sua aliquo precio aestimentur, omnes priscos rerum scriptores sibi vexandos ac lacerandos desumpsit."

Ibid., p. 195: Valla "dixit Romanum ibi esse ubi Romana lingua dominatur. Quis hoc, unquam, modo insolentissima bestia, locutus est? Ubi nam legit Romanam linguam dici pro Latina? Ubi nam audivit linguam Romanam dominari? Dominantur homines, non lingua. Praeterea lingua Romana est, et ea vulgaris qua sola utuntur Romani, ut si quibus dominetur Romanis ubi est in usu, non aliis dominetur. At linguam latinam dicere voluit stultissimus barbarus, quae nemini dominatur, sed in usu et in precio apud multos."

Ibid., p. 203: "Latinorum verborum proprietas, vis, significatio, constructio non tantum ratione, quantum veterum scriptorum autoritate constant. Qua sublata latinae linguae fundamentum et sustentaculum pereat necesse est. Latine enim loquendi usus semper fuit magister, qui solum autorum priscorum libris et scriptis continetur. Iste vesanus convitiator, superorum omnium autoritate semota, nova sensa verbis indidit, novum scribendi morem introducit, tanta praesumptione usus, ut sibi soli plusquam reliquis omnibus tribuat autoritatis."

My summary is based also on passages from *Oratio III*, in *Opera omnia*, i, p. 239, and *Oratio V*, ibid., p. 243.

68.   In his letter to Alamanni, Poggio indicated that Rinuccini considered more than one figure: "Habet haec civitas saltem quatuor qui in tradendis eiusmodi [*sc.* artis rhetoricae] praeceptis nulla in re cederent *illis quos* Rinuccinus iudicat advocandos" (Ep. XIII, 3 [27 June (1455)] [Tonelli III, 184]). Rinuccini's letter to Alamanni referred to those figures who helped establish Florence's reputation in eloquence: Bruni, Marsuppini, Manetti, and George of Trebizond, whom "ego saepius apud librariam Vespasiani nostri tabernam coeuntes, adolescentium turba circunfusos ac de maximis rebus egregie disputantes audivi" (*Lettere ed orazioni*, p. 11). Poggio praised also the first three figures, noting that they were self-taught, but omitted George: "Nam quod queritur, apud tabernam nescio quam librariam nullas fieri inter doctos homines disputationes, sicut hactenus fieri consuetum putat, non opinor neque Iannotium neque Carolum Arretinum, neque Leonardum penes eum locum more graeculi pedagogi disputare in triviis, aut bene vivendi institutiones tradere consuetos" (p. 187). Poggio's dispute with George in the early 1450s at Rome involved a physical confrontation in the papal curia as well as, possibly, hired assassins. Poggio chased George from Rome, and George was unable to return even after Poggio left Rome for Florence in 1453. George had taught rhetoric with distinction at the University of Florence in the 1440s, and at the time of the Studio controversy, in early 1455, he probably would have been happy to return. This disposition would have continued at least through 8 Apr. 1455, the date of the election of Calixtus III, since the early favorite among papal candidates was another of Trebizond's enemies,

tempt to convince his students that eloquence depended on wider studies of rhetoric and on a knowledge of Greek. At about the same time
that he wrote Andrea Alamanni in favor of the four Florentines, Poggio
wrote to Domenico Sabino, who had been lecturing at Florence, probably on an interim basis, and who was also seeking the Studio chair.
Poggio praised Sabino for concentrating on the *fontes*, not the *rivuli*, of
eloquence. From Cicero, Poggio emphasized, I have learned what little
I know of eloquence; only idiots prefer to study Quintilian for the
rules.[69] Poggio thought the lecturer should simply explain the ancient
texts. Able to read and appreciate a variety of texts, the student could
then begin to develop his own style, adopting whatever form the occasion demanded. In his letter to Andrea Alamanni, therefore, Poggio
could have been concerned with one issue only: the appointment of
someone who held impressive credentials as a teacher of rhetoric.

It is difficult to reconstruct exactly what happened to the Studio controversy after Poggio's letter of 27 June 1455 to Andrea Alamanni. Donato Acciaiuoli's last letter on the question, undated and fragmentary,
follows in his letterbook a letter of 16 June 1455. Addressed again to
Andrea Alamanni, the letter at first hints at resignation: "As for our
concern for the Studio, . . . what more can I say?" But Donato urged
Andrea to continue fighting for the *communis litterarum utilitas*.[70]

Soon, it appears, a compromise was worked out, probably by Piero
de' Medici, one of the Ufficiali dello Studio, and the "Marsuppini chair"
was divided. It was divided not by having the salary meted out, as in the
proposal of February 1455, but through a division according to the several disciplines.[71] The *Ufficiali* offered John Argyropoulos a position in
early August 1455 and again for the following year—although the Byzantine did not actually begin teaching until January or February 1457. In
effect he took over the philosophical section of the "universal chair"—
with a salary comparable to that offered Marsuppini—and he began instruction in Aristotle's dialectics, ethics, natural philosophy, and metaphysics, according to a systematic program laid out in advance.[72] An-

Cardinal Bessarion. The election of Calixtus, which caused most humanists to flee
Rome, allowed Trebizond to return as secretary (for these details of George's life, see
J. Monfasani, *George of Trebizond*). The problem with George of Trebizond as a Studio
candidate is that there is no evidence apart from whatever Rinuccini's and Poggio's letters may offer (cf. Monfasani, ibid., which does not mention the Studio controversy).

69.   Ep. XII, 32 (Tonelli III, 176–77). See also my *"Studium Florentinum* Controversy,"
pp. 53–54, n. 39.

70.   Magl. VIII 1390, fol. 20–20v.

71.   For Piero's role, see nn. 93 and 94, below.

72.   For his first appointment, see n. 18, above. The records of a notary for the Monte
Comune show a payment to John Argyropoulos of 115 florins, representing approxi-

other part of the "universal chair," that of Greek language, was taken over by one of the four original candidates, Francesco da Castiglione, at a rather low salary.[73] The remaining part, the "traditional" portion of the chair, that of rhetoric and poetry, became the prize to be won by the remaining rival candidates, Landino, Rossi, and Nuti, who were joined by 1456 by Bartolomeo Scala. By the autumn of 1456 Landino managed to win a minor lectureship in the Studio with a salary of about 45 florins yearly; this very likely was for lectures on Dante.[74] He continued to seek the chair in rhetoric and poetry and finally won it in January 1458, with the title (*ars oratoria et poesis*) and salary (100 florins per year) close to those of the original proposal.[75] Bernardo Nuti became a teacher of some note, but whether his lectures were public or private is not known.[76] Antonio Rossi quit Florence for the Accademia Pomponiana in Rome (ca. 1460).[77] Bartolomeo Scala became a tutor and secretary for the Medici family, chancellor of the Parte Guelfa in 1459, and finally chancellor of Florence in 1465.[78] Of the minor candidates, Guglielmo Becchi pursued successfully an ecclesiastical career. The non-Florentine

mately one-third of his annual salary, for public lectures in early 1457 (Not. Antec. D 66 [Niccolò di Michele Dini, 1456–1458], unfoliated [f. 13 by count, at document dated 26 Feb. 1456/57]). I discuss the dating and subject of his first lectures in Chapter v.

73.   By late 1456 Francesco was no longer considered as a major candidate for the chair in rhetoric. He seems to have lectured on Greek irregularly in the Studio from 1446 to 1462 (see n. 36, above).

74.   Field, "Cristoforo Landino's First Lectures on Dante," esp. p. 33, n. 71.

75.   Gherardi, ed., *Statuti*, p. 467 (document dated 5 Oct. 1458, reconfirming the appointment from the previous January 1457/58).

76.   For the school of Nuti, see the sources cited above, n. 36.

77.   In his *Storia dell'Accademia platonica*, Della Torre promised an appendix on Rossi (p. 383), but this was not published. There is some information in Della Torre's *Paolo Marsi da Pescina: Contributo alla storia dell'Accademia Pomponiana* (Rocca S. Casciano, 1903), pp. 107–9 (reference owed to the late John D'Amico). Alamanno Rinuccini commended Rossi to Iacopo Ammannati, in Rome, in a letter dated 4 Mar. 1460 (*Lettere ed orazioni*, pp. 48–50). Pierfilippo Pandolfini also wrote to Rossi, 17 Aug. 1460, professing friendship and asking for news and letters from Rome (Magl. VI 166, fols. 113–14v; cited by Della Torre, *Paolo Marsi*, pp. 108–9). This Rossi (surname spelled "Rufus" or "Rusus" in earlier testimony) is almost surely the Antonius "Roscius" who wrote an *Oratio de laudibus scientiae* (Magl. VI 183, fols. 1–28v) and translated some Lucian, each dedicated to Berardo Eroli, cardinal of Spoleto (see Kristeller, *Iter*, II, 43, 245, 306). He is identified in a manuscript at Oxford, Bodleian Library, cod. lat. misc. e 81, fol. 118, under a section entitled "Libros quos Rome habeo" (by Gentile Becchi? Antonio Pelotti?), as "Antonius Roscius Florentinus cardinalis Spoletani secretarius." This note dates from the 1460s: see Kristeller, *Studies*, I, 154–56, and C. Grayson, "Poesie latine di Gentile Becchi in un codice bodleiano," in B. Maracchi Biagiarelli and D. E. Rhodes, eds., *Studi offerti a Roberto Ridolfi* (Florence, 1973), pp. 285–303. In 1466 Rossi delivered to Leonardo Dati in Rome a copy of Matteo Palmieri's *Città di vita*: see Dati's letter of thanks, in his *Epistolae XXXIII*, ed. L. Mehus (Florence, 1743), pp. 59–60.

78.   Brown, *Bartolomeo Scala*, pp. 21, 22–41, 42.

Domenico Sabino asked both Donato Acciaiuoli and Poggio Bracciolini for their support, won from them warm praise only, and apparently found academic fields more fertile elsewhere. Of Agnolo da Lecco, possibly a candidate, nothing is known.

That Landino and Argyropoulos could have competed with one another for a chair at the University of Florence in 1455 now seems most unlikely. No solid evidence suggests that their professional interests overlapped. Moreover, their salary expectations diverged too greatly for them to have been in actual competition for any academic post created by statute. In these years Argyropoulos would command a salary some three or four times that of Landino, and Landino's own salary would not approach that of the Byzantine until the 1470s.[79] But was Argyropoulos the central figure in the polemics surrounding the controversy? When he began to lecture most members of the Acciaiuoli circle became his students. Some of them indeed spoke of him, after he arrived in Florence, as if he were the new Marsuppini, and they reinforced this notion by praising his eloquence as well as his philosophical learning.[80] Yet he came to Florence as a professor of philosophy, and that he remained. Unlike Marsuppini or Filelfo, Argyropoulos was never in a position where he could have "absorbed" the "traditional" parts of the "universal" humanistic chair, nor did his salary, which indeed approached Marsuppini's, absorb those salaries assigned to poetry and rhetoric. His appointment could not, therefore, threaten seriously the academic ambitions of Cristoforo Landino.

The most conclusive evidence for this, hitherto ignored in discussions of the Studio controversy, appears in the *pratica* debates over Poggio's tenure as chancellor, which took place in late 1456 and early 1457. Hoping to have Poggio reappointed, on 27 December 1456 the counselors to the Signoria suggested that a second chancellor, Antonio di Mariano Muzi, be selected to assist Poggio, who would also have four humanist assistants, two of whom, with a combined salary of two hundred florins, would lecture at the university as well. These four are named: Cristoforo Landino, Antonio Rossi, Bernardo Nuti, and Bartolomeo Scala. These were the four original major candidates, except that Scala is listed in-

79.   In the 1460s Landino's salary gradually rose to 200 florins (Gherardi, ed., *Statuti*, pp. 473–74; Park, "Readers at the Florentine Studio," p. 309) and then reached 300 florins in 1471–72 (ibid., p. 310; cf. Verde, *Lo Studio fiorentino*, II, 174–75).

80.   For example, Donato Acciaiuoli's proem to his commentary on the *Nicomachean Ethics* (ca. 1463–64), to Cosimo de' Medici (Magl. XXI 136, fol. 1; cf. ed. 1478, sig. A1 [for these sources, see Chapter VIII, n. 24, below]): "Cum post interitum quorundam doctissimorum hominum studia Florentina magna ex parte remissa viderentur, venit in hanc urbem Argiropylus Bizantius vir ingenio prestans summusque philosophus, ut iuventutem litteris grecis ac bonis artibus erudiret."

stead of Francesco da Castiglione. The counselors gave these reasons for this rather ingenious scheme: Poggio needs assistance, and "la facoltà oratoria et morale è senza maestri."[81] To be sure, at this time Argyropoulos had not yet begun teaching, and he would not begin for several weeks. But the counselors' proposal suggests strongly that Argyropoulos's appointment, originally made in 1455 and renewed in the autumn of 1456, was not then considered to include the chair of rhetoric and that his appointment was not so generally defined as to supersede the proposal of 1455.

We can adduce some other evidence that Argyropoulos was not at the center of the original controversy. When Argyropoulos was offered an appointment in August 1455, Alamanno Rinuccini drafted the letter urging him to come. Rinuccini had to apologize for not having written since Argyropoulos's departure from Florence—that is, for about a year.[82] Nor are there letters during the entire time of the Studio controversy between Donato Acciaiuoli and Argyropoulos. That the polemical letters during the controversy were addressed to Andrea Alamanni could also point to the central role of Filelfo, since it seems likely that Alamanni was in Milan with his friend Filelfo during most of 1455.[83] At some time in the 1450s, it seems, Andrea attempted to induce Cosimo to remove the Florentine ban on Filelfo.[84] Moreover, if Argyropoulos was at the center of the controversy, then the original candidates, including Antonio Rossi, would have had to oppose him. But one of Rossi's supporters, Franco Sacchetti, enthusiastically embraced Argyropoulos and became one of his leading patrons.[85] Finally, in 1460 Filelfo would scold Acciaiuoli for not writing enough, hardly forgivable, he noted, for one who "had wanted to use me as a teacher."[86] The next year

81.   Ed. E. Walser, *Poggius*, pp. 404–6; cf. Brown, *Bartolomeo Scala*, pp. 20–21. The unnoticed report on the Poggian Chancery (Cons. e Prat. 54, fols. 49v–50), referred to by me in my *"Studium Florentinum* Controversy," p. 57, n. 68, has now been edited and discussed by Black, *Benedetto Accolti*, pp. 92–93n.

82.   *Lettere ed orazioni*, p. 12: "Vereor ne forte desideraris officium meum, quod tam fuerim hactenus in scribendo piger, ut nihil ad te post discessum tuum dederim litterarum; quod non oblivione tui aut negligentia factum existimes velim. Quo pacto enim mihi liceat oblivisci quem ego propter admirabiles virtutes . . . [etc.]."

83.   Giustiniani, *Alamanno Rinuccini*, p. 91.

84.   See below, pp. 101–102.

85.   See the sources cited above, n. 34, and Vespasiano, *Vite*, II, 215–17.

86.   *Epistolae*, fol. 118v: "Non possum non probare tuam tam longam taciturnitatem, cum existimem te uti voluisse me magistro. . . . " But Filelfo is promising to send Acciaiuoli a requested copy of an oration before Pius II at the Congress of Mantua, 1459, and perhaps here his role as *magister* consists in this.

Acciaiuoli alluded also to Filelfo's role as teacher: I now have, he wrote, Argyropoulos aiding my studies *viva voce* and you helping *litteris*.[87]

Landino's appointment to the chair in rhetoric in January 1458 was not a sop thrown to his supporters after their defeat by the Acciaiuoli/Argyropoulos forces. Rather, it reflects Landino's victory over the other candidates and a fulfillment of the funding for the humanist chair approved in February 1455. Was the delay of almost three years in the appointment of Landino to the chair of poetry and rhetoric due to the strengths of his rival candidates—Rossi, Francesco da Castiglione, Nuti, and Scala—or was it due rather to some other cause? Was there continued opposition from the Acciaiuoli circle, which yet held hopes, even after the appointment of Argyropoulos, that an outside professor in the humanities such as Filelfo could be appointed?

The latter seems unlikely. A letter from Filelfo in May 1456 implied his defeat. He wrote Acciaiuoli that he had recently seen Argyropoulos and expected him to return to Florence to begin the autumn lectures. Congratulating the young Florentines on their choice, Filelfo noted that "among the Greeks"(!) they could have found no one better.[88] Soon Filelfo's letters would suggest that things were not so bad in Milan after all.[89] Why was Filelfo eliminated as a candidate? For one thing, Argyropoulos's anticipated lectures in moral philosophy, and his obvious skills in the Greek language, would preempt some of Filelfo's strengths. It also would have been difficult to get a law passed to fund another position so expensive. Moreover, political developments in Florence from 1455 would have tended to bolster Medici opposition to the appointment of their old enemy in Milan. From the summer of 1455 until the Parlamento of 1458, as we have seen, the Medici party steadily lost power, and Cosimo could hardly have welcomed talk of Filelfo's return. (A story was told that Cosimo was overheard at confession promising to forgive his enemies. Would he then, Andrea Alamanni asked, revoke

87.   Edited in part in Della Torre, *Storia*, p. 395.

88.   Dated 31 May 1456, in *Epistolae*, fol. 94v: "[Johannes Argyropulus] transivit ad Transalpinos: rediturus ad vos ad constitutum tempus. Te vero et reliquam Florentinam iuventutem non possum non laudare, quod talem tantumque et oratorem et philosophum graeca vobis instituendis disciplinis praefeceritis. Nam sentio neminem inter Graecos hoc uno viro omni disciplina praestantiorem."

89.   Adam, "Filelfo," I, 40 (citing a letter to Mariotto Tertini, 30 Oct. 1457). Unfortunately, a gap in Acciaiuoli's letterbook leaves us no letters (except one, irrelevant to this section, a consolatory letter to Pandolfo Pandolfini, discussed below, Chapter VIII) from July 1455 until 1460, and we can only guess how (1) Poggio's open opposition to Filelfo's return (June 1455), (2) the first appointment of Argyropoulos (August 1455), and (3) the growing loss of Medici control over the government (especially noticeable from the summer of 1455), may have affected Acciaiuoli's relations with Filelfo.

the ban on Filelfo? Cosimo replied: "I'm still the good sort who forgives those who offend me, not yet the perfect sort who 'prays for those who persecute.' When I join the perfect, however, let's talk it over."[90]) Open criticism of how Poggio handled—or, rather, avoided—his duties as chancellor, which eventually, in the late summer of 1456, drove him from office, likewise would have made speculation of Filelfo's return to Florence disturbing to many. Filelfo's talents and international prestige would have made him a strong candidate to replace Poggio as chancellor—especially if a period of residence in Florence as its leading humanist lecturer should affirm his popularity and patriotism.[91]

One reason for the delay in appointing Landino to the chair of rhetoric could have been simply the growing tightfistedness of the Florentine government. The economy was slow and Florence was defaulting on debts; in times of economic hardship university salaries were often not paid and positions not filled. The appointment of Landino to the chair of rhetoric, on 18 January 1458, fell exactly one week after a bill was passed to reform the *catasto* and hence generate more money.[92] The compromise from the summer of 1455, therefore, probably authored by Piero de' Medici, which included a public appointment of Argyropoulos and, apparently, the assumption that the positions in rhetoric and poetry would be filled later, seems to have ended the Studio controversy. Several members of the Acciaiuoli circle credited Piero, and sometimes Cosimo, with the appointment of Argyropoulos.[93] Letters and

90.   Poliziano, *Detti piacevoli*, p. 72, no. 181; *Tagebuch*, pp. 86–87, no. 178.

91.   When Benedetto Accolti died in 1464, Cristoforo Landino sought to become the new chancellor. He outlined his credentials in a letter to Lorenzo de' Medici and warned against appointing either a jurist or an "outside orator" (Filelfo?) who could not be trusted with state secrets (ed. M. Lentzen in his *Studien*, pp. 203–10). The Medici accepted his warning and appointed a Florentine humanist—but it was the Medici secretary Bartolomeo Scala, who had the support of the Argyropoulos circle (Brown, *Bartolomeo Scala*, pp. 42–45).

92.   The law of the catasto was passed 11 Jan. 1458 (Gutkind, *Cosimo*, p. 27).

93.   Most of the manifold evidence for Piero's role has been collected by Della Torre, *Storia*, p. 381, n. 3. Only rather late accounts (Vespasiano, *Vite*, II, 203, and a letter of Alamanno Rinuccini, 1489, in *Lettere ed orazioni*, p. 189) credit Cosimo alone. Cammelli has rejected the evidence for Piero's role (*Argiropulo*, p. 73n.), viewing the several dedications and letters as rhetorical flourishes and taking the position, followed since by many others, that the Acciaiuoli/Argyropoulos forces were strongly anti-Medici. But Cammelli overlooked the fact that many of the "rhetorical" laudations of Piero were contemporary with the events (e.g., Rinuccini's dedication of a work, dated 28 Feb. 1457, within a few weeks of Argyropoulos's first lectures: *Lettere ed orazioni*, p. 23); he supposed, incorrectly, that the Medici in these years had outright control over academic appointments and public salaries; and he assumed that Argyropoulos was competing for one of the positions of the proposal of February 1455.

dedications of Landino show similar gratitude toward Piero, although, since there were rival candidates (some of whom were Landino's friends), they are less explicit.[94]

By the autumn of 1456 Landino still had not gotten the appointment in rhetoric, but he did manage to receive a less lucrative position in the Studio, probably a lectureship on Dante. For that year John Argyropoulos held a lectureship in philosophy, though he did not begin teaching until January or February 1457. That the appointments were considered jointly, as part of a compromise, may be inferred from a letter that Alamanno Rinuccini wrote to Donato Acciaiuoli, dated 9 November 1456, in which both Argyropoulos and Landino are called "ours": "You should know that our Landino, on the same day you wrote your letter to me, began his lectures, before a large group of listeners and with a splendid and refined adornment of words. This I heard from others: I was in the country and could not attend. From our Argyropoulos, however, who aroused such great hope for his lectures, which we were so anxious to begin attending, there is not even a word."[95] Whether the "our Landino" indeed indicates a compromise, and one cheerfully accepted, is unclear. Since the Acciaiuoli circle had so publicly let it be known that the several original candidates were "unworthy" of Marsuppini's chair, some bitterness no doubt lingered, especially for Landino, who had been the focus of attack. Yet this attack was probably less virulent than modern scholars would wish, and it seems highly unlikely that Acciaiuoli's most serious attack upon Landino and his supporters (in the letter dated 15 April 1455) was ever published.[96] Nor even privately (as far as we know) did Acciaiuoli make the famous statement that Landino was "unworthy of a small town like Prato."[97] While there

94. In 1458 or early 1459 Landino dedicated to Piero, whom he called his "Maecenas," his first major work, the collection of poems called *Xandra* (*Carmina*, ed. A. Perosa: see the introduction, p. xxxviii). See also two letters of Landino to Piero, edited ibid., pp. 181–90). Piero's young son, Lorenzo, was in these years one of Landino's students (Rochon, *La jeunesse de Laurent de Médicis*, p. 35).

95. *Lettere ed orazioni*, p. 18.

96. Field, "*Studium Florentinum* Controversy," pp. 39, 55, n. 47.

97. The quotation has been applied directly to Landino by Garin and others ("Donato Acciaiuoli cittadino," pp. 200, 260). Acciaiuoli's original letter shows that it is the entire provision for the humanistic chairs—that is, the choosing of only two lecturers, the limiting of the provision to rhetoric and poetry, and the small salary—that is "etiam Pratensi oppido . . . indignum" (ed. Fossi, *Monumenta*, p. 81). Acciaiuoli's aspersions on "Prato" may indicate more than a random choosing of the nearest small, "bourgeois" town. In a short letter to Piero de' Medici, 10 May 1455, one Iacopo Zanobi mentioned Prato in the context of the Florentine Studio; I could not determine, however, what issue was at stake (MAP XVII, 122).

is no evidence that Rinuccini or Acciaiuoli attended Landino's lectures regularly, Rinuccini's notice that he missed the inaugural oration because he was "in the country" should probably be taken at face value. Certainly by 1462, and probably much earlier, the personal elements of the controversy had been pushed aside, as a warm letter from Acciaiuoli to Landino at this time shows.[98] By the early 1470s Landino brought Acciaiuoli and Rinuccini into his dialogue, the *Disputationes Camaldulenses*.[99] Finally, in 1478, it was Landino who was selected to deliver the funeral oration on Donato Acciaiuoli.[100]

If we can exclude Argyropoulos as the central figure in the Studio controversy of 1455, not a shred of evidence remains that Poggio, Landino, or anyone else we can name opposed the appointment of that Byzantine philosopher to a chair at the university. Poggio's own position toward the new philosophical studies in Florence, usually considered so conservative, now becomes far more interesting. Consider a passage from his letter on the Studio controversy to Andrea Alamanni, dated 27 June 1455:

> At the age of twenty-five Cicero delivered the orations *Pro Cluentio* and again *Pro Roscio* so elegantly that none of his orations are more eloquent in their adornment of words or gravity of opinions. But we read that he had no teacher: rather, by the assiduous reading of eloquent men, by study, by diligence, and by practice, he reached that grade of speaking that no Latin has since approached. Afterward he crossed over into Greece—not for the sake of eloquence but for the sake of philosophy.[101]

That Cicero "transivit postmodum in Graeciam non eloquentiae sed philosophiae gratia"—that is, that Latins can properly turn to Greece for philosophy but not for rhetoric—would seem curious words indeed for one who opposed Argyropoulos! If Rinuccini and Acciaiuoli, still in their twenties at the time of this controversy, had wanted to follow the

---

98. Landino, *Reden*, pp. 90–91.

99. Ed. P. Lohe (Florence, 1980).

100. Landino, *Reden*, pp. 81–89.

101. Ep. XIII, 3 (Tonelli III, 185): "Cicero ipse in vigesimo quinto suae aetatis anno pro Cluentio et item pro Roscio oravit adeo eleganter, ut nulla eius oratio tum ornatu verborum tum sententiarum gravitate sit copiosior. At eum nullum dicendi magistrum legimus habuisse, sed assidua eloquentium virorum lectione, studio, diligentia, exercitatione scimus pervenisse ad eum dicendi gradum, ad quem nullus inter latinos accessit. Transivit postmodum in Graeciam non eloquentiae, sed philosophiae gratia."

Poggian model of Cicero, they could have found in the chancellor's words only an endorsement of their philosophical pursuits. As Poggio admitted elsewhere, he himself had never taken up philosophy. But he did encourage others in the new studies.

The Studio controversy of 1455 fell at a time when the principal lines of the philosophical renaissance in Florence were not yet drawn. Some commonplaces regarding the patrons of that renaissance and the parties to the Studio controversy must now be revised. Landino and Poggio did not, on the one side, oppose Argyropoulos—or so it seems. Nor in clinging to rhetorical traditions did they oppose philosophical innovation. Moreover, no corpus of ideas associated with Argyropoulos—be it "Aristotelian" or "civic"—can explain the arguments of those Florentines who opposed the feared "outsider." Filelfo in Florence would have scared the Medici and embittered Poggio. He would surely have damaged and possibly have ruined Landino's career in the Studio. From the other side, Acciaiuoli and Rinuccini had no ideological reasons whatsoever to oppose Landino. They could and, at least for some years, did, look on him with some aloofness, as one who offered Florentines a mere "mercantile" education, who could not quite get the hang of Greek, and whose livelihood (like that of any nonaristocratic humanist) depended on a salary plus whatever patronage he could muster.

The Medici were able to effect a compromise and satisfy, at least outwardly, the parties of the controversy. The controversy involved scholars and public appointments, and, as we should expect, the role of patrons and politicians had to be great. But it seems very likely that the Medici and its party intellectuals sought only to accommodate intellectual forces already in existence, as long as such an accommodation would keep Poggio's pride intact and Filelfo out of Florence. Those elements of Medicean cultural hegemony, which reached their fruition in the Age of Lorenzo, had little play in the Studio controversy—and here I must disagree with those scholars who read ideological controversies into the dispute. There is no evidence that the Medici entered the controversy either to create a speculative philosophical culture or to block the development of Aristotelian, "civic" ideals, which scholars have so recklessly associated with Argyropoulos and his circle. More than anything else the students of Argyropoulos looked to their teacher as one who could bring their cultural and intellectual education to completion. As we said earlier, scholars have not sufficiently appreciated the role of the intellectuals themselves in shaping the new culture. That Cosimo de' Medici was anticipating the *Theologia Platonica* in the 1450s makes only a little more sense than Ficino's assertion, late in life, that some of his best conversations with Cosimo took place after the latter's death.[102] To assess the impact of John Argyropoulos we must abandon imaginary plans and imagined discussions; instead, we should do what his students did, and sit in on a few of his lectures.

102.   *Opera omnia*, pp. 843–44, 1537.

V

THE
TEACHING OF
JOHN ARGYROPOULOS

L ET US now turn to the actual formal expression of the ideas of the
philosophical renaissance, looking first at the mentor of the Acciaiuoli circle, John Argyropoulos. Of primary concern here is his
role in the revival of Plato. But we shall also investigate his ideas more
generally, in order to discover why Acciaiuoli and his circle were attracted to his teaching and how they would depart from it.

In September 1463, about a year after Cosimo de' Medici and Marsilio
Ficino had founded their Platonic Academy, Donato Acciaiuoli described for a Castilian friend of Vespasiano da Bisticci recent intellectual
changes in Florence. "Never before," he wrote, "have the humanities so
flourished in this city," and many young Florentines are "so well versed
in the Aristotelian and Platonic teachings that they seem to have been
brought up in the Academy." To whom did Acciaiuoli credit this revival? Not the Medici, nor even Ficino, but the Byzantine immigrant to
Florence, John Argyropoulos.

> With great elegance, in the manner of the ancients, he has taught
> and is teaching moral and natural philosophy. Many books of Ar-

This chapter, a revised version of my "John Argyropoulos and the 'Secret Teachings' of
Plato," in J. Hankins, J. Monfasani, and F. Purnell, Jr., eds., *Supplementum Festivum:
Studies in Honor of Paul Oskar Kristeller* (Binghamton, N.Y., 1987), pp. 299–326, attempts
in part to reexamine some commonly held hypotheses concerning the teaching of John
Argyropoulos in Florence. It touches only peripherally on Argyropoulos's place in the
Latin and Greek scholastic traditions, and such a study, which I am not qualified to
make, would no doubt clarify and perhaps emend some of the conclusions that follow.
The cited article includes a section, omitted here, on Argyropoulos's exposition of the
Platonic Ideas. Also, where I quote from Argyropoulos in the text, the article regularly
provides the Latin in the notes.

istotle he has translated into Latin, and he has diligently opened
up Plato's beliefs, and those secrets of his and the hidden teaching
as well, to the great wonder of those who hear him lecture (*Platonis opiniones atque arcana illa et reconditam disciplinam diligenter
aperuit non sine magna audientium admiratione*).[1]

Ficino himself did not dismiss the role of the Byzantines.[2] From Byzantium, he wrote in 1464, the "spirit of Plato" had flown to Italy. But for
Ficino the "spirit" had flown with the Greek text of Plato, and it had
landed in his Academy.[3] Very soon after Acciaiuoli's description of the
philosophical renaissance, Ficino would emphasize his own role in the
revival of Plato. To learn the "basic tenets of philosophy" (*prima philosophiae sacra*), Ficino wrote in 1464, Cosimo de' Medici commissioned
translations of Aristotle from John Argyropoulos. Then, to learn the
"inner secrets of wisdom itself" (*intima sapientiae ipsius arcana*), Cosimo
turned to some Hermetic writings and Platonic dialogues. In these
works, which he translated, Ficino wrote, are revealed "all precepts of
life, all principles of nature, all mysteries of theology."[4]

While there have been important and detailed studies of the Neoplatonism of Marsilio Ficino, little effort has been made to investigate the
Platonism of John Argyropoulos. At the same time many scholars, led

1. Letter to Alfonso de Palencia, 24 Sept. 1463, written for Vespasiano da Bisticci, ed.
Fossi, *Monumenta*, pp. 61–62. See also A. Mondó, "Una lletra d'Alfons de Palència a
Vespasià da Bisticci," in *Studi di bibliografia e di storia in onore di Tammaro de Marinis*
(Verona, for the Biblioteca Apostolica Vaticana, 1964), III, 271–81. There are several
other editions of this letter, the most recent in Alfonso de Palencia, *Epístolas latinas*, ed.
R. B. Tate and R. Alemany Ferrer (Barcelona, 1982), pp. 71–74, 122 (the shelf mark cited
should be corrected from Magl. VIII 1939 to Magl. VIII 1390).

2. For Ficino and Byzantium, see the general remarks of P. O. Kristeller, "Byzantine
and Western Platonism in the Fifteenth Century," now in his *Renaissance Thought and Its
Sources*, pp. 161–62.

3. M. F., *Prooemium* to trans. of ten dialogues of Plato, to Cosimo de' Medici, ed. in
Kristeller, *Supplementum Ficinianum*, II, 104: "[E] Bizantia Florentiam spiritus eius ipsis
in licteris vivens attica voce resonus ad Cosmum Medicem advolavit." A. Brown, "Platonism in Fifteenth-Century Florence," pp. 389–90, unites this statement of Ficino with his
later, positive opinion of Pletho's lectures and states, inaccurately in my opinion, that
Ficino meant that Plato's "spirit" arrived in Florence when Pletho began his Platonic lectures in 1439.

4. *Prooemium* to trans. of Xenocrates, *De morte* (i.e., *Axiochus*), in *Opera omnia*, p. 1965:
Cosmus, ut "in primis philosophiae sacris initiaretur, nonnullos Aristotelis libros con-
verti ab Ioanne Argyropylo viro doctissimo voluit, eosque diligentissime legit. Deinde
ne intima sapientiae ipsius arcana sibi deessent, divi Platonis libros decem et unum Mer-
curii e Graeca lingua in Latinam a nobis transferri iussit, quibus omnia vitae praecepta,
omnia naturae principia, omnia divinarum rerum mysteria sancta panduntur." See also
Kristeller, *Supplementum Ficinianum*, I, cxxxvi–vii. For Ficino's conception of the historical importance of his Academy, see also Kristeller, *Il pensiero filosofico di Marsilio Ficino*
(Florence, 1953), pp. 11–20.

by Eugenio Garin, have stressed the central role of Argyropoulos in the revival of Platonic studies in Florence.[5] According to Garin, Argyropoulos not only wove Platonic doctrines into his public lectures on Aristotle but also directly explained, privately to his students, his preferred Platonic texts. University rules alone kept his public activity confined to Aristotle.[6] Taking up the passage from Acciaiuoli's letter, quoted above, Garin has maintained that Argyropoulos taught a "secret and hidden doctrine" of Plato and hence embraced the hypothesis of a secret, Hermetic teaching passed on by Plato and his followers.[7] The common distinction between Argyropoulos's Aristotelianism and Ficino's Platonism, according to Garin, is due to Marsilio Ficino's cunning attempt to elevate his own role and that of his Medici patrons in the new Platonic studies.[8] Garin's conclusions are now widely accepted. Not unusual is the recent summary by George Holmes: the evidence that John Argyropoulos "filled his pupils with enthusiasm for Plato" is "not abundant but it is decisive."[9]

To his future students, Argyropoulos appeared to have stepped into Florence from antiquity itself. He spoke of the ancient philosophers as if he knew them firsthand, and his strong accent sounding through a full beard represented an otherworldly and ancient lore.[10] Donato Acciaiuoli's description of him in 1454 is telling: "He seemed to me not only erudite (as I had heard before I met him) but also wise and venerable, as if he had come from Greece of old."[11] Physically the impression re-

---

5.   See especially Garin's "Donato Acciaiuoli cittadino," pp. 199–267; "Platonici bizantini e platonici italiani," pp. 153–190; *La cultura filosofica*, pp. 102–8; and "La rinascita di Plotino," pp. 89–129. For other works, see *Bibliografia degli scritti di Eugenio Garin, 1929–1979* (Rome, 1979).

6.   "Donato Acciaiuoli cittadino," pp. 226–27; "La rinascita del Plotino," pp. 98–100.

7.   "Donato Acciaiuoli cittadino," pp. 226–29, 233. The expressions Garin uses, *arcanam illam et reconditam disciplinam* (p. 226) and "l'arcana e riposta disciplina" (p. 233), are inaccurate. The original is *arcana illa et reconditam disciplinam* (see p. 108, above). For this study the distinction is important: I argue that Argyropoulos was never interested in explaining any "secret teaching" of Plato.

8.   "Donato Acciaiuoli cittadino," p. 265; "La rinascita del Plotino," pp. 96–97.

9.   G. Holmes, *The Florentine Enlightenment, 1400–50* (London, 1969), p. 263.

10.   In 1477, when Argyropoulos returned to Florence from Rome, Niccolò Michelozzi mentioned that he still had his accent but no longer his beard, and he "didn't look Greek anymore" (cited by G. Cammelli, *Argiropulo*, p. 159, and now edited in part by Verde, "Giovanni Argiropolo e Lorenzo Buonincontri," p. 280; cf. Angelo Poliziano, *Detti piacevoli*, p. 46, no. 15; and *Tagebuch*, pp. 11–12, no. 15). Describing the lay and clerical Greeks at the Council of Florence, 1439, Vespasiano da Bisticci noted that they were dressed in the same "serious and dignified manner" that had been in use among the Greeks for "fifteen hundred years or more" (*Vite*, I, 18–19).

11.   Letter to Iacopo Ammannati, 5 Aug. 1454, ed. G. Zippel, "Per la biografia

quired little from the Florentine imagination. Since the period when the Eastern church sent to Florence its philosophers and theologians for the great ecumenical council in the late 1430s, no Florentine painter of the Adoration could neglect to include the portrait of a bearded Byzantine sage as one of the Magi.[12] Constantinople's fall to the Turks in 1453 left Florence with an exile, one of these wise men from the East.

In Florence, Argyropoulos was a teacher. He did little else professionally, except prepare a great number of Latin translations, mostly of Aristotle, which he presented to patrons.[13] The argument that Argyropoulos introduced Platonism to Florence is based principally on the testimony of his students and on evidence drawn from his lectures. Of these lectures several of the more formal prefatory orations or preliminary lectures (the *praefationes* or *praelectiones*) have modern editions.[14]

---

dell'Argiropulo" (1896), p. 181: "Vir . . . mihi visus non solum eruditus, ut fama audieram, sed etiam sapiens, gravis et vetere illa Grecia dignus."

12. Domenico Ghirlandaio included a portrait of Argyropoulos as a magus in his *Adoration of the Magi*, 1487. The two bearded figures in Benozzo Gozzoli's *Voyage of the Magi*, completed in 1459, merit closer attention. For the Renaissance representation of the magus, see R. Hatfield, *Botticelli's Uffizi "Adoration": A Study in Pictorial Content* (Princeton, 1976) [p. 90, n. 78, for Ghirlandaio's Argyropoulos], and his "The Compagnia de' Magi," *Journal of the Warburg and Courtauld Institutes* 33 (1970), 107–61. For contemporary portraits of Argyropoulos, mostly miniatures, see the plates in Cammelli, *Argiropulo*, and in Lampros, *Argyropouleia*.

13. See Cammelli, *Argiropulo*, pp. 183–84, for a list. See also C. Frati, "Le traduzioni aristoteliche di G. Argiropulo e un'antica legatura medicea," *La Bibliofilia* 19 (1917), 1–25.

14. From Ricc. 120, K. Müllner has edited six pieces from John Argyropoulos's introductory lectures: *Reden und Briefe*, pp. 3–56. The manuscript has been considered a possible autograph, but the hand is Donato Acciaiuoli's (see S. Caroti's note on Ricc. 120 in the section "La rinascita della Scienza" of the exhibition catalog *Firenze e la Toscana dei Medici nell'Europa del Cinquecento: La corte, il mare, i mercanti* . . . [Florence, 1980], p. 136, no. 1.7, and my "John Argyropoulos and the 'Secret Teachings' of Plato," pp. 303–4, the plate on p. 305, and the appendix on p. 326). Although the titles and style of the six pieces in Ricc. 120 would seem to indicate six separate lectures, some of the separate pieces in the manuscript are made up of several introductory lectures, and the "secunda lectio" for the course on the *De anima* (Müllner, ed., pp. 48–53; Ricc. 120, fols. 31–34) should be loosely considered "a following lecture," probably the third for that academic year, 1460–61. Some of the divisions can be clarified by comparing Donato Acciaiuoli's notebooks for the regular lectures themselves (Naz. II I 104; Naz. II I 103; Magl. V 42). These contain some but not all of the introductory lectures from Ricc. 120, as well as other introductory material. For these notebooks, see n. 28, below. In the notebooks the separate lectures are more clearly distinguished (labeled "1a," "2a," etc., or separated by vertical lines, pen changes, or such tags as "pridie dicebamus"). It should be mentioned that since Ricc. 120 is an Acciaiuoli autograph, the dates assigned in the Acciaiuoli notebooks, long recognized as autographs, no longer serve as corroborating evidence for the dates of Ricc. 120. (For problems with Acciaiuoli's autograph dates, see Chapter IV, n. 31, above.) But I think they are roughly accurate. While I find few errors in Müllner's editions, Ricc. 120 should probably be reedited with a fresh reading of the manuscript and with the material from Acciaiuoli's notebooks added and compared. For one problem with the edition, see Brown, "Giovanni Argiropulo on the Agent Intellect," p. 161, n. 4.

There are also unedited lectures, only sporadically utilized by modern scholars, which are in manuscript notebooks diligently copied by Donato Acciaiuoli.[15] (Acciaiuoli had the "fastest hand" in Florence, a *mano velocissima*, according to Vespasiano da Bisticci, which could "take down in writing everything that Argyropoulos said in voice."[16]) Three of these notebooks are extant, and they include some fifteen hundred pages of text covering lectures delivered before 1462–63, when the Platonic Academy was founded and when Ficino began his direct and systematic study of the Platonic corpus.[17] Hence there are abundant sources, for the most part unedited, that should permit careful analysis of Argyropoulos's role in the revival of Platonism in Florence.

To be sure, affixing or removing the tag "Platonist" to a Renaissance philosopher can be risky. For Argyropoulos's "Platonism" one could look at his status within the Byzantine tradition, in relation to its earlier history from Psellus to Pletho. Platonism so permeated Byzantine philosophical culture that few Byzantines, even ardent Aristotelians, can escape being called Platonists in some sense of the word, even if they would not have so described themselves. Moreover, in the Plato-Aristotle controversy of the Quattrocento, Argyropoulos sided with the "harmonizers" by praising Bessarion's defense of Plato against George of Trebizond's rigid Aristotelianism.[18] For this too one might term Argyropoulos a "Platonist." The concern in this chapter is different, defined by the question I raised earlier: Is there evidence that the Platonic teaching of Argyropoulos heralded that approach toward Plato taken by Marsilio Ficino and hence that it ushered in the Neoplatonic movement itself? Did Argyropoulos, that is, attempt to convince his Florentine students that certain Platonic doctrines, express teachings and hidden ones as well, were consonant with their proper "human condition," essential to their self-understanding, and beneficial or even necessary to their desire to attain happiness?

What, we may ask, did Donato Acciaiuoli mean when he wrote that

15.   For the notebooks, see n. 28, below. Although Acciaiuoli's notebooks have been called "lecture notes," they should properly be called "lecture drafts," or *reportationes*. In these the student prepares the drafts from notes, usually attempting to reproduce faithfully the lectures and sometimes in consultation with the lecturer himself. Any close reading of the corrections and style of Acciaiuoli's notebooks reveals that they cannot possibly contain actual lecture notes.

16.   Vespasiano, *Vite*, II, 25.

17.   See n. 28, below. For Ficino's early Platonic studies, see Kristeller, *Studies*, pp. 196–98, and his "Marsilio Ficino as a Beginning Student of Plato," *Scriptorium* 20 (1966), 41–54. For dating the beginning of the Academy, see below, Chapter VII, n. 96

18.   Argyropoulos, letter to Bessarion, ed. in L. Mohler, *Kardinal Bessarion als Theologe, Humanist und Staatsmann* (1923–42; rept. Aalen, 1967), III, 601–2.

Argyropoulos opened up the "secrets" and the "hidden teaching" of
Plato? The expressions appear in a letter composed on behalf of a Florentine book dealer, Vespasiano da Bisticci, and addressed to a foreign
customer, where exaggerated statements of Florentine cultural and intellectual accomplishments should abound. Secret and hidden teaching
could mean the doctrine of a *prisca theologia* like that of Marsilio Ficino.
According to Ficino, secret teachings of natural and divine wisdom had
been passed down by a succession of ancient sages from the Egyptian
Hermes Trismegistus to Orpheus and to others, and thence to the divine Plato and his followers. Some of these could be found in ancient
writings (the Hermetic texts known to Ficino as the *Pimander*, the
Orphic Hymns, the *Chaldaic Oracles*); others required an enlightened
interpretation of Platonic dialogues and letters. They were "secret" because they had been cunningly kept from the masses of men, because
they were "hidden" in express teachings of philosophers and poets, or
because they were "removed" from one's ordinary way of looking at the
world.[19] Acciaiuoli's description of Argyropoulos's role in the new studies, in September 1463, falls just a few weeks before Tommaso Benci
published his Italian translation of Ficino's Latin rendering, published
the previous April, of the *Pimander* of Hermes Trismegistus. The Hermetic texts were very popular, and in underscoring the importance of
ancient secret lore Acciaiuoli could have simply been reflecting current
fashion.[20] We shall argue, however, that in ascribing to Argyropoulos
the idea that Plato had a "hidden teaching," Acciaiuoli was using expressions that had a particular meaning of their own.

To contemporaries Argyropoulos's wisdom was neither inscrutable
nor esoteric: the common tag applied to it was that it was "systematic."
One of Argyropoulos's students, Alamanno Rinuccini, described in
1489 the Byzantine's early lectures. After traveling through France, Ger-
many, and England (1456), Argyropoulos returned to Florence and

> began to teach philosophy, in no backward or piecemeal way,
> but—a thing which is a great aid to learning—in the order in
> which it was written out by Aristotle. Taking his beginning from
> dialectics, he went thence through his teachings on natural science
> and went forward in his teaching up to metaphysics, explicating
> Aristotle's twelve books on it over a two-year period.[21]

19.   See esp. D. P. Walker, *The Ancient Theology: Studies in Christian Platonism from the
Fifteenth to the Eighteenth Century* (London, 1972), pp. 1–21.

20.   For the Benci translation, see the sources cited below, Chapter VII, n. 7.

21.   Rinuccini, *Lettere ed orazioni*, p. 189.

Indeed an important, and, for the Florentines, unconventional part of
Argyropoulos's teaching was his consideration of Aristotle's philosophy
as a unified whole. Leonardo Bruni and the humanists of the early Quattrocento worried about the Stagirite's eloquence and enjoyed his ethics;
they avoided Aristotle's speculative philosophy or treated it eclecti-
cally.[22] In the universities teachers in the arts and medicine lectured on
standard texts of Aristotelian logic and dialectics, as well as on those
other works of Aristotle that served as a groundwork for the professions. But Argyropoulos saw how the several parts of the Aristotelian
corpus fitted together: to study philosophy, he argued, one had to begin
with logic and dialectics; then one studied, in order, ethics, natural philosophy, mathematics, and finally metaphysics. When Argyropoulos
spoke of education in more general terms, he added grammar and rhetoric to the beginning of the list—but these were two basic and preliminary disciplines, not part of philosophy.

This scheme of sciences was Platonistic, and seems to have originated
in late antiquity with the Greek Neo-Platonic commentators on Aristotle. The theory then was that one proceeded up through hierarchies
from things humanly perceived to the divine essences themselves.[23] In
Byzantine philosophical culture the scheme was commonplace. Even
the scourge of Renaissance Platonism, George of Trebizond, followed
the same ascending order of logic, natural philosophy, mathematics,
and metaphysics.[24]

Each step forward in the *cursus* of sciences required a grasp of the
earlier sciences. In one of his first public lectures in Florence, in early
1457, Argyropoulos pointed out the necessity of preliminary instruction
in logic:

> After the art of grammar and oratory, if we wish to proceed to
> philosophy, we must first look to the art of arguing and reasoning,
> which is customarily called logic. Without logic—and this is as
> clear as noonday—nothing can be perfectly perceived or known in

22. For an especially useful synopsis of Aristotle in the early Renaissance, see E. Garin,
"Le traduzioni umanistiche di Aristotele nel secolo XV," *Atti e memorie dell'Accademia
fiorentina di scienze morali "La Colombaria"* 16, n.s., 2 (1947–50 [1951]), pp. 55–104.

23. B. Tatakis, *La philosophie byzantine*, suppl. 2 to E. Bréhier, *Histoire de la philosophie*
(Paris, 1949), pp. 179, 191, 196–97; J. A. Weisheipl, "Classification of the Sciences in Medieval Thought," *Mediaeval Studies* 27 (1965), 58–62.

24. George of Trebizond, *Comparationes phylosophorum Aristotelis et Platonis* (Venice,
1523; rept. Frankfurt, 1965), book 1, chaps. 3ff. His list of the sciences in his *divisio operis* at
the end of 1,2, however, reads *rationalis* (including the *copia dicendi*), *naturalis*, *metha-
physica*, and *mathematica*, with *moralis* separated out. But in discussing these in the following chapters, he reversed mathematics and metaphysics; the earlier order would seem
to be due, therefore, to a mental lapse or an editorial or scribal error.

the active or speculative life. Afterward we should proceed at once
to moral philosophy.[25]

The transition from moral to natural philosophy Argyropoulos described in an introductory lecture on the *Physics* (1458). After dialectics,
our entrance to philosophy, ethics serves as our preparation for more
advanced study: "For when the soul is well disposed and purged of vice,
and all moral disturbances have been stilled, one may proceed to this
natural philosophy." Then, he argued, one must not proceed "at once"
to divine philosophy (metaphysics), for while through natural philosophy we know that the "essence of the soul" and "certain separated substances" exist, we are not able to perceive these things perfectly without
mathematics.[26] Studies of mathematics, as Plato said, serve as "steps"
that lead to metaphysics.[27]

  This order of sciences indeed provided Argyropoulos with his actual
program of studies. The chronological evidence we have for his lectures,
from the notebooks of Donato Acciaiuoli, from extant *praefationes* and
praelectiones, and from the testimony of his students, demonstrates con-
clusively that Argyropoulos did adhere to his order of sciences. That is,
after private lectures in logic (always labeled "first" in contemporary testimony, though it seems that they must have been given at the same
time as the early lectures on ethics), Argyropoulos taught moral philosophy (the *Nicomachean Ethics*, 1457–58, and soon thereafter, on feast
days, the *Politics*) and then went through natural philosophy (*Physics*,
1458–60; *De anima*, probably 1460–61; and *Meteorologica*, beginning in
1462).[28] After 1462 he may have taken up more natural philosophy.

25. *Praefatio in libris Ethicorum quinque primis* (4 Feb. 1457), in Müllner, ed., *Reden und Briefe*, p. 16 (cf. Ricc. 120, fol. 8v).

26. Naz. II 1 103, fol. 8v (from the *accessus*, explaining the position of natural philosophy within the *ordo scientiarum*).

27. *Praefatio . . . in sexto libro Ethicorum* (i.e., introductory lecture to second series of
lectures on the *Ethics*, 1 Feb. 1458), in Müllner, ed., *Reden und Briefe*, p. 20 (cf. Ricc. 120,
fol. 12v): "[S]unt . . . res mathematicae mediae inter naturales et supernaturales, ne ab
extremo ad extremum sine medio fiat transitio, unde Plato scalas appellare haec solebat,
quibus ab inmersis in materia ad purissimas substantias ac separatas ab omni materia
posset accedi." That autumn, in an introductory lecture to Aristotle's *Physics* (Naz. II 1
103, fol. 2v), Argyropoulos made the same argument but may have given Plotinus as the
source: ". . . post philosophiam naturalem in ordine perdiscende sunt mathematice, quas
Plotinus ille summus philosophus apellavit scalas." This image of the "steps" toward
metaphysics appears in Plato, *Rep.* 6. 511b, and Plotinus, *Enn.* 6.7.36. Two lectures later
Argyropoulos would again speak of the intermediary sciences and mention Plato alone
(Naz. II 1 103, fol. 8v: section quoted in my "John Argyropoulos and the 'Secret Teachings' of Plato," p. 310, n. 28).

28. For dates, see the introductory lectures edited by Müllner, *Reden und Briefe*, pp. 3–
56, from Ricc. 120. Acciaiuoli's draft of the *Ethics* course, Naz. II 1 104, is undated at the

There were no texts of Aristotle for mathematics, and it is unlikely that Argyropoulos used other, standard texts; rather, he probably wove into his regular lectures on Aristotle a careful explanation of the function of mathematics.[29] Argyropoulos concluded the series with two years of lectures on Aristotle's *Metaphysics*.[30]

The system of sciences not only determined Argyropoulos's sequence of courses but also helped shape his method of lecturing. One advanced to the higher science after mastering the lower one. Hence in his lectures on ethics Argyropoulos relied heavily on Aristotle's logic. And so, too, natural philosophy depended on ethics. Here, however, we can not expect the relation to be strikingly evident in the lectures themselves. Eth-

---

beginning, but the date "1456" (s.f.) appears at the top of fol. 29, at the beginning of Book 2, an indication that the second book was probably begun before 25 Mar. 1457. For the course on the *Politics* we have testimony only: a letter of Pierfilippo Pandolfini to Xanthus Viriatus, Magl. VI 166, fols. 111–112v, and Vespasiano, *Vite*, II, 13, 26 (who also mentions other courses). Acciaiuoli's lecture draft of the *Physics* course, Naz. II I 103, is dated at the beginning 3 Nov. 1458 (fol. 1) and at the end 2 Aug. 1460 (fol. 260v). The manuscript is complete for *Physics* 1–3, covered by Argyropoulos in 1458–59 (cf. the *praefatio*'s title edited by Müllner), but does not include most of the rest of the *Physics* (i.e., 4–8), except part of Book 8. Acciaiuoli probably missed the lectures at the beginning of the academic year 1459–60; he may have been at the Congress of Mantua (see Pandolfini's letter, autumn 1459, p. 122, below; A. C. de la Mare, "Vespasiano da Bisticci, Historian and Bookseller" [Ph.D. diss., University of London, 1965], II, 325–26; de la Mare, "New Research on Humanistic Scribes," p. 404). As Argyropoulos was lecturing on the *Physics*, he was preparing a new Latin translation of the work (see Ricc. 122, a manuscript owned by Pierfilippo Pandolfini and partly copied by Donato Acciaiuoli, which contains this translation and has the following colophon, fol. 183v: "Finis octavi libri naturalis auditus Aristotelis qui dum ab Johanne Argiropolo Florentiae legerentur sunt ab eodem in latinum conversi. Anno MCCCC°LX"). Acciaiuoli's notes from the course on the *De anima* (Magl. V 42) are dated, at the beginning, 5 Nov. 1460 (fol. 1). For the *Meteorologica* we have an introductory lecture only, edited by Müllner, pp. 53–56, as "In libro Mechanicorum" (Ricc. 120, fol. 35: "In libro Methaurorum"), dated, at the beginning, 21 Nov. 1462. In an early article Garin pointed out the correct subject of the course ("Le traduzioni umanistiche di Aristotele," pp. 85–86n.). Somewhat more problematic are the courses in logic and dialectics: see my "John Argyropoulos and the 'Secret Teachings' of Plato," p. 311n. Important for our argument is that Argyropoulos did adhere to his system, and the notion that he abandoned or distorted it to create a "civic" Aristotle, or to pander to his civic-humanist friends, cannot be supported by the available evidence. Cf. Garin, "Donato Acciaiuoli cittadino," pp. 202–3, 240–41, 245. See also Garin's "Platonici bizantini e platonici italiani," where he reviews favorably F. Masai's *Pléthon et le Platonisme de Mistra* (Paris, 1956). Masai regards Argyropoulos as the Italian exponent of the pagan movement of Pletho, who wanted to use a form of Platonism as the ideological foundation of political renewal and reform. For Masai's thesis, see the cogent remarks of Monfasani, *George of Trebizond*, p. 160, n. 124, and pp. 202–3.

29. In a letter on education to his son, Alamanno Rinuccini adhered strictly to Argyropoulos's order of studies and recommended for mathematics the *Sphaera* of Johannes de Sacrobosco, the *Planetarum Theorica* of Gerardus de Sabbioneta, and Euclid (*Lettere ed orazioni*, p. 100 and n.).

30. See the quotation from Rinuccini, p. 112, above; cf. Vespasiano, *Vite*, II, 13, 26.

ics shaped not future lectures but future students. Ethics was to produce students cured of vice and rid of moral disturbances, good and hard-working, and eager to master the higher branches of philosophy. But for the Florentines the transition from moral to natural philosophy presented special problems. For those seeking a general, humanistic education, natural philosophy was a new science.[31] Midway through Argyropoulos's lectures on the *De anima* (1460–61), Alamanno Rinuccini would write that, from Book 2 of Aristotle's work, the students could relate only to the fifth chapter, *De gustibus* (on eating and drinking).[32] Much later he would describe the typical Argyropoulos student as Ennius described Neoptolemus, as one, that is, who was willing to learn philosophy only part way.[33] Indeed, from his first lectures in Florence John Argyropoulos himself described all philosophical learning as difficult and learning in speculative philosophy as especially difficult. He underscored the problem by identifying repeatedly the principles of philosophy as *arcana*. After logic and dialectics, he said in 1458, we must move on to the *arcana* of philosophy, beginning with ethics.[34]

This was indeed John Argyropoulos's characteristic definition of *arcana*: secret teachings were those difficult to grasp.[35] These *arcana* embraced not just the speculative wisdom hidden in the writings of the *prisci philosophi* or the *prisci poetae* but the teachings of all philosophy, including the relatively easy subject of Aristotle's *Ethics*.

Argyropoulos described some of the difficulties in an early lecture on Aristotle's *Physics*, in October or November 1458, when he attempted to outline the philosopher's method (the *modus procedendi*, one of the several categories surveyed in a scholastic *accessus*):

> The method of proceeding seems to be now divisive, from which he defines, now demonstrative, partly from causes, partly from effects. He also seems to proceed by way of definition. Thus he uses these three methods. Now and then he also uses the resolutive (for

31. See Rinuccini's letter on education to his son, 1474, where he says that, to get a good education, it is *now* considered necessary to pass beyond rhetoric to philosophy (*Lettere ed orazioni*, p. 97).

32. *Ibid.*, pp. 55–56.

33. Letter to Roberto Salviati, 1489, ibid., pp. 187–90 (ref. at pp. 189–90).

34. Naz. II I 103, fol. 8v. For the quotation, see my "John Argyropoulos and the 'Secret Teachings' of Plato," p. 310, n. 28.

35. In a preface to a translation of some of Aristotle's logic, for instance, Argyropoulos argued that all should avidly move on from studies of rhetoric to the "archana philosophiae sententiasque persubtiles Aristotelis": ed. Seigel, "Teaching of Argyropulos," p. 258.

there are four methods), that he might discover the cause from the effects.[36]

Although these four dialectical methods were common divisions of the Greek commentators, Argyropoulos's description (if Acciaiuoli's draft of the lectures is here faithful) is almost stammering.[37] And well it should be, as we may note as the passage continues:

> Nevertheless in this [that is, his method] as in his other things [relating to this work], he is most difficult [to follow], and not only in the old Latin translations, but also in Greek. For at one moment he seems too laconic, at another too prolix—out of this variety the difficulty arises. . . . And this not without reason, but so that the sciences might lie hidden and with difficulty be mastered, and so that men, stirred by the excellence of the subject matter, would despise the labor necessary so long as they obtained outstanding benefits and hence emerged from the discipline more perfect.

Argyropoulos then turned to the problem of the origins of scientific thinking.

> One should also realize . . . that the sciences had a beginning, not only in our opinion but also in that of the pagans, who nevertheless held that the sciences have continuously sprung up: because at one time things were lost through a flood (one which did not cover the whole world), and at another time things were recovered. Therefore they admit that the sciences were invented in some part of the world, as in Greece after the flood of Deucalion, but that in the world there were always sciences. They say that the Egyptians did not have the flood of Deucalion and thus the Greeks were helped by them.

Argyropoulos went on to explain that early science was necessarily unsystematic.

> Therefore the sciences seemed to be crude in the beginning. For there were many philosophers who taught science obscurely and in verse—nevertheless many things were worthy and outstanding. Afterward came Pythagoras, who seems to have extended philosophy. Later came Plato, who avoided verse and provided most

36. Naz. II I 103, fol. 9v.

37. For the four methods, see N. W. Gilbert, *Renaissance Concepts of Method* (New York, 1960), pp. 24, 104–5.

fully a teaching—although he preserved some old practices by des-
ignating the principles of things in the mathematical way. Then
Aristotle treated the principles of things as natural, and he did not
seem to speak about the parts of the world, but as if the world had
never been, not presuming any existence but only quiddity.
Nevertheless he maintained the obscurity.[38]

Thus in the systematization of natural philosophy even Aristotle retained some of the confusion of the earlier philosophers: the poetic obscurities of a former age, which the Stagirite cleared up in several disciplines, yet have remained in natural science.

Aristotle could be systematic only because he stood at the end of a
great philosophical tradition, one that was unified and that should be
studied in its unity.[39] After the simple preservation and transmission of
many Greek texts, the doctrine of a unified philosophical tradition must
rank as the most strikingly evident Byzantine contribution to Renaissance Platonism. Marsilio Ficino seized on the hypothesis at once.[40] But
Argyropoulos placed Aristotle at the pinnacle of this tradition. As for
the pre-Socratic poetic philosophers, theirs was no "oracular wisdom"
or secret teachings that the good philosopher should want to recover
and pass on; rather, the *prisci philosophi* were crude and unscientific. If
their teachings were "hidden away" it was because they were obscure.
Aristotle's text itself gave Argyropoulos ample opportunity to explore
pre-Peripatetic philosophical traditions: directly or indirectly Aristotle
referred often to earlier traditions, and Argyropoulos was either clever
enough to identify the indirect references or diligent enough to look
them up in available commentaries. Our concern here is his attitude
toward Platonic and pre-Socratic (or pseudo–pre-Socratic) "secrets."

In the lectures, we find that the "unity" of ancient philosophy was not
something that Argyropoulos accepted passively; rather, he critically
and carefully identified three stages of ancient wisdom: the pre-Socratic
or poetic, the Platonic, and the Aristotelian. He analyzed each in terms
of what it contributed to the development of the specific sciences, ethics,
natural philosophy, mathematics, and metaphysics. Argyropoulos in-

38. Naz. II 1 103, fols. 9v–10. For similar themes from the lectures, see Naz. II 1 104,
fol. 29, and Magl. v 42, fol. 231v.

39. *Too* unified, one might say, for in an *accessus* Argyropoulos has Aristotle studying
"sub praeceptore Socrate primo [!] deinde Platone" (*Praefatio in libris Ethicorum quinque
primis*, in Müllner, ed., *Reden und Briefe*, p. 15; cf. Ricc. 120, fol. 8). Noted by E. B.
Fryde, *Humanism and Humanist Historiography* (London, 1983), p. 63.

40. *Opera omnia*, p. 1537. See also A. Keller, "Two Byzantine Scholars and Their Re-
ception in Italy," *Journal of the Warburg and Courtauld Institutes* 20 (1957), 363–66, and
Kristeller, "Byzantine and Western Platonism,"pp. 161–62.

cluded the earliest philosophers, from Zoroaster to Anaxagoras, within the "unified tradition," but he ignored them in his lectures except where Aristotle himself spoke of an earlier tradition. When he took up these pre-Socratics, as in his remarks quoted earlier, Argyropoulos mentioned their "obscurity" and their philosophizing "in verse." An excellent summary of Argyropoulos's opinion of the first centuries of philosophy appears in an early lecture on Aristotle's *De anima* (1460). In this passage, Argyropoulos passed by the earliest philosophers and poets in favor of the three figures who created the classical philosophical tradition—Socrates, Plato, and Aristotle:

> There were three outstanding geniuses. I omit Zoroaster and many others up through Anaxagoras who taught philosophy obscurely and in verse. There were, then, three: Socrates, Plato, and Aristotle. Socrates drove men to the sciences through discourses on moral philosophy: thus he is called a moral philosopher although he was a speculative philosopher of first rank. He saw that the men of his time were devoted to forensic eloquence; he called them away from this and urged them on to the study of wisdom and self-perfection. For man is born imperfect, but he has the power to perfect himself and then also to perfect others. In this way, therefore, Socrates drove on the rest. After him was the divine Plato, most perfect in every discipline, supreme in poetry and the most eloquent of all, a moral, natural, mathematical, and especially a speculative thinker, as we may understand from his writings: he, however, followed Socrates' practice of not putting the sciences in order. After him came Aristotle, who studied under Plato for twenty-one years [*sic*] and gave the supreme order to the sciences.[41]

Argyropoulos never gratuitously wove Platonic teachings into his lectures on Aristotle. To be sure, he did follow standard academic practice in his introductory lectures, or *praelectiones*, and outline a variety of ancient teachings. In a prefatory section on the definition of philosophy he reproduced the Pythagorean definition ("amor sapientiae"), the Platonic ("cognitio eorum quae sunt," or "similitudo qua deo similis homo quoad possit fieri potest," or "excogitatio mortis"), and the Aristotelian ("artium ars scientiarumque scientia").[42] But these highly schematic, formal listings implied no endorsement of any one position—and a

41. Magl. v 42, fol. 2v.

42. *Praefatio in libris Ethicorum quinque primis*, in Müllner, ed., *Reden und Briefe*, p. 5 (cf. Ricc. 120, fol. 2).

scholar's recent attempt to isolate the Platonic definitions as Argyropoulos's favorite has not been backed by supporting evidence.[43]

It cannot be denied, however, that Argyropoulos took up the Platonic
teachings with much care and empathy. Argyropoulos's overall opinion
of Aristotle's critique of Plato followed well-worn paths: (1) Aristotle is
really criticizing not Plato but common opinions attributed to Plato,
opinions taken up by some of Plato's followers; (2) Aristotle's arguments against Plato are artificial, disputatious, and sophistic, designed
solely to impress his audience with the distinctiveness of his own doctrine. (Argyropoulos avoided, however, the heavy-handed moralistic
judgments common to humanist exegesis, that the Stagirite was a *discipulus ingratus.*) Where Aristotle criticizes Plato's theory of Ideas (for
example, in passages in the *Nicomachean Ethics* and the *De anima*), Argyropoulos examined the respective positions at some length.[44] According to Vespasiano da Bisticci, Argyropoulos indeed fancied himself
something of an authority on the Platonic Ideas.[45]

Plato's major contribution, emphasized Argyropoulos, was to be the
first to present a "clear," unfettered teaching of certain philosophical
principles. Taking up some Pythagorean and corpuscular theories, Argyropoulos explained to his students why the teachings appear so curious: philosophy at that time was thoroughly confused (*vehementer in-
digesta*).[46] Early teachings on the soul reflect this confusion, and certain
doctrines, especially where the soul is defined purely by physical characteristics, should be accepted as metaphors.[47]

The earliest philosophers may indeed have been "obscure," but they
were by no means "subtle." Their thinking was necessarily limited, in
that dialectical reasoning had not yet been invented. In his lectures on
the *Nicomachean Ethics*, Argyropoulos took up Aristotle's distinction between two kinds of universal term, one predicable of the agent and the
other of the object (7.3.6/1147a). Aristotle, Argyropoulos stated, always
takes the middle ground with such distinctions. Plato, he continued,

43.   Garin, "La rinascita di Plotino," p. 99.

44.   See my "John Argyropoulos and the 'Secret Teachings' of Plato," pp. 317–20.

45.   Vespasiano, *Vite*, I, 346–47.

46.   Lectures on the *De anima*, Magl. V 42, fol. 43.

47.   Ibid., fols. 44, 55, 199. Argyropoulos began describing such doctrines as metaphori-
cal in his lectures on the *De anima* (1460–61), and this terminology may be due to the
influence of his Florentine contemporaries. One quotation (fol. 55) reads: "Sed hec [*sc.*
opinio de anima] Platonis est vehementer subtilis accipiendo eam non ut verba sonant
sed ut significatur per verba methaphorica." And later (fol. 199): Aristotle spoke "con-
fusedly" about the *phantasia*, following the *prisci philosophi* who called it *imaginatio*. We
shall discuss it "proprie et non methaphorice."

"was the first to have discovered these ways of making distinctions." Later Aristotle made wide use of these methods of distinguishing, so that "all those 'ironies' of the sophists, whom he always hated intensely, could be removed."[48] Later, in lectures on the *De anima*, Argyropoulos repeated the theme with the question of whether there could be color without sight. One must distinguish, he said, between "color itself" and "color" in any particular circumstance. "Before Plato," Argyropoulos explained, "these distinctions were not made, and people spoke in a simple manner." Later Aristotle "in a wonderful fashion amplified on these methods."[49]

The lectures of Argyropoulos as recorded by Donato Acciaiuoli repeat these themes time and again, whenever the Byzantine is compelled by the text of Aristotle to take up Platonic theories. Nothing in the lectures reveals the "Platonic enthusiasm" scholars have suggested they contain.

To be sure, other evidence for Argyropoulos's Platonism has been adduced. Eugenio Garin has argued at length that Argyropoulos had already studied a codex of Plotinus before Marsilio Ficino had acquired the skills to do the same. No one has yet demonstrated how such study, if it indeed did take place, affected any lectures in the classroom.[50] Acciaiuoli's notebooks give no solid evidence that Argyropoulos was promoting Plotinus before his students.[51] Garin also has argued that once in a lecture on the soul, Argyropoulos, opposing Aristotle, insisted on the autonomy of the mind in respect to the sensible phantasm. "Sed dominus Ioannes exponit quod . . . intelligit quando vult, et non indiget presentia phantasmatis": so reads Acciaiuoli's draft of the lectures, cited by Garin. But an examination of the manuscript reveals that Argyropoulos is not opposing Aristotle at all. He is here (at *De anima* 3.430a 14–15) simply explaining the textbook doctrine of the agent intellect, an intellect that, unlike the possible intellect that uses phantasms, uses intelligible species as objects of thought.[52]

There remains one important and well-known piece of evidence for Argyropoulos's Platonism. It appears in a letter of one of his students, where we learn that the Byzantine, at least once, taught Plato privately.

---

48. Naz. II I 104, fol. 110.

49. Magl. V 42, fol. 192v.

50. "La rinascita del Plotino," pp. 91ff.

51. See n. 27, above. This is the only instance I have seen, in some 1,500 pages of Acciaiuoli's notes, of any reference to Plotinus.

52. See my "John Argyropoulos and the 'Secret Teachings' of Plato," pp. 321–22, n. 58, for a lengthy analysis of Argyropoulos's gloss and Garin's interpretation of it.

In the autumn of 1459 Pierfilippo Pandolfini sent Donato Acciaiuoli a description of John Argyropoulos's teaching of Plato. The oft-quoted letter seems to demonstrate Argyropoulos's enthusiasm for Plato and could suggest, as Garin has argued, that only academic constraints kept his public lectures tied to the texts of Aristotle. The relevant section from the letter follows:

> The afternoon of the last day of September, a Sunday, Vespasiano and I went to John and found him reading Plato. Several of our group were with him. He put his book aside and spoke with us for a while. After many words were bandied about we at last brought him to a discourse, one which would have pleased you immensely—on Plato, namely, whom he praised with enthusiasm and of whom he related some things incredible and truly unheard-of. "With many words (he said) I shall show you how great was the prudence and wisdom of Plato, whom all, even if they do not know his teaching, admire greatly." At once he began: "I shall explain to you this man's dialogue entitled *Meno*. You ought to be satisfied with this one, for how great is its doctrine, eloquence, prudence, and wisdom you will surely observe if you wish to hear." Then he explained it, with such systematization, such elegance, such richness, and such variety of expression that as much as we marveled at Plato himself, whose many divine teachings we heard, we marveled no less at the eloquence of John.[53]

What does the letter reveal? We have no transcription of the described "lecture," and any conclusions as to its content must remain speculative. We shall venture a few anyway. First, the lecture was on the *Meno*, and this dialogue was one of the poorest Argyropoulos could have chosen had he wanted to outline for his students something close to Ficino's "Platonic theology."[54] The *Meno* begins with the distinction between the thing-in-itself (that is, virtue in itself) and the particular thing (any virtue); to illustrate this distinction, Plato has Socrates ask whether "white" is "color" or "a color" (74C). Here we do not have to stretch our imaginations far to imagine how Argyropoulos would describe what he saw as a marvelous Platonic invention in the field of logic and

53. Magl. VI 166, fol. 108–108v (cf. Garin, *La cultura filosofica*, p. 119). The letter is undated, one of several from Pierfilippo Pandolfini in a fragmentary section of the ms. (fols. 104–15v) containing letters from August 1459 to August 1460. The last day of September 1459 was a Sunday, and the date therefore seems secure. See also n. 28, above.

54. This conclusion is somewhat impressionistic and could be tested through a complete index of Ficino's works. Those indexes now available (Kristeller, *Il pensiero filosofico*, as well as some recent editions of Ficino) show few direct citations of the *Meno*.

dialectics. The dialogue deals also with the theory of recollection, whether certain ideas are held innately or acquired by our efforts; it includes the famous episode where Socrates educes certain mathematical principles from an uneducated boy. This, too, is a theme ideally suited as a backdrop to Argyropoulos's conception of Aristotelian science. Even if Pierfilippo Pandolfini maintained that what Argyropoulos taught were *inaudita*, we can yet surmise that on that Sunday afternoon Argyropoulos's students heard some rather familiar themes, developed, to be sure, with a "richness" and "elegance" (as the letter reads) unsuited to a class lecture. Indeed, the letter states that the students marveled at Argyropoulos's "eloquence" and "systematization." Did the Byzantine leave his students thirsty for more Platonic wisdom, doctrines of the soul and of love, the secret teachings and wonderful metaphors contained in the *Phaedo, Philebus*, or the *Symposium*? Possibly, but only because they were not getting such doctrines from their Florentine maestro. As Argyropoulos said before he began talking about the *Meno*: "You ought to be satisfied with this one." Indeed, within a year Pierfilippo Pandolfini would once again refer to Argyropoulos's teaching: I have heard so many divine things, he wrote, that "now for the first time I have begun to admire Aristotle as the prince of the philosophers."[55]

Argyropoulos's accomplishments in Florence were many. He showed how Aristotelian philosophy was a unified whole, whereas Florentines had before been accustomed to study the Peripatetic discipline (as Rinuccini later implied) "in a backward or piecemeal way."[56] He introduced the Florentines to the "hidden teaching" of ancient poets and philosophers: Plato had been the first to outline expressly many of the doctrines and methods that became part of the Aristotelian system, and the early poetic philosophers with their obscure figments had given the system its first form. He was fascinated by this Aristotelian system and knew that it had a history, that the sciences had a "beginning." Hence he praised the pre-Socratics, Socrates, and Plato. And his students could, and many did, move freely between his lectures and those of Marsilio Ficino. Yet Argyropoulos could never praise Plato at Aristotle's expense, and his only serious endeavor in Florence was an explanation of the Aristotelian system. So devoted was he to the "true Aristotle" that in his first lectures in Florence, on the *Nicomachean Ethics*, he inserted a running critique of Leonardo Bruni's translation of the text—Filelfo

---

55. Letter to Xanthus Viriatus, Magl. VI 166, fol. 112: "In quorum [*sc.* librorum philosophiae naturalis] declaratione tot et tanta audiuntur divina ut nunc primo Aristotelem philosophorum principem admirari incipiam." For Xanthus Viriatus, see E. Raimondi, *Codro e l'Umanesimo a Bologna* (Bologna, 1950), pp. 32n., 33.

56. See p. 112, above.

warned him at once that he was treading on hallowed and sensitive ground.[57] Even more boldly (according to later testimony of Politian) Argyropoulos claimed that Cicero did not know his Aristotle.[58] These "indiscretions" underscore his diligence. By the sixteenth century, classical scholars would credit Argyropoulos, not Leonardo Bruni, with having broken with the medieval tradition of translating Aristotle.[59] In his own time, with his skillful, careful explanation of Aristotle, based on the original sources, he remained at the forefront of Florentine intellectual life.

As noted earlier, in the mid-1460s Marsilio Ficino claimed that, through Cosimo's efforts, he had translated the works of Plato while Argyropoulos had made available Aristotle. Our conclusion here is that Ficino has described rather well Argyropoulos's influence: the Byzantine recreated for the Florentines the system that Aristotle had built. While Ficino had from the beginning an independent, theoretical, dialectical relationship with the Platonic corpus, so that he was continuously adding to what he had accomplished previously, Argyropoulos described his project from the beginning—a reconstruction of the Aristotelian system—and he set about to fill in the details. Perhaps it was fitting that in 1471, lured by Sixtus IV, he left Florence for Rome: by now he had surely completed both the lecture series and the translations of Aristotle.

The nature of Argyropoulos's teaching, as outlined above, may explain the curious silence between him and Marsilio Ficino. Ficino's sole reference to Argyropoulos was cited earlier; Argyropoulos seems never to have mentioned Ficino. (There is complete silence between Ficino and Argyropoulos's most loyal student, Alamanno Rinuccini. Between Ficino and Argyropoulos's most enthusiastic student, Donato Acciaiuoli, nothing is heard until the 1470s, when Ficino urged Donato to play the patron to an impoverished son of Carlo Marsuppini.[60]) However

57.   If Acciaiuoli's notebook is at all faithful, from his first lectures on the *Nicomachean Ethics* Argyropoulos often quoted the Greek and then gave his students a translation "correcting" that of Leonardo Bruni (Naz. II 1 104). Filelfo's warning—this is the only negative thing I am hearing about you from Florence—appears in a letter of November 1457 (ed. E. Legrand, *Cent-dix lettres*, p. 93).

58.   E. Garin, "'Ενδελέχεια e ἐντελέχεια nelle discussioni umanistiche," *Atene e Roma*, 3d ser., 5 (1937), 177–87; J. Kraye, "Cicero, Stoicism, and Textual Criticism: Politian on κατόρθωμα," *Rinascimento*, 2d ser., 23 (1983), 83–87. Politian's testimony may be true, although Argyropoulos's critique of Cicero does not appear where one might expect it, in Acciaiuoli's redaction, that is, of the lectures on the *De anima* (Magl. V 42).

59.   C. B. Schmitt, *Aristotle and the Renaissance* (Cambridge, Mass., and London, 1983), pp. 69–72.

60.   Ficino, *Opera omnia*, p. 655. In describing this silence I have followed Kristeller,

highly Argyropoulos may have regarded Ficino's translations or his other attempts to *reproduce* Greek antiquity, it seems likely that, with his particular view of the progress of the disciplines, he could only have considered the Ficinian "Platonic theology" as philosophically retrogressive. Aristotelian science had developed through three steps, from the *prisci philosophi* to Plato to Aristotle, and Ficino was demonstrating far too much enthusiasm for the first two—for the early, secret wisdom, the poetic obscurities, and the Platonic metaphors—for his philosophy to be palatable to an Argyropoulos. Ficino was throwing the sciences, as they had naturally developed, into confusion.[61] From the other side, Ficino, as it seems according to the style of his philosophical discourse, would likely have considered Argyropoulos a skilled expounder of Aristotle, a learned translator, but limited in scope and imagination. We would have to agree with Ficino, if indeed that was his opinion, save for the tag "limited," which ill suits the leading Peripatetic of early Renaissance Florence.

John Argyropoulos offered his students the high road to philosophical learning, a systematic study of all branches of Aristotelian philosophy. A positive acquisition of learning ideally suited the young merchant-aristocrat of the Acciaiuoli stamp: here was an increasing body of knowledge decorating the ever more cultivated individual. But what-

---

"L'état présent des études," p. 68, who raises this as a question yet to be answered. Other possibilities exist. First, as we have seen, there was much nastiness in the controversy between Argyropoulos's students, led by Donato Acciaiuoli and Alamanno Rinuccini, and the supporters of Cristoforo Landino, who presumably included Poggio Bracciolini and Marsilio Ficino, over the status of the humanist chairs at the University of Florence. While I argue that John Argyropoulos was not at the center of the controversy, it is possible that he had a greater role than I described, and it is true that several of his future students engaged in polemics with the supporters of Landino. Cardini has argued that in 1458 Argyropoulos and Landino exchanged barbs in their inaugural orations at the university (*La critica*, pp. 71ff.); see also pp. 241–43, below. Second, Argyropoulos evidently viewed Latin philosophers generally as second-rate thinkers (see p. 124, as well as n. 61, below). Latins took the Greeks as vain and too willing to conceal their intellectual borrowings. The latter opinion is particularly evident in Poggio Bracciolini and Cristoforo Landino, but it also appears, in its own way, in Ficino's endorsement of the pre-Greek *prisca theologia*. Third, as I mentioned earlier, Argyropoulos attacked Bruni's translation of Aristotle. This of course was an attack on a Florentine chancellor, could only have infuriated Ficino's friend Poggio Bracciolini, and may also have provoked a "patriotic" reaction from Ficino himself. Fourth, Argyropoulos appears at times to have been sympathetic to Averroist doctrines, which Ficino condemned strongly (see my "John Argyropoulos and the 'Secret Teachings' of Plato, pp. 319–20). Fifth, Ficino and many of his circle were not, particularly in the earlier period, the social equals of the better-born disciples of John Argyropoulos. See also Chapter III, n. 14, above.

61.   Whom did Argyropoulos consider to be the best interpreter of Plato? According to Vespasiano da Bisticci, Argyropoulos thought that "among the Latins" (!) none could approach Narcissus Verdunus! (*Vite*, I, 346–47).

ever Argyropoulos's accomplishments as an individual, we strain to find
his mark on the cultural and intellectual life of the early Platonic Academy. His sympathetic treatment of Plato no doubt smoothed for many
the transition to Ficino's Academy. But Argyropoulos created no
school: he certainly did not sponsor the civic humanism incorrectly associated with him, nor did he sponsor a Neoplatonism or a revival of an
ancient theology. Alamanno Rinuccini complained in 1461 that the students of Argyropoulos were growing restless in the classroom; decades
later he said the typical student of Argyropoulos lacked the skill or en-
ergy to see the Byzantine's program of studies through to completion.[62]
Much of his impact was owed to the diligence of Donato Acciaiuoli,
who published in 1463 or 1464 a redaction of Argyropoulos's lectures on
the *Nicomachean Ethics*. This commentary, which circulated widely, has
long been considered nothing more than an "eloquent" version of Argyropoulos's own lectures. I shall argue, however, that Acciaiuoli departed from Argyopoulos in a Platonic direction. And his departures
from Argyopoulos, it seems, were owed to influences from Marsilio
Ficino's Platonic Academy. But before examining how Argyopoulos's
ideas would change and survive, we should take up the Florentine Academy.

62.   *Lettere ed orazioni*, pp. 55–56, 189–90.

PART THREE

THE
FLORENTINE
ACADEMY

VI

SCHOLASTIC
BACKGROUNDS

IN Marsilio Ficino's earliest datable work, a letter of 13 September 1454 to his close friend Antonio Serafico, he contrasted their usual elegant and humanistic style of writing with a new form:

> Frequently when I contemplate what I may call the "necessity" of our friendship, my Antonio, that kind of writing we first employed is wont to seem entirely strange and different. For the letters that pass between us are crammed with those prefatory statements, circumlocutions, and overly obliging phrases. I confess that it is I in particular who have hitherto busied myself with this sort of writing and have devoted much time and labor to words, especially in the case of relationships as close as ours. But we, I think, have no need for that persuasion through words, nor for those excessive praises and that belabored manner of elegant speaking that we would use if we were complete strangers seeking to generate some new favor. Therefore let us abandon that old style that those babbling lightweights use—I think you know the ones I am talking about—so that we may speak in the manner of philosophers (*more philosophorum*), despising everywhere words and bringing forward weighty utterances.[1]

---

1. Ed. Kristeller and A. Perosa, in Kristeller, *Studies*, p. 146: "Alienum penitus ac diversum Antoni mihi sepenumero amicitie nostre necessitudinem ut ita dixerim contemplanti vetus a nobis initum scribendi genus videri solet. Nam exordiis(?), circuitionibus prolixisque nimium verbis inter nos referte littere circumferuntur, quo in genere me potissimum hactenus fateor esse versatum ac plurimum temporis presertim in tanta hominum quanta nostra est coniunctione verbis operam tradidisse. Non enim nobis ut mihi

Ficino then made an extended and thoroughly scholastic discussion of a problem of natural philosophy.

Early in the next decade, lecturing on Virgil's *Aeneid*, Ficino's close friend Cristoforo Landino came to the section in Book 5 where Virgil described a footrace between Nisus, Salius, Euryalus, and others. Near the end of the race Nisus loses his footing and falls in mud; victory now impossible, he rises up and bowls over Salius so that his friend Euryalus can win. Before the judges Salius cries foul. But the tearful entreaties of Euryalus prevail, helped by his "virtue more attractive because of his beauty" (*gratior et pulchro veniens in corpore virtus*) [5.344].[2] The scribe of the lectures, Giovanni di Bartolomeo Guidi, recorded the following as Landino's gloss:

> In the book entitled *City of God* Augustine censures Virgil for this passage and says that virtue does not increase on account of beauty. Augustine is speaking the truth, and Virgil did not depart from it. For this truth, which depends on a philosophical account (*est ex ratione philosophica*), Virgil chose not to speak; rather, he described what then happened to Euryalus, whose virtue grew, was reckoned greater, and was held in more esteem because of beauty.[3]

From Marsilio Ficino's letter to Antonio Serafico, we may conclude that we are at the advent of a new form, a self-styled attempt by a humanist to abandon a rhetorical for a philosophical form of discourse. The quotation from Landino's lectures could indicate the degree to which the two forms of speaking were consciously distinguished in the

---

quidem videtur verborum persuasione ulla est opus, neque preter modum laudibus lepidique labore sermonis, quo inter nos tanquam inter ignotos et extraneos aliqua nova gratia constituatur. Quamobrem iam veteri stilo dimisso quo levissimi omnium garrule— nosse te opinor de quibus dicam—uti consueverunt, deinceps philosophorum more loquamur verba ubique contempnentes et gravissimas(?) in medium sententias adducentes."

2.   Landino later quoted the "controversial" passage in describing Donato Acciaiuoli: see below, p. 202.

3.   Lectures of 1462–63, Casanatense 1368, fol. 187–187v (after quoting favorable opinions on the power of beauty from Aristotle and Statius): "Augustinus vero in libro qui inscribitur De civitate dei reprehendit in hoc loco Virgilium et dicit quod virtus ex pulchritudine non crescit. Sed tamen Augustinus verum dicit. Et Virgilius non erravit. Noluit enim hoc dicere quod est ex ratione philosophica, sed id quod tunc Eurialo eveniebat, cuius virtus crescebat et maior existimabatur et maiori favore afficiebatur propter pulchritudinem." For the identification of the scribe, see Chapter IX, n. 25, below. Cf. the other manuscript, probably based on these same lectures (see ibid.), Laur. 52, 32, fol. 125v (again after quoting Aristotle and Statius): "Contra autem Augustinus in libro De civitate dei virtutem non crescere ex forma corporis. Sed uterque recte. Nam Virg(ilius) id quod apparet nunc sequitur et non ipsam phylosophiam."

early Platonic Academy. Of course many Florentine humanists before Ficino not only knew how to engage in a philosophical or scholastic discourse but often had to. The great Trecento and early Quattrocento Florentine humanists were law-school dropouts (Petrarch, Salutati, Bruni, Alberti, and Poggio, to name only a handful). In their schools they had studied and practiced the scholastic *quaestio disputata*, an exercise where situations of legal ambiguity were posed and then analyzed for their proximity to cases where legal formulas had already been drawn up, which were then applied toward a solution.[4] The method served the humanists well when they composed their dialogues and treatises: humanists could pose questions as disputations and examine opposing opinions side by side, underscore the moral ambiguity of a problem, or even keep their moral distance from or feign jocularity over a controversial but favored view.

In more speculative philosophical circles physicians and theologians took up the *quaestio* in its four traditional categories: *an sit* (does it exist?), *quid sit* (what is it?), *quia sit* (does it have a given characteristic?), and *propter quid* (why?).[5] These were the categories, mastered by the schoolmen, which Ficino used in his earliest philosophical writings in natural and speculative philosophy, such as the tract to Antonio Serafico, writings that reflect his early training in philosophy and medicine at the University of Florence.[6]

A close association with scholastic philosophers, particularly theologians, was by no means new to Florentine humanists. Many humanists, especially in the earlier period, learned their Latin and sometimes their Greek from monks. Once educated, these humanists often found monasteries to be ideal meeting centers, and here they could only have become acquainted with speculative philosophy, albeit in the form of scholastic theology. The Augustinian monk Luigi Marsili of the convent of Santo Spirito was nominally the head of the humanist circle of Salutati and others of the late Trecento, out of which the entire Quattrocento Florentine humanist tradition sprang. Then in the early fifteenth century, at the convent of Santa Maria degli Angeli, the Camaldulensian monk Ambrogio Traversari (1386–1439) met regularly with other humanists and theologians. The group included the humanists Niccolò Niccoli, Giannozzo Manetti, Matteo Palmieri, and Carlo Marsuppini;

4. There is much literature on this. I am following H. Kantorowicz, "The quaestiones disputatae of the glossators" (1939), in his *Rechtshistorische Schriften* (Karlsruhe, 1970), pp. 137–85.

5. J. A. Weisheipl, "Scholastic Method," *New Catholic Encyclopedia*, vol. 12 (1967), 1146.

6. For these early writings, see Kristeller, "The Scholastic Background of Marsilio Ficino," in his *Studies*, pp. 35ff.

the poet and canon of the church of San Lorenzo, Leonardo Dati; and, occasionally, the man of affairs Cosimo de' Medici.[7] Arnaldo Della Torre has theorized that the diverse political allegiances of the group made political discussions unattractive.[8] Traversari's own interests, translating the Greek Church Fathers, would suggest that religious subjects dominated.

Others joined remnants of the Traversari circle in the 1440s to form what Della Torre has labeled the *contubernium* of Niccolò della Luna.[9] Besides the obscure figure della Luna, to whom the others seemed to defer as head, the group included Manetti, Palmieri, Leonardo Dati, and several members of what we have called the Acciaiuoli circle: Donato himself, Alamanno Rinuccini, Andrea Alamanni, and Antonio Rossi. Nearly every discussion we know of from this group has a religious theme: God's indulgence to the sinner at the hour of death, Adam's fasting before and after the Fall, whether the righteous sin seven times daily or not at all, why God created some rich and some poor.[10]

In a famous letter written late in the Quattrocento Alamanno Rinuccini stated that before his generation—that is, before the 1450s—no Florentine, except those dedicated to religion and medicine, had studied in depth natural and speculative philosophy. The one exception he offered was Giannozzo Manetti.[11] Indeed, as I noted in an earlier chapter, Manetti was exceptional: he could hold his own in a scholastic debate. In 1450, for instance, when questioned by Donato Acciaiuoli about the damnation of unbaptized infants, Manetti responded at length, producing an impressive array of scholastic arguments.

Manetti could keep a foot firmly planted in the scholastic camp and use scholastic arguments for questions that called for a scholastic answer. But there is no evidence that the scholastic method, aside from that developed in the law schools, had any appreciable influence on the early humanist movement in Florence or that it was applied to any questions not purely theological. One might want to object at once that the damnation of the "unbaptized innocent" might touch on the humanist theme of the dignity of man. But Manetti's scholastic answer was the "non-humanist" one: those babies were indeed damned, even if they

---

7.   Della Torre, *Storia*, pp. 226ff.

8.   Ibid., pp. 227–28.

9.   For the *contubernium* (the term appears in one of della Luna's letters), see ibid., pp. 286ff.

10.   Ibid., pp. 312–15. Less religious was a question of natural or perhaps moral philosophy, the "phlegmatic" temperament (p. 314).

11.   *Lettere ed orazioni*, pp. 188–89.

had done nothing "on their own" to deserve it. Donato Acciaiuoli, with his more humanistic, commonsense, and eclectic approach, wanted to permit somehow their salvation.[12]

Even well after the Platonic Academy was founded, humanists continued to fall back on scholastic methods and scholastic arguments when the subject matter seemed to call for it. Ficino's *Theologia Platonica* is thoroughly scholastic. At other times, however, as in many of his letters, his philosophizing was much less formal. Donato Acciaiuoli, in a sermon on the Eucharist before the Compagnia de' Magi in 1468, also pointed toward a new approach: "Let us leave behind the many subtle investigations that are made by sacred doctors . . . ."[13] But Cristoforo Landino, in his sermon on the Eucharist before the same confraternity, was much more conservative, and he launched at once into a scholastic *distinctio partium*. The most faithful doctors of holy letters, he stated, divide this sacrament "into two principal parts":

> First one looks at the essence of the most sacred body of Christ, and in the second place at its composition. The first part is divided into three: one looks first at its essence in itself; in the second place through its confrontation with him who receives it; and in the third place one shows the true body of Christ to be contained in the species, not the accidents, of the bread. And again one divides the first part in three, since first one looks at the dignity of the sacrament . . . [etc.].[14]

Whether one "departed" from scholasticism, for these humanists their own methods and those of the scholastics tended to remain distinct.

Florentine scholastic traditions, by contrast, were affected by the humanist movement. In universities and monastic centers doctors and theologians had numerous contacts with humanists—some could boast of an education under a humanist teacher, a claim most humanists themselves could not make. The theologian who probably taught Ficino his Greek, Francesco da Castiglione, was a student of Vittorino da Feltre, and Francesco proudly publicized the relationship by writing a biography of his illustrious humanist teacher.[15] Another of Ficino's scholastic mentors, Lorenzo Pisano, a canon of San Lorenzo, gave his humanist

---

12. See the sources cited above, Chapter III, n. 89.

13. See below, p. 225.

14. Ed. in Lentzen, *Studien*, pp. 246–54 (passage quoted on p. 247).

15. I have examined Ambros. F 4 sup., where, as evidently in other manuscripts, this biography and other biographical notes are subsumed under a life of Saint Antoninus. For Castiglione, see Chapter IV, n. 36, above.

friends and associates major roles in his dialogues.[16] Ficino's teacher of
Aristotle, Niccolò Tignosi, boasted far and wide of his humanist contacts, apparently numbering among his humanist friends and supporters
figures with whom he was only casually acquainted.[17] These scholastics
cultivated their humanist ties in other ways. Many of course shared patrons with the humanists. They also used humanist translations of Aristotle and other Greek philosophers and of Greek poets in their dialogues and lectures.[18] Most importantly, they distinguished their own
scholastic method from that of the "sophists," which held "inextricable
knots": in other words, their scholasticism was not jargon-ridden. By
stopping short of the heavy formalism of many scholastics they reached
a degree of eloquence that made a dialogue with the humanists possible.

I shall make here only a few remarks on the problem of "humanist
religiosity." As has been often repeated, in the Middle Ages a comfortable division of labor existed between the clerics, who looked after spir-
itualities, and merchants, artisans, knights, and serfs, who took care of
secular matters. The religious exchanged rewards of their extra merits
for what those who worked were able to produce or for the protection
offered by knights and their dependents. This sort of symbiosis continued through the Renaissance as merchants gave gifts "for the love of
God" and hired monks, in their testaments, to sing masses for them.
But in lay confraternities the division became blurred as the lay brethren
performed pious acts on their own. These included not only almsgiving
but fasts, vigils, lay sermons, and flagellation.[19] Intellectually, laymen
also created for themselves a moral sphere less dependent on monastic
norms. Bolder thinkers viewed activity in the world as equally pleasing
to God and began to consider the merchants' good works as valid in
their own right. Some humanists helped create a "counter-hegemony"
to those monastic ideals which aimed toward molding character around

16. For these dialogues, see my discussion below.

17. See below, n. 92.

18. See the general remarks of Kristeller, *Renaissance Thought and Its Sources*, p. 101.
Tignosi's use of humanist translations will be discussed shortly. I have not attempted to
trace Lorenzo Pisano's sources: he tended to leave quotations in the Greek, but he or a
scribe often provided a Latin version in the margins. In quotations from Dionysius the
Areopagite, the Latin version is that of Ambrogio Traversari (e.g., *Dialogi humilitatis*,
Vat. lat. 961, fol. 5v; cf. *Dionysiaca: Recueil donnant l'ensemble des traductions latines* . . .
[Bruges, 1937], I, 101–2).

19. There is much literature on the subject. The devotional, as opposed to the social or
functional, aspects of confraternities are emphasized by John Henderson, "Piety and
Charity in Late Medieval Florence," chaps. 2–3. For the confraternities and the Platonic
Academy, see Kristeller, "Lay Religious Traditions and Florentine Platonism," in his
Studies, pp. 99–122.

the imitation of saints' lives. Those active in the world created the "surplus" that allowed "good works" to flourish; mendicants "lived off the labor of others," consumed that surplus, and benefited neither themselves nor others. Even usury theory was affected by new critical analyses and legal formulas.[20]

At the dawn of the philosophical renaissance, humanists moved freely in lay-confraternal settings, with scholasticizing priests as spiritual mentors, to whom, for the most part, were left the weightier questions of theology. Humanists opposed some scholastics only in particular economic questions, such as usury, or where there was moral tension, as in defining the nature of the good life, worthwhile activity in the world, or the merits of the active and contemplative life. In education there was some rivalry. In their pursuit of eloquence the humanists distinguished sharply their own method from that of the scholastics.[21] Outside Florence traditions differed: humanists such as Lorenzo Valla developed antischolastic methods of treating scholastic questions; hence, as has often been noted, in this sphere Valla was more "creative" than his Florentine counterparts.

Even if the Florentine humanists did not consider themselves authorities on everything in the heavens and on earth, their intellectual net covered the lowest sphere rather well, and the net was being extended outward. The humanist monk Ambrogio Traversari was turning the Greek Church Fathers into Latin, letting them speak eloquently and directly to humanists and to those merchants who had a classical education.[22] More and more religious texts were making their way into merchants' libraries.[23] This wide use of religious authorities, which historians sometimes view as evidence of Quattrocento medievalism or conservatism, or as a "return to religion" away from civic ideals, can also been seen as laymen's usurpation of spheres of activity normally reserved to others.

The humanists I shall focus on in the early development of the Platonic Academy—Ficino, Acciaiuoli, and Landino—felt quite at home in the lay confraternal or other religious setting. From each, in fact, there is at least one extant sermon delivered either before a religious company

20. See, e.g., the sources cited above, Chapter II, n. 61.

21. See H. H. Gray, "Renaissance Humanism: The Pursuit of Eloquence," in P. O. Kristeller and P. P. Wiener, eds., *Renaissance Essays* (New York, 1968), pp. 199–216.

22. Cf. Stinger, *Humanism and the Church Fathers*. Like many other historians, Stinger sees the Greek Fathers capturing the humanists rather than vice-versa.

23. See, e.g., Bec, *Les livres des Florentins*.

or before a lay audience.[24] The ideas promoted in the confraternal meetings of clerics and other scholastics, merchants, and humanists in the mid-Quattrocento are difficult to determine: safer conclusions can be and have been drawn for the period from the 1470s, where we have some of the sermons and a great number of the religious plays.[25] Generalizations about the earlier period are based on companies' charters and some descriptions of their rituals. Perhaps the earliest datable humanistic speech before a confraternity (not named) is from 1457, by Alamanno Rinuccini. He emphasized the love, harmony, and union of the group's members.[26] While these may seem to be "Christian commonplaces," they may yet be noteworthy. After all, Rinuccini did not emphasize those "role-playing" themes endorsed by the companies' charters and idealized in the companies' plays, the performance, that is, of good works and the imitation of saints' lives. "Love and harmony" for Rinuccini were goals—he did not attempt to give the themes an intellectual content. But he was writing in 1457. Indeed, these were themes appreciated and explored by the emerging Platonic Academy.

Marsilio Ficino's own religious mentor was once considered to be Saint Antoninus (d. 1459), the archbishop of Florence. But Ficino's early works show no influence of the archbishop's heavy-handed moralizing. Kristeller has argued that the hypothesis, based on testimony of Fra Zenobi Acciaiuoli in the early sixteenth century, that Antoninus's warnings against paganism drew Ficino temporarily away from Platonic studies in the late 1450s, is very likely inaccurate.[27] Kristeller has offered more probable mentors: Francesco da Castiglione, Antonio degli Agli, Lorenzo Pisano, and Niccolò Tignosi.[28] Francesco da Castiglione, who probably taught Ficino Greek from 1456, left few early works.[29] Antonio degli Agli left a short, philosophical dialogue dedicated to Ficino in the

24. For Ficino's sermons, see Kristeller, *Studies*, pp. 110ff. Acciaiuoli delivered a sermon before the Compagnia de' Magi, 1468 (see below, pp. 225–26); Landino's, before the same confraternity, is undated (ed. in Lentzen, *Studien*, pp. 246–54).

25. For the ideological function of the confraternities, see Weissman, *Ritual Brotherhood in Renaissance Florence*, esp. pp. 1–105.

26. *Lettere ed orazioni*, pp. 22–23. Perhaps the speech was before the Compagnia de' Magi: see Giustiniani, *Alamanno Rinuccini*, pp. 107–14.

27. Kristeller, *Studies*, pp. 200–201. See also pp. 180–81, below.

28. See his "Florentine Platonism and Its Relations with Humanism and Scholasticism," *Church History* 8 (1939), 201–11, and his "L'état présent des études," p. 70.

29. See Chapter IV, n. 36, above, and Chapter VII, n. 34, below. While I have examined the printed catalogs of the Biblioteca Laurenziana and the Biblioteca Nazionale Centrale in Florence, as well as Kristeller's *Iter*, I have made no systematic attempt to look for Castiglione's early works. I have seen no notice that his commentary on the *Psalms*, praised by Ficino, is extant.

mid- to late 1450s: we shall look at it briefly at the end of this chapter.[30] Much more can be learned from Lorenzo Pisano, a priest and canon of the Church of San Lorenzo in Florence. In several of his dialogues older priests and scholastics and younger scholars and humanists discuss themes of the good and religious life. In a letter to Cosimo de' Medici, Ficino said that in Lorenzo's commentary on Solomon's *Song of Songs* "hardly anything of importance to theology is excluded."[31]

In the letter, Ficino mentioned that Niccolò Tignosi of Foligno, the physician and Aristotelian philosopher, also praised the work. As Cardinal Mercati once suggested, Tignosi is probably the "Nicolaus medicus" who appears in Lorenzo Pisano's *Dialogi quinque* of the late 1450s or early 1460s.[32] In the dialogues "Nicolaus" opposed the "simplicity" of pure Christian and philosophical wisdom to the "snares" of classical eloquence. The latter, he argued, captivate the impressionable youth.[33] Between the Aristotelian "rusticity" of Niccolò Tignosi, the Platonizing Augustinianism of Lorenzo Pisano, and the humanist pursuits of the better-born youth stood Marsilio Ficino. Perhaps he is literally in this same dialogue as the unnamed adolescent described as dedicated "not only to music but also to the *recondita studia*."[34]

Ficino shared a religious or "confraternal" background with many others who helped shape the philosophical renaissance; his medical background was more exclusively his own, and his fellow students under Niccolò Tignosi, the forenamed Antonio Serafico, as well as, perhaps, Michele Mercati, are known for little other than receiving some of Ficino's earlier works. But Tignosi's ideas entered humanist thinking through another route. For the widely read Poggio Bracciolini took over and adapted many of Tignosi's ideas into his legal humanism. Before returning to Lorenzo Pisano and his "religious philosophizing," then, let us look briefly at Ficino's scholastic background in the field of medicine.

30.   *De mystica statera*, Naples, Biblioteca Nazionale, cod. VIII F 9, fols. 19–33. For Agli see Kristeller, *Supplementum Ficinianum*, II, 335; A. D'Addario, in *DBI*, vol. I, 400–401; N. H. Minnich, "The Autobiography of Antonio degli Agli (ca. 1400–77), Humanist and Prelate," in *Renaissance Studies in Honor of Craig Hugh Smyth*, ed. A. Morrogh et al. (Florence, 1985), I, 177–191; and R. Fubini, "Ficino e i Medici," pp. 3–52 *passim*.

31.   *Letters*, I, 48; *Opera omnia*, p. 615. Quoted in part, p. 12, above.

32.   G. Mercati, *Codici latini Pico Grimani Pio . . . esistenti nell'Ottoboniana*, Studi e testi 75 (Vatican City, 1938), pp. 284–85.

33.   Laur. S. Marco 457, fol. 5v: "Omni enim sapientia fatuitas et rusticitas ista scripturarum sapientior est. . . . Verum enim vero quanquam minime ignorem adolescentiores qui adsunt scripta quae carent venustate, luce et munditia multa verborum pompa quoque arte locata voculis infractis non suscipere . . . ." For this work, see n. 130, below.

34.   See n. 124, below.

Niccolò Tignosi's Critique of the Active Life

As a gloss on Aristotle's notion that each art has its own good (*Eth. Nic.* 1.7.1/1097a), Niccolò Tignosi da Foligno (1402–74) pointed out that when Filippo Brunelleschi was constructing the dome of the Florentine cathedral, the art that chiseled out and that which dug up and shaped the stones had different ends but that each existed for the sake of the ultimate end, the creation of the cupola.[35] The point is obvious enough, and Tignosi wanted only to give his Florentine audience an identifiable and vivid illustration of Aristotle's own argument. At the same time, Tignosi's illustration of Brunelleschi is but one part of a detailed scheme of how means relate to ends and how different ends relate to one another in the several disciplines. The arguments of Ficino's teacher of philosophy are highly theoretical and are based on careful constructions of intellectual and volitional hierarchies.

In considering these arguments let us look first at Tignosi's own career as a doctor of medicine and his conception of the dignity of his own science. What little is known of Tignosi's life points to his attachment to the Italian university; if any detail is striking it is the degree to which he cultivated and exploited his humanist ties.[36] Born of a noble family

35.   Florence, Biblioteca Nazionale Centrale, cod. Gino Capponi 314, fol. 18v; Laur. 76, 49, fol. 14 (for these manuscripts, see n. 44, below): Philosophus "[p]onit exempla . . . de edificio, de quo mirabiliter apparere potest nostris temporibus in testitudine Beatae Reparatae apud Florentiam. Nam ars quae caelio utitur et quae marmora secat et saxa cavans et in filum dirigens diversos fines habent, quamvis in unum ultimum denique coeant quae omnes sunt inferiores et gratia illius ultimi a quo compraehenditur aliarum unaqueque. Hae inter se differunt et in uno contentae rursus ab alia differunt. Huius admirabilis edificii Phylippus Brunelliscus Florentinus extitit archytectus et quasi Dedalus alter habitus est, quod tam ingens edificium struxerit nulla subeunte armatura quae ad substentandos arcus dum fiunt supponi solet." Cf. G. B. Canfield, "The Florentine Humanists' Concept of Architecture in the 1430s and Filippo Brunelleschi," in *Scritti di storia dell'arte in onore di Federico Zeri* (Venice, 1984), I, pp. 112, 118, n. 14 (she cites an earlier draft of this chapter, which I had sent her). Ficino much later, in his letter *Quinque quaestiones de mente*, used a similar analogy of the architect and his assistants (*Opera omnia*, pp. 675–82 at p. 676): "Nisi . . . absoluta totius aedificii forma praescripta sit architecto, nunquam diversi ministri eo ordine qui ad totum ipsum conducat ad diversa opera movebuntur."

36.   Unfortunately nearly all of the work on Tignosi has focused on his last few years (ca. 1473–74) when, at the Pisan branch of the University of Florence, he entered into the Plato-Aristotle controversy. The absence of any reference to a few important biographical details (see nn. 37, 50, below) would seem to indicate that his most important work before 1470, his commentary on the *Nicomachean Ethics*, has not even been completely read by modern scholars. Except where otherwise noted, the following sketch of Tignosi is based on M. Sensi, "N. T. da Foligno: L'opera e il pensiero," *Annali della Facoltà di Lettere e Filosofia*, Università degli Studi di Perugia 9 (1971–72 [1973]), 359–495. For Tignosi's earlier connections with Arezzo, see now Black, *Benedetto Accolti*, pp. 14–15, who promises to publish a documentary study in the future. Works still useful include Della Torre, *Storia*, pp. 487, 495–500; L. Thorndike, *Science and Thought in the Fifteenth*

of Foligno in 1402, he won his doctorate in the arts at Bologna or Siena in the 1420s. In the later 1420s, at Siena or Perugia, he studied under the most famous professor of logic of the early Quattrocento, Paul of Venice.[37] At Perugia in 1429 he began teaching medicine. The early 1430s found him in Florence for a political assignment. By the end of that decade he had married into the famous Marsuppini family in Arezzo and, in 1439, gained Aretine citizenship.[38] Also in 1439, when the University of Florence reopened (after a two-year closing for plague), he won an appointment to teach "theory," that is, logical texts preliminary to studies in medicine. He no doubt extended whatever humanist contacts he had during this period; he refers later to his presence in Florence during the ecumenical council.[39] Probably in the 1440s Tignosi managed to induce the humanist Giovanni Tortelli to prepare a new translation of Aristotle's *Posterior Analytics*. Tortelli dedicated it to Tignosi, who then used it in a commentary on the work.[40] Notarial and other

---

Century (1929; rept. New York, 1963), pp. 161–79; A. Rotondò, "N. T. da Foligno (Polemiche aristoteliche di un maestro del Ficino)," *Rinascimento* 9 (1958), 217–55; E. Berti, "La dottrina platonica delle idee nel pensiero di N. T. da Foligno," in *Filosofia e cultura in Umbria tra Medioevo e Rinascimento: Atti del IV Convegno di Studi Umbri, Gubbio, 22–26 maggio 1966* (Perugia, 1967), pp. 533–65.

I shall be looking at Tignosi in the context of Florentine culture in the mid-Quattrocento. As in my treatment of Argyropoulos, an analysis of Tignosi's thought in the context of scholastic traditions will be wanting. According to a communication of Dillwyn Knox, there is an affinity between Tignosi's ideas and those of the late thirteenth- and early fourteenth-century Augustinian hermit Henricus de Vrimaria.

37. This has not been noted before, even though in all three of his major commentaries, on Aristotle's *Posterior Analytics*, *Nicomachean Ethics*, and *De anima*, Tignosi manages to throw in somewhere the fact that Paul had been his teacher. In the first and last of these Paul is called merely "doctor meus" (last only cited by Sensi, "N. T. da Foligno," p. 408n., who does not seem to draw the conclusion that Paul had actually been Tignosi's teacher; the first is Ricc. 110, fol. 110). The reference in the *Ethics* commentary is graphic (cod. Gino Capponi 314, fol. 85v; Laur. 76, 49, fol. 62): "Multi abhorrent allia ut Lucas Perusinus nostri temporis medicus et phylosophus clarus; et Paulus Venetus cunctos nostri temporis excellens cui ego fui discipulus pulpas pullorum plurimum abhorrebat." Lucas Perusinus was Luca di Simone Perugino (G. B. Vermiglioli, *Biografia degli scrittori perugini* . . . [Perugia, 1828–29], II, 201–5). According to A. R. Perreiah, "A Biographical Introduction to Paul of Venice," *Augustiniana* 17 (1967), 458–59, Paul of Venice was in Perugia from November 1424 and then in Siena in 1427. The real question we may be asking ourselves here, however, is not when Tignosi studied under Paul of Venice but what garlic and chicken have to do with Aristotle's ethics!

38. According to a communication of Frank Dabell, who is studying archival material on Aretine culture. See now Black, *Benedetto Accolti*, pp. 14–15.

39. He mentions the council in his commentary on the *Ethics*: Laur. 76, 49, fol. 68v.

40. Cod. Ricc. 110: see the description by G. Mancini, "Giovanni Tortelli cooperatore di Niccolò V nel fondare la Biblioteca Vaticana," *Archivio storico italiano* 78 (1920), 198ff. The commentary is preceded by a letter from Tortelli to Tignosi and the latter's reply (each ed. in part by A. Rotondò, "N. T. da Foligno," pp. 221n., 224). In his letter Tortelli stated that he had prepared the translation at Tignosi's request, and Tignosi's reply (in-

records place him again in Arezzo in the 1440s: none indicate definitely
that he resided there.[41] At any rate, when the University of Florence
opened in 1451 (again after a closing for plague), Tignosi began once
again to teach "theory" and probably medicine. Just before this second
Florentine period Poggio Bracciolini used him as the major interlocutor
for his *Secunda disceptatio convivalis*, the second and most important dialogue of his *Historia tripartita* (1450), which, set in Terranova in 1447,
included the humanists Carlo Marsuppini and Benedetto Accolti.[42]

   At Florence Tignosi lectured on Aristotle, and among his students
was Marsilio Ficino.[43] From his lectures Tignosi completed in 1459 or
1460 a commentary on the *Nicomachean Ethics*, based on Leonardo Bruni's translation, which he dedicated to Piero de' Medici in 1461.[44] Soon

---

cipit, fol. 1: "Glosaturus sum [?] opusculum quod meo nomine traduxisti") points toward Tignosi's authorship of the commentary as a whole, as does the internal evidence
cited above, n. 37). Tignosi referred to his commentary on the *Posterior Analytics* in his
commentaries on the *Ethics* (Laur. 76, 49, fol. 185) and on the *De anima* (noted by Rotondò, pp. 221–22n.), as well as in his treatise on the antiquity of Foligno (ed. Sensi, in
"N. T. da Foligno," p. 484).

41.   Sensi, "N. T. da Foligno," pp. 376–77.

42.   I shall cite both the Basel edition (1538) of the second dialogue (*Opera omnia*, I, 37–
51) and that of E. Garin, in his *La disputa delle Arti nel Quattrocento* (Florence, 1947), pp.
15–33, and shall simply choose what I regard as the better readings in each, without noting variants. G. G. Visconti is currently preparing a new edition.

43.   That Ficino was a student of Niccolò Tignosi is based on the following: (1) Ficino
was at the University of Florence studying Aristotle in preparation for a career in medicine, and for this Tignosi was an ideal teacher; (2) Ficino's close friend and *confilosofo* in
Aristotle studies, Antonio Serafico, owned a codex of Tignosi's commentary on the *Nicomachean Ethics* (Gino Capponi 314); (3) Ficino's letter praising Lorenzo Pisano's commentary on Solomon's *Song of Songs* mentions Niccolò Tignosi's shared opinion; (4)
probably Tignosi and possibly Ficino appear in Lorenzo Pisano's *Dialogi quinque*; (5)
Ficino's sixteenth-century biographer, Piero Caponsacchi, describes him as a student of
Tignosi (ed. in R. Marcel, *Marsile Ficin*, pp. 705, 731). This evidence (except no. 4) is
discussed by Della Torre, *Storia*, pp. 495–501. Cod. Ricc. 135 contains Leonardo Bruni's
translation of the *Nicomachean Ethics*, with a marginal commentary, all in Ficino's hand
and dated May 1455. Della Torre, *Storia*, pp. 499–500, and Rotondò, "N. T. da Foligno," p. 228 (following Della Torre), have argued that these marginalia would be taken
from Tignosi's lectures on Aristotle. However, in my somewhat cursory comparison of
these marginalia with Tignosi's published commentary on the *Ethics*, I found no obvious
connection. Certainly the manuscript merits further study. (When I examined the manuscript, the marginalia in the inner margins were difficult to read because of the manuscript's tight binding; my microfilm copy taken from the Riccardiana's negative microfilm proved more legible.) For Ricc. 135 see now *Marsilio Ficino e il ritorno: Mostra*, pp.
14–15, no. 12 (the shelfmark for the Tignosi commentary cited there should be corrected
to cod. Gino Capponi 314).

44.   Four codices are extant, with two different dedications, an earlier one to "the
reader" (inc.: "Quisquis has glosulas lecturus es") and a later one to Piero de' Medici,
"vexillifer iusticiae" (inc.: "Neque argentum neque aurum").
    1. Laur. 76, 49, is the dedication copy, with of course the second dedication only. Pi-
ero's name appears both on the title page (fol. 1v) and in the dedication (fol. 2), and the
correction at the very end of the commentary (COMENTUM [*sic*] . . . AD COSMUM [corr.

thereafter he dedicated to Cosimo de' Medici a short work defending this commentary.[45] Meanwhile he published a *De laudibus Cosmi* dedicated to Cosimo's son Giovanni.[46] His other works include a tract on the fall of Constantinople, an astrological treatise, and a work on the antiquity of Foligno (emphasizing, one might note, the role of the Tignosi family in the early history of Umbria!).[47] About 1470 he wrote a treatise *De ideis*, a critique of Donato Acciaiuoli's attempt to harmonize Plato and Aristotle;[48] then, while at the Pisan branch of the University of Florence, he completed a commentary on Aristotle's *De anima*, based on the Latin translation of John Argyropoulos.[49] He died in 1474.[50]

to PETRUM]) was probably a scribe's error (fol. 198v). On this same folio is written "Liber Petri de Medicis Cos(mae) F(ilii)." Elegant and in a humanist script, the codex has a small miniature portraying Tignosi, an embroidery (fol. 2), and lemmas in red. That one entire gathering (fols. 183–90) has the folios in the wrong order is not noted in the margins, nor has it been noted since (between fols. 182 and 191: the sequence 186, 185, 184, 183, 190, 189, 188, 187, would restore the correct order of the text).

2. Laur. 76, 48, less elegant, also with the dedication to Piero.

3. cod. Gino Capponi 314 (Biblioteca Nazionale Centrale, Florence) is even less elegant, has only the earlier dedication, and includes Books 1–9 only. At the bottom of the front flyleaf and on the last page (fol. 205v) is named the owner, Antonio Morali da San Miniato (i.e., Antonio Serafico), Ficino's *confilosofo* in Aristotle studies. (For the problem of the manuscript's shelfmark, see Kristeller, *Iter*, I, 166.)

4. Perugia, Biblioteca Comunale Augusta, cod. L 79, with both dedications. Folio 1r is blank; fol. 1v has the earlier, anonymous dedication, entirely crossed out; fol. 2r has the new dedication to Piero; fol. 2v begins the commentary. But the script of fol. 1v more closely resembles that of 2v than that of 2r, which would suggest that the scribe knew a new dedication was planned and left room for it. The codex has some additions and corrections.

For the dating, the dedication to Piero de' Medici, *vexillifer iustitiae*, gives us a *terminus ante quem* of January-February 1461, when Piero was Gonfaloniere di Giustizia. Tignosi mentioned the Parlamento of (August) 1458 in the body of the commentary (it appears in those manuscripts with an earlier dedication as well as the copy dedicated to Piero: Perugia Com. L 79, fol. 184v; Gino Capponi 314, fol. 194v; Laur. 76, 49, fol. 166v). The manuscript must have been written between late 1458 and the beginning of 1461, and, since two versions contain the earlier dedication, it likely circulated in some form before 1461.

For simple references I shall cite the dedication copy (Laur. 76, 49 – L). But for passages quoted I shall compare the manuscript of Antonio Serafico (Gino Capponi 314 – N) and important variants will be noted. In the case of difficult readings, the Perugia manuscript (Bibl. Com., cod. L 79) will be compared also.

45. Ed. M. Sensi, in "N. T. da Foligno," pp. 466–82.

46. Ibid., pp. 447–65, based on Laur. 53, 11, and Laur. 54, 10 (the latter Scala's *Collectiones Cosmianae*).

47. The first and last ed. M. Sensi, in "N. T. da Foligno," pp. 423–31, 483–95; the astrological treatise is mentioned in the panegyric of Foligno (at p. 484 of ed.).

48. *De ideis*, ed. in Thorndike, *Science and Thought*, pp. 332–63; cf. pp. 308–31.

49. Thorndike, *Science and Thought*, p. 164; Rotondò, "N. T. da Foligno," pp. 218, 241–42.

50. Was Tignosi a poet? Evidently, for Porcellius praised his poetic pastime (cited by Della Torre, *Storia*, p. 496n.). Tignosi was criticized for citing poets in his commentaries

In a recent monograph on Tignosi, Antonio Rotondò has argued that Tignosi's interest in logic, from the time of his commentary on the *Posterior Analytics* of about 1440, depended on the common medical notion that the superiority of medicine as a discipline was based on "its rational character and on its direct derivation from nature."[51] Indeed, a study of the commentary on the *Ethics*, which Rotondò did not make, confirms the hypothesis: again and again Tignosi iterates the *dignitas disciplinae* theme. As early as 1450 Tignosi had no doubt won considerable fame for the theory of the natural superiority of the medical discipline, as his role as defender of medicine against law in Poggio's *Historia tripartita* indicates. Much of the theoretical groundwork of the humanist critique of the legal science was established by Tignosi (and by Poggio's use of him in the dialogue), and we shall look at his theory at some length.

As Tignosi said in the Brunelleschi illustration, each art has its own end: the stone mason need not know the final purpose of the architect. As an academic and professor of medicine, Tignosi took up the favorite humanist and academic dispute on medicine and law by weighing the function of the physician within the medical profession against the lawyer and his profession. In the *Nicomachean Ethics*, a passage at the end of Book 1 (1.13.7/1102a) would seem to have caused him difficulties. Aristotle argues that a politician should know something about the soul, just as the physician healing the eye should consider the state of health of the entire body; indeed, such knowledge is more important in politics "inasmuch as politics is a higher and more honorable art than medicine." Tignosi resolved this difficulty by showing how medicine as a discipline is closer to politics than is law: Our lawyers, he wrote, are not

> those who enact law, for this is a function of the council, the people, or the prince, to whom even theologians are subject, so that they might live in a civil fashion; but they are . . . those who bring to the people those statutes, plebiscites, laws, and edicts, and who interpret them if anything in them appears confusing. However, the things said today by them are more confusing than the sayings of the sibyls or of Apollo! These lawyers are subordinate to the makers of law as are the craftsmen to the architect. Since the physician has a free science and does not convey another's—but is the

---

(see the *Opusculum* in defense of his commentary on the *Ethics*, ed. Sensi, "N. T. da Foligno," at p. 479). Tignosi did quote in the commentary some verses of Panormita (Laur. 76, 49, fol. 165) and some other verses ("volui hos versus apponere") that I have been unable to identify and may be Tignosi's own (ibid., fol. 184v, inc.: Verum cuncta dari profert arcana clientes).

51. "N. T. da Foligno," p. 222.

craftsman of his own science—he is to be placed in a rank well ahead of those lawyers they call judges or advocates.[52]

The notion of a "free science" (*scientia libera*) of medicine involves precisely the notion that the highest activity in whatever discipline defines the perfection of that discipline. The lawyer has no such freedom, being subordinate to the makers of law; the physician on his own sees to the health of the body. In his commentary on Book 10 of the *Ethics*, Tignosi extended his critique of lawyers to a general critique of the "sophists," meaning here rhetoricians and orators as well as lawyers. Closely following Aristotle (10.9.20/1181a), who argues that the sophists are ignorant of the very nature of politics and of "the subject with which it deals," Tignosi turned this condemnation into a scholastic formula: on politics the sophists know neither "what it is" (*quid sit*) nor "what its end is" (*quis finis eius*). Politics, Tignosi continued, is not the "instrument of another science"; rhetoric is, and hence is subject to politics:

> Politics deems those to be good who are in charge of laws, who interpret them correctly, and who see to their execution. It hears the raillery and exhortations of the rhetoricians; nevertheless, it is not moved from what is right. If they knew what politics was, and what matters it dealt with, then they would not "think that it is easy to legislate for one who collects excellent laws" [10.9.20/ 1181a]. Making these laws is indeed a part of politics. The sophists persuaded themselves that such a construction was easy since it seemed easy "to be able to select the best laws" [ibid.]. They thought that it was enough to have a legislator who knew the approved laws select and systematize them.

By once again using a medical analogy, Tignosi showed how the sophists are in a "twofold error":

> In the first place to recognize or gather together the laws found or approved and to make a judgment on them is not enough to make

---

52.   Gino Capponi 314, fols. 36v–37; Laur. 76, 49, fol. 27; cf. ed. Rotondò, "N. T. da Foligno," p. 228: "Nostri legistae, ut vocabulo Arabo utar, non sunt muthachali, idest qui leges sanciant—nam hoc est senatus, populi vel principis cui etiam theologi sunt subiecti, ut civiliter vivant—sed sunt alphachi, idest in populum illa statuta vel plebiscita vel senatus consulta vel edicta promulgantes et interpraetantes si quid in illis nodosum est, quamvis hodie dicta ipsarum [ipsorum *L*] sybillarum vel Apollinis dictis sint enigmaticiora [enigmatiora *L N*]. Subsunt ergo legum conditoribus sicut artifices archytecto. Cum ergo medicus scientiam liberam [liberalem *N*] habeat nec sit alterius promulgator sed ipsemet suae scientiae artifex, longe legistis istis, quos iudices vel advocatos nominant, praeponendus est."

a good legislator. One must know how to invent new laws, for when new things emerge new deliberation is required: one must then dispose them in accordance with the condition of the commonwealth. Likewise knowing and collecting good remedies does not make a good physician: a good physician must know how to find and apply them when and to what cases they are appropriate. In the second place the sophists seem to err when they think that there is no need for carefully chosen reasons or keenness of intellect in selecting laws, "as if the selection did not demand understanding" [ibid.].[53]

Here we see that Tignosi has not simply opposed the "superior" medicine to the "inferior" law; rather, he showed how in each discipline one has a proper method of proceeding, based on a skillful subordination of means to ends. To be sure, this method was more readily apparent to a physician, Tignosi believed, than to a sophist or lawyer of his own day, and his arguments can only be viewed as a critique of the legal discipline.

To what extent, for Tignosi, was law a science? Need lawyers abandon their mundane, sophistic perspective in favor of the broader outlook of the better doctors and politicians? Or should the lawyers be like Brunelleschi's stonemasons, who would confuse their tasks if they *ceased* to be mere functionaries? Tignosi constantly reminded his readers of the variability and even discrepancy of human laws and customs. Even though, he argued at one point, "governing the family" is deemed "good" by common custom, you "never find two people governing it in the same way." Likewise, what was honest at Rome was evil elsewhere. In "our time" cremation is forbidden, while among other peoples it is held most holy. While laws may indeed be "customs" written down and

---

53. Not in *N*; Perugia, Bibl. Com., cod. L 79, fol. 277–77v; Laur. 76, 49, fol. 197v (the lemmas are from Leonardo Bruni's translation): Res "polytica illos bonos reputat qui leges custodiunt et recte interpraetantur et praestant executionem. Cavillationes et suasiones rhetorum audit; non tamen a recto movetur. Si scirent quid est res polytica et circa quae versatur non *putarent esse facile leges ferre colligenti praeclaras leges* quas condere pars est polyticae. Facilitatem hanc sibi ipsis suadebant quia ipsis facile videbatur *posse optimas eligi*. Sufficientem esse legis latorem putabant qui leges approbatas scivisset eligere et in unum colligere vel congregare. At hi dupliciter errant. Uno modo quia non satis est inventas aut approbatas cognoscere vel congregare et secundum illas ferre iudicium ut quis fiat bonus legis lator. Sed opus est ut sciat novas invenire, quoniam quae de novo emergunt nova indigent deliberatione, et illas pro statu rei p. ordinare. Non sufficit ad esse bonum medicum scire et colligere inventa remedia, sed opus est ut nova sciat invenire et approximare quibus et quando opportet. Alio modo videntur errare putantes non esse opus rationibus exquisitis et intellectu perspicaci ad ipsas inveniendas, *quasi electio non sit intelligentiae*."

approved, customs themselves "even in the same city" undergo continuous change and depend on human opinion. San Bernardino brought about an end to gambling in Siena and Perugia but was unable to do it elsewhere.[54] Interpreters of the law, then, are not engaged in a science.

The "variability" argument was the theme of Tignosi's speeches in Poggio Bracciolini's dialogue on law and medicine, the *Secunda disceptatio convivalis* of 1450.[55] In the dialogue, in which Poggio and Carlo Marsuppini play passive roles, Tignosi opposed the jurist Benedetto Accolti by showing how medicine's greater nobility lay in its derivation from philosophy or "nature herself," whereas law changed as customs changed.[56] Law is merely an instrument, a tool used by the stronger to subject the weaker. People everywhere and at all times have resisted this subjection: hence the first lawgivers, including Moses, attached a numinous authority to their laws so that the people would obey them.[57] Pointing to the variety and inconsistency of law, "Tignosi" described law as essentially a function of power. Greek and Roman cultural vigor and political strength lay not in their laws but in their use of force.[58]

54. Laur. 76, 49, fols. 5v–6v.

55. The arguments that follow are developed much more thoroughly in the excellent analysis by Krantz, "Poggio," esp. pp. 143–51.

56. *Opera omnia*, I, 38; Garin, *La disputa*, p. 17: "Nostra . . . ars ducem habet rationem, hoc est ipsam naturam, in qua sua iecit fundamenta. Leges pro voluntate maiorum conditae. Maior profecto pars hominum illis caret; suo more vivunt regna ac populi, aut obtemperantes imperantium arbitrio aut sua consuetudine aut usu a maioribus tradito contenti."

    Opera omnia, I, 39; Garin, *La disputa*, p. 18: "Quanto naturali philosophiae moralis cedit, tanto leges medicinae concedant necesse est. Opus nostrum naturali continetur philosophia."

    Opera omnia, I, 39–40; Garin, *La disputa*, p. 18: "Iureconsulti in urbe solum docti habebantur; extra urbem indocti. At medicinae ars firmiori in sede residet, ut quae ab ipsa philosophia, hoc est ab ipsa natura quae semper est eadem, movetur neque moribus aut cuiusquam arbitrio tollitur vel mutatur" etc.

57. *Opera omnia*, I, 47–48; Garin, *La disputa*, p. 28: "Constat enim eas [*sc.* leges] invitis ac repugnantibus hominibus introductas, ut qui se in servitutem quandam redigi existimarent; adeo vero illas populis invisas constat fuisse, ut primi earum latores semper ab aliquo numine illas se, quo eas obiecto deorum metu suaderent populis, finxerint accepisse. Primus apud Aegyptios Menes" etc. " . . . Nonne Moyses noster leges suas, ut verum erat, a Deo se accepisse ostendit, quas repugnanti plebi imponeret?"

58. *Opera omnia*, I, 48–49; Garin, *La disputa*, p. 29: "Non Athenienses nisi eorum ampliata re publica studiis litterarum domicilium praebuissent. Non philosophia, non eloquentia, non caeterae bonae artes in lucem inventae atque excultae prodissent. Summa semper imperia litteris et doctrinae aditum praebuere. Non Romanorum gesta, non caeterorum praeclarissima legerentur, sed silerent litterae, muta esset eloquentia, conticescerent bonae artes, omnis liberalis doctrina obdormivisset; praeclara opera, ingentia aedificia cessassent omnia, si obsequendo vestris legibus suo quisque contentus aetatem in ocio absumpsisset."

Poggio had always emphasized the variability and concreteness of the *res humanae* (law, customs, language, fortune, and so forth), and his arguments followed naturally from these earlier humanistic interests. His own motivation for writing the dialogue may have been a current legal difficulty he was in, a desire to defend the "illegitimate" Medici regime, and his patriotic interest in justifying the expanding Florentine empire.[59] The major point of the dialogue, in fact, is that each power should make its own law instead of relying on some derivative construct (for example, Roman law) and that derivative legal interpretations inherently undercut the power of the actual makers of law.[60]

Let me now attempt to place Tignosi's analysis of the disciplines in the context of his philosophy as a whole. Just as the good physician seeks the "end" of the health of the body, so each species within a genus seeks an "end" or "good" for that genus, which is pleasure (*voluptas*). At the same time not all species that have sense or intellect seek the same pleasure: man, horse, the young, and the old (to use Tignosi's examples) are by disposition different. Each, however, has a "best disposition":

> All do not seek the same thing, although all seek pleasure, because pleasure is the best thing for all. Nevertheless, they do not seek the same pleasure, just as there is not the same disposition for all. To look at the matter further: it may be said that all men seek the same pleasure according to natural appetite (*appetitus naturalis*), not, however, according to each individual judgment, since all do not judge the same pleasure to be the best. In a *natural* sense, nevertheless, all incline toward the same thing as if toward the best, as, namely, toward the contemplation of truth, because all men by nature desire to know.[61]

59. Cf. Krantz, "Legal Thought," pp. 274–75n.

60. *Opera omnia*, I, 49: Garin, *La disputa*, p. 30: "Sua quaeque civitas iura civilia disponit, suum quodque oppidum privatum ius sibi condit. Florentini privatis institutis magis quam publicis, hoc est Romanis legibus, utuntur. Multa enim condentium aetate conferebant, quae nunc tempore et conditione urbium sunt immutata. Itaque in singulis urbibus leges in suam rem accommodatas condere necessitas impulit, quae iuri Romano anteferuntur."

61. Gino Capponi 314, fol. 161; Laur. 76, 49, fol. 141: "[A]lia est optima dispositio hominis, alia equi, iterum alia iuvenis alia senis, et cum unicuique adsit quod ipsum delectat, inde est quod non omnes idem appetunt, quamvis omnes expetant voluptatem, quia voluptas est omnibus optima. Non tamen eandem, sicut nec omnibus eadem dispositio. Et potest dici omnes homines eandem voluptatem secundum naturalem appetitum expetere, non tamen secundum proprium iudicium, cum non omnes iudicent eandem voluptatem esse optimam. Naturaliter tamen omnes inclinantur in eandem sicut in optimam ut puta in veritatis contemplationem secundum quod omnes homines natura scire desiderant."

Within the larger frame of these "natural" tendencies one may study the particular desires, the "voluntaristic" ones: these are the more problematical, the true subject of ethics. While "voluntarism" was no longer a major controversy in humanist circles, it was still lively in scholastic ones, especially when voluntaristic arguments were injected into questions of virtues as they relate to man's "genus" and "natural disposition." Among the critics that Tignosi names in his *Opusculum* defending his *Ethics* commentary were those who would "reduce everything to fate."[62] In the commentary Tignosi argued that moral virtues "are generated through customs, vary, and are not present from nature," and he referred to the determinists, here identifiable with Stoics, as follows:

> But many say that there are naturally present in the reason of man certain principles naturally known both of things knowable and of things to be done, which are the seeds of intellectual and moral virtues, and also in the will there is present a certain appetite toward the good, and it exists according to reason, and in this way virtue is natural to man *as a species*. It is also able to be present to man *as an individual*, to wit, on account of the disposition of the body rendering that individual more suited than others to acquiring virtues. Thus they infer that virtue is present to man from nature according to a certain beginning or aptitude but not perfected by actuality or habit, for the habit is acquired by the custom of acting well.[63]

The theme of Poggio—*res hominum variantur*—provided Tignosi his answer: In doing the good one must always look to the circumstances, because "at one time one thing is moral and at another the same is subject to blame."[64] Most striking is how voluntaristic emphasis is placed on the side of the *medical* discipline: physicians have a higher regard for the principles of selection and choice dependent on rational activity than do the schematic lawyers. The rationality of medicine is based not simply on its derivation from nature but on its more correct assessment of

62. Ed. in Sensi, "N. T. da Foligno," pp. 475–78.
63. Gino Capponi 314, fol. 43v; Laur. 76, 49, fol. 31v: "Verum multi dicunt quod in ratione hominis naturaliter insunt quaedam principia naturaliter cognita, tam scibilium quam agendorum, quae sunt seminaria intellectualium et moralium virtutum, ac etiam in voluntate inest quidam appetitus ad bonum, et is est secundum rationem et isto modo virtus est homini naturalis ex parte suae speciei. Potest etiam inesse ex parte individui, scilicet propter corporis dispositionem reddentem illud individuum caeteris facilius ad virtutes acquirendas. Ex quo inferunt virtutem inesse homini a natura secundum quandam inchoationem et aptitudinem, non tamen actu vel habitu perfectam; sed habitus acquiritur assuetudine bene faciendi."
64. Laur. 76, 49, fol. 31v.

its discipline, with its more cunning and intellectual regard for this discipline. Traditionally in the disputes *de dignitate disciplinarum* the "voluntaristic" argument was the lawyer's last and strongest card; the physician, it was said, ignored questions of the will and looked toward the health of the body alone. Such, indeed, had been Salutati's approach in his famous *De nobilitate legum et medicinae*.[65] "Benedetto Accolti" relied on the same argument in Poggio's dialogue: when you, Tignosi, praise medicine you are, to use Cicero's words, "creating a fortress out of a sewer" (or, in an alternate reading, "creating an art out of the toilet").[66]

Throughout the commentary on the *Ethics* Tignosi hammered away at the notion of the reality of the external world and the necessity for intellectual cunning in dealing with it. The highly variable external world requires intellectual rigor in judging tendencies of each particular thing, relations of parts to the whole, motions to their place of rest. An "understanding of ends" brings many benefits to our life, he said early in the commentary, but our own end, happiness, is not the ordering principle of our life; rather, we are ordered to something which, if we attain it, makes us happy. By subordinating means to ends, by "proper reason" (*per propriam rationem*), man can become "lord of his actions" (*dominus suorum actuum*).[67]

The principles of moral conduct, then, find their order through one's activity and will. Thus intellectual endeavors alone, the "*quieta rerum contemplatio*" of the Stoics, do not embody the whole man. In isolation, intellectual activity lacks the *appetitus sensitivus*.[68] With the will and intellect united one has free choice (*liberum arbitrium*), by which we differ from beasts, who are moved "by nature's stimulus alone."[69] Man not only seeks his own end within his genus (as do all creatures), but he also has a certain "teleological principle" (*ratio finis*). Objective standards, or ordering principles, therefore exist for us: these are pleasure and pain.

> These two seem to be particular rules of human actions. They accompany the end of the action, on which account they have in some way a teleological principle, and their end is the rule of those

65. Ed. E. Garin (Florence, 1947).

66. Poggio, *Opera omnia*, I, 40; Garin, *La disputa*, p. 19: "Verum mihi videris, Nicolae, id quod olim Ciceroni in oratione, ut opinor, pro Plancio est obiectum, te 'arcem [artem *Op.*] facere ex cloaca.'" Cicero of course reads *arcem* (*Planc*. 40.95), but *artem* and *arcem* would have been pronounced alike or nearly alike and often written alike, and a pun may have been intended: diagnoses of the medieval doctor depended on urinalysis.

67. Laur. 76, 49, fol. 4v.

68. Ibid., fols. 33–34.

69. Ibid., fols. 42v, 47–47v.

things which are directed to it. For moral goodness and evil principally consist in the will. . . . The end is that in which the will comes to rest. The state of rest of the will, and of whatever appetite, in the good is pleasure: if one finds joy in the good he is called good; if he suffers pain or unhappiness he is called bad. Although it is said in the tenth book of the *Metaphysics* that the first thing in any genus (*primum in genere aliquo*) is the rule of all things which are under that genus, but that in moral philosophy desire and love seem to precede pleasure, it is answered that they are prior by generation, not by intention, since pleasure in respect to them has a teleological principle, which is a rule which at least is uniform (as every rule should be) in that it is the state of rest in any good, in which, if it does not find rest, it suffers.[70]

Here we see the beginnings of Ficino's more highly developed doctrine of the *primum in aliquo genere*: each genus defines the hierarchy of its parts in an objective way, and the first thing in the genus determines the structure and participation of them.[71] For Tignosi the genus itself regulates man's precise position in the hierarchy; man senses this rule through pleasure and pain.

In moral conduct Tignosi emphasized the central role of the intellect in finding proper ends according to the particular circumstances and in subordinating the available means to these ends. Not all, he argued, have even the capacity for clear thinking: some are moved simply by a "credulity acquired through custom or authority." For youth the "impetus of passions is stronger than the judgment of reason," and they need strong guidance from an early age.[72] Because of his emphasis on the "scientific" status of medicine, it seems, Tignosi's arguments on the "passions" or "enticements of the senses"—emphasized not only by

70. Gino Capponi 314, fol. 48; Perugia, Bibl. Com., cod. L 79, fol. 45; Laur. 76, 49, fol. 34v: "Igitur haec duo videntur regulae particulares operationis humanae. Concomitantur enim finem quapropter habent quodammodo rationem finis, et finis est regula eorum quae in ipsum fiunt. Bonitas enim et malitia moralis principaliter in voluntate consistit. Utrum autem voluntas sit [sib *L*] bona vel mala, excedens vel deficiens ex fine habetur. Finis vero est in quo voluntas quiescit. Quies autem voluntatis et cuiuslibet appetitus in bono est voluptas [voluntas *L*] in quo si gaudet bonus ille dicitur, si vero dolet aut moleste ferat malus est. Et si dicitur ex decimo Methaphysice quod primum in genere aliquo est regula omnium quae sunt sub illo genere, sed in morali desyderium et amor videntur praecedere voluptatem, respondetur quod sunt priores generatione non tamen intentione, quia voluptas respectu illorum habet rationem finis qui est regula quae ad minus in hoc est uniformis, qualiter [qualem *L*] omnem regulam decet esse, quia est quies in aliquo bono, in quo si non quiescat dolet."

71. For Ficino and the *primum in aliquo genere*, see Kristeller, *Il pensiero filosofico*, pp. 153–79.

72. Laur. 76, 49, fol. 7–7v.

scholastic theologians by also by many humanists of the Platonic Academy—never came to dominate his discussion. Instead, the major impediment to true intellectual understanding, from which moral action follows, was what he called the *scientia sophistica*, knowledge based on sophistries, legalistic thinking, and formulas. Such, he says, is only "scientia" by a license of speech (*largo modo dicendi*). This type of thinking belongs to the "clouded mind."[73] Here again the purely moral position is subordinated to the highly intellectual one. Clear thinking requires right reason (*recta ratio*): right reason depends on using the correct arts and doctrines to achieve the end desired. Man knows that he has done rightly when the end is reached. The only external limits to such deliberation are that one must seek an obtainable object; hence Tignosi's pungent observation that "de hora qua sitit bos et leo stimulatur ad coitum nemo consultat."[74]

By about 1460 Niccolò Tignosi had found the individual who embodied that intellectual cunning that could examine all aspects of civil life and set in order the republic. He was the greatest private citizen living or dead, Cosimo de' Medici. "Just as by nature birds are born to flying, panthers to leaping, horses to running, and lions to acting ferocious, thus to this man a quickness and agility of mind is natural and proper."[75] Thus reads Tignosi's not particularly happy series of metaphors for the gout-stricken, often bedridden old man, but perhaps the philosopher's eye was so riveted on the internal workings of the mind that he could not avoid them.[76] The treatise *De laudibus Cosmi*, dedicated to Cosimo's son Giovanni, was the offshoot of a discussion held at Perugia, Tignosi claimed, on whether contemporary men could equal the men of antiquity. All agreed that Cosimo proved they could.

In her study of the *De laudibus Cosmi* genre of literature, Alison Brown has shown how before the 1450s Cosimo had been praised for his practical virtues, expressions of his political and financial power.[77] Cosimo's deeds Tignosi also recounted, both the architectural (the church of San Lorenzo, the library of San Marco, his own palace), and the political (the extension of the Florentine *imperium* and the honors

---

73. Ibid., fol. 104v.

74. Ibid., fol. 107.

75. *De laudibus Cosmi*, ed. Sensi, "N. T. da Foligno," p. 456 (cf. Laur. 53, 11, fols. 51v–52): "Nam sicut avis ad volandum, pardi ad saltum, equi ad cursum, leones ad sevitiam a natura gignuntur, sic huic homini naturalis et propria est mentis agitatio atque solertia ." Cf. Quintilian, *Inst. or.*, 1.1.1.

76. J. R. Hale, *Florence and the Medici: The Pattern of Control* (London, 1977), p. 27, has also noted the impropriety of this comparison.

77. Brown, "Humanist Portrait of Cosimo," pp. 186–221, esp. p. 196.

given him by foreign powers).[78] But these outward signs, Tignosi said, lead us to the inner mind of Cosimo: were we actually able to gaze upon it, "what a beautiful image we would find there, and what a complete idea of things to be done!"[79] Tignosi praised Cosimo in terms taken directly from his commentary on the *Ethics*, as if Cosimo were the perfect example of the *genus humanum*, as if, in fact, he were the *primum in genere humano*. Cosimo is the "rule of living and ruling," where "will and knowledge accompany the power of acting."[80] Just as the soul rules the body, Cosimo guides the other citizens. As a result, "all the minds of men, all desires, all single pleasures, whatever is in error, whatever is in decline, or whatever should be held stable and firm, whatever soldiers, intellectuals, citizens, artisans, or rustic lower classes seek after— all of these come together in the reason of his mind."[81] Thus it is no accident that Florence has reached the optimal state: the genius of Cosimo has correctly measured and set in order the disciplines within it. In showing the inner reason of Cosimo's genius, Tignosi brings together the humanist and philosophical themes of human diversity, the dignity of the disciplines, the nobility of the soul, with the theme of the contemplative life:

> However much the soul is separate from the bodies, man from other creatures, animate things from metals, so much is reason deemed more noble than the corporeal, sensible, and transient. Thus our mind is to be placed before all other things. For its activity proves its origins to be celestial. The use of reason varies among men: many give themselves up to the mechanical arts; many waste time buying and selling merchandise (antiquity thought Mercury ruled them); some choose arms and make every effort to prove themselves sons of Mars; many choose priesthood and seek Jupiter's presence with their prayers; excellent persons follow after the laws which Justinian collected in volumes; more than a few love Plato and Aristotle; Galen and Avicenna have made many disciples; many desire facility of speaking and seek to extend their patrimony with their eloquence. Thus "each has his

78. Ed. in Sensi, "N. T. da Foligno," pp. 455–56.

79. Ibid., p. 460 (I am changing the punctuation slightly): "Si animum huius tanti tamque clarissimi viri liceret inspicere, quam pulchram effigiem completamque rerum agendarum ydeam, cuncta trite accurateque considerantem intueremur!"

80. Ibid., p. 455.

81. Ibid., p. 465 (I am changing the punctuation slightly): "[O]mnes hominum mentes cuncta desideria singulaeque voluptates quid erret quid labatur siquid stabilis firmique debet haberi sive milites expetant sive docti sive cives artifices vel plebs rusticana in ratione huius hominis sunt adnexa."

attendant spirit" and is led by his own pleasure. Not only in these things is there diversity, but also in manners and nationality. For the same thing is not agreeable to the Greek, Roman, and the barbarian, and the laws of cities are various and diverse, and there is a great difference of opinions and wills.

But the man who applies himself to more noble works is recognized as the more thoroughly prudent and wise. And since governing the republic and acting in the interests of the people justly and piously surpass other human arts (for there is need for prudence, wisdom, and intellect, which comes only with great and long experience), I have no doubt that he ought to be preferred before all the others who has shown himself to surpass all others with noble and singular action.[82]

Great states in the past, such as Athens and Sparta, where the *res civilis* presided over and dominated the other faculties, had their rulers stand before the others just as the architect stands before the hands of the craftsman. Yet even these states fell apart. Led by their own pleasure, men formed factions through which they sought to rule. The men could no longer live as one because they were not of "one mind."[83]

Tignosi's ability to look behind the deeds of the civic leader to the mind—the ability, that is, to understand or at least to appreciate the inner harmony and order of the individual as it relates to his works—extended also to his approach toward the texts he commented on. One

---

82.   Laur. 53, 11, fols. 42v–43v (cf. ed. cit., p. 448): "Quanto quidem anima corporibus interest homoque coeteris et animata metallis, tanto corporeis ipsis sensibilibus et caducis ratio discernitur esse praestantior: hinc nostra mens quibusvis rebus anteponenda est. Nam eius agitatio atque solertia suam originem coelestem esse demonstrat, cumque rationis usus inter homines varius videatur—nam plures mechanicis artibus indulgent, in emendis vendendisque mercimoniis multorum tempora conteruntur quibus Mercurium praeesse putavit antiquitas, arma nonnulli quo se Martis filios experiantur deligunt et omnibus conatibus prosequuntur, sacerdotium plerique qui suis votis Iovem adesse voluerunt, praecipui iura sectantur quae Iustinianus in volumina recollegit, quamplures amant Aristotelem et Platonem, Galienus et Avicena multos fecere discipulos, multi facundiam dicendi cupiunt nitunturque sua eloquentia patrimonium ampliare—sic quisque suos patitur manes [cf. Virgil, *Aeneid* 6.743] et a sua trahitur voluptate. Nec in his solum apparet diversitas sed in moribus et natione. Nam idem graeco, romano barbaroque probabile non est, et civitatum leges variae atque diversae. Opinionum etiam atque voluntatum magna est differentia. Penitus prudentior sapientiorque cognoscitur qui se [*sic*] nobilioribus operibus iam adheret. Sed quoniam rem publicam gubernasse, populis sancte iusteque consuluisse coeteros humanos actus exsuperat, ubi prudentia opus est sapientia et intellectu quae non sine magna longaque experientia nanciscimur, nequaquam illum coeteris anteponendum dubito, qui hoc digno singularique facinore monstrat cunctos alios praecessisse. Talem tantumque virum multo quilibet admiratione digniorem esse iudicabit quam fuerit Helena vel Medusa vel quisquis alius qui" etc.

83.   Ed. cit., pp. 449–50.

of Tignosi's major concerns was to present the text in a "clearer" manner than had previously been done. Thus, while being a product of the scholastic world and never leaving it, Tignosi criticized severely some scholastic attempts to interpret classical authors, both in their translations and commentaries. Tignosi greeted with enthusiasm the new translation of Aristotle's *Posterior Analytics* made by Giovanni Tortelli: through your superior Greek, Tignosi wrote Tortelli, we can now abandon the harsh and rough old translation and attempt to gloss a text "clear, faithful, and elegant, and directed toward Aristotle's intention."[84] The *interpretatio ordinata ad mentem philosophi* seems to have become an obsession with Tignosi: in the commentary on the *Ethics*, he mentioned that such an interpretation, now possible with the new translation by Leonardo Bruni, would be his goal.[85] He then later defended his "method" when his commentary came under attack.

The attack came from a variety of quarters, as the *Opusculum* in defense of his commentary indicates.[86] Some, he said, criticized his Latinity, claiming he failed to follow the best Latin authors; some said he was *too* eloquent, avoiding the "sophistries, intricacies, and sibylline poems" appropriate to scholastic discourse; some disliked his use of technical terms, preferring a more *maternus sermo* or even the *volgare*; some, wanting to reduce all things to fate, disliked his attitude toward free choice; some said he should not have quoted poets. In a section on the "duty of the commentator," Tignosi maintained that the most important consideration is to interpret the work according to the "mind and true teaching" of the author, so that the reader can understand the end according to which the work is to be read, understood, and taught. While words should be carefully chosen to express the opinion of the author—and here some technical terms are necessary—eloquence itself is not an important consideration. On "things more than words," Tignosi concluded, the commentator must focus.[87]

It would seem that Tignosi, like Poggio, is emphasizing concrete realities as opposed to the sophistic concern with words alone as is characteristic of lawyers. For lawyers disputed about one work of late antiquity, Justinian's codification of law, and were limited to the words of that codification, while physicians (for instance) looked to "nature herself." To what extent, then, can Tignosi be harmonized to the Poggian

84. Rotondò, "N. T. da Foligno," p. 224. See also E. Garin, "Donato Acciaiuoli cittadino," pp. 230–31.

85. Laur. 76, 49, fol. 2.

86. Ed. Sensi, in "N. T. da Foligno," pp. 466–82.

87. Ibid., p. 469.

wing of the humanist movement? Poggio did seem to find some simi-
larities in choosing Tignosi as an interlocutor. But in the *verba* and *res*
question, Poggio had always shown that the meaning of words change
as the reality they describe changes; the critique of law was based largely
on the notion that the "words" of Roman law were describing a reality
far different from that of the Italian city-state.[88] As I argued earlier, his
concern for eloquence was as great as that of his rivals, the philological
school headed by Lorenzo Valla; in practice, in the elegance of his prose
style, he left Valla far behind. Tignosi, by contrast, was convinced that
the "realities" could be described without eloquence. In his original
preface to the *Ethics* commentary, he began: "You who are about to read
these glosses, since they are written without elegance I pray that you
will be a good Latin and not be haughty. For all people cannot do all
things."[89] The philosopher's duty to follow *res*, not *verba*, finds an echo
in Marsilio Ficino's letter to Antonio Serafico (another of Tignosi's students) of September 1454, quoted at the beginning of this chapter. Our
friendship, he said, does not require the humanistic niceties: let us turn
instead to the pure truth of philosophy. Ficino contrasted their customary form of writing—eloquent, humanistic, with careful attention to
words—with the "new," scholastic form, based on realities.

Ficino's letter may be interpreted as more evidence of the shift from
a grammatical and rhetorical culture to a philosophical one. Such, indeed, it does illustrate. But even if Ficino took his arguments on *verba*
and *res* (or *sententiae*) from his scholastic background (as it would
seem), the letter shows also that the intellectual worlds of Ficino and
Tignosi could never merge. For Tignosi the philosophical method of
writing was the only one he knew or cared about, and he defended it
with passion. For Ficino that method was a particular way of handling
a particular question, a method of writing, arguing, and thinking identified as such, which he could use, parody, joke about, or choose to
ignore, and which in itself did not limit his way of thinking. And indeed
that section of the letter to Serafico quoted at the beginning of this
chapter is about as classical a Ciceronian period as one could ask for.

This limitation of Tignosi may well be the main reason he had no
continuous, direct influence on the development of philosophical studies in the 1460s. His concern for language never extended beyond his
condemnation of the *nexus inextricabiles* of the sophists. While he wel-

---

88.   See the remarks of Krantz, "Poggio," pp. 128–29.
89.   Perugia, Bibl. Com., cod. L 79, fol. 1v; Gino Capponi 314, fol. 1: "Quisquis has
glosulas lecturus es, quoniam eleganter [elegantes *N*] minimum conscripte sunt, precor
Latio conveniens pone supercilium. Non enim omnia possumus omnes."

comed the translations of Aristotle by Bruni, Tortelli, and Argyropoulos, he never himself felt it necessary to learn Greek. The other "pure philosopher," John Argyropoulos, could begin his lectures on the *Ethics* by showing that Aristotle's τἀγαθόν ("the good," 1.1.1./1094a) could mean either a relative end (*finis propinquus*) or an absolute end (*finis remotus*), and that a better translation than Bruni's "*summum bonum*"— the only translation Tignosi chose to use—could be found.[90] More importantly, Tignosi's commentary, except to the most ardent Peripatetic, must have been monumentally boring. Even though the text of Aristotle itself forced Tignosi to look at a variety of circumstances, he continuously, and tediously, returned to the same arguments in the same way. There is indeed salt in the commentary, but none of it is rhetorical; the piling up of unrelated and, by humanist standards, indecorous *exempla* demonstrates rather the breadth than the depth of Tignosi's knowledge. In his dedication of the commentary to Piero de' Medici, Tignosi noted that he would be sufficiently honored to have the commentary grace Piero's bookshelves, should public affairs prevent him from reading it. On library shelves the commentary has remained to this day.[91] Tignosi influenced a few students, no doubt; he seems to have contributed significantly to Poggio Bracciolini's legal humanism; but as for a direct influence on any philosopher or humanist of note, after the 1450s there is no evidence of any whatsoever.

We must, therefore, describe Niccolò Tignosi as an intellectual and cultural figure of minor importance.[92] At the same time, if one likes to describe the thought of a figure as an "objectification" of an age's political or social world, the ideas of Niccolò Tignosi provide a field day. The apotheosis of Cosimo is glaring and gross. From the standpoint of intellectual history, Tignosi's political theory would well be studied through Poggio Bracciolini's own theory, whose *diversitas* comes from the soul and not the mind alone. We, however, are interested in the thought of Tignosi in its moment, not the richness of its source: our summary will have to be one-sided.

From Tignosi, it seems, Ficino got his first taste of how "philosoph-

90. Naz. II 1 104, fol. 11v: "*Summum bonum*: secundum translationem Leonardi. Hoc modo salvari potest:" etc., concluding: "Intelligendum . . . quod grece Τἀγαθόν quandoque significat bonum, quandoque etiam summum bonum, quasi ipsam bonitatem, ipsum bonum."

91. See nn. 36, 37, and 50, above, and the description of Laur. 76, 49, n. 44, above.

92. Tignosi made rather strained attempts to place himself in the mainstream of Florentine intellectual life. I discuss these at length in a paper which I have decided not to publish but will make available to any scholar upon request.

ical thinking" differed from "humanistic thinking": we will now, he wrote Antonio Serafico in 1454, act seriously and look after propositions rather than words. More specifically, Ficino learned that philosophizing involved putting the realities of the external world into order. In any true science the categories of thought must be founded on the categories of reality. With medicine, Tignosi argued, true scientific thinking was possible, for the subject matter of the medical discipline mirrored the external world. A true philosophical discipline, then, could never derive from the particular exigencies of the external world: just as the mind ruled the body and the architect ruled the stonemasons, so did philosophy rule the derivative sciences. In one of his earliest writings (ca. 1454), an invective against pedagogues to one Guardavilla da Volterra, Ficino seemed to pick up one of Tignosi's themes. The pedagogical discipline, he argued, almost inherently leaves one dependent on the status of one's student, and the subject matter of pedagogy is never the "highest studies" but the derivative ones, the books of civil law, inelegant commentaries and glosses.[93]

Ficino even seems to have shared some of Tignosi's (or Poggio's) more particular political insights on the relation of law and power. In a letter to Giovanni Cavalcanti written in 1471, he opposed the lawgiver Lycurgus to the subtle disputant Carneades:

> The Greeks once admired the power of expression, memory and sharpness of intellect in Carneades and, as you say, your friends praise the same qualities in Giovanni Guidi, and often call him Carneades because of a certain likeness. But you say he follows in the tradition of Lycurgus because of his discovery of laws. You also ask which is more praiseworthy, to be like Carneades or Lycurgus. Carneades in his arguments promoted discord, but Lycurgus resolved it. The cleverness of Carneades was more often useless than useful; indeed it was seldom useful to anyone anywhere. The teaching of Lycurgus is always useful and necessary everywhere to all men. Finally, insofar as it is better to live well than talk well and to be happy than seem to be, so far is the talent of Lycurgus more excellent than that of Carneades.[94]

The political thought of Tignosi and Poggio, as I suggested in Chapter II, may be viewed as part of an emerging ideology of the Medici party: the materialization of law seems bound to the new political real-

93. E. Cristiani: "Una inedita invettiva giovanile di Marsilio Ficino," *Rinascimento*, 2d. ser., 6 (1966 [1967]), 209–22.

94. *Letters*, I, 90; cf. *Opera omnia*, p. 631. The occasion of the letter was the selection of Giovanni di Bartolomeo Guidi, whom Ficino was comparing to Lycurgus, as a prior of the Florentine Signoria (i.e., in 1471): see Chapter IX, n. 25, below.

ities of Medici power. Most scholars would describe the political economy of the Trecento in terms of rising power of the corporations, where
the great guilds, and the lesser ones, asserted themselves most fully. Cut-
ting through these structures was an emerging economic elite, described
variously as an aristocracy or an oligarchy. Whether the Medici attempted to dominate these or merely to provide them their political
direction—I have argued elsewhere that the latter better describes early
Medici rule—it must yet be acknowledged that in the Quattrocento
unifying political forces were at work. Francesco Ercole described this
evolution through a study of public law in his *Dal comune al principato*.[95]
Jacob Burckhardt himself had merely called the Florentine republican
polity a "less clear" expression of the princely state as a work of art.[96] As
politics became a question no longer of individual, corporate forces but
of the unified structures of one great corporation, should we not then
expect that law should lose its normative role, a giving "to each its own,"
as the body politic becomes more like a giant corporate body?[97]

   And should we not then expect to see ideas mirroring the new corporate entity? Should not law lose its association with justice, its mediating role between the goodness and will of God and the whims of
the particular? And should it not be more instrumental, regulating the
crew (in that favorite humanist analogy) for the sake of the ship? Indeed
for Cristoforo Landino, Virgil's Aeneas is much like Cosimo, one who
could guide the ship through stormy seas to a safe harbor. Aeneas saw
the necessities of the course as a whole, avoiding the particular and apparent good.[98] In a more abstract form this "philosophy of ends" appears in a lengthy excursus by Landino, in his *Disputationes Camaldulenses*, on evil's relation to the highest good: evil, he says, is whatever results
beyond the intention of one carrying out any action.[99] In the same dialogue he would also describe, in a hyperbole, the ideal citizen as one
who stood above the others, at the gates of the city, inviting in the useful and good and throwing out the useless and dangerous; and then this
sage would put the city in order by seeing to its littlest detail.[100] In his
De iciarchia of the late 1460s, Leon Battista Alberti would also emphasize a leader's need to regulate the particular not according to ethical
norms but for the good of the whole. The city, he said, was like a large

95.   Florence, 1929.

96.   Burckhardt, *Civilization of the Renaissance in Italy*, pp. 40–41.

97.   For this theme, see now Brown, "Platonism in Fifteenth-Century Florence."

98.   *Disputationes Camaldulenses*, ed. P. Lohe, books 3, 4.

99.   Ibid., pp. 97–109.

100.   Ibid., pp. 28ff. For Landino's source, see E. M. Waith, "Landino and Maximus of
Tyre," *Renaissance Quarterly* 13 (1960), 289–94.

family.[101] And he had compared the family head (in his *Della famiglia*) to a spider in the middle of a large nest, with strands going out in all directions. If anything touched any strand, the spider would feel the movement at once and take action.[102] The highest expression of the philosophy of ends of course comes from Machiavelli: "in human affairs, . . . where there is no court of appeals, one looks to the end."[103]

One might want to account for the thought of Marsilio Ficino and his idea of the contemplative life as but one expression, albeit a rather elaborate one, of the new political ideal of the unified Renaissance state. As Tignosi argued, the particular things of the world have to be analyzed in their interrelatedness: over them the mind stands sovereign and divine. Indeed Ficino's contemplative life requires the mind not to be absorbed by the world but to rule it, to understand externals as interrelated realities that, once understood, can be controlled.

The origins of the Platonic Academy might so be explained if we were looking merely at the calm, rational student of Niccolò Tignosi, studying his notes on Aristotle but realizing that Plato offered broader perspectives for exploring the contemplative life. But what is this young student doing outside the classroom, apart from studying his Greek and reading up on his Latin philosophical sources? Is he the rational scholar alone? Or is he also the unnamed adolescent, or like this adolescent, who joins with laymen and clerics in evening discussions of the Christian virtues, discussions led and recorded by that priest and canon of the Medici church of San Lorenzo, Lorenzo Pisano? During a discussion this young man is so moved by the contemplation of the divine that he assumes for a time a trancelike state, filling the faces of the assembled brothers and laymen with smiles and tears of joy.[104] Such meetings in Florentine churches and convents provided Lorenzo Pisano with the themes for his dialogues of the 1450s and 1460s, lengthy works which, as Ficino pointed out to Cosimo, "hardly anything of importance to theology is excluded."[105]

Lorenzo Pisano's New Laws of Wisdom

Lorenzo Pisano (ca. 1391–1465) is a strange, elusive figure.[106] He wrote a commentary of at least eighteen books on Solomon's *Song of Songs*, a

---

101. In *Opere volgari*, ed. C. Grayson, vol. 2 (Bari, 1966), pp. 266–67.

102. *Della famiglia*, pp. 215–16.

103. *Il principe*, ed. S. Bertelli (Milan, 1960), chap. 18.

104. See below, pp. 159, 168.

105. *Opera omnia*, p. 615; *Letters* I, 48–49.

106. For Lorenzo Pisano, see the early biographical sketch by his nephew Teofilo, in

poem strange and elusive in itself, which only by heavy allegorizing and the embarrassment of tradition has been preserved in various canons of sacred writings. Marsilio Ficino wrote to Cosimo de' Medici that Solomon wove an "intricate knot" into the work, which Lorenzo Pisano had taken eighteen books ("if I remember aright") to unravel.[107] The allegorical commentators then and now have viewed the erotic song of Solomon as God choosing his people or Christ taking as his bride the Church. Lorenzo Pisano's commentary has not come to light, but he understood the erotic content of the poem, as he explained elsewhere, under the theme that one who seeks beauty must also seek the truth.[108] Ficino was convinced, for he later wrote that just as we are not troubled by the erotic passages in Solomon's *Song*, so should we not be bothered by similar passages in Plato's *Phaedrus*.[109] Beauty, truth, and love permeate the dialogues of Lorenzo Pisano. During the 1450s he gathered some of the best and brightest young Florentines into his circle. He had to cajole some, who naturally adhered to the "passions of youth"; others were too dispassionate, allured not by the sexual enticements of girls but by the beauty of eloquence. But the best of the youths, even if they pursued eloquence, were rosy-cheeked, bright-eyed, impressionable, and unblemished by sexual intercourse. When the interlocutors hit the proper chord a youth would swoon, press into the sides of an older companion, and go into a trance; all would wait, moved and speechless, as he recovered himself.[110] These youth were all that Lorenzo Pisano knew of eros: in love he would gather them under his wings, "as a hen gathers chicks."[111] This love was spiritual and erotic: it would soon find its echo in the "love letters" of Marsilio Ficino.

Lorenzo Pisano's background is curious—so curious that Cardinal Mercati has argued that there might be two figures of that name. Yet to the Lorenzo Pisano praised by Ficino the following *curriculum* seems to

---

cod. 688, Biblioteca Universitaria, Pisa, in two versions, fol. 95v and fols. 113–15 (see Appendix A); Moreni, *Continuazione delle memorie istoriche*, II, 192–97; Gherardi, ed., *Statuti*, pp. 415, 441; A. Mancini, "Laurentius canonicus pisanus," *Bollettino storico pisano*, I, no. 1 (1932), pp. 33–47; Kristeller, *Supplementum Ficinianum*, II, 349; Mercati, *Codici latini*, pp. 84–86, 98–105, 274–86; Mercati, *Ultimi contribuiti alla storia degli umanisti* (Vatican City, 1939), fasc. I, pp. 68–70. See also the works cited in n. 127, below. For the problem of the two Lorenzo Pisanos, see Appendix A.

107. See p. 12, above.

108. *De amore*, Magl. XXI 115, fol. 118.

109. Commentary on the *Phaedrus*, ed. in M. J. B. Allen, *Marsilio Ficino and the Phaedran Charioteer* (Berkeley, 1981), p. 79.

110. For Lorenzo's description of the youths, see especially the *De amore*, Magl. XXI 115, fols. 3, 12v, 24, and *passim*; for "swoonings," ibid., fol. 5v, and the *Dialogi quinque*, Laur. S. Marco 457, fol. 55v.

111. *De amore*, Magl. XXI 115, fols. 12v–13: his source of the image is Matt. 23:37.

belong.[112] The son of one Giovanni, he was born about 1391 in Terriciola, a small town between Pisa and Volterra.[113] Pisan parentage or citizenship probably gives him the tag *Pisanus*. He came to Florence in the early fifteenth century as a gold- and silversmith but quit the profession in a huff when a work commissioned for Florence was rejected by the government.[114] Abandoning the world for religious studies but not wanting to become a "priest for peasants" (according to his nephew's biography), he began studies in theology under Evangelista da Pisa, a lecturer at the Augustinian school of the convent of Santo Spirito and a teacher to Giannozzo Manetti.[115] Humanistic studies, including evidently some Greek, were probably under another of Manetti's teachers, Ambrogio Traversari.[116]

Then in 1428 Cosimo de' Medici's father, Giovanni di Bicci, created a canonry for him and another for Antonio degli Agli at the Medici church of San Lorenzo.[117] This prestigious position suggests that Lorenzo Pisano had an aristocratic background, and the nineteenth-century chronicler of San Lorenzo, Domenico Moreni, offered the Pisan family Gambacorta as a possibility.[118] Certainly he appears to have been from a better family. Lorenzo's sister, Bartolomea, had married into the noble Palmieri family of Pisa (and the philosopher of some note, Mattia, not to be confused with the Florentine humanist, Matteo, was her son).[119]

112. See Appendix A.

113. Mancini, "Laurentius canonicus pisanus," p. 35.

114. Mentioned by Lorenzo Pisano, *De misericordia*, in preface to Cosimo de' Medici, Munich, Bayer. Staatsbibl., Clm 109, fol. IV, and in Teofilo's biographical sketch (see Appendix A), Pisa, Bibl. Univ., cod. 688, fols. 95v, 113–113v.

115. Teofilo, *Vita*, cod. cit., fols. 95v, 113v (Teofilo mentions also studies in Bologna and Ferrara), and Mancini, "Laurentius canonicus pisanus," p. 37.

116. Mancini, "Laurentius canonicus pisanus," p. 37. See also Traversari's letter to Niccolò Niccoli, ed. and discussed by Mercati, *Ultimi contributi*, pp. 68–70.

117. Lorenzo Pisano mentions his rescue by Giovanni di Bicci in the preface to his *De misericordia* (Munich, Bayer. Staatsbibl., Clm 109), fol. IV. See also Moreni, *Continuazione delle memorie istoriche*, II, 192–93. The provision for the canonry appears in MAP CLV, fols. 1ff.; fols. 10ff. for the selection of Lorenzo Pisano. It was created on 28 November 1428 and paid for through the Monte Comune (fol. 3v). The provision, creating two canonries (the other for Antonio degli Agli), prohibited the canons from being absent for more than two continuous months, and even then substitute masses had to be arranged (fol. 5v). I have seen no evidence that Lorenzo Pisano had to renounce his canonry when, for instance, he was *cubicularius* at Rome under Nicholas V. Antonio degli Agli renounced his canonry, apparently for good, on 17 December 1436 (ibid., fol. 17v).

118. Moreni, *Continuazione delle memorie istoriche*, II, 193.

119. Lorenzo Pisano refers to his son-in-law, Mattia, and Mattia's translation of Herodotus, in his *Dialogi quinque* (see the citation of Mercati, *Codici latini*, pp. 284–85, and Laur. S. Marco 457, fol. 57; cf. fols. 85, 161v). The Pisan catasto of 1428 lists Bartolomea,

In 1431 and 1435 Lorenzo lectured on Dante at the University of Florence.[120] From the 1430s until his death in September 1465 we know little, except that he evidently spent a period of time in Rome during the 1440s and the 1450s.[121] He dedicated or attempted to dedicate a work to every pope from Eugenius IV to Paul II.[122] From the figures appearing in Lorenzo's dialogues we can deduce that he moved in high intellectual circles. Among Florentine clerics appear Evangelista da Pisa, Antonio degli Agli, and Leonardo Dati. The "Paulus" of one dialogue, identified as a physician and natural philosopher knowledgeable in Latin, Greek, and Arabic is very likely the famous Paolo Toscanelli.[123] The argumentative doctor named "Nicolaus," I suggested earlier, is probably Niccolò Tignosi. Other figures in the dialogues test the imagination: the unnamed adolescent dedicated to music and Plato could well be Ficino himself.[124]

Lorenzo Pisano left many works, most of which are extant in unique manuscripts.[125] His short, early compendium of maxims, an *Enchiridion*, dedicated to Leonardo Dati, seems to have had the widest circulation.[126]

---

aged thirty-six, as the wife of Giovanni di Michele de' Palmieri, aged forty-one, and, among the children, Mattia, aged four and a half (B. Casini, ed., *Il catasto di Pisa del 1428–29* [Pisa, 1964], p. 69, no. 303).

120.   Gherardi, ed., *Statuti*, pp. 415, 441. Teofilo, *Vita*, cod. cit., fols. 95v, 113v, mentions these as well as lectures on the *Psalter*.

121.   Teofilo, *Vita*, fols. 113v–14. Teofilo calls him a *cubicularius* of Nicholas V. Lorenzo evidently died 3 or 4 September 1465, and his death is recorded on 4 September in records of San Lorenzo, Archivio di San Lorenzo, vol. 2413, fols. 36v, 39v. The date of death mentioned by Teofilo (cod. cit., fol. 114v), "1466," by the way, is correct as written in the Pisan style (the new year beginning, like Florence, 25 March, but, unlike Florence, advancing a year).

122.   See the texts cited below, p. 162, and in Appendix C.

123.   Noted by Mercati, *Codici latini*, p. 285.

124.   The *Dialogi quinque* refer to an "adolescens ingenuus praestantis indolis moribus fortuna bene ornatus et non solum ad musicam sed etiam ad recondita studia ingenio facili et arguto solers, qui etiam superioribus orationibus adfuerat, coetanus nostro [*sc.* Matthiae Palmerio] et in amoribus pudicus [pudicis *cod.*] et litterarum certaminibus indivisus comes" (Laur. S. Marco 457, fol. 203). This Mattia Palmieri was born about 1424 (see n. 119, above), so Ficino, born 1433, was roughly "coetanus"; the "fortuna bene ornatus," which I take to indicate wealth, seems less fitting. In the dialogue, this youth quotes from the sibyls, speaks of the *mens primae intelligentiae*, cites Hermes Trismegistus (from Apuleius's *De deo Socratis*) and Plato, and finally, after arguing that the world was full of spirits, mentioned that "in omnibus omnia semper rediguntur ad unum in illo genere primum" (fol. 206). For Ficino's possible presence in Lorenzo Pisano's *De amore*, see pp. 168–70, below.

125.   For some of Lorenzo Pisano's minor works, see Appendix C.

126.   This collection of maxims is not especially relevant to our study. I have seen Vat. Ottob. lat. 368, fols. 41v–66 (pref. inc.: Mea quidem sententia; text inc.: Cor simplex liberum), two versions copied by Teofilo, in the Pisan cod. cit., fols. 2–27v, 105–12v, and the version in Vat. lat. 6301, fols. 69–99. The work described by Kristeller, *Supplementum*

None of his works has been studied, although the *De amore* has received some scholarly attention.[127] His lengthy commentary on the *Song of Songs*, praised by Ficino, has not come to light. Three long dialogues are extant: the *Dialogi humilitatis*, dedicated to Nicholas V,[128] the *De amore*, probably from the late 1450s,[129] and the *Dialogi quinque*, probably from the early 1460s.[130] Since we are interested in Ficino's scholastic background, we must be careful with the latter two, since Ficino may already be influencing Lorenzo Pisano—it is possible, as I said, that he is an unnamed interlocutor in either or both. The dialogues are of the "virtues and vices" genre, broadly from an Augustinian perspective. The author tended to assign each book of the dialogue one title based on its theme and a second title after its chief interlocutor. Some of these names correspond to figures we can identify; each has a personality and probably corresponds to one of Lorenzo Pisano's contemporaries.[131] Though Lorenzo may have been creative in constructing scenes, his imagination, unlike that of some of his humanist contemporaries, did not run wild, and we may speculate that some of the more dramatic confrontations between conservative clerics and humanistic and paganizing laymen, between the censorious elderly and the poetic young, did take place and that the opinions expressed by the interlocutors correspond to actual views of his contemporaries. Unlike the humanists, Lorenzo offered no dialogue labeled as formal or disputatious.

Ficinianum, II, 349, as Lorenzo's *Paradoxa theologorum*, printed Basel 1569, is a version of this *Enchiridion*.

127.   Discussed briefly by P. Zambelli, "Platone, Ficino e la magia," in E. Hora and E. Kessler, *Studia humanitatis: Ernesto Grassi zum 70. Geburtstag* (Munich, 1973), pp. 127–29, and M. A. Iusim, "Neopublikovannyi traktat Lorentso Pizano," *Srednie veka* 42 (1978), 122–44. A translation of parts of the latter was kindly read to me by the staff of the Associazione "Amicizia URSS–Italia," Rome.

128.   Vat. lat. 961 (pref. inc., fol. 1: Quando mihi ingenii singularitatem; text inc., fol. 3v: Cum die qua a fidelium ecclesia).

129.   See Appendix B.

130.   In two manuscripts: Laur. S. Marco 457 (which I shall be cite) and Ottob. lat. 2051 (for the latter, see Mancini, *Codici latini*, pp. 278, 284, and Kristeller, *Iter*, II, 435). Book 2, "De natura demonum," and Books 3 and 4, "De tentatione," may be revisions of works composed earlier (see Appendix C). The manuscript in the Laurenziana, S. Marco 457, was given by Cosimo de' Medici to the San Marco library (noted on flyleaf, now fol. 3v; see also Ullman and Stadter, *Public Library*, p. 238, no. 967). The first dialogue is entitled *De casu primae intelligentiae*, the title used for the whole work in Teofilo's *Vita*, cod. cit., fols. 95v, 114. The work is late. Lorenzo refers to a *De invidia* he had once sent to Calixtus III (reference in Laur. S. Marco 457, fol. 185v). There is also a mention (fol. 56) of "Iacopus . . . hodie pater generalis fratrum minorum" (see Appendix B). Lorenzo sent the dialogues and an accompanying oration to Pius II (cited Appendix C).

131.   This point has been made by Mercati, *Codici latini*, p. 286.

Lorenzo Pisano's world is set in a convent and ruled by love. The world embraces laymen, however, often identified as young and humanistic. Following a *topos*, Lorenzo had the world expand as the dialogues progress: new people join, "drawn by the news of the previous day's discussion." He treats most broadly of love in his *De amore*, of course; the *Dialogi humilitatis* deal with man's desires and how they can be controlled; the *Dialogi quinque* emphasize the nature of sin. The theme of all the dialogues is how and why man moves upward from or through the world toward God.

As Lorenzo explained in his *Dialogues of Humility* (early 1450s), man's difficulty in striving upward was best described by Paul: man's animal nature exists before his spiritual nature, for the former is with man from birth but the latter is bestowed only through grace (1 Cor. 15:46–47).[132] Natural man, like everything else, is ruled by desire, and he possesses naturally only his intellectual faculties. The will, however, is free and can lead man out of his natural state.[133] Lorenzo is characteristically graphic in describing the difficulty:

> Who will readily turn the nature of the body and the senses, weak and always prone to carnal things, and the phantasms always bent down and seeking the blooming cheeks and pretty lips of girls— who, I ask you, will turn these to an obedience to temperance, to a clean heart and to a mind not corrupted with evil desires?[134]

With some degree of humility, however, the vices into which man naturally falls promote an internal sadness. This sadness leads to grief, then to penitence, which then leads to the wisdom to avoid the same vices. Paul, who boasted of "weeping with those who weep" and "rejoicing with those who rejoice" (Rom. 12:15) expressed this also: "I rejoice not because you were grieved, but because you were grieved into penitence" (cf. 2 Cor. 7:9).[135]

Through a variety of steps, Paul explained, the body can be chastened and the spirit made free. The highest earthly state is reached when the soul either through a gift of God or through a *habitus* of virtue (itself a

---

132. Vat. lat. 961, fol. 44v: "Doctor . . . ipse gentium ante alios virtutis et sapientie gratia venerandus primum inesse homini quod animale quam quod spirituale constantissime asseverat, quia animale a natura homini cohabitat, spirituale gratia largitur."

133. Fol. 45–45v.

134. Fol. 47–47v: "Quis, rogito vos, naturam corporis sensuumque infirmam perpronamque ad carnalia et phantasmata semper inclinata et ad petentia puellarum floridas genas et labella concinna saviis ad obediendum temperantiae, cordique pernitido mentique neque infectae malis desideriis retorqueret?"

135. Fol. 61v.

gift of God) overcomes its natural forces and rests in the enjoyment of
the eternal. In overcoming worldly cares we become dead in the world,
"for you are dead and your life is hidden away with Christ in God" (Col.
3:3).[136]

Humility, Lorenzo argues, is a sort of "rule" and a "proper and correct measure of the appetite," necessary because desire can find no rest
without it.[137] Its opposite, pride, is the queen of the vices: she will not
bow her high head to eternal laws or to God himself. Other vices can be
corrected through an internal order of penitence (which operates even
among pagans); pride is without order and leads all to destruction.[138]

The restraints upon the appetite and its fulfillment in its object, therefore, are neither arbitrary nor accidental. There is a hierarchy of desires,
ruled by a single ordering principle, humility. This "measure," however,
is nothing more than man's means of proceeding through the hierarchy
and uniting one's desire with God. Lorenzo Pisano persists in describing the passions and their objects as ordered, hierarchical realities. God's
grace does not have to look about and search, define the substance of
the sinner's travail, or strike a particular chord according to the moment.
The final stage is when we are seized to the divine. But first we make a
step upward, and then a second, and then others follow in order: these
are not simple, and "some are known to us and some are not known."
But objectively they are there.[139]

Since they are objective, they have appeared in all places and all times,
and they were known in some form in pagan antiquity. Indeed Lorenzo
Pisano notes that pagan philosophers themselves understood humility:
they described, in their way, the grief and penance that follow after mis-
placed desires.

136. Fol. 82v: "Ultimus gradus est cum anima, vel dei dono raptim ad divina raptatur
vel cum virtutum habitu qui et ipse munus est dei, naturales excedit vires et in divinis
ludit." See also n. 139, below. For the entire argument, see fols. 82v–101v.

137. Fols. 106v–7: ". . . humilitas veluti regula quaedam ac propria rectaque mensura
appetitus per sese semper errantis adnitentisque."

138. Fol. 120v: "Sola superbia habet aversionem a deo hoc ipso quod non vult legibus
aeternis deo ipso suaeque bonitati altum caput subicere, et naturam ipsam divinamque
voluntatem bonum ipsum leges inrefragabiles in contrarium mutare sua pre libidine pro-
perat festinatque ⟨et⟩ ardet. Idcirco caetera peccata in ordine divinae legis cum corrup-
tione et turpitudine aliquo modo secundum extremam consonantiam stant. Sola superbia ab omni ordine recedit."

139. Fol. 82v: "[S]icuti ad Iohannem evangelistam scribens adseverat beatus Dyonis-
ius, sunt iustis in hac vita futurorum bonorum pregustationes. Medius qui primo subse-
quitur gradus, sicuti reliqui ipse quoque suos habet gradus, et ipsi gradus nec simplices
sunt, qui cum multis constet affectionibus et habitibus partim nobis cognitis partim in-
cognitis."

Although there be to some extent a difference, and the things said in the manner of philosophers are at a variance (for they have with great vigilance investigated such things, or, as our people think, they refer all such things to the mind of inner man), since such things are regarded by the wise solely through the intuition of the mind and lack proper appellations, and since external things are quite similar to internal things, investigating their teaching in the proper measure will in no way hurt you.[140]

The question of the value of pagan philosophy generates most of the tension in Lorenzo's dialogues. The discussions are rife with quotations from the prophets and the Christian scriptures, and from the Church Fathers: Is not their wisdom sufficient to lead us to the good life? In the first dialogue on humility, the priest "Nicolaus," described as learned both in Latin and in Greek, opposed the "pure and sincere wisdom of the Church fathers" to the degeneracy of pagan philosophy. He chided Lorenzo Pisano as follows:

At one time when you were younger you so avidly pursued, day and night, sacred letters, that whenever we came to you we found you meditating on and speaking about the law, the prophets, and the gospels. At present, however, you while away your time with I know not what insoluble questions of the sophists—those "pure trifles" Paul warned us to avoid—and you devote yourself to them with your whole heart.

Where now do you think the mind of Aristotle is, corrupted by envy against his teacher, with its circuits of dialectics and Menandrian subtleties and petty teachings ground to dust? Where the lasciviousness of Plato, whom it never shamed to fill nearly all his dialogues with the loving kisses of boys? Where the knotty snares of the Stoics and the insensibility of Diogenes redounding with pride? Where the weak and effeminate madness of the Epicureans? In the choirs of angels, my friend?

O would that that pure and sincere wisdom of the ancient Fathers had flourished, a flower yet fresh and giving off the scent of

140.   Fol. 61v: "Prima affectio quae penitentem hominem ac reflectentem vestigia ex superbiae aviis obsitis spinis ac vepribus ad humilitatis planitiem tangit, profecto interna tristitia est, que etiam sua vehementia in corpus per dolorem redundat. Qui utique motus est asperior? sensibus alienus? . . . Verum enim vero licet diversum admodum sit, plurimum dissideant [dissidant *cod*.] ista e more philosophorum, qui cura [*lege* cum ?] multa vigilantia talia indagarunt aliter ut nostris placet, qui omnia ad interioris hominis mentem referunt, tractare dumtaxat, tum quia talia solo mentis intuitu sapientibus contuentur nominibusque carent, tum quia plurimam similitudinem cum interioribus exteriora [interioribus cum exteriora *cod*] servant, de sententia eorum minime vos penitebit."

eternal life! O would that through this great reverence the mouths
barking out shameless things should come to their senses and become greatly ashamed to cry out I know not what fables and lies
of the pagans![141]

When another participant in the dialogue, the humanistic and philosophizing priest Leonardo Dati, heard Lorenzo so rebuked, he turned
bright red: he, after all, had adorned his own poetry with such pagan
follies.[142] Dati then smiled and indicated that he would not engage in
subtleties. So "Nicolaus" resumed with a long oration in praise of the
Virgin and on the gifts of humility.[143]

The next day (the dialogue "Leonardus"), before a larger group
("drawn by the news of the previous day's oration"[144]), Leonardo Dati
led the discussion and opposed his method to that of his predecessor:

> Although from the things spoken by you, with great talent and
> much care, the learned are able to understand what humility is
> (since the first thing in an oration is to delimit the nature of the
> question through definition), in this matter your arguments are
> not easily repeated to nor in common use by the slower and less
> learned, nor are your arguments self-evident. Clearly your method
> of speaking is of long standing: nor is this method uncultivated or
> alien to the wise. But these times have changed along with many
> other things your type of teaching, and they have given us new
> and not unpleasant laws of wisdom.

141.   Fol. 4 and ed. in Mercati, *Codici latini*, p. 100: "Olim tu iunior cum esses vehe-
menti quodam ardore inremissoque tempore die et nocte sacras litteras ita animo invol-
vebas, ut nunquam iremus ad te, quin aliquid de lege et prophetis deque evangeliis te
meditantem ac loquentem non offendissemus. In presentiarum autem nescio quibus in-
determinatis sophistarum quaestiunculis, quin meris nugis, quas Paulus cavere monuit,
ita attonite ut ita loquar vacas hisque toto incumbis pectore. . . . "

Fols. 4v–5: "Ubinam Aristotelis infectam in magistrum invidia [invidae *cod.*] mentem
suis dialeticae gyris atque Menandreis acutulis minutisque ad pulverem detritis doctrinis,
lasciviamque Platonis quem nequaquam dispuduit puerorum amoribus ac saviis ferme
omnes replere dyalogos, Stoicorum involutas tendiculas, Diogenis duritiam redundan-
tem superbia, Epicureorum enervem effeminatamque vesaniam, esse creditis? Forte inter
angelorum choreas, mi hospes, tu arbitrare? O viguisset illa priscorum patrum pura
sinceraque sapientia, flos illabatus redolens vitae aeternae odoribus, ut dispuderent tanta
reverentia ora impudibunda latrantia nescio quas gentilium fabellas atque fallacias clami-
tare et resipiscerent."

142.   Fol. 5 and Mercati, *Codici latini*, p. 101: "Noster etiam Leonardus cum haec perho-
nesta convitia in me iactari advertisset, haud sine rubore tulit, eo quod ipse carminibus
suavissimis illectationibus ilarique prorsus illitis modestia solitus sit ludere." For concur-
ring contemporary opinions of Dati's poetry, see Della Torre, *Storia*, pp. 295–97.

143.   Fols. 5–38v.

144.   Fol. 39: "Equidem arbitror licet nostras frequenti celebratione viserent aediculas,
hesterne orationis rumor illos traxisse. . . . "

Therefore I am prepared to attempt to look first at what humility is, and, in order to make it stand more easily before our eyes, I believe we must examine step by step what part of the soul it is located in: whether in one part or many; if in one part, whether it is always there or has been taken from another part; if it has different powers at different times, whether it should be described with some words at some times, and other words at other times.[145]

Here Dati is of course outlining a series of scholastic questions. What is interesting is how philosophy is applied here not to make an argument more sophisticated and subtle but simply to make it clear—more easily grasped by the "slower and less learned." This may seem a curious use of terms, particularly if one wants to follow most historians' opinions of the philosophical renaissance, that it was a movement away from simple, humanistic studies toward the esoteric obscurities of Platonism. I shall merely pose the problem now. It may be worth recalling also Ficino's letter to Antonio Serafico of September 1454, quoted at the beginning of this chapter: in taking up philosophical categories he is consciously moving toward a simpler discourse, away from the elegant and elaborate way of speaking common to the humanists.

For Lorenzo Pisano, Platonic teachings of the *reversio animi* especially helped point the way toward suppressing earthly desires and making, as Paul said, the world dead for us. In the *Dialogues of Humility* he railed against the "shameful deeds and insolent words" of the "lazy and gluttonous" monks. How much more are they to be condemned in that Plato, a "pagan alien from God and from the gifts of Christ," yet described well the dangers of earthly desires: "He said that death was when the soul, as yet situated in the body, with philosophy as a guide despises bodily attractions and roots out the insidious snares of desires and the other passions of worldly cares."[146]

---

145. Fol. 40–40v: "Tametsi ex tuis ingenio acri multa et cura peroratis colligi possit a doctis quid humilitas sit, quod primum in oratione est naturam rei per diffinitionem constringere, nequaquam dumtaxat sunt tua tardiusculis et semidoctis dictu facilia usuque obvia nec per se dilucent. Vetus tuus fuit plane mos orare, minime equidem rudis abque sapientibus alienus. Sed tempora ipsa cum ⟨multa tum⟩ [mul-/(fol. 40v)tis tuum *cod.*] illud docendi genus immutavere, et sapientie novas nec ingratas ⟨dederunt⟩ [dedit *cod.*] leges. Idcirco imprimis quaesitum ire me accingam, quid humilitas sit, quod ut facilius pre oculis obversetur peraccurate pedetentim indagandum arbitror, qua animae parte suas locarit sedes, unane an plurimis; sin una, semper insit an ab alia susceptarit; sin diversis pro tempore potentiis diversetur, aliis aliisne verbis describi debeat." The page break at *multis tuum* and the grammatical confusion may point toward a lacuna in the text.

146. Fol. 94: "Mortui enim estis et vita vestra abscondita est cum Christo in deo, ut stomachabundus probra infamissima et convitia dedecore plena haud aniculis delirisque senibus sed nostri ordinis hominibus perditissimis deditis somno et ventri obiiciam. Talia Platonem hominem gentilem alienum a deo et a Christi muneribus ex parte non

Platonic doctrines play a greater role in Lorenzo Pisano's dialogue *De amore*, set in Florence perhaps in the late 1430s or the early 1440s and written probably in the late 1450s, with the interlocutors Evangelista da Pisa, Antonio degli Agli, one Cipriano perhaps to be identified with Cipriano Rucellai, and several other figures unnamed or unidentifiable.[147] For any dialogue set in the 1440s an appearance by Marsilio Ficino (b. 1433) would have required great imagination; but by the time the dialogues were composed Ficino may well have been influencing Lorenzo Pisano. Indeed, early in the dialogue an unnamed adolescent appears, virginal and modest in appearance, learned in both Greek and Latin, and excelling in music and the inner secrets of philosophy. He had been found reading Plato's *De amore* (that is, the *Symposium*), one of the participants mentions, and not with a "simple reading" but with such care and intelligence that he was "almost out of his senses." The youth confessed that he had been absorbed in the work, and he even promised to translate the *De amore* into Latin if all so urged it. But he said he was unworthy to explain it before such a dignified gathering. Then Antonio degli Agli, identified as his friend and former teacher, urged him on, quoting from Virgil: "Not with the pipe alone, but with voice do you match your master" (*Eclogues* 5.48).[148] The adolescent then contrasted two ways of philosophizing:

---

fugerunt, unde aiebat: mors enim dicitur cum anima adhuc in corpore constituta corporeas illecebras philosophia ducente contemnit et cupiditatum dulces insidias reliquasque curarum ex se [ex se] sese *cod.*] eruit passiones." Cf. *Phaedo*, 64c–68c.

147.   For the dating of the work, see Appendix B. The preface states that the dialogues took place at Santo Spirito not long before the death of Evangelista da Pisa. This Evangelista was an Augustinian friar at the convent of Santo Spirito, where he taught Manetti logic, and was also a teacher of logic at the University of Florence. Nothing is known about him after 1435 (see the sketch by Vespasiano da Bisticci, *Vite*, II, 393–94, and A. Greco's notes to same). If the Cipriano in the dialogue is Cipriano Rucellai (see the next note), then a setting in the 1440s seems likely.

148.   Who is this adolescent? The text does not seem to be clear, and often the transitions in Lorenzo Pisano's dialogues are confusing. In the Budapest manuscript of the *De amore* (Clmae 185), this Cipriano is described in the title of the first dialogue (fol. 1): "Presbyteri Laurentii Pisani dialogus primus de amore qui dicitur Cyprianus ab adolescente ingenuo et liberalibus disciplinis et lingua greca et latina adprime peritissimo." The dialogue names at the beginning Lorenzo himself, an adolescent Cipriano, and Antonio degli Agli, who were visiting Evangelista da Pisa. Antonio begins, addressing Evangelista and asking him to explain divine love. This Evangelista says a few words and then explains that such a question is almost beyond human understanding. Then Lorenzo introduces an unnamed adolescent. This adolescent is the mysterious Platonizing figure referred to. After mentioning his interest in Plato, the adolescent and his *magister* Antonio degli Agli exchange a few words, the adolescent resumes, and Evangelista da Pisa says a few words. Finally (Magl. XXI 115, fol. 6v) an adolescent identified as Cipriano begins speaking, as if resuming the earlier unnamed adolescent's arguments. It would appear that Cipriano was the adolescent speaking all along (as evidently assumed by Mercati and P. Zambelli, who have looked at these passages). But still another adolescent, dedi-

There are two principal types of discourse. . . . One is liberal and pleasant, enveloped to an extent with a hidden art and worthy of a learned and noble man, of which I heartily approve, but which has grown out of fashion and which the philosophers of our time reject. In my opinion, Plato was the most distinguished exponent of this approach, and among Latin authors our Cicero flourished in it beyond all others. The other approach—the one our native philosophers confess to use, and they say they are emulating Aristotle—is terse, dry, crafty, and full of thorns and reservations, and not only does it require dazzling erudition and indefatigable talent, but it has need of sibyls and oracles![149]

What was Plato's golden eloquence and clear discourse expounding on? That the world was ruled by love.

If indeed from the highest and first creature to the final dregs of nature, inert and unformed matter, you make one world (*mundus*), also called *mundus* ["elegant"] from its very beauty, it clearly is necessary that all things be folded, bound, and tied together by a certain bond and by reciprocal ties, in such a way that all things

---

cated to the liberal arts, interrupts Cipriano (fol. 7). Later it becomes evident that many youths are present.

M. A. Iusim, "Neopublikovannyi traktat Lorentso Pizano," tentatively identified this Cipriano with Cipriano Rucellai (p. 127). This identification seems highly probable. Vespasiano da Bisticci (*Vite*, II, 369–70) gave one Cipriano Rucellai a brief biographical sketch, saying little about him except that he was learned in Greek and Latin, was celibate, died "very young," and had held great intellectual promise. The given name Cipriano appears in the "Berlinghieri detto Bingeri di Naddo" branch of the Rucellai family (L. Passerini, *Genealogia e storia della famiglia Rucellai* [Florence, 1861], table II), but the dates for the three Ciprianos there could not fit our figure. Vespasiano da Bisticci's figure is surely the Cipriano Rucellai mentioned by Leonardo Dati in his preface to his commentary on Matteo Palmieri's *Città di vita*. He stated that this youth, after his death, appeared to Matteo in a dream or vision in 1451 and again in 1455 and showed him the nature of the angels, the celestial spheres, and the human soul, inspiring him to write out the great poetic work (ed. in A. M. Bandini, *Catalogus codicum latinorum Bibliothecae Mediceae Laurentianae* . . . [Florence, 1774–78], V, 79–84). With the striking description of this Platonizing "Cipriano" by Lorenzo Pisano, may we not speculate that the delay in founding the Academy, desired by Cosimo de' Medici from the late 1430s, was due to the tragic, early death of Cipriano Rucellai?

149. Magl. XXI 115, fols. 3v–4; Budapest, Clmae 185, fol. 3v; P. Zambelli, "Ficino, Platone e la magia," pp. 138–39, n. 39 (cf. E. Garin, "Donato Acciaiuoli cittadino," p. 230n.): "Duo sunt disserendi precipue genera, uti omnes plane nostis: liberale unum et iucundum, recondita arte dumtaxat perplexum [proplexum *Magl.*] et docto ingenuoque homine dignum, quod plurimum plane adprobo, licet inoleverit et nostri temporis philosophi illud aspernentur. In quo namque mea de mente Plato princeps fuit, et apud nos noster Cicero omnibus prelonge plurimum effloruit. Alterum autem est quo nostrates philosophi se uti fatentur et Aristotelem emulari dicunt, breve, aridum, argutum, plenum sentibus et scrupulis et non solum acri detritoque eruditione eget [aget *codd.*] ingenio, sed sibyllis et oraculis opus habet."

may continuously persist and endure. And if therefore we contemplate and diligently investigate with our minds each and every
thing, we shall find it to be nothing other than love which unites
and congeals all things into one, by means of similar repelling and
antagonistic qualities with which their natures are endued. For
truly no thing and no first nature . . . acts immediately through its
essence, but through qualities, appetites, and forces innate to it it
carries out its works.[150]

Others in the dialogue—Antonio degli Agli, Evangelista da Pisa, and
unnamed figures—join in the arguments. God is the father of all things,
who alone is all things in all things (quoting Hermes Trismegistus). He
ties all things together in uninterrupted series. All things are thus bound
together in "pleasing harmony."[151] Each thing in its place has a "natural
appetite" toward its own good, its peace, its beauty. Its end is unity.
Man is led by various "loves": one is of the body, the other of the spirit.
Love dwells naturally in man, leading man to the beautiful and good.
According to Plato friendship is natural to all. Love leads one to another. When one sees in another something beautiful and honest, one
burns with a recollection of the one Good. Then one becomes inflamed
by love. The lover becomes bound to the beloved through an insepara-
ble tie, making the two into one.[152]

The Platonic arguments of the dialogue do not arise without challenge. One man, *quidam semipaganus*, objected to the mingling of poetic
fallacies with philosophical truth;[153] another, who "had studied so much
Aristotle that he had nearly lost his tongue," went into an incomprehen-
sible scholastic discourse, then, finding himself ignored, shouted in de-
fiance and stalked out.[154] It is openly questioned by another whether
Virgil was really dedicated to Platonic teachings or merely happened
now and then to hit upon a "Platonic" doctrine when rapt in divine

150. Magl. XXI 115, fol. 7v; Budapest, Clmae 185, fol. 7; P. Zambelli, "Platone, Ficino e
la magia," p. 128: "Atqui si a summa primaque creatura ad ultimas rerum feces inertem
rudemque materiam unum mundum facitis, qui etiam ab ipso decore mundus dicitur,
necessarium plane est vinculo quodam mutuisque nexibus omnia complicari, constringi,
illigari, uti simul stent omnia permaneant perseverentque. Itaque si singula et universa
mente contemplabimini et diligenter indagabitis, non reperietis nisi amorem illum esse,
qui solum per similes qualitates resilientes repugnantesque indutas naturis in unum omnia adsotiet coaguletque. Nulla enim prorsus res nullaque natura . . . immediate per essentiam suam agit, sed per qualitates, appetitus, virtutes sibi insitas sua pernavat opera."
151. Magl. XXI 115, fols. 8v, 11, 26.
152. Ibid., fols. 25v–26, 32v, 74v, 96v–97.
153. Ibid., fol. 14v.
154. Ibid., fols. 34v–35. After the man left, Lorenzo noted, "cachinum continere nequi-
vimus" (fol. 35).

frenzy.[155] Another older theologian present, rather censorious in aspect, explained carefully that love's diffusion should be considered as the instrument of the Holy Spirit and that arguments drawn from non-Christian sources range from the misleading to the nonsensical.[156] The dialogue ends in harmony. One person says, as if to conclude:

> Both philosophers and theologians agree with poets, and those maddened with a subtler muse agree with those who naturally seek what is right, and I think none of our group would deny, that love . . . is nothing other than that wonderful sweetness and ineffable pleasantness which from communion, union, and common experience flows forth and conciliates all things with each other. . . . Whether in animated things or in things lacking a soul, . . . it is nothing beyond the essence of unity, simplicity, and goodness, which we call God and which we worship, as every ancient religion professes.[157]

If we wish to find the prototype of the Platonic Academy, we need look no further than the theological symposia sponsored by Lorenzo Pisano.[158] Specifically they are far closer to the Ficino model than the

155. Ibid., fol. 11; Budapest, Clmae 185, fol. 10v: "Noster vates an divino furore fuerit insanus an Platonis vestigia secutus licet ignorem, tamen haec preclara admodum ac prope divina in eius sexto protulit: 'Principio coelum ac terras . . .' [*Aen.* 6.724ff.]."

156. Magl. XXI 115, fols. 112v–16. This figure is Iacobus de Sarzuela, identified as Lorenzo Pisano's teacher. Lorenzo, a true *discipulus ingratus*, stated that this Iacobus began by quoting Plato's *De legibus* in Greek, but his pronunciation was so bad that all burst out laughing, and so he continued in Latin (fols. 112v–13). Then, when Iacobus paused in his attack on pagans, an older man present urged him to continue his arguments, but with less bitterness (fol. 116).

157. Magl. XXI 115, fols. 150v–51; Budapest, Clmae 185, fol. 161: "Philosophi una et theologi simulatque cum poetis etiam qui argutiori musa hac materia furentes dulce pansere [*sic*] cum reliquis probe ingeniatis viris quod nullum nostro grege abnuere arbitror asseveravere amorem . . . nil aliud utique esse [esset *Budapest*] nisi mel illud perdulce suavitatemque illam ineffabilem quae ex communione unione usu rerum similium effluit quae invicem omnia conciliat. Omnia enim trifariam primo discernuntur in rebus animatis et anima carentibus merisque corporibus et spiritibus ab materiei fece porro disiunctis, hec ultra nil esse preter essentiam unitatis simplicitatis et bonitatis quam [qua *Budapest*] deum dicimus et colimus quod omnis vetus religio fatetur."

158. Finding the model of the modern or early modern Academy, the scholarly gathering dedicated to the rational, scientific pursuit of truth, was a major aim of Arnaldo Della Torre, *Storia dell'Accademia platonica di Firenze* (for his summary of the model, see p. 237). He described carefully the types of learned gatherings before Ficino: but he was writing before Mercati and Kristeller and hence overlooked Lorenzo Pisano. According to Della Torre, the move away from the humanistic, "skeptical," disputatious type of discussion toward the "associazione del lavoro" and "correzione reciproca" is largely due to the nearly complete collapse of humanist erudition in Florence in the mid-Quattrocento—a necessary step, in his view, for the emergence of the Academy (ibid., pp. 237–

humanist disputations, where the speeches as often as not are *gratia exercitationis* and the personalities of the interlocutors are to a greater or lesser extent suppressed. Pisano sponsored a diversity of personalities, all speaking freely and each seeking truth. Those with whom he disagreed were still "good men"; the edge of his patience only wore when he found arrogance, pomposity, or intolerance. The participants' reactions to the speeches differ according to their age and temperament. But all emerge from the dialogues better, dedicated more than ever to truth and to love. Here also we could display the banner of the Platonic Academy: *A bono in bonum omnia diriguntur.*[159]

If Niccolò Tignosi provided Ficino his intellectual rigor, Lorenzo Pisano provided the poetry. If Tignosi stirred the intellect, Lorenzo moved the will. Lorenzo Pisano contributed especially in two significant areas to the Florentine philosophical renaissance. First, he showed how philosophy was important for the *reversio animi*: the soul, exiled in an earthly prison, can escape only by seeing through and seeing beyond the images presented to it, correcting its judgment, and raising itself toward the divine. Pagan philosophy provides a method for examining the internal structure of the soul as it assimilates the images before it. Second, philosophy enables us to understand the inner workings of the universe and the bond of love that connects the impulses of its apparently chaotic parts. An understanding of either sphere is aided by philosophy: categories need to be defined and related to one another. These relations can best be formulated through a logical and dialectical method, the "new laws of wisdom" learned from the philosophers. This idealism—the reality and comprehensibility of the world of ideas—is the most important link between Lorenzo Pisano and Ficino.

Yet even if Lorenzo was well ahead of his contemporaries in cultivating the philosophical method, he was far behind, even "medieval," in his philosophical positions and in his approach toward his sources. In the *Dialogues of Humility* he showed how man is naturally led to vice and afterward penitence: pagans and Christians alike are under this eternal law, the natural tendency of the intellect to grasp the corporeal. To the extent that pagans understand this, their philosophy can lead us to humility, and we can at least overcome this natural tendency to evil. This single, universal truth is that described by Jesus and by Paul, the

38). Della Torre views Giannozzo Manetti's consolatory dialogue on the death of his son (see pp. 70–71, above) as exceptional for the early Quattrocento: here Manetti's own arguments are effectively broken down by his adversary, and the conversation becomes a process of true discovery and learning (ibid., pp. 234–37).

159.   For the inscription of the Academy, see Ficino's letter to Francesco Musano, in *Opera omnia*, p. 609. Cf. n. 124, above.

"one light which enlightens all things" (cf. John 1:9).[160] Lorenzo is antihumanist in his lack of concern for getting at the complete Plato or the complete Aristotle, for understanding the relation of them, as individuals, toward their works, for appreciating their possible motivations for writing, for examining the works in their original corpus (despite, it seems, some knowledge of Greek), and for seeing any basis of comparability of human experience outside of the "natural" framework. The pagan works, that is, are simply tapped. The "true light which enlightens every man" Lorenzo seems to have taken literally: Neoplatonic humanists of the Ficino circle later tried to show how the notion should not be interpreted to mean an external source of wisdom, for such would unduly circumscribe the divinity and individuality of the human soul.[161]

Finally, Lorenzo Pisano was unable or unwilling to explore the limits of pagan philosophy for its general as well as its specific doctrines. He used philosophy to resolve particular theological questions. To be sure, such were important for many laymen, but here the appeal could only have reached a specific type of personality or mood. The problems Lorenzo addressed and his means of answering them were not the sort that would make many Florentine nobles eagerly seek his counsel (except, perhaps, on holy days) or copy his works (as the manuscript diffusion seems to indicate). Such figures as Ficino, Acciaiuoli, and Landino were far more aware of the variety of interests and personalities of educated and noble Florentines as a whole. When Ficino, in particular, decided to resolve the "problems of the age" through the use of philosophy, he found he had to turn to the classical sources themselves.

The strains in Ficino's relationship with his scholastic mentors show themselves early. In Antonio degli Agli's dialogue *De mystica statera,*

160.   Vat. lat. 961, fol. 57v.

161.   Antonio degli Agli also discussed the "divine light" in his *De mystica statera* (see below) to Marsilio Ficino (Naples, Bibl. Naz., cod. VIII F 9, fols. 21v–22), where he distinguished for Ficino the "one source" of truth from the world's deceptions. In his later work, *De immortalitate animae,* Agli identified this "divine light" as the one true source of human intelligence, separating man from other animated creatures (Vat. lat. 1494, fols. 91–97v; ref. at fol. 95). The Florentine Neoplatonists, I suspect, worried that the passage could support Averroist doctrines of the unity of the intellect. Marsilio Ficino quoted the passage from John in his *Di dio et anima* of 1458 but used it as an argument for human *diversity*: the light shone in the darkness, but the darkness *comprehended it not* (ed. in Kristeller, *Supplementum Ficinianum,* II, 140–41; cf. John 1:5). In book 3 of his *De anima,* Landino discussed the passage at length, noting that it had been the source of great error for many Christians, who used it to argue that the agent intellect was separate from the human soul. The passage from John, Landino argued, merely meant that humans were created with a capacity for understanding. For thinking humans the process of reasoning took place *nulla externa luce adiuvante* (Book 3 [ed. cit. below, Chapter IX, n. 30], pp. 30ff.).

probably composed in the mid- to late 1450s, Antonio acts as one interlocutor to warn the other, Marsilio Ficino, that pagan thinking leads to
vanity and error.[162] In seeking the highest good, he stated, follow the
"mystical balance" of divine truth: "Tarry not in turning yourself back
to the knowledge of God, and leave Plato and others of his sort behind!"[163] "Marsilio" thanks "Antonio" for this fatherly advice and then
attempts to assure "Antonio" that his studies could only lead him to
reject falsehoods. Even in this dialogue, however, "Marsilio" defends his
studies, and the Ficino in real life, of course, would continue his "pagan" studies with ever greater intensity.[164]

When Marsilio Ficino, in his own works, began to describe the *reversio animi*, the soul's attempt to leave the world and return to its true,
celestial homeland, he found a soul free from every necessity of the
world yet bound in the utter necessity of divine love. Niccolò Tignosi
had described for him the soul's freedom, its dignity and rule over the
world regulated by law. Lorenzo Pisano described a soul moved by divine love and battered by various desires: his soul was set free from the
world by this divine love but ever more tightly bound, in this love, to
God and to the community created by his love. Marsilio Ficino's philosophy of the contemplative life freed Tignosi's cosmos from its rigid
rationalism and fired it with poetic frenzy; it restrained Lorenzo Pisano's Christian exuberance and gave it philosophical rigor, universal-
izing it to the human experience. Most importantly, Ficino removed the
philosophers from the classroom and the convent. Human dignity
would now reign in Florence; and Platonic love would unite all Florentines together, bringing the Florentines ever closer to each other and
ever farther from their bodies, their material goods, their political statuses, or the other things of this world.

162.   Naples, Bibl. Naz., cod. VIII F 9, fols. 19–33. Since the dialogue is between Antonius, a *magister*, and Marsilius, an *adolescens*, and Ficino's surname is spelled *Fecinus*
(found often in his early writings), the work appears to date from the 1450s. The preface
is edited in Kristeller, *Supplementum Ficinianum*, II, 369–71. For the manuscript as a
whole, see Kristeller, *Iter*, I, 427, and J. H. Swogger, "Antonio degli Agli's 'Explanatio
symbolorum Pythagore': An Edition and a Study of Its Place in the Circle of Marsilio
Ficino" (Ph.D. diss., University of London, 1975 [copies at the Warburg Institute, London, and the American Academy in Rome]), pp. 19–21, 58–62. The title is inspired by a
passage from Job (6:2) [see fol. 19v].

163.   Cod. cit., fol. 33: "Ad hanc [*sc*. dei scientiam] itaque Platone aliisque huiusmodi
relictis convertere te non differas."

164.   Ibid., fol. 33. See also pp. 180–81, below.

VII

MARSILIO FICINO
AND THE
PLATONIC ACADEMY

W̶E have looked at the two worlds of Marsilio Ficino's youth: first, the academic, where he learned scholastic categories and systematic thinking, and second, the religious, where he learned of the love of man and God and of philosophy's role in knitting the two together. There was also the world of humanism, where Ficino could find, in mid-Quattrocento Florence, secular conceptions of the contemplative life and the dignity of man.[1] Humanism would also push him constantly toward a direct study of his revered philosophical texts. A fourth world was that of the Florentine patrician. Economic necessity forced him there in search of employment and patronage. There he also found friends, and many patricians discovered in Ficino their guide to the good life. Ficino assumed the role gladly, and at last came to view his position in Florence as that of the Socrates for the new Athens.

Since the subject of this study is the origins of the Platonic Academy in Florence, not simply the formal development or expression of the Platonic ideas themselves, I shall be emphasizing the ethical teaching that Ficino offered the young Florentine merchants and nobles; the Academy's "success" can be measured by the degree to which the better-born Florentines accepted Ficino's leadership and teaching, thus turn-

---

1. For a good summary of the "dignity" theme, see P. O. Kristeller, "The Dignity of Man," in his *Renaissance Thought and Its Sources*, pp. 169–181. I shall not emphasize the theme in a general sense, in part because it has been treated at great length by others and in part because I am not convinced that the mid-Quattrocento figure most often associated with it, Giannozzo Manetti, had any influence whatsoever on Marsilio Ficino, at least in those works of Ficino appearing before the 1470s. As to humanist influences on Ficino, however, I shall be making a few remarks on Poggio Bracciolini.

ing the philosopher's Platonism into a philosophical movement. This is
not to say that Ficino's relationship with the ruling class explains either
his teaching or his appeal: his Platonism was taken up by humble monks
and scholars, artists, priests, and other intellectuals within Florence, as
well as figures of various classes and strata in other cities and nations. A
symbol of Ficino's early international influence was his correspondence
with Cardinal Bessarion in 1469.[2]

As for the content itself of Ficino's Platonism, what is striking is the
degree to which his ideas were *removed* from the better-born Florentines' "normal" way of looking at the world. Seemingly more appropriate to the Florentine aristocrats—those, that is, who aspired to culture—is the Manettian ideal described in Chapter III, the attempt to
reach an ever fuller and more complete intellectual and political life. Ficino's isolation from the "immediate interests" of the ruling class—if not
from the ruling class itself—shows itself early. In 1457, while the business
and political leader Giovanni Canigiani was attempting to salvage the
Medici party in the Florentine government, Marsilio Ficino was outlining for his son, Antonio, the philosophers' teachings on moral virtues
and the highest good.[3] That same year, Pellegrino degli Agli, from another leading family, was applauded by Ficino for having departed from
the world altogether: you are a rare soul, Ficino wrote him, whom divine frenzy has visited.[4] Then on 13 June 1458, the very day the Medici
counselors in the Florentine government were arguing that "necessity is
impending" and that the government would have to be retaken by force,
Ficino would describe for Agli a world of perfect freedom: "Our minds
occupy neither space nor time," he wrote, and "they can run at once
through the entire world."[5] Finally, at the founding of the Platonic
Academy, after Cosimo de' Medici had supported or caused every material, political, diplomatic, and artistic success imaginable, and while
the orators were pronouncing him father of his country and the greatest
private citizen in the history of the world, Marsilio Ficino convinced

2.   Ficino, *Opera omnia*, pp. 616–17.

3.   Early works to Antonio Canigiani were *De virtutibus moralibus*, 1 June 1457 (ed. in
Kristeller, *Supplementum Ficinianum*, II, 1–6), *De voluptate*, 29–30 Dec. 1457 (*Opera omnia*, pp. 986–1012), and perhaps *De quattuor sectis philosophorum* (see Kristeller, *Supplementum Ficinianum*, I, cxxxix). See also V. R. Giustiniani, "A. C.," in *DBI*, vol. 18 (1975),
81–82. For Giovanni Canigiani's political activity in 1457, see Cons. e Prat., vol. 54; cf.
M. Mallett, in *DBI*, vol. 18 (1975), 93–94.

4.   *Opera omnia*, pp. 612–15 (*De divino furore*).

5.   Cons. e Prat. 55, fols. 21v, 22 (for the expression "necessitas imminet"). Ficino's letter
to Agli is ed. in Kristeller, *Supplementum Ficinianum*, II, 85–86 ("Quid enim prohibet
mentes, cum extra omne tempus locumque sint nec ullum temporis aut loci spatium oc-
cupent, universum orbem temporis momento percurrere?").

him that the "things of the world" were really of little importance.[6] And Cosimo was no anomaly: at this time, as we said earlier, Ficino's most esoteric work to date, his translation of the Hermetic *Pimander*, was eagerly being read by Florence's merchant-nobility.[7]

Marsilio Ficino was born in 1433 in Figline, a town in the Arno valley about a half-day's ride by horse from Florence.[8] His father emigrated to Florence and began to teach and practice medicine; though of modest social standing, he numbered Cosimo de' Medici among his clients, and he also came to know, at some point, Antoninus, archbishop of Florence.[9] He sent Marsilio to the University of Florence, where Marsilio took up the humanities as well as Aristotelian logic and natural philos-

6. See above, pp. 3–4.

7. For the diffusion of the *Pimander*, see Kristeller, "Marsilio Ficino as a Man of Letters," p. 22; *Marsilio Ficino e il ritorno: Mostra*, pp. 41–43, no. 30; and now Kristeller, "Marsilio Ficino and His Work," p. 167.

8. For Ficino's life see Della Torre, *Storia*, pp. 479ff.; Kristeller's introductions and notes to his *Supplementum Ficinianum*; and R. Marcel, *Marsile Ficin*. For some important corrections to Della Torre and Marcel, see Kristeller, "Per la biografia di M. F.," in his *Studies*, pp. 191–211, and *passim*. See also Kristeller, "L'état présent des études," and now his "Marsilio Ficino and His Work," pp. 15–196 and plates, which, among other things, brings up to date the secondary literature, the Ficino manuscripts, and Ficino's own works. New documentary information is ibid., pp. 171–180, and P. Viti, "Documenti ignoti per la biografia di M. F.," in *Marsilio Ficino e il ritorno: Studi*, I, 251–83. I am now investigating the possibility, for which the evidence is so far inconclusive, that some of Ficino's close ancestors were Jewish.

A few minor notes may be added here. The Bancus arithmetra, to whom Ficino wrote in August 1458 (*Opera omnia*, p. 656; Kristeller, *Supplementum Ficinianum*, I, 39–40), is further identified in the Florentine *notarile* as "Bancus olim filius Pieri Andree vocati Piero Porro magister arismetrice" (Not. Antec. G 616, 2 [Simone Grazzini], fol. 100: document dated 11 Oct. 1458): this confirms Kristeller's hypothesis that this Banco is not to be identified with the figure from the Acciaiuoli circle named Banco da Casavecchia (*Supplementum Ficinianum*, I, 124). For the late 1450s this section of the notarile contains many documents relating to the Ficino circle, mentioning, for example, Giovanni Pigli (fol. 35), Cristoforo Landino (fol. 51–51v), Antonio Canigiani (ibid.), Lorenzo Pisano (fol. 101), and Ficino's father Dietifeci (fols. 167–68v). Similar documents from the same notary, for the mid-1450s, are in Not. Antec. G 616, 1 (including a document concerning Comando Comandi, fols. 66v–67) and, for the early 1460s, in Not. Antec. G 616, 3 (including a document concerning Antonio degli Agli, fol. 186).

In a survey of Tuscan archives, under Volterra, Archivio Guidi, there is a note by the late Mario Luzzatto of a "carteggio" of Giovanni di Salvatico Guidi with Marsilio Ficino (*Archivio storico italiano* 114 [1956], 679). I pointed out the reference to Professor Paul O. Kristeller, who inquired and found out that the archive is now deposited with the Archivio di Stato in Florence. With the kind assistance of Dott. Maria Vittoria Palli d'Addario, I went through those filze most likely to contain early letters, and I found no letters to or from Marsilio Ficino. I did discover, however, in letters of 1498 and 1499 testimonies concerning Ficino (filze 120 and 564), and those may possibly have been the source of Luzzatto's notice. See my descriptions of the Archivio Guidi in P. O. Kristeller, *Iter Italicum*, vol. 5 (forthcoming).

9. R. Marcel, *Marsile Ficin*, pp. 122–27, 164–66, 735–40; *Marsilio Ficino e il ritorno: Mostra*; Kristeller, *Studies*, p. 171.

ophy: he was supposed to be studying for a career in medicine. Like many students and scholars, Ficino supported himself as a tutor for wealthy Florentine patricians. A document of 1451 shows that he was teaching Piero de' Pazzi the logic of Paul of Venice; he may also have tutored Cosimo de' Medici's most promising son, Giovanni.[10] Ficino's early training in the humanities was probably under two rather obscure grammarians, Luca da San Gimignano and Comando Comandi.[11] He also came to know the humanists Carlo Marsuppini (probably), Cristoforo Landino, and Poggio Bracciolini.[12] During the early 1450s, also, Ficino began studies under Florence's most prominent lecturer in medicine, Niccolò Tignosi.[13] Ficino's "miserable" status as a tutor and several scholastic categories learned from Tignosi combined to produce one of Ficino's first works, an invective of 1454 against pedagogy, directed to one Guardavilla da Volterra. Pedagogues never deal with the highest sciences, he wrote, for they are restricted to the particular studies of their clients. They are forced to petty subjects, rudimentary grammar and the glosses of law.[14]

In 1454 and 1455 appear Ficino's earliest philosophical works, addressed to fellow students and derived largely from Aristotelian scholastic studies at the university.[15] But already we detect a particular interest in Plato. On 13 September 1454, he wrote from Florence to his close friend Antonio Serafico da San Miniato, who, like Ficino, studied under Niccolò Tignosi, a letter (quoted in part at the beginning of the last chapter) that was actually the first of a series of tracts dealing chiefly with questions of natural philosophy.[16] The content is thoroughly scholastic, but we find in the work an early form of the philosophical "unity" of love that was to become characteristic of the Platonic Academy. We formerly, Ficino began, had to write in the ornate style: let us abandon this, and in the manner of philosophers (*more philosophorum*) look more

10.   S. J. Hough, "An Early Record of Marsilio Ficino," *Renaissance Quarterly* 30 (1977), 301–4; see now Sillano, ed., *Le ricordanze di Giovanni Chellini da San Miniato*, p. 183. For Ficino and Giovanni de' Medici, see Della Torre, *Storia*, pp. 527–29, and Kristeller, *Supplementum Ficinianum*, I, cxli–ii; II, 79–80.

11.   Della Torre, *Storia*, pp. 489–95.

12.   For Landino and Poggio, see below. For Ficino and Marsuppini, see Kristeller, "L'état présent des études," p. 65 and n. Paris, Bibl. Nat., cod. Nuov. acq. lat. 650 contains some brief autograph notes of Ficino on Marsuppini's funeral: see the description in Kristeller, *Iter*, III, 282.

13.   See above, Chapter VI, n. 43.

14.   E. Cristiani, "Una inedita invettiva giovanile di Marsilio Ficino," pp. 209–22. For Cristiani's manuscript source, see Kristeller, "Marsilio Ficino and His Work," p. 157.

15.   See the descriptions and editions in Kristeller, *Studies*, pp. 35–96, 139–50.

16.   Ibid., pp. 139–50.

closely at propositions than at words. After surveying the propositions, Ficino mentioned how pleased he was that Antonio too burned greatly with the desire to play the philosopher.[17] That same year, or perhaps the next, Ficino wrote for another close friend, Michele Mercati da San Miniato, a more far-reaching series of tracts covering several aspects of dialectics, natural philosophy, and metaphysics.[18] Again the content is scholastic, with the work serving as a compendium so that Michele "might participate, in some way, in those studies which Plato ordered."[19] Already appears a theme Ficino later explored in depth: just as the craftsman must have the idea or exemplar of the thing he creates first in his mind, so God contains in himself the forms of all natural things; but we would not recognize these forms if our mind was not similar to God.[20]

Ficino's "closeness" to his fellow philosophers based on "common studies" is an old humanistic and philosophical theme. That God is a craftsman and that man has an affinity with his creator seems to be more closely based on the recent studies under Niccolò Tignosi: the mind of the creator contains the forms of the created things and gives them their definition and order. This theme of affinity marked Ficino's first work of real philosophical innovation, a letter of August 1455 to his brothers and sisters.[21] Focusing on filial piety, Ficino first showed how God, author of the world, had necessarily to communicate to the world his perfection. Better things give their goodness to things less good; the lesser things must be capable of participating in the good. Similarly the father creates his sons and imparts his goodness to them. And so likewise the sons owe obedience to their father and ought to preserve his rules voluntarily. Just as God likes to see men, whom he made, united as parts of his work, so sons ought to preserve a fraternal harmony in the family: nothing is better than this peace and concord. Sons should look not to

17.   Ibid., p. 150: "Vale ac ut cepisti flagrantissime philosophare, quod dum feceris, nihil mihi gratius acidere poterit."

18.   Ibid., pp. 55–96.

19.   Ibid., p. 56: "[D]ialetice simul et philosophie compendiosum hunc tibi tractatum mictere decrevi, ut illorum iam studiorum aliquantulum particeps efficiaris, quibus etatem nostram, quantacunque futura sit, Platonis nostri precepta iubent penitus exercendam."

20.   Ibid., pp. 64–65; for other themes in this work that Ficino would later develop, see Kristeller's remarks, p. 48.

21.   Ed. in Kristeller, *Supplementum Ficinianum*, II, 109–28. The main themes seem to derive from Ps. Dionysius Areopagita. Wedged into the "loftier" statements is Ficino's argument that he, as the eldest child, should serve at times like a father to his brothers and sisters. A domestic dispute probably prompted the letter. Documentary evidence for such disputes in Ficino's family, at other times, is not wanting.

their own gain but to that of all: disharmony characterizes those who
have rejected their humanity and become beasts.

Here, applied to the family, we see a simple, early form of the philosophical basis of the Platonic Academy: souls, created by God, participate in his goodness and are drawn to one another in his unity. In terms
of the sort of philosophizing that Ficino would soon undertake, however, the letter is limited: Ficino does not identify his insights as the
product of his philosophical studies; he does not emphasize the appli-
cability of his notions to society at large; and he is not preoccupied with
the novelty and historical significance of his own ideas.

Ficino evidently spent the years 1455 and 1456 in intense study, moving
boldly away from the scholastic compendia learned in the schools and
toward a wide variety of philosophical teachings found in sources available in Latin. His notebooks are filled with quotations from Cicero's
and Seneca's philosophical works, from Apuleius, Lactantius, and Augustine. The passages from these authors illustrate Ficino's growing interest in Plato and the Platonists.[22] Even where, as in the tract to Michele
Mercati of ca. 1455, he relied on Aristotelian categories, he described the
studies as those "which Plato ordered." His enthusiasm for Plato was
now great—too great, as we said in the last chapter, for his scholastic
mentor and a friend of Lorenzo Pisano, the Florentine cleric Antonio
degli Agli. In Agli's *De mystica statera* of about 1455 (or a few years later),
Agli warns Ficino to adhere to the "mystical balance" of divine law and
to "leave Plato and others of his sort" behind. This "Marsilio" created
by Antonio degli Agli tries to defend his studies: "At present I am going
through certain profane books, not that I may become acquainted with
falsehoods but that I may with greater authority and eloquence repel
those who are becoming acquainted with them."[23] This is similar to the
traditional Christian defense of pagan studies, where the aim is to answer pagan lies more efficaciously with Christian truths. But here, it
seems, the pagan studies assist in answering "falsehoods" in general—
that is, they in themselves lead toward truth. "Antonio" is not convinced
by "Marsilio," however, and warns him, at one point, about citing
Platonists and Stoics: "Those whom you have just now named," he ex-

22. See S. Gentile, "In margine all'epistola 'De divino furore' di Marsilio Ficino," *Rinascimento*, 2d. ser., 23 (1983 [1984]), 33–77.

23. Naples, Bibl. Naz., cod. VIII F 9, fol. 33: "Tibi o Antoni habeo gratias eo quod me
ut filium monuisse videris. Agam vero pro viribus ea omnia que deus in quem spem
meam omnem iamdudum conieci subgesserit. Ideo tamen ad presens prophanos quos-
dam libros percurro, non ut discam mendacia sed ut discentes maiori auctoritate facund-
iaque propulsem."

claims, "have no authority with me!"[24] In Lorenzo Pisano's dialogues, Antonio degli Agli is described as "stern" and "censorious": one may wonder if, in the early sixteenth century, Fra Zenobi Acciaiuoli confused this Antonio with the famous Antoninus when he stated that Antoninus's warnings about paganism caused Ficino for a time to abandon his studies of Plato.[25]

At any rate, whether Ficino accepted Agli's warnings or parlayed them, he continued in his Platonic studies, and in 1456 produced his first major, lengthy work, his four books of the *Institutiones ad Platonicam disciplinam*, dedicated to Cristoforo Landino.[26] The work is not extant. It dealt in part, it seems, with a theme Ficino read in Plato's letter to Dionysius (2.312e): "Around the king of every thing is each thing, and similar to him is every thing, and he is the cause of all goods."[27] The work seems, therefore, to have included a discussion of the theme of "affinity" that Ficino explained in 1455 in his letter to his brothers and sisters. It surely was based on available Latin translations of and commentaries on Plato. Kristeller has suggested that it may be identical to a work Ficino would soon be describing as his "commentary on the *Timaeus*."[28] It also seems likely that Ficino's letter *De divino furore*, written to Pellegrino degli Agli in December 1457, was largely an excerpt from these *Institutiones*.[29]

In his *De divino furore* Ficino took up two interrelated themes that we shall examine separately and in some detail. One is the theme of the contemplative life; the other is the role of philosophy in leading to human perfection. For the first of these, Ficino described for Agli "two wings" the soul used to return to its divine origins: Plato, he wrote, believed that we "fly back to heaven" through "two virtues, one relating to moral conduct and the other to contemplation. One he names with the common term 'justice,' and the other 'wisdom.'" Ficino then referred to a second theme, the role of philosophy: "Socrates teaches in the *Phaedo* that we acquire these by the two parts of philosophy, namely the active and the contemplative. Hence he says again in the *Phaedrus*

---

24.   Ibid., fol. 31: "Eorum quos modo nominasti nulla apud me auctoritas valet."

25.   For Ficino and Antoninus, see Kristeller, *Studies*, pp. 171, 200–201. For the "censorious" Agli, see Lorenzo Pisano, *Dialogi quinque*, Laur. S. Marco 457, fol. 225v: " . . . unus ex amicis presbiter Antonius vir moribus maturus fronte severus et natura censor." Cf. Lorenzo's *De pace*, Lucca, Bibl. Statale, cod. 366, fol. 30v.

26.   For the *Institutiones*, see Kristeller, *Supplementum Ficinianum*, I, clxiii–iv.

27.   Ficino, *Di dio et anima*, to Francesco Capponi, 24 Jan. 1458, in Kristeller, *Supplementum Ficinianum*, II, 132.

28.   Kristeller, *Supplementum Ficinianum*, I, clxiv.

29.   See my "Cristoforo Landino's First Lectures on Dante," pp. 34–35.

that only the mind of the philosopher regains wings."[30] In some of his works, particularly where he is more traditional and academic in defining his terms, Ficino continued to treat the active and contemplative life as he did in his letter to Pellegrino degli Agli: philosophy, that is, points the way toward the perfection of either life. In his scholastic *Divisio philosophiae*, one of the tracts of ca. 1454–55 to Michele Mercati, Ficino reproduced the traditional distinction between "speculative" and "active" philosophy. Speculation concerns God, separated intelligences (spirits), separated substances yet participating in matter (that is, demons and airy spirits), and physics; active philosophy concerns ethics.[31] Likewise in his *De voluptate* (1457) to Antonio Canigiani, Ficino pointed to the "divinity" of the contemplative life, while once again affirming the importance of each.

> With two arguments especially Mercurius Trismegistus, the wisest of the Egyptians, attempted to root out this abominable stain [that is, pleasure] from the souls of men. He thought that that was good for each thing which either maintained in its own nature the very thing to which it is attached, or led it to a better result. Of the first sort are those virtues which regulate action: to them it is proper to render the soul tranquil and free from every tumult of passions . . . . To the second sort clearly belong those virtues which have to do with contemplation. For in fact these virtues, through the understanding and pursuit of divine things, raise up and exalt the mind in some way above human nature, so that it seems to approach as closely as possible to the life of God, which consists in contemplation alone. But it is clear that the condition of pleasure is contrary to both.[32]

Here, and elsewhere, tradition alone forced Ficino to consider the two lives, active and contemplative, as separate, while the science of the latter, concerned ultimately with God, had to be the higher.

30. Ficino, *Letters*, I, 43 (trans. altered slightly); cf. *Opera omnia*, p. 613. For this letter, see now S. Gentile, "In margine all'epistola 'De divino furore.' "

31. In Kristeller, *Studies*, p. 95.

32. *Opera omnia*, p. 991: "Mercurius Trismegistus Aegyptiorum omnium sapientissimus duabus potissimum rationibus hanc nefariam labem ex animis hominum extirpare conatur. Id enim cuique bonum esse censet quod aut rem ipsam cui quidam [quidem *ed.*] adsit in propria natura contineat aut ad meliorem frugem perducat. Primi generis esse virtutes eas quae in actione positae sunt videmus; earum namque proprium est animum ab omni perturbationum tumultu liberum tranquillumque reddere. . . . Secundi generis eas virtutes quae in contemplatione versantur esse constat. Quippe cum animum rerum divinarum studio intelligentiaque supra humanam quodammodo naturam erigant atque extollant, ut ad Dei vitam, quae duntaxat in contemplatione consistit, quam proxime videatur accedere, voluptatis vero conditionem utrique contrariam esse patet."

The year 1456 seems to mark a new course in Ficino's studies. For one thing, when Cristoforo Landino and (according to Ficino's later testimony) Cosimo de' Medici read the *Institutiones ad Platonicam disciplinam*, they praised the work but urged Ficino to begin approaching the Platonic sources directly.[33] At this point, it seems, Ficino began studying Greek, probably under Francesco da Castiglione.[34] Also from 1456 and 1457 Ficino moved out of his more narrow scholastic circles toward a greater philosophical confrontation with Florentine patricians. Earlier these contacts were more circumscribed or pedagogical. Moreover, Ficino was now boldly recreating philosophical traditions. From Lorenzo Pisano, and through independent study, he knew that the "theme" of his *Institutiones*—Plato's statement that "around the king of every thing is each thing, and similar to him is every thing, and he is the cause of all goods"—was remarkably similar to certain teachings of Hermes Trismegistus found in his *Asclepius*.[35] Last, Ficino was becoming impatient with the traditional Aristotelian divisions of philosophy into the "practical" and "speculative" sciences, where the mind "learns" through each perfection in either discipline. Even in the letter on divine frenzy, where he described the "two wings" of philosophical ascent, Ficino discovered that Pellegrino degli Agli was moving upward by objective processes he was only partially or afterward aware of—that is, he had been seized by divine frenzy, and he was being moved by love.

To study the "objective" process Ficino's philosophizing took a curious turn: he began to study Epicurean teachings.[36] The reasons for this have never been described successfully: one problem is that two of his Epicurean works of 1457, a commentary on Lucretius and a treatise

33. See Kristeller, *Supplementum Ficinianum*, I, clxiii.

34. This seems likely, since in 1456 no one else was available. (Perhaps as early as 1457 John Argyropoulos began teaching some Greek, but these lessons may have been only private and for better-born Florentines, and even if some lectures were public it seems unlikely that Ficino would have attended them: see Chapter IV, n. 18, above.) There is an early letter from Ficino to Castiglione (*Opera omnia*, p. 616), and Ficino's close friend, Pellegrino degli Agli, we know from other evidence, studied Greek under Castiglione (see Kristeller, *Supplementum Ficinianum*, II, 322). I could not find, however, any obvious affinities between Ficino's autograph Greek-Latin lexicon, Laur. Ashburnham 1439, ed. as Ficino, *Lessico greco-latino*, by R. Pintaudi (Rome, 1977), and the Greek-Latin lexicon owned by Castiglione, Laur. Acq. e Doni 92.

35. Lorenzo Pisano, *De amore*, Magl. XXI 115, fol. 11. See also the description of Ricc. 709 by S. Gentile, "In margine all'epistola 'De divino furore,' " p. 73ff.

36. For the extant works, see Kristeller, *Studies*, p. 49. F. Gabotto, "L'Epicureismo di Marsilio Ficino," *Rivista di filosofia scientifica* 10 (1891), 428–42, focuses on Ficino's *De voluptate* of 1457 and compares Ficino's general approach with that of Lorenzo Valla (in his *De vero falsoque bono*).

called *Physiognomia*, are not extant.[37] Some doctrines do appear in a few
letters of 1457 and 1458. Like the doctrine of God as craftsman imparting
his goodness to his handiwork, a notion that seems to depend on Tignosi's rationalization of the sciences, the Epicurean teachings also appear to have a scholastic inspiration. They arise, that is, in Lorenzo Pisano's dialogues. Lorenzo described a world ruled by love, where from
the basest matter to the highest God things were interconnected, bound
by actives and passives, bonds of love. That is, like the Epicurean cosmos, there were objective interconnections of the things of the world,
not simply a spirit informing matter or God's grace acting inscrutably.
Man's will freely ranged through this hierarchy, and desire led him
either to God or to sin. Humility provided a rule and measure; divine
love reigned over the whole. In Lorenzo Pisano's *De amore* the adolescent discovered reading Plato's *Symposium*—who, we argued, is perhaps
to be identified with Ficino himself—twice quoted the proto-Epicurean
Empedocles as an authority for the notion that even things of the natural world are ruled by love.[38] Lorenzo's "measure" or "rule" described
in the *Dialogi humilitatis* of the early 1450s seems to be echoed in Antonio degli Agli's *De mystica statera* dedicated to Ficino. God has done all
things, Agli wrote, with weight, number, and measure: he has infused
all things with a sense of what is just and unjust. These are weighed on
God's mystical balance.[39] It would seem absurd, "Marsilio" interjects,
for divine things to be weighed by a "balance." But it is indeed so, "Antonio" replies, and not only are "all things weighed by a balance, but
they are also examined, judged, and known" by the divine light, the
light that enlightens all men.[40]

We are here fully in the world of Lorenzo Pisano, where humility and
love lead man out of the world and toward God. Too often, Agli wrote,
men seek after the beauty of the world and not that of their own soul.
For if you, "Marsilio," could only perceive that "you were born for
greater and more difficult undertakings," you would then strain to be-

37.   For the lost Epicurean works, see Kristeller, *Supplementum Ficinianum*, I, clxiii.

38.   Magl. XXI 115, fol. 6: "Haec Agrigentinus ille . . . : Omnia que in rerum natura to-
toque mundo constarent queve moventur ea contrahere amorem dissipareque discor-
diam. . . . Empedoclem quoque haud incelebrem philosophum amorem causam esse
bonorum, litem vero malorum nequaque asseverare penituit." (If I understand correctly
the force of his prose, Lorenzo Pisano seems to have been unaware that the "Agrigen-
tine" and Empedocles are the same figure.) For similar citations, see Ficino's *Summa philosophiae* to Michele Mercati, ca. 1455, ed. in Kristeller, *Studies*, at p. 74. See also p. 50,
above.

39.   Naples, Bibl. Naz., cod. VIII F 9, fols. 19v–20.

40.   Ibid., fol. 20: "Est enim non solum statera qua appenduntur omnia sed lux evangelio teste qua examinantur, diiudicantur, agnoscanturque universa."

come and be recognized as a "son of God," not a "Platonist." And if you do not step back, with Plato you will be hurled "into outer darkness."⁴¹

Through this world ruled by desire, passion, and love, Ficino looked beyond these theological and scholastic admonitions toward the "Platonic" and philosophical truths. And he would use philosophical guides wherever he found them. (If you are going to quote Plato to me, "Agli" told "Ficino," you may as well quote Epicurus and Brahmins!⁴²) In a letter to Antonio Serafico, of 1457, Ficino seized on a passage of Lucretius describing Epicurus the philosopher (*De rerum natura* 6.24–28): "He purged men's breasts with words of truth. He set bounds to desire and fear. He demonstrated what is the highest good after which we all strive, and pointed the way by which we can win to it, keeping straight ahead along a narrow track."⁴³

In this letter, and in others of this period to Michele Mercati and Piero de' Pazzi, Ficino spoke of the soul being buffeted about in various directions and how difficult it was to chart one's course.⁴⁴ The soul, born into the world, was either tricked by pleasures or tortured by agonies but was always subject to one or another domination. The world he described to his friends was troublesome indeed. "One must not only not fear the threats of tyrants and avoid being snared by their charms," he wrote Piero de' Pazzi in about 1457, "but one must wholly despise them inwardly, if one wishes to follow the gentle and divine king."⁴⁵ On 1 November 1457, writing from Florence, Ficino congratulated his close friend Antonio Serafico on his victory:

> You are happy in the midst of calamities. Fear does not make you lose heart; sadness excruciates not; pleasure does not corrupt nor desire inflame. In the thickest thorns you gather delicate and fair flowers, from dung you extract pearls, in the deepest darkness you see, impeded and held by chains you run like one who is free.⁴⁶

---

41.   Ibid., fol. 32: "Si novisses, maioribus augustioribusque natum te perspexisses, plurisque profecto faceres te dei filium ac etiam deum quam Platonicum vel fore vel appellari. Platonicum inquam, quia maximo opere Platonem sectari videris, a quo non nisi recedas una cum eo in tenebras te deturbari exteriores [cf. Matt. 8:12] denique opus erit."

42.   Ibid., fol. 31.

43.   Dated 29 Nov. 1457, ed. in Kristeller, *Supplementum Ficinianum*, II, 82–84. The translation of Lucretius is that of R. E. Latham (Baltimore, 1951).

44.   Ed. in Kristeller, *Supplementum Ficinianum*, II, 81–82, 82, 84–85; another letter of similar content, dated 4 Jan. 1459 but with no address, is ibid., II, 86–87.

45.   Ibid., II, 85: "Etenim tirannorum nec minas reformidare nec illecebris capi atque irretiri, sed contempnere penitus et oblivisci decet, siquis mansueto divinoque regi obsecuturus sit."

46.   Ibid., II, 82: "Felicem te puto . . . qui in mediis quoque calamitatibus sis beatus,

But by the end of that month Ficino warned Serafico of external, competing forces ("friends and enemies") affecting his soul. To achieve tranquility of soul, which is the highest good,

> you must first of all examine who are your friends, who are your enemies, and who are neither. Friends bring tranquility, enemies take it away, those numbered among neither group diminish and impede it. Now there are two friends in preference to all others, four enemies, and those who hold the middle position are infinite. But since from our conversation I think you know this, by no means shall I reveal it publicly, lest the sweetest bread of the sons, as the wise man warned, be given to the dogs [cf. Matt. 15:26]. Since indeed you know all these things, take care for your friends as diligently as you are able, lest they become strangers. Drive out without delay your enemies if they hold your house, and if they are out of doors take care lest they invade it. From among these enemies two are fawning with their flatteries, lay ambushes, whisper idle prophecies, and creep up on you in secret. The others rush in violently and impetuously. If they occupy your house, they will throw you out of doors at once.[47]

It seems likely, though it is difficult to prove, that Ficino's new emphasis of the latter 1450s, on the power of those forces that compete for the human soul, was inspired by humanists as well as by philosophers—in particular, that is, by Poggio Bracciolini. Ficino's teacher, Niccolò Tignosi, it will be remembered, was a close friend of Poggio and led the discussion of Poggio's *Secunda disceptatio convivalis* of 1450.[48] Poggio's

---

quem nec metus exanimat nec dolor excruciat nec voluptas corrumpit nec libido inflammat, qui inter densissimas spinas molles ac candidos flores legas, qui ex putrido stercore margaritas eruas atque effodias, qui in profundis tenebris videas, qui compedibus gravatus et vinculis circumstrictus velut liber solutusque percurras."

47.   Ibid., II, 83: "Ut autem hanc ipsam quietem tranquillitatemque quam isti [*sc.* quidam Epicurei disputantes] summum bonum putant facile consequaris, discutiendum imprimis est, qui tibi amici quive hostes qui denique neutri sint. Amici namque tranquillitatem prestant, hostes auferunt, qui vero neutrorum numero censentur minuunt atque impediunt. Duo vero potissimum amici sunt, inimici quattuor, qui medium tenent innumeri [cf. Plato, *Republic* 445c]. Quod cum te iam pro nostra consuetudine intelligere putem nequaquam vulgo aperiam, ne suavissimus filiorum panis quod sapiens ille monet canibus detur. Cum vero hec omnia noveris, amicos tuos quam diligentius poteris ne alieni fiant caveto, adversarios si domum teneant absque mora pellito, quod si foris sunt ne domum tuam invadant curato. Ex eis quippe duo blanditiis mulcent, insidiis capiunt, presagiis allucinantur, latentes surrepunt; ceteri vi impetuque irrumpunt. Si domicilium occupaverint, te quam primum foras eiicient."

48.   Other links between Ficino and Poggio *may* be some mutual friends: e.g., Giovanni di Bartolomeo Guidi (see Chapter IX, n. 25, below), Cristoforo Landino, and Cosimo de' Medici.

legal humanism seems to have affected Ficino only through Tignosi: Ficino's writings, unlike those of Landino, are rather bare of "legal language." (But this is not surprising, since Ficino had not gone to law school.) But Ficino also came to know Poggio directly, serving as a witness for him in a legal transaction of March 1459.[49] Although, as I noted earlier, Poggio had written in 1455 that "philosophiae ars a me deest," he also wrote that same year a rather remarkable "proto-philosophical" dialogue, *De miseria humanae conditionis*.[50]

The dialogue was set in Florence in the mid-1450s, with the interlocutors Matteo Palmieri and Poggio himself attempting to convince Cosimo de' Medici that the world was not as happy as it appeared. Formally the dialogue may have been intended in part as an "answer" to Giannozzo Manetti's *De dignitate et excellentia hominis* of 1450.[51] Manetti was now out of favor with Florence and the Medici, due presumably to his pro-Venice stance toward the end of the midcentury wars, at a time when Florence and the Medici were courting the Sforza. If Manetti had described a world where "ours are the foxes, ours are the wolves, ours are the water-snakes," Poggio's world was owned by man-hunting carnivores, rabid dogs, and vipers.[52]

The humanism of Poggio had always looked to the "concreteness of things"; the humanism of Manetti and his disciples looked to exemplars and ideals. A decade before, at the death of Leonardo Bruni (1444), both Manetti and Poggio wrote funeral orations on Florence's late hero. In describing Bruni's early life, Manetti had him come to Florence with an "incredible desire" of pursuing the humanities. Poverty forced him, for a time, to the study of law, but when the apt *praeceptor* Emanuel Chrysoloras arrived in the Arno republic, Bruni turned from law to the humanities and gave himself over especially to the study of Greek. Manetti has here described, of course, the "high road" to the humanities, the road nearly every humanist thought he had taken. Poggio's biographical sketch departs significantly: even after his studies under Chry-

49. Cited in several studies: see now *Marsilio Ficino e il ritorno: Mostra*, p. 174, no. 138.

50. *Opera omnia*, I, 86–131. For Poggio's letter on philosophy, see p. 43, above.

51. The dialogue also honored Cosimo, and was perhaps meant to console him and to comment, obliquely, on Florentine affairs: in it the folly of the world is juxtaposed to the wisdom and dispassion of Cosimo. The dialogue was written in 1455 (see Walser, *Poggius*, pp. 305ff.), at the time, that is, when Cosimo was beginning to lose power in Florence. The entire work ends with Cosimo's remark, "[Q]uanquam hi nostri sermones plurimum mihi voluptatis attulerint, reliquorum voces aliquando molestia non carent" (p. 131).

52. Poggio, *Opera omnia*, I, 110 (you would think "ursos, leones, apros, lupos, serpentum genus in nostrum interitum conspirasse"); Manetti, *De dignitate et excellentia hominis*, p. 81 ("nostre vulpes, nostri lupi, nostre natrices," etc.: cf. pp. 67, 68–69, above).

soloras, Bruni returned to law, "which promised property and wealth to its cultivators." Poggio then implied that it was only after a secretarial position in the papal curia had been secured for him (by Poggio himself and Salutati) that Bruni returned wholly to his preferred studies in the humanities.[53]

While Manetti charted a straight course to virtue, Poggio knew the human condition was marked by vicissitudes. In the *De miseria humanae conditionis* of 1455, the course of human life is described as Virgil's entrance to Hell, where "grief and avenging cares have made their bed," with diseases, old age, fear, famine, want, and death (*Aeneid* 6.272ff.).[54] Is it not right to say, "Poggio" asks, that we are all in a state of vice, plagued by physical infirmities, and is not humankind marked by the forces of greed, pride, and ambition? Is not the proper description of the human race the image of Heraclitus, weeping over the foolishness and misery of man?[55]

"Cosimo" responds that a better image of man is that of Democritus, who laughed rather than wept at man's errors.[56] "Poggio" reminds Cosimo that he himself has little to complain of—just a little gout—while the general lot of man is one of misery.[57] "Palmieri" later argues (quoting Cicero) that "unless the soul is made sound, which cannot happen without philosophy, there will be no end of misery": but our condition is weak, and no one seeks to be healed by philosophy.[58] Then, after lengthy descriptions by "Poggio" and "Palmieri" of the disasters of ancient and recent history, where all things human have been marked by misery and grief, "Cosimo" at last concedes that man by nature is weak and fragile and his life follows an uncertain course. But if, he concludes, from the restrictions of the senses and the snares of pleasures we call back our mind to contemplation, if we attempt nothing that in itself will force us to be penitent, we can look to those things that are under our law (*nostri iuris*): even if fortune takes away our wealth, health, and family, "the soul is free from its domain."[59]

---

53. This summary is based on F Krantz, "Legal Thought" pp. 141–42, who discusses the orations in a different context.

54. *Opera omnia*, I, 94.

55. Ibid., I, 90.

56. Ibid.

57. Ibid., p. 91 (and quoting Terence: "Tu si hic sis aliter sentias"!).

58. Ibid., p. 108: "Illa . . . eiusdem [*sc.* Tullii] egregia est sententia: nisi sanatus animus sit, quod sine philosophia fieri non possit, nullum fore miseriarum finem. Sed nostra palam est imbecillitas, nullos a philosophia ut sanentur quaerere: igitur miseri omnes sunt ex(is)timandi."

59. Ibid., pp. 130, 131: "Ea [*sc.* vera libertas] erit, si vitiorum reiecta contagione mentem

Poggio, of course, who quietly confessed in 1455 that "philosophiae ars a me deest," could do little more here than stress the freedom of the soul and the value of contemplation. The ancients, for him, became immortal as he conversed with them, and in old age, as he was battered by upstart foreign philologists and politically punished and humiliated by domestic lawyers and the *popolo*, he knew his own immortality would have to be secured through his writing.[60]

Ficino would later, in the first book of his letters, insert a series of declamations entitled "De stultitia et miseria hominum," sounding themes very much like those developed by Poggio.[61] Here he described Heraclitus weeping over the human condition and Democritus laughing at man's folly; a painting so depicting the two decorated Ficino's studio at Careggi, the official site of the Platonic Academy.[62] We might indeed want to say that the latter 1450s was not simply Ficino's "Epicurean" period but his "Poggian" period as well.[63] As we stated, he now began to show much less concern for philosophy as a discipline, divisible into its active and speculative components, and more for philosophy's effects on the individual. He would now describe the connecting links between the active and contemplative lives and show how philosophy leads man from one life to the other.

Poggio's "resolution" of the problem of the human condition offered little, if anything, in the way of concrete philosophical direction. Philosophically it merely described the "problem." But Poggio understood that human difficulties were real, not imagined, and that they certainly could not be "thought" out of existence through Stoic dispassion. Ficino's attempt at a resolution was "Epicurean" in that he described man's

---

ad suimet contemplationem cogitationemque revocaverimus, si contemptis sensuum deliniamentis ac spretis voluptatum illecebris parebimus imperio rationis, si virtutem tanquam ducem nostrorum operum secuti, eius praeceptis veluti bene vivendi magistrae obsequemur. . . . Id autem praeceptum in promtu est habendum, ut nihil agere conemur ex quo ulla poenitendi ratio oriatur. . . . Animus a fortunae imperio liber est, si opes aufert, si vires, si valitudinem, si uxorem, si liberos."

60. See, e.g., Poggio's letter to Petrus de Monte, probably early 1456 (Ep. XIII, 18 [Tonelli III, 216–17]): It was in part this "conversation" that was being threatened by the philologists of the Valla school, who insisted on picking apart and criticizing the ancients.

61. *Opera omnia*, pp. 636–38. See also Kristeller, *Il pensiero filosofico*, pp. 315–17.

62. See Kristeller, *Il pensiero filosofico*, pp. 316–17.

63. Poggio's influence on the early philosophical revival may be seen even more clearly in Landino's inaugural oration before lectures on Cicero's *Tusculans*, probably delivered in 1458: see Chapter IX, below. Poggio's dialogues, orations, and letters are so rife with Stoic opinions that the Epicurean element in his thought can easily be overlooked. For Poggio's Epicureanism, see the succinct remarks of R. Fubini, "Il 'Teatro del Mondo' nelle prospettive morali e storico-politiche di Poggio Bracciolini," in *Poggio Bracciolini 1380–1980: Nel VI centenario della nascita* (Florence, 1982), pp. 27–29.

passions as objective, interrelated realities. He found that the objects of
man's desires could be placed in hierarchies and that what man seeks
was not the product of man's inscrutable will but an identifiable object.
The interrelationships appeared in his earliest writings, as in his letter
on filial piety to his brothers and sisters: God gives his goodness to his
creatures, and they participate in it. Ficino's conception of the *primum
in aliquo genere*—that the highest thing in any genus determined, actually and not ideally, the other things in that genus—could not have
come from the "nonphilosophical" Poggio. Indeed the notion had been
developed by scholastic philosophers out of several ancient teachings.[64]
The academic Tignosi described an artist and his idea, with an external
world shaped by a true *scientia*; the theologian Lorenzo Pisano described an external world ruled by love where man could conform his
own will to the "measure" ordained by God.[65] Ficino's early themes of
"affinity" certainly owed much to these scholastic mentors. But he gave
these opinions a new philosophical form with his *primum in aliquo genere*: the highest thing in any genus exists objectively, defines each thing
within its genus, creates the hierarchies, and leads the participants toward itself. As early as his *De voluptate* to Antonio Canigiani, in 1457,
Ficino described this *primum*: Hermes Trismegistus, he wrote,

> asserts that in all genera of things there is one greatest and highest
> and that by participating in it the other things are placed in the
> same genus; as, for instance, all warm things become warm
> through the nature of fire, to which the greatest warmth is intrin-
> sic, and all good things must be called good because they follow
> and imitate the highest and first good.[66]

When Ficino became less "ontological" and more "ethical," he began
to divide human existence itself into stages of perfection. In 1464, for
instance, he used man's "ages" as an artificial schema to link his early
translations of ten dialogues he attributed to Plato. "At a tender age,"
Ficino wrote Cosimo in his dedication to the translation early in 1464,

64. See Kristeller, *Il pensiero filosofico*, pp. 153–79, esp. pp. 159–60.

65. For Tignosi's *"primum in genere aliquo,"* see pp. 148–49, above. In his *Dialogi
quinque*, probably from the early 1460s (Laur. S. Marco 457), Lorenzo Pisano formalized, to an extent, his earlier theories by arguing that a good adheres naturally to the
good closest to it (fol. 48: he or the scribe gave "Maximus Trimagister" [!] as the authority); that a *res* is *plena* if to it "in suo genere nihil amplius accedere potest" (fol. 10v); and
that "in omnibus omnia semper rediguntur ad unum in illo genere primum" (fol. 206:
cf. Chapter VI, n. 124, above). Both Pisano's doctrines and his language, however, may
here be reflecting Ficino's influence.

66. *Opera omnia*, p. 991. The translation is from Kristeller, *The Philosophy of Marsilio
Ficino* (1943; rept. Gloucester, Mass., 1964), p. 146; cf. *Il pensiero filosofico*, p. 153.

men are deceived by their senses and by common opinion, and they reckon the good to be a possession of material objects, so that their whole impulse is directed toward their possession. Hence I have put the book *De lucri cupiditate* [that is, *Hipparchus*] first in order. When men have advanced in age and been incited by reason, they begin to love the understanding of divine things as a good. The love of wisdom is "philosophy": therefore the book *De philosophia* [that is, *Amatores*] is assigned the next place, second in order.[67]

Here Ficino has the higher form of life rule the lower: there are not simply the two wings, as described earlier in his *De divino furore*, but a higher, contemplative life ruling the active. Ficino even went so far as to argue that the outstanding virtue of the active life, which he termed "justice," could not lead even to temporal happiness without the virtue of the contemplative life, or wisdom. Again to Cosimo in January 1464 Ficino attempted to explain the essence of Plato's dialogue *De summo bono* (that is, *Philebus*):

All men want to act well, which is to live well. But they live well if they are endowed with as many good things as possible. Now these good things are said to be riches, health, beauty, strength, nobility of birth, honors, power, prudence, as well as justice, fortitude, and temperance, and above all else wisdom, which indeed comprehends the whole essence of happiness. . . . Wisdom ensures that we rightly use riches, health, beauty, strength, and the other things which are called good. For this reason knowledge is the cause of good and successful action, in the possession, use, and working of every gift. The man who possesses many gifts and uses them without intelligence is injured the more, the more he possesses, since he has more to misuse. . . . Thus none of those qualities which above were called good are good in themselves, for if they are dominated by ignorance they are worse than their opposites, insofar as they can plentifully supply the means of crime to an evil leader. . . . Clearly, from these things Plato placed as the highest good in the soul, not acting but contemplating the pure intelligence of truth.[68]

---

67. Kristeller, *Supplementum Ficinianum*, II, 104: "Verum in tenera etate homines sensibus et opinione decepti rerum mobilium possessionem bonum existimant, unde ad illam toto impetu perferuntur, quo fit ut de lucri cupiditate primus sit in ordine liber. Quoniam vero etate provecti ac ratione quandoque admoniti divinorum cognitionem tamquam bonum amare incipiunt, amor autem sapientie philosophia est, liber de philosophia proximum locum secundum ordinem est sortitus."

68. Ficino, *Letters*, I, 32–34 (altered very slightly); cf. *Opera omnia*, p. 608. The last sen-

At this same time, Ficino was beginning to discover a parallel structure to describe the several "levels" of virtues. In his *argumentum* to his translation of *Alcibiades II* (1464), a dialogue he attributed to Plato, Ficino identified the four virtues as the *civiles, purgatoriae, animi iam purgati*, and *exemplares*, which four ranged from the human virtues to the divine.[69] His source was probably Macrobius's commentary on the *Dream of Scipio* (1.8.5 seqq.), who listed his source as Plotinus's *De virtutibus* (that is, *Ennead* 1.2).[70] Matteo Palmieri had already used the Plotinian or Macrobian *virtutes* as the frame for the soul's ascent in his *Città di vita* of the 1450s, and in the early 1460s Landino was using them also, in his lectures on Juvenal and Virgil.[71]

By the late 1460s, in his commentaries on Plato's *Symposium* and *Philebus*, Ficino described in more detail the several ages of man that he had outlined for Cosimo. These he handled variously. He always had the *vita voluptuosa*, man's life as he lived the life of a beast, at the bottom, and the *vita contemplativa*, man's life as he lived the life of a god, at the top. The middle, *vita activa*, the life "proper" to man, Ficino sometimes subdivided. In his *Philebus* commentary, drafted in 1469 for Michele Mercati out of lectures surely delivered earlier, Ficino explained (as had Plato) how wisdom relates to pleasure as the highest good. The principle of things, which is the good, draws all things toward itself. All things, therefore, necessarily desire the good.

By this impulse, as Plato says in the *Republic*, things divine something to be the good. But what it is they know not. Yet they divine that it must be something sufficient and perfect. Thus whatever

tence is my own translation, following the earlier form of this letter (ed. in Kristeller, *Supplementum Ficinianum*, I, 37): "Ex iis perspicuum est Platonem summum in animo bonum non agente iam, sed potius contemplante puram veritatis intelligentiam posuisse [potuisse *ed.*]."

69. *Opera omnia*, p. 1134. Ficino evidently inserted the passage on the four virtues just before publishing the work in 1464: see Kristeller, "Marsilio Ficino as a Beginning Student of Plato," p. 51.

70. The virtues were formalized by Porphyry, out of Plotinus's *Enn.* 1.2 ("De virtutibus"), in his *De occasionibus*, a text Ficino would translate much later into Latin (see Kristeller, *Supplementum Ficinianum*, I, cxxxv). It is possible that Ficino was using a scholastic source, e.g., Thomas Aquinas, who mentioned the virtues often: see L. Schütz, *Thomas-Lexikon* (1895; rept. Stuttgart, 1958), s.v. "virtus" (sect. e).

71. M Palmieri, *Città di vita*, ed. M. Rooke as *Libro del poema chiamato Citta di vita composto da Matteo Palmieri Florentino*, Smith College Studies in Modern Languages, 1–2 (Northampton, Mass., 1927–28), book 3. (Roberto Cardini is currently preparing a new edition.) Palmieri had already surveyed these virtues in his *Della vita civile*, pp. 52ff. They were also mentioned in Petrarch's *De vita solitaria*, ed. G. Martellotti (Turin, 1977), p. 56 (citing Macrobius and, from Macrobius, Plotinus). For Landino, and other sources, see Chapter IX, n. 90, below.

seems to have the aspect of sufficiency or perfection they choose as the good. Men, therefore, proceed by different routes; they strive, nevertheless, toward one end, that is, to attain a way of life that is sufficient. Some think sufficiency belongs to the life of pleasure, others to the military life, others to the civil life, others to the life of contemplation. Thus the four inclinations of men, through the four types of life, seek one and the same thing, sufficiency. But only those who contemplate reach it. For the contemplative life is nearer to the good itself, God. This life seeks nothing externally, it is content with internal things, it has need of very few things. By fleeing the body it avoids the evils which afflict it.[72]

For Ficino there was but one route from the active to the contemplative life, and this was through philosophy. The function of philosophy is to change, to lead the individual from an inadequate, unhappy life to the life of contemplation. Since this life is man's highest good, philosophy had to be closely related to religion, and the philosopher must be similar to the priest. This relationship is strikingly evident in the title of Ficino's greatest systematic work, his *Theologia Platonica* of the 1470s. Yet even in a youthful oration before the Florentine Studio, his *De laudibus philosophiae*, Ficino had already pointed to a *prisca theologia* from the time of Hermes Trismegistus, a theology carried to Greece by Pythagoras, Heraclitus, and Plato, taken up directly by Dionysius the Areopagite (who was "first a Platonic and then a Christian"), and then continued by Saint Augustine.[73] Some of the most simple truths, Ficino knew, were explained by both theologians and philosophers. In an Italian letter of consolation (ca. 1460) to his cousin on the death of her sister, Ficino explained that "all theologians and philosophers would have it that each of us is not that which is seen and touched, but that the soul is the substance of whatever we are, and the body is the prison and tomb in which man is bound over and buried the first day he takes on the body."[74]

Hence, well before the founding of the Platonic Academy at Careggi, Ficino began to distinguish his own philosophizing, which concerned itself with the spiritual health of the soul, from that purely formal phi-

72. M. J. B. Allen, ed., *Philebus Commentary*, pp. 310–13 and nn. The translation generally follows that of Allen, but I have changed a few things for stylistic reasons.

73. *Opera omnia*, pp. 757–58.

74. Kristeller, *Supplementum Ficinianum*, II, 174: "[E] theologi e philosophi tutti vogliono che ciascuno di noi non sia quello che si vede e tocca, ma che la anima sia la substantia di qualunque di noi et il corpo la prigione o sepultura in che l'uomo è legato e sepellito il primo dì che piglia 'l corpo."

losophy taught in the universities. To Antonio Serafico, on 1 November 1457, Ficino alluded to the two methods of philosophizing: you, on whom heavenly frenzy has breathed, "follow the footsteps of Socrates and Christ by philosophizing in action as well as in disputation. Continue as you have begun, philosophize even when fortune wills you not to, cultivate philosophy, even if you must be the only one to do so, with your whole heart, even as others do so merely with their tongues."[75]

For Ficino the Platonic doctrine of the contemplative life was especially important for the Florentine youth. He saw how the "several lives" of men, from the life of pleasure to that of contemplation, tended to coincide with the periods of man's life. How remarkable was the case of Pellegrino degli Agli, who, when Ficino wrote to him his letter *De divino furore*, was but seventeen! Indeed, wrote Ficino,

> when I consider your age and those things which come from you every day, I not only rejoice but indeed marvel at such great gifts in a friend. I do not know which of the ancients whose memory we respect, not to mention men of our own time, achieved so much at your age. This I ascribe not just to study and art, but much more to divine frenzy.[76]

The letter *De divino furore* attempted not merely to praise Agli's pursuit of the contemplative life but to point to what Ficino called the "most potent proof" of the "divine force" that dwells in our soul. This frenzy is only the beginning of the contemplative life, what Plato calls "the first attempt at flight."[77] Later, in his *Philebus* commentary (drafted in 1469), Ficino outlined the three things necessary for understanding the divine: "One must have long experience in all things, be bolstered by knowledge in all fields, and lead the mind completely away from the customary vision of the eyes. Since adolescents lack all of these things, they cannot yet grasp the reasons of divine things."[78] How do philosophers deal with these problems and point the youth toward the true nature of things? The *prisci theologi* first showed the way by pointing to the "traces" of

75. Ibid., II, 82: "Felicem te puto mi Seraphice, . . . quem . . . celestis furor afflaverit, qui Socratis et Christi imitatus vestigia non minus agendo quam disputando philosopheris. Perge igitur ut cepisti, invita etiam fortuna philosophare, philosophiam toto pectore quam reliqui lingua dumtaxat colunt solus tu cole."
76. *Letters*, I, 42; cf. *Opera omnia*, p. 612.
77. *Letters*, I, 42, 45; cf. *Opera omnia*, pp. 612, 613–14.
78. *Philebus Commentary*, p. 233: "Oportet enim ad divinorum intelligentiam et longo rerum usu callere et scientiis omnibus esse fulctum, et mentem ab oculorum consuetudine prorsus abducere. Cumque his omnibus adolescentes careant, rationes divinorum nondum assequuntur."

divine things that were hidden in the observable world. Later, by perfecting logic and dialectics, Socrates (and Plato) could show others the true nature of their desires and the true possibilities of their fulfillment.[79]

In Ficino's role as a "philosopher for youth," we see also his transition from a young scholarly intellectual to his role of ethical leadership to the Florentine youth. Ficino himself insisted that his philosophy required a transformed spirit, a turning away from the world to the *vita contemplativa*. This obviously required no mere "meditation" but a new way of life. By Ficino's own terms the contemplative life must rule the active life: the Ficinian philosophy could never require one set of norms to govern life in the world and another to govern pure thought. In taking up one scholastic topos, the *utilitas disciplinae*, in his *Symposium* commentary (1469), Ficino examined at some length the usefulness and hence practical consequences of one aspect of the Platonic doctrine, Socratic love. Ficino indicated first both the private and public benefits: Socratic love "benefits Socrates himself for recovering the wings by which to fly back to his homeland"; it also "benefits his city greatly for living virtuously and happily. Certainly men, not stones, make a city." Ficino then showed how difficult it was to effect a Platonic philosophy.

> But men at a tender age are like quite tender trees: they have to be looked after and pruned straight for the most bountiful harvest. Parents and pedagogues have the care of children, but youths no sooner escape the supervision of parents and pedagogues than they are corrupted by wicked association with the crowd. Certainly they would follow that higher level of living received at home if they were not deflected from it by the customs and habits of wicked men, especially of those who entice them.

Socrates will take action on behalf of the Athenian youth, Ficino next argued, although whatever legal remedies he makes will be ineffective.

> What, therefore, will Socrates do? Will he permit the youth, who is the seed of the future commonwealth, to be corrupted by the contagion of shameful men? But where is his love of country? And so Socrates will come to the aid of the country and will free its sons—nay, his own brothers—from destruction. He will perhaps prescribe laws which will segregate lascivious men from the company of youths. But we cannot all be Lycurguses and Solons. To few is the authority given to make laws; very few obey laws that are made. What then? Will he use force and by his own hand drive

---

79. Recognition of the divine and then fuller discovery through dialectic are common themes in Ficino. See, e.g., *Philebus Commentary*, pp. 247–49.

away the older men from the youth? But only Hercules is said to
have fought with monsters; for anyone else, violence of this sort
is most dangerous. Perhaps he will warn, rebuke, and scold the
wicked men? But the disturbed soul scorns the words of him who
warns and, what is worse, rages against the warner. For this reason, Socrates is struck with the fist by one, with the heel by another, when he tries that method.

Finally, Ficino shows Socrates' solution: "Only one way of saving the
youth remains, the companionship of Socrates."[80]

If Marsilio Ficino viewed himself as the Socrates of the Florentines,
we have some idea of how he might wish the Platonic Academy to help
create in Florence a new way of looking at the world. Its function was
primarily educational and ideological, designed to win over and hold
the Florentines, particularly the young, to the contemplative life. The
glue of the new society was Platonic love. The human soul, created by
God, contains his divine splendor. Attracted by this beauty, another
soul is moved toward it. Man's true existence is his soul; his body is like
a prison for it. When one loves another, one abandons this prison and
is left "stranded" if this love is not received or returned by the other.
The "true and eternal unity" of God means that souls, created by God,
are actually closer to one another than are the souls of individuals to
their own bodies.[81]

---

80.   The translation is partly my own, but I have freely used sections of the two translations by S. Jayne: *Marsilio Ficino's Commentary on Plato's Symposium*, University of Mis-
souri Studies, 19 (Columbia, Mo., 1944), pp. 233–34, and Marsilio Ficino, *Commentary
on Plato's* Symposium *on Love* (Dallas, 1985), pp. 172–73. Cf. the edition by R. Marcel,
Commentaire sur le Banquet de Platon (Paris, 1956) [hereafter *De amore*, ed. Marcel], pp.
260–61: "Queritis quid amor socraticus conferat? Primo quidem ipsi Socrati plurimum
ad alas recuperandas, quibus in patriam revolet, deinde civitati sue magnopere ad honeste feliciterque vivendum. Civitatem profecto non lapides sed homines faciunt. Homines vero a tenera etate, quemadmodum arbores a tenerioribus curandi sunt et ad frugem optimam dirigendi. Puerorum curam parentes habent et pedagogi. Adolescentes
autem limites parentum et pedagogorum non prius transgrediuntur quam iniqua vulgi
consuetudine depraventur. Superiorem quippe vivendi normam domi inhibitam seque-
rentur, nisi ab ea improborum hominum, eorum presertim qui illis blandiuntur, usu con-
suetudineque deflecterentur. Quid ergo Socrates faciet? Num permictet ut flagitiosorum
contagione adolescentia, que future rei publice semen est, corrumpatur? At ubi patrie
caritas? Succurret itaque patrie Socrates filiosque illius, suos autem fratres, a pernitie li-
berabit. Leges fortasse conscribet, quibus lascivos viros ab adolescentum consuetudine
segregabit. Sed non omnes Solones aut Lycurgi esse possumus. Paucis legum condenda-
rum datur auctoritas; paucissimi legibus latis obtemperant. Quid ergo? Vim inferet et
manu iniecta seniores a iuventute depellet? At solus Hercules monstris dicitur decertasse;
ceteris periculosissima est huiusmodi violentia. Forsitan scelestos homines monebit, cori-
piet, obiurgabit? Ceterum perturbatus animus monentis verba contemnit et, quod dete-
rius est, sevit in monitorem. Qua de causa ab alio pugno, ab alio calce, dum id tentaret,
percussus est Socrates. Unica restat iuventuti via salutis, Socratis consuetudo."

81.   For the early form of "Platonic love," see Kristeller, *Il pensiero filosofico*, pp. 301ff.

A form of this theme is already evident in Ficino's letter to his brothers and sisters (6 August 1455), where domestic harmony is preserved
through the children's common participation in the creation and hence
love of the father.[82] In Ficino's later writings Platonic love answers to a
variety of circumstances of daily life. In October 1462, for instance, after
the death of his brother Anselmo, Ficino wrote a letter of consolation
to his parents, brothers, and sisters in which he described a spiritual
voice of joy from his brother just after his death. "Rejoice in the present
day," the voice said, "rejoice and make merry, since from servitude into
freedom, from shadows to light, from sleep to wakefulness, and from
death to life your Anselmo has by the greatest God been transferred."
All things proceed from the highest good and return to it.

> Grieve not that you cannot see me. Now no less than before you
> can see me. What you saw in the past was my vestment and tomb.
> You never did recognize me with human eyes. When you thought
> of my soul wrapped up in that vile matter you saw me with mental
> eyes. With these you may now see me in equal measure when you
> think of me. And if you should say, "Alas, how immeasurable is
> the grief that we are not able to be together as we were in the
> past!"—I answer that we are now much closer together than we
> were earlier. . . . Thus do not look for me outside of yourselves,
> since in you do I live and think, just as you yourselves do.[83]

Ficino exploited identical themes in his letters to associates. In 1458 he
informed Pellegrino degli Agli, in Ferrara, that he did not miss him even
a little: one misses only those things one is without, and you, Pellegrino,
are as assuredly with me as I am with myself.[84] Four years later he as-
sured Leonardo di Tone Pagni that Leonardo was closer to Marsilio

---

Kristeller argues convincingly that the "consciously 'erotic' coloring" of Ficino's correspondence ought never to be viewed as a "fantastic or exaggerated sentimentalism" or as
a "more-or-less veiled homosexuality" (from the English version: *Philosophy of Marsilio
Ficino*, p. 282). See also p. 159, above.

82. Ed. in Kristeller, *Supplementum Ficinianum*, II, 109–28.

83. Ibid., II, 163, 164: "Orsù per lo amore paterno, materna carità, fraterna benivolentia, exultate nel presente giorno, exultate dico et fate festa che di servitù in libertà, di
tenebre in luce, di sonno in vigilia, di morte in vita Anselmo vostro è dal sommo Iddio
transferito. . . . Ancora non vi dolete di non poter vedermi. Non meno al presente che
prima vedere mi potete. Quello che pel passato riguardavi, era la veste et sepultura mia.
Me con occhi di corpo non conoscesti mai. Quando pensavi all'anima mia che era in
quella vile materia involta vedevi me con occhi mentali. Per la qual cosa equalmente ora
ad me pensando mi vedrete. Et se dicessi: Omè, che smisurato dolore è che noi non pos-
siamo essere insieme come pel tempo preterito, ad questo rispondo, che molto più siamo
ora insieme che prima. . . . Adunque non cercate me fuora di voi, che in voi sono vivo et
penso come voi medesimi."

84. Ibid., pp. 85–86.

than Leonardo was to himself.[85] And Ficino could jokingly even use the theme as an excuse for not writing.[86]

While some scholars have insisted that the Platonic Academy was an elite, isolated band of philosophers, drawn out of Florence and to Careggi by the Medici and there nurtured on Platonic wisdom by Marsilio Ficino, the membership requirements for the Platonic Academy appear to have been far from strict.[87] One had to pursue the contemplative life and (hence) be united in love with the other members. One need not become a professional philosopher or give up any activity in the world. A striking illustration of this is the fate of Ficino's translation into Latin of the *Pimander* of Hermes Trismegistus, completed in April 1463. By the following September his close friend Tommaso Benci, a cloth merchant, had prepared an Italian version for his friends, whom he described in the preface as merchants interested in philosophy but ignorant of Latin.[88] While Ficino was united with Hermes Trismegistus, Socrates, and Plato as a philosopher-theologian, he was united with Benci and other Florentines—be they professional philosophers or professional bankers—in love.

Hence Ficino viewed his Platonic philosophy as suited to a wide variety of persons and professions. His own "professional" interests, it should be emphasized, he viewed as special. As early as 1458, in an eclectic tract to Francesco Capponi, he mentioned parenthetically his particular talents as an expounder:

> Although it would appear to be arrogant and rash that I, at so tender an age, should undertake to explain such obscure enigmas and secrets [that is, Hermetic teachings on God and the soul] never before laid bare, by anyone I have read, in so many centuries, my love for you is so great that it forces me, for your sake, to make an attempt at this so arduous and difficult subject.[89]

Careggi for Ficino could only confirm his special position. Early in 1464, dedicating to Cosimo his translation of ten dialogues he attributed

---

85. Ibid., pp. 167–69.

86. For the theme of whether an exchange of letters was necessary between friends, see the letters cited in the above two notes. See also Kristeller, *Il pensiero filosofico*, pp. 302–3.

87. That the Platonic Academy was "isolated" and "elite" has now become a commonplace of Renaissance historiography. See, e.g., G. Brucker, *Renaissance Florence* (New York, 1969), pp. 265–66.

88. Ed. in Kristeller, *Supplementum Ficinianum*, I, 98–101.

89. *Di dio et anima*, ibid., II, 134: "E benché paia la mia arrogantia e temerità, ch'io in tenera età pigli a dichiarare tanto scuro enigma e velame da nessuno in tanti secoli ch'io abbia lecto mai exposto, niente di meno l'amore inverso di te è tanto, che mi constringe a qualunche ardua e difficile materia per te tentare."

to Plato, he noted that when Cosimo first received the Greek manuscripts "the spirit of Plato flew from Byzantium to Florence."[90] In affirming the importance of Byzantium as the medieval locus of the Platonic spirit, Ficino also affirmed his own historical position, for he had reassumed the Platonic spirit directly from its sources rather than from the Christian Patristic or Latin and Greek medieval traditions. He knew that he was unique in introducing the real Plato to the Latins, and he jealously refused to allow anyone in the 1460s or 1470s to copy from his translations of Plato until they could be put in final form.[91] Yet he viewed his status as a "professional philosopher" as more than historical, for he began to recognize in his own melancholic temperament a disposition of soul that made him particularly suited to be a philosopher.[92]

As one born under a special configuration of stars, Ficino had the talent to be a "priest of the Muses" and, assisted by steady Medicean patronage, live a life separated from the world as far as humanly possible. He never demanded such a literal devotion from his friends, and, indeed, among them professional philosophers are rare indeed. Cristoforo Landino became a philosopher of sorts, but he was primarily a poet and scholar, and his "purer" speculative efforts depended on Ficino. Pico della Mirandola was influenced by Ficino but was not part of the Academy. In fact, from Giovanni Corsi's biography of Ficino in the sixteenth century to Paul Oskar Kristeller's manuscript searches and studies in our own, only one name clearly emerges, besides Ficino's, as the Academy's philosopher, a rather obscure sixteenth-century figure named Francesco da Diacceto.[93]

Ficino's Platonism, indeed, "permitted" a variety of professional pursuits, only one of which was philosophical and each of which had its ideal form. The historian of the Academy, Arnaldo Della Torre, has traced each of these ideas under its own rubric and according to the individual figures who pursued each ideal: he identified the ideal poet, rhetorician, jurist, businessman, philosopher, priest, physician, and mu-

90.   See Chapter v, n. 3, above.

91.   See the letter to Michele Mercati, 1 April 1466, now ed. in Kristeller, "Marsilio Ficino and His Work," pp. 32–33.

92.   See Kristeller, *Il pensiero filosofico*, pp. 224–27, and especially R. Klibansky, E. Panofsky, and F. Saxl, *Saturn and Melancholy* (Cambridge, 1964), pp. 255ff., an outgrowth and translation of Panofsky's and Saxl's fundamental study *Dürers "Melencolia I"* (1923).

93.   See Kristeller, *Studies*, pp. 112–13n. See now Francesco da Diacceto, *De pulchro libri III; Accedunt opuscula inedita et dispersa necnon testimonia quaedam ad eumdem pertinentia*, ed. Sylvain Matton (Pisa, 1986). Perhaps the fifteenth-century theologian Sebastiano Salvini should be considered a philosopher as well. See P. O. Kristeller, "Sebastiano Salvini: A Florentine Humanist and Theologian, and a Member of Marsilio Ficino's Platonic Academy," in *Didascaliae: Studies in Honor of Anselm M. Albareda*, ed. S. Prete (New York, 1961), pp. 205–43.

sician.[94] A variety of these figures, identified in their professional capac-
ities, appear as interlocutors in Ficino's commentary of 1469 on Plato's
Symposium.[95] These men could live in the world and yet be united in
Platonic love and in their pursuit of the contemplative life.

It should be noted, finally, that scholars have attached far too much
importance to the Academy's "isolation" at the Medici villa in Careggi.
It now appears that the Academy's seat there was largely symbolic—a
symbol, that is, of the contemplative life removed from the affairs of the
world. Plato's birthday was often, but not always, celebrated there. And
it now appears likely that "Careggi" for Ficino was annual profits from
a farm and a studio in the Medici villa, not his regular residence or place
of work.[96] Ficino's house was on Via Sant'Egidio, in the heart of Florence; of Ficino's letters bearing dates, about three are from Florence for
every one dated Careggi.[97] His lectures on Plato were in Florence,
mostly at the church of Santa Maria degli Angeli.[98] In his *De mystica
statera*, probably written in the mid- to late 1450s, Antonio degli Agli
attempted to convince Ficino that, for the Christian, life in the country
is better: You, I know, he scolded Marsilio, enjoy life in the city, with
its urban charms. The embarrassed "Marsilio" then had to reply: Yes,
and did not my Plato locate his Academy outside the city, so that the
youth would not be corrupted?[99] Modern scholars ought not to wrest

94.   *Storia*, pp. 654ff.

95.   *De amore*, ed. Marcel, p. 136.

96.   It now seems likely that Cosimo, in 1462, established the "Academy" in the Medici
villa at Careggi, while only in April 1463 did he endow Ficino with a nearby villino and
farm: see *Marsilio Ficino e il ritorno: Mostra*, pp. 175–76, no. 140.

97.   This ratio is based simply on a count of letters bearing a date. For Ficino's house,
see *Marsilio Ficino e il ritorno: Mostra*, pp. 174–75, no. 139.

98.   Della Torre, *Storia*, pp. 568ff.; Kristeller, *Studies*, p. 111 and n.; M. J. B. Allen, introduction to Ficino, *Philebus Commentary*, pp. 522–23, n. 31.

99.   Naples, Bibl. Naz., cod. VIII F 9, fol. 30v: "[Antonius:] Cumque denique ingenioli
modum ac vires mei optime iam tenuissem, cum magnis amplisque negotiis ineptum
parumque idoneum me deprehendissem urbem relinquere statui, rus concessi, idque
quoad potui ac licuit colui, ruri ut nosti iamdiu permansi. Non enim rusticum ingenium
urbis lautiis ac delitiis convenire congruereque posse putavi. Urbes enim presertim ut
nostra est urbanis, hoc est delicatis excultisque conveniunt ingeniis, ut est tuum, ut etiam
peregrini nostri, utque aliorum complurium quorum gratiam, leporem, suavitatem,
atque animi altitudinem inclita hec civitas ita sibi rapere solita est, ut mei similes continere consueverit. . . .

   "[Marsilius:] Miror equidem verba hec. Plerique enim egregii et ingenio et doctrina
viri hanc vitam adamasse manifestum. Ait siquidem beatus Hyeronimus in libro contra
Iovinianum: 'Multi philosophorum relinquerunt frequentias urbium, et ortulum subur-
banum elegerunt. . . . Ipse etiam Plato, cum esset dives et thoros [= toros] eius Diogenes lutatis pedibus conculcaret, ut posset vacare philosophie elegit academiam villam
ab urbe procul' [Jerome, *Adversus Jovinianum*, II, 9 (337–38); *PL* 23, 311–12]."

Ficino from the urban charms mentioned by Agli. At the Academy's founding, its "isolation" was largely symbolic, or, at most, what the villa has always been, a quiet place in which to think.[100]

In the first half of the Quattrocento the great humanist educator Guarino da Verona said that in Florence he found only conspiracies, not friendships.[101] In the world idealized by Marsilio Ficino there were only friendships, never conspiracies. He took the young Florentines and showed them how an excessive attachment to the things of the world, from their material goods to their political statuses, degraded them from their true nature and led ultimately to unhappiness and spiritual torment. He explained how justice could be a virtue of the active life only and could never be a virtue in itself unless ruled by the contemplative life. In this way Marsilio Ficino, who separated himself as thoroughly as possible from the world, resolved Florence's "problem" of friendship and thereby gave the Medici party's dreams of unity an ideological substance: he showed the young Florentines that they were closer to one another than they were to their very own selves.

100. D. R. Coffin, *The Villa in the Life of Renaissance Rome* (Princeton, 1979), pp. 9–16, surveys several early Quattrocento opinions on the villa. For economic aspects and the problem of the "villa psychology," see Goldthwaite, *Private Wealth in Renaissance Florence*, pp. 246–51.

101. See Guarino's letter cited by R. Sabbadini, *Vita di Guarino Veronese* (Genoa, 1891), p. 18.

VIII

DONATO ACCIAIUOLI'S
COMMENTARIES ON
ARISTOTLE

I N his funeral oration on Donato Acciaiuoli (1478), Cristoforo Landino first named the public offices Donato had held in the Florentine territories: these were at Pisa, Volterra, the Casentino (at
Poppi), San Miniato, Montepulciano, and Pistoia.[1] He then described
Donato's special embassies: he was a legate to Paul II, to the king of
France, to Siena, to Sixtus IV, and finally to France again, a commission
he did not survive. Landino next praised Donato's virtues: his continence, justice, fortitude, assisted by his beauty (quoting Virgil: "gratior
et pulchro veniens in corpore virtus"[2]). Then Landino changed directions: while in Donato we do indeed find the many great "civil" and
"purifying" virtues (*virtutes civiles et purgatoriae*), "let us leave Leah and
Martha behind, and ascend to Rachel and Mary. For our citizen not
only was distinguished in that way of life centered in action, but he also
took himself up to the contemplation of higher things."[3] From his early
years he learned Latin and Greek, the poets and historians of both languages, and the precepts of rhetoric. But "when he reached the age to
fulfill the duties of the republic, and he read in Plato that republics are
happy when philosophers rule, he turned himself wholly to the study of

1. Ed. M. Lentzen, in Landino, *Reden*, pp. 65–76.
2. *Aen.* 5. 344; cf. p. 130, above.
3. *Reden*, p. 72: "Multas tamen ac maximas fuisse in eo affirmabo, neque solum huiuscemodi virtutes ea ratione, qua civiles sunt, verum etiam qua purgatoriae appellantur,
habuisse contendam. Sed nos iam Lya Marthaque omissis ad Rachelem Mariamque as-
cendimus, quandoquidem non solum in eo vivendi genere, quod in actionibus versatur,
floruerit noster civis, verum . . . ad altiores res contemplandas sese erexerit."

wisdom."[4] And so, Landino continued, Donato began to follow the systematic order of studies taught by the great philosopher of our age, John Argyropoulos. He first mastered dialectics. Then he took up moral philosophy. From these studies he produced an outstanding commentary on Aristotle's *Ethics*, "which is in the hands of all."[5] (The commentary was printed in Florence that very year, 1478.[6]) Donato then learned natural philosophy from Argyropoulos and, through many years of contact with the Byzantine philosopher, even picked up some mathematics.[7]

Landino may now have paused in his speech and turned toward Argyropoulos himself, back in Florence from Rome for a final, brief assignment as lecturer in philosophy and hence present at the funeral:[8]

> I fear that while I am following these things in their own order someone would believe that I am more concerned with the division of philosophy than with the learning of the man. But his most serious teacher stands here as a witness, and he will not permit me to lie. Therefore I have said that Donato was an excellent citizen: he was an outstanding orator, a skilled dialectician, a clever natural philosopher, and a superior mathematician. Now I shall not fear also to call him a metaphysician, since he investigated not only those things which the Platonists and Aristotelians said about God, but also the things from Christian theology.
>
> For when he knew that our souls were produced not from matter but by the immortal God himself, in his image and likeness and out of nothing, and that they were created immortal with no secondary cause interceding, and that they were not able to find rest unless, insofar as they were able, they were conjoined to God, he took himself out of this lowest mire of earth up to the highest heavens, and, although he held by an indubitable faith those things which we can investigate by no human reason, nevertheless with his skill and genius he pursued those things which, by an established reason, lead to the first truth of faith.[9]

4. *Reden*, p. 72.

5. Ibid.

6. *Donati Acciaioli Florentini expositio super libros Ethicorum Aristotelis in novam traductionem Argiropyli Bisantii* (Florence: San Jacopo di Ripoli, 1478 [*GW* 140]) [hereafter "ed. 1478"].

7. *Reden*, pp. 73–74.

8. For Argyropoulos's return to Florence, see now Verde, "Giovanni Argiropolo e Lorenzo Buonincontri," pp. 280–81.

9. *Reden*, pp. 74–75: "Vereor dum haec omnia suo ordine prosequor, credat me quispiam eius potius quae de philosophia est divisionis quam hominis doctrinae rationem habuisse. Sed testis adest gravissimus praeceptor suus, is me mentiri non patiatur. Dixi

Landino concluded the oration with an imaginary speech of grief by the prophet Jeremiah and an exhortation to young Florentines to become like Donato Acciaiuoli.

Argyropoulos may have been willing to testify that Acciaiuoli knew his metaphysics; but we may rightly wonder if the label "metaphysician" is indeed proper. Merely the curriculum of Acciaiuoli's studies raises doubts. As I said in Chapter v, John Argyropoulos taught Aristotelian philosophy systematically: he began with logic and dialectics, then took up moral philosophy, natural philosophy, and metaphysics. But Acciaiuoli published commentaries only on Aristotle's *moral* philosophy, the *Nicomachean Ethics* (1464) and the *Politics* (1472).[10] (His only other philosophical works were a short disputation of 1464, *Utrum bene an male operari sit facilius*, which treats of ethics, and a *protesto* on justice delivered in 1469.[11]) In the late 1480s Alamanno Rinuccini would argue that almost no one in Florence successfully completed Argyropoulos's program of study. The Florentines, according to Rinuccini, were like Ennius's Neoptolemus, willing to sip from the vessel of philosophy but unwilling to drink from it deeply. Perhaps Rinuccini meant to include Acciaiuoli among the Florentine failures. The students of Argyropoulos, he said, were distracted from their philosophical studies by "family matters" and "affairs of state."[12] Acciaiuoli was married in 1461 and then regularly began to hold public offices, first as unofficial legate to France

---

igitur illum civem omni ex parte probatissimum, dixi oratorem egregium, dixi dialecticum acutissimum, phisicum ingeniosum, mathematicum non mediocrem. Nunc metaphisicum quoque illum nominare non verebor, cum ea quae de Deo non solum ab Aristotelicis Platonicisque, verum quae a Christiana theologia dicuntur, investigaverit, nam cum sciret animos nostros non ex materia productos, sed ab ipso immortali Deo ad suam imaginem et similitudinem ex nihilo nullaque secunda causa intercedente immortales creatos nec posse unquam conquiescere, nisi se Deo, quoad fieri potest, coniungant, ex hoc infimo terrarum limo ad summum usque caelum penetravit et cum ea, quae de Deo nulla ratione humana investigare possumus, indubitata fide teneret, acerrimo tamen ingenio ea prosequebatur, quae ad primam fidei veritatem certa ratione producunt." The last part of the quotation states a Thomistic position.

10.   A misreading of a section of a manuscript of Niccolò Tignosi's *De ideis*, by F. Fiorentino, in his *Il risorgimento filosofico nel Quattrocento* (Naples, 1885), p. 250 n. 28, led him to conclude that Acciaiuoli wrote a commentary on Aristotle's *Metaphysics*. For the correct reading, see L. Thorndike's edition in his *Science and Thought*, p. 332.

11.   The former ed. A. Perosa in his *Giovanni Rucellai e il suo zibaldone*, vol. 1: *"Il zibaldone quaresimale"* (London, 1960), pp. 125–33; cf. pp. 91–102. The tract, an answer to Giovanni Nanni da Viterbo, argues that doing evil is "easier" than doing good because of the strength and variety of man's appetites and passions. Evil lures man with several choices; the unique "good" in any circumstance can be found by reason alone. The *protesto* is ed. in E. Santini, "La *Protestatio de justitia* nella Firenze del sec. XV," *Rinascimento* 10 (1959), 32–106 at pp. 48–54.

12.   *Lettere ed orazioni*, pp. 189–90.

(1461) and then *vicarius* at Poppi (1462).[13] Acciaiuoli kept careful notes from Argyropoulos's lectures, but if there were any of these after 1461 they have not come to light. The last of the notebooks was on Aristotle's *De anima*, before, that is, the lectures on the *Metaphysics*.[14]

But it is not Acciaiuoli's academic curriculum alone which has led scholars to conclude that he could have had little or no interest in metaphysics. He was too committed to the principles of the active life and the humanistic studies that reinforced a civic ideology. One scholar has Acciaiuoli shocked and embittered by Argyropoulos's decision to teach natural and speculative philosophy.[15] Another, Eugenio Garin, has stressed the "insurmountable distance" between the logical, rhetorical, ethical, and political interests of the Acciaiuoli circle and the metaphysical and theological concerns of the Ficino group.[16] Landino indeed seemed somewhat hesitant about labeling Donato Acciaiuoli a "metaphysician." It may be significant that for this area alone Landino did not name Argyropoulos as the specific channel for Acciaiuoli's learning: instead of systematic instruction, Landino implied that there had been some sort of "absorption" of metaphysics from Platonists, Aristotelians, and Christian theologians. To be sure, Landino tended to impress rather energetically ancients and moderns into the camp of speculative, Platonic philosophy. In his *Disputationes Camaldulenses* of the early 1470s, Landino argued that the Acciaiuoli circle and Ficino's Academy each sought, in its own way, the same goal; more boldly, he turned Leon Battista Alberti, the late champion of the *vita attiva e civile*, into an allegorizing Platonist.[17] But before we speculate further on whether Landino was churning up a Platonic vortex so wide that anything and everything would get sucked into it, let us look briefly at Acciaiuoli's early philosophical studies and look particularly at the background to the

---

13.   A. d'Addario, in *DBI*, vol. 1, 81, 82; Della Torre, *Storia*, pp. 408–12 (and nn.); and now Ganz, "Humanist as Citizen," pp. 290–91. He held a few minor offices and accompanied a few embassies before 1461: see Ganz's checklist, as well as the evidence concerning embassies to Milan, 1452 (Chapter IV, n. 30, above), and to Mantua, 1459 (Chapter V, n. 28).

14.   He also transcribed Argyropoulos's introductory lecture on Aristotle's *Meteorologica*, 1462: see Chapter V, n. 28, above.

15.   Ganz, "Humanist as Citizen," chap. 3, "Anticipation and Disappointment: Iohannes Argyropulos," pp. 83–142 (esp. pp. 83–84, 122ff., 132ff.). Ganz does make one point that may be worth noting: there is "no word" of Acciaiuoli "submitting any of his works" to Argyropoulos "for critical comment" (p. 137). See also Ganz's "Ambition and Accommodation in Medicean Florence: Agnolo and Donato Acciaiuoli," *Stanford Italian Review* 4 (1984), 48.

16.   E. Garin, "Donato Acciaiuoli cittadino," pp. 202–3.

17.   *Disputationes Camaldulenses*, esp. pp. 64, 69.

work we are especially interested in, his commentary on the *Nicomachean Ethics*, written for Cosimo de' Medici in 1463–64.[18]

As we have said, Acciaiuoli's interest in philosophy predated the arrival of Argyropoulos in Florence in 1457. Before 1450 he took courses in logic at the University of Florence and studied privately the logic of Paul of Venice under a friar identified by Vespasiano da Bisticci as Agnolo da Lecco.[19] From a letter of 1451 we know also that he owned a codex of dialectics, but he noted that he planned to put off studying it to hear Carlo Marsuppini's anticipated lectures in Latin rhetoric and Greek.[20] He made some progress in Greek in the early 1450s, but it seems that he did not study it intensely until the end of the Italian wars in 1454. The breadth of his philosophical culture by 1457 cannot be determined exactly: from codices he owned and marginal citations in his lecture notes we can detect a growing familiarity with a wide range of Latin scholastics: Thomas Aquinas, Albertus Magnus, Giles of Rome, Walter Burley, Johannes Buridanus, Paul of Venice, and Caietanus de Thienis.[21]

In Chapter III, on the students of Argyropoulos, I argued that Donato Acciaiuoli was one of a group of Florentines who, influenced largely by Giannozzo Manetti, sought individual perfection through full active participation in public offices, especially the elective embassies, through commitment to religious good works, and through a full development of the intellectual faculties. The last of these required him to master the humanities, including Greek, as well as those branches of philosophy (natural philosophy and metaphysics) outside the humanist curriculum. Like most others in his circle, he sought a suitable *praeceptor* to direct the new studies. A course in logic, therefore, under Agnolo da Lecco could be for Acciaiuoli only a basic course. Donato feared also that another Florentine philosopher and theologian, the Augustinian Guglielmo Becchi, would pass himself off as an orator and win a university position as one of the candidates for the position in rhetoric and poetry proposed early in 1455. In many ways, however, John Argyropoulos, with his exposition of the Aristotelian system as a whole, and from the original sources (or nearly so), was an ideal teacher. At the beginning of 1455, therefore, Donato Acciaiuoli had many reasons to be hope-

18. For the dating, see n. 24, below.

19. See the sources cited above, Chapter III, n. 87.

20. Letter to Iacopo Ammannati, 10 Oct. 1451, ed. in C. Marchesi, *Scritti minori*, pp. 11–12.

21. Donato Acciaiuoli's copy of Johannes Buridanus, *Quaestiones in Aristotelis libros X ethicorum*, is Naz. II I 81. As I noted earlier, Acciaiuoli studied Paul of Venice under Agnolo da Lecco. The references to the other figures are in the marginalia of Acciaiuoli's drafts of the lectures of Argyropoulos (Naz. II I 104, Naz. II I 103, Magl. V 42).

ful. Postwar prosperity would free him from the family business and give him leisure for study. Prosperity would also allow Florence to hire an outstanding outside orator, such as Filelfo, who would teach Florentines Latin and Greek eloquence. The happiest of unhappy occurrences, the fall of Constantinople to the Turks, would permit John Argyropoulos to teach the Florentines Greek philosophy. Out of all of this Donato would be able to reach the age when he could begin to hold the more prestigious public offices and embassies (that is, during the early to mid-1460s) with a well-rounded humanistic and philosophical education.

Acciaiuoli's outrage at the Florentine Councils' attempt to draft two "orators" for the university, with a combined salary of up to 250 florins per year, stemmed in part from his strict separation of the higher life of the philosopher from the servile life of "action." His anger was directed not toward Landino and what he stood for (be it Platonism, Ficinianism, scholarly detachment, or Medicean hegemony) but toward those who would reduce academic life in Florence to preparation for the *res mercenariae*. In the latter category fell his older cousin Agnolo, who not only supported Landino but had held Donato "captive" in the "mercenary life" during the war. The salary being offered the orators would tend to reduce Florence, the natural center for wisdom, to the petty, mercantile level of a small town ("like Prato," as he put it). The basic disciplines, rhetoric and poetry, would turn young Florentines into good, literate merchants: they could not make them into true aristocrats or complete men. On the immediate Studio question Donato failed, and the marvelously complementary instruction of the two outstanding intellectuals of Greek culture, Filelfo and Argyropoulos, who together would turn Florence into a "new Athens" in a way it had never been before, was not to be. Donato, then, made the best of what was available: he resumed his studies of logic and dialectics, the preliminary courses necessary to Argyropoulos's systematic teaching, and, through the teaching of Francesco da Castiglione, he perfected his Greek.

Acciaiuoli's aristocratic intention of becoming a philosopher and his determination to be a *virtuoso* in his chosen discipline led him toward one of the most extraordinary achievements in notetaking of the entire Quattrocento, his notes to Argyropoulos's lectures on Aristotle. For four and a half years, from the beginning of 1457 to the summer of 1461, Donato heard and recorded the lectures, amassing nearly fifteen hundred pages of notes in a small hand. And it would appear that he did not miss a word. Recorded almost always as if they are Argyropoulos's own words, the notes describe each logical step of Aristotle's teaching: no argument is cut short, no sentence is truncated, no word is mis-

spelled, slips of the pen and lapses of concentration are few. While the
extant notebooks are almost surely a second draft of the lectures, they
indeed appear almost always to be verbatim records. In his life of Acciaiuoli, Vespasiano da Bisticci marveled at Acciaiuoli's accomplish-
ment: he could "take down in writing everything that Argyropoulos
said in voice."[22] The completeness of the notes reveals an almost mania-
cal attempt to follow exactly the Argyropouleian route to systematic
philosophical knowledge.

To his draft of the lectures on the *Ethics* Acciaiuoli added many marginalia. Argyropoulos's lectures were based on Leonardo Bruni's translation, which, as I noted earlier, the Byzantine criticized frequently. The
Greek passages under scrutiny are sometimes included in the body of
the lecture notes; but often Donato added them in the margin, apparently on his own, when this would clarify the argument of the lecture.
Simple expository material also appears in the margins, accompanied by
a mark showing its correct place in the text. These may be Acciaiuoli's
additions as he compared his lecture drafts to his original notes (that is,
a correction of a lacuna due to incomplete notes or inexact recopying),
Acciaiuoli's own interpretation added on his own, or Argyropoulos's
clarification of a passage that Donato heard after the formal lectures and
added at a later time. These additions are crammed into whatever space
in the margins is available. We know from Vespasiano and others that
Acciaiuoli frequently had questions for Argyropoulos after the lectures
and that the Byzantine was more than willing to respond.[23]

The content of these lectures on the *Ethics* we have already looked at
in Chapter v. As I said, Argyropoulos's attempt to put Aristotle's philosophy into systematic hierarchies, with metaphysics at the top, may
have been based on a Neoplatonic cosmology; but Argyropoulos was
consciously an Aristotelian who saw Plato's doctrines as necessarily obscure and insufficiently systematic. Although he discussed Plato with
empathy in his lectures when the text of Aristotle mentions or alludes
to Platonic teaching, and while he underscored Plato's contribution to
the history of philosophy, Argyropoulos was wholly an Aristotelian

22.   *Vite*, II, 25. For the notebooks, see Chapter v, nn. 14 and 28. Spelling eccentricities
in them are of the most common sort: Latin words having Greek equivalents, where the
Greek has a voiceless stop or liquid, often have a "wandering" aspiration (e.g., in Naz. II
I 104, fol. 16, "methafisicis"). Such errors as this are rare, and Acciaiuoli moved gradually
toward correct orthography. Virginia Brown exaggerates only slightly when, in describing Acciaiuoli's notes on the *De anima*, 1460–61 (Magl. v 42), she says that he "never"
has the *h* in the wrong place ("Giovanni Argiropulo on the Agent Intellect," p. 162).

23.   *Vite*, I, 13, 26; Alamanno Rinuccini noted this also, *Lettere ed orazioni*, pp. 189–90.

who believed that a correct, systematic study of Aristotle led to moral and intellectual perfection.

From his draft of Argyropoulos's lectures Donato Acciaiuoli wrote a commentary on the *Nicomachean Ethics*, which he completed for Cosimo de' Medici in late 1463 or 1464 and published under his own name.[24] In the preface to the work, dedicated to Cosimo, Donato first praised Argyropoulos's lectures and new translation of the *Ethics*. He was preparing the commentary, he wrote, for those who had been unable to attend the lectures, so that they could understand, on their own, at their own pace (*pro arbitrio*), "the things we learned through Argyropoulos's own words." Indeed Donato promised only a redraft, differing from the original in using a more diffuse style, "so that a clear explanation can be accessible to all."[25] Some differences with the original were

24. Vespasiano, *Vite*, II, 210–11: Cosimo "[v]olle per passare tempo, inanzi circa uno anno che morissi, farsi legere l'Etica d'Aristotile a meser Bartolomeo da Colle, cancelliere in palagio, et pregò Donato Acciauoli che arecassi in ordine gli scritti aveva ricolti sotto meser Giovanni sopra l'Etica, et secondo che Donato emendava egli mandava e' quinterni a Cosimo, et meser Bartolomeo legeva, et lessela tutta, et questo comento che c'è oggi dell'Etica di Donato fu quello s'emendò, mentre che Cosimo se la faceva legere." For the confusing label "cancelliere in palagio" (Scala was not yet chancellor of Florence), see D. Marzi, *La Cancelleria*, p. 238; cf. Brown, *Bartolomeo Scala*, p. 36. Acciaiuoli evidently had already begun sending the fascicles to Cosimo de' Medici by early November 1463 (see Rinuccini, *Lettere ed orazioni*, p. 62), and Vespasiano's dating here seems accurate. See also the *Vite*, II, 49, 50, and Brown, *Bartolomeo Scala*, p. 36. That what Acciaiuoli sent Cosimo was the commentary we shall be considering, and not his draft of the lectures (i.e., Naz. II I 104), is clear from Vespasiano's remarks, the dates attached to the draft of the original lectures (see Chapter V, nn. 14 and 28, above), and the fact that the revised commentary was dedicated to Cosimo.

For Acciaiuoli's commentary, we shall be following the autographs, Magl. XXI 136 (182 fols.), covering Books 1–3 and part of Book 4; Magl. VI 162, fols. 54–86v, covering the rest of Book 4 and part of Book 5; and Magl. XXI 137 (258 fols.), Books 7–10. The manuscripts have an original foliation in the lower right, which reveals that the three manuscripts were originally a unit. The section now missing, from Book 5, would begin "Et primo ostendit quo pacto operatio" and be foliated 204–33 in the lower right (the section from sig. Q3v, line 14, to sig. R8v of the 1478 printed edition). Where the text is quoted, I shall also cite the respective section of the 1478 edition (see n. 6, above).

Eugenio Garin has asserted that Naz. II I 80, owned by Alessandro Acciaiuoli, is a Donato Acciaiuoli autograph (*La cultura filosofica*, p. 69n.), but this is incorrect (de la Mare, "New Research on Humanistic Scribes," p. 479, has now identified the scribe as Agnolo di Iacopo de' Dinuzi), and in at least one place this manuscript is inferior to the printed edition (cf. Naz. II I 80, fol. 250–250v and ed. 1478, sig. [I]I7v–8). Garin has also identified "appunti e abbozzi" to the commentary in Magl. VI 102 ("Donato Acciaiuoli cittadino," p. 251n.): but surely he meant Magl. VI 162, which does not contain notes but part of the missing section described above.

25. Magl. XXI 136, fol. 1–IV (cf. ed. 1478, sig. A1): " . . . ut ii qui adesse non potuerunt et harum rerum desiderio tenerentur, hec que nos ex eius [*sc.* Argyropuli] ore accepimus percipere et ipsi pro arbitrio possent. Quare traductionem illius ac ordinem explicandi pluribus verbis sequuti sumus, lata interdum et diffusa oratione utentes, ut explanatio aperta magis magisque omnibus esset communis."

necessary. The "diffuse style" permitted more introductory and summary material than the original lectures. In addition, Acciaiuoli was now
using Argyropoulos's own translation, so that the continuous references
to the Greek and to the problems of Bruni's translation could be left
out. Some of Acciaiuoli's own marginalia are brought into the text, such
as the opinions of Aquinas, Walter Burley, and other Latin expositors.
Quotations from Cicero, particularly the *Tusculans*, while not absent
from Argyropoulos's lectures, are more frequent. Aside from these differences, the bulk of the commentary is a verbatim reproduction of Argyropoulos's own argument in his lectures. Donato even used the de-
ceptive device of putting apparent quotations from Argyropoulos's
lectures, which then included an "ut mihi videtur" or "meâ sententiâ,"
directly into his commentary, without even altering the pronoun of the
first person.[26]

Acciaiuoli's "debt" to Argyropoulos in "his" commentary on the *Ethics* has long been recognized. Eugenio Garin too has recently emphasized Acciaiuoli's verbatim "borrowings," but he has also pointed to a
slight change in emphasis ("Chi confronti con cura la redazione del
commento dell'Acciaiuoli con le lezioni dell'Argiropulo deve riconos-
cere che lo scrittore fiorentino non fece che ordinare, ritoccando, l'opera
del professore bizantino. L'originalità, se di originalità di contributi può
parlarsi, è tutta in qualche accento").[27] The only specific difference Garin
refers to is Acciaiuoli's deliberate "suppression" of the "Neoplatonic"
elements of Argyropoulos's lectures. In distinguishing Donato Acciaiuoli's approach from the new Platonizing tendencies, Garin has pointed
to one passage from the Argyropoulos lectures, a digression into "Platonic theology" that describes a supreme god creating second, third, and
fourth gods, which passage Donato marked in his notebook with the
catchword "De ideis." In his commentary, according to Garin, Acciaiuoli chose to omit the passage.[28] The digression is an attempt to show
how Aristotle's criticism of Plato (*Eth. Nic.* 1.6) is "sophistic" and "apparent" only, for Plato meant simply that the ideas existed "causatively"
in the mind of God but "essentially" in the second god created by the

26.   For example, from the lecture draft (Naz. II I 104, fol. 164, on *Eth. Nic.* 9.4.10/
1166b): "Totus iste ordo, ut mihi videtur, conrespondet ex opposito illi quem tenuit philosophus, quando ennaravit ea superius que tribuenda sunt bonis." And in Acciaiuoli's
commentary (Magl. XXI 137, fol. 176 [cf. ed. 1478, sig. (F)F8v]): "Notandum quod totus
iste ordo, ut mihi videtur, conrespondet ex opposito illi quem tenuit philosophus,
quando enarravit ea superius que competunt bonis."

27.   "Donato Acciaiuoli cittadino," p. 251, n. 66; cf. ibid., p. 229.

28.   Ibid., pp. 228–29.

first god's self-reflection.[29] In his commentary Acciaiuoli glossed the passage of Aristotle (at the beginning of 1.6), where Argyropoulos discussed the theory of Ideas, in another way entirely, by giving a simple, literal explanation of Aristotle's argument.[30] Likewise he did not answer each of Aristotle's arguments against Plato by showing that they were "sophistic." Yet Garin's conclusions are incorrect nonetheless. In delivering lectures Argyropoulos had to take up Aristotle's arguments one by one and not leave his students in suspense over the course of several lectures; in a written commentary Acciaiuoli could allow the reader to proceed at his own pace (*pro arbitrio*, as he said in the preface), and he could include more theoretical, "digressive" material according to what was fitting for the commentary as a whole. And in fact we find the essential elements of Argyropoulos's "Platonic digression" in Acciaiuoli's commentary, and in an expanded form, as a gloss on a different passage of Aristotle, near the end of 1.6 rather than at the beginning.[31]

Elsewhere Acciaiuoli is independent of his teacher. In a passage in Book 8 (8.4.5/1157a), for instance, where Aristotle argues that friendship on account of pleasure and friendship on account of utility are unlikely to coincide, to Argyropoulos's gloss as it appears in the draft of the lectures Acciaiuoli added a long, marginal commentary on the same passage, which concluded as follows: "This exposition seems to be more in accord with the mind of the philosopher than the one placed within [that is, than the one within the margins, or the exposition recorded from the lectures]."[32] Whether Donato's gloss was based on another commentary, his own ingenuity, or a changed opinion of Argyropoulos in response to Donato's questions, it did differ from that of the lectures, and the marginal correction is the gloss Donato chose for his own commentary on the *Ethics*.[33]

To examine the more general distinctions between the commentaries of Acciaiuoli and Argyropoulos we must finally turn to the question

---

29. See my "John Argyropoulos and the 'Secret Teachings' of Plato," pp. 318–19n.

30. Magl. XXI 136, fols. 25v–26v.

31. Argyropoulos began his Platonic "digression" at 1.6.1/1096a, where Aristotle states that "perhaps it is desirable that we should examine the notion of a Universal Good, and review the difficulties that it involves, although such an enquiry goes against the grain because of our friendship for the authors of the Theory of Ideas" (here, as in other citations from the classics, I follow the Loeb editions). Argyropoulos continued referring to the theory, as he had to, throughout 1.6. Acciaiuoli waited until 1.6.14/1096b–97a, where Aristotle argues that a knowledge of the Ideas (and the Ideal Good) may be beneficial in acquiring those goods that are attainable (Magl. XXI 136, fols. 33–36v).

32. Naz. II I 104, fol. 147: "Hec expositio videtur esse magis ad mentem philosophi quam intus posita."

33. Magl. XXI 137, fol. 139–139v.

raised earlier, that of Acciaiuoli as "metaphysician." It has been argued by others that Acciaiuoli avoided the sort of "pure" metaphysical speculation characteristic of the Platonic Academy: Acciaiuoli's single-minded interest in moral philosophy accentuates his commitment to the *vita activa* of the real world. But as is evident in Ficino, and as will be explored in Landino, humanists in the 1450s and 1460s were increasingly turning to speculative philosophy for answers to concrete problems of public morality. Consciously departing from an exclusive interest in the humanist *verba* fortified now and then by philosophical *sententiae*, humanists learned from the scholastics that the philosophical way of inquiry (the *mos philosophicus*) involved an investigation of the "things themselves" (*res ipsae*). While one could draw upon, as had Leonardo Bruni, the philosophical teachings of the *Nicomachean Ethics*, one had also to view the "ethical man" in terms of the reality of the soul and the very nature of the ideas that the mind held. To describe this reality Acciaiuoli turned to metaphysics—the study of the nature of God and of the separated substances—and played these back on several notions of Aristotelian ethics. The attempt was sporadic, and we cannot now hope to elucidate what Acciaiuoli's "metaphysics" was, if he indeed "had" one. But I shall attempt to show how Acciaiuoli now and then departed from Argyropoulos in a "metaphysical" direction and thereby turned his teachings into a "commentary" on society.

Like Niccolò Tignosi, Donato Acciaiuoli read the *Nicomachean Ethics* as a theoretical critique of civil society. Tignosi, it will be recalled, emphasized the relation between the artist and his work and the necessity of subordinating means to ends; on such a basis, laws, the "foundation" of civil society, lacked the "scientific" quality of medicine. Acciaiuoli shared the basic premise (while never revealing any desire to defend the medical *scientia* as such), and he too praised the "good politician" for creating rather than interpreting laws. But while Tignosi praised the good politician as a virtuoso in his craft, as a supreme artist, Acciaiuoli examined in greater depth the premises of human society as a whole and the nature of the human condition. He found two levels of human conduct, one "civil" and based on necessity and the other "speculative" and based on friendship and the true nature of man.

Like that of Tignosi (and Poggio Bracciolini), Acciaiuoli's critique of civil society depended on the notion of human "variety." Aristotle himself provided a good starting point for the critique. As stated in Book 5 of the *Ethics*, the very activity of men in human society varies: some produce shoes, others produce houses. From this diversity of activities arise basic material needs, which require a measure of some sort for the several activities. This measure is coined money (*nummus*), the only thing in human society that appears "stable" and permanent. Yet to a degree this stability is illusory, because money itself rests on human convention: we see that its name, *nummus*, derives from νόμος, meaning law.[34] From these premises, adapted from Aristotle, Acciaiuoli argued that in the world of needs and necessities, laws provide certain standards; but the diversity of human affairs means that there can be no fixed rule, and so the laws should be subject to rulers, not to jurists. Hence the "justice" (*iustitia*) of the lawmaker (a giving to each his own) contains in itself no ethical norms: to it must be added "goodness" (*bonitas*) and a "sense of equity" (*aequitas*).[35]

Yet for Acciaiuoli the *aequitas* was not a general mediating principle, be it immanent or transcendent, leading man toward the good or regulating human society toward the good. On the contrary, each person seeks happiness by pursuing his pleasure, and human pleasures are so diverse that one can scarcely find in them any sort of standard at all. Paraphrasing Aristotle (10.5.8–9/1176a), he argued that the different pleasures for the different animals ought not to be contrasted with the pleasures proper to man; rather, men have different pleasures, as do the various species of animals. In fact, to each species of animal certain pleasures seem fitted, yet for man "some things delight some, others delight others; some things disturb some, others disturb others."[36]

A simple examination of what man "desires," therefore, cannot define man: there are both "desires" and an activity (*operatio*) in seeking them. Pleasure, indeed, must follow *operatio*. This poses an especially difficult problem for man, for while animals are borne naturally to their pleasures,

> man carries out his actions by reason and choice, and thus he has great variety. For some have corrupt judgment, others good judgment, and thus they produce different actions, and hold to and pursue different and various pleasures. Indeed the other animals are acted upon and do not act in the proper sense. Man on the other hand has free choice, reason, and will, and, following things pleasant in different ways (for some things please some, others please others), he pursues diverse pleasures.[37]

---

34. Cf. *Eth. Nic.* 5.3–5.

35. Ed. 1478, sig. R5–R5v (on *Eth. Nic.* 5.10/1137a–38a) [this section wanting in the Acciaiuoli autographs (see n. 24, above)].

36. Magl. XXI 137, fol. 221–221v.

37. Ibid., fol. 222v (cf. ed. 1478, sig. [I]I2) [10.5.11/1176a]: "Dicendum quod alia animalia feruntur instinctu nature ad suas voluptates; homo vero ratione et electione agit suas operationes, et ideo habet multas varietates, quia alii habent iudicium corruptum,

In man there are two types of *operationes*, the active and the speculative.
For each type of *operatio* there must be one pleasure that is supreme, for
in each genus there must be one thing distinctively best (*optimum in
aliquo genere*).³⁸ For the just *operatio* of the active life the *optimum* exists
in the mind of the just person: "The just act toward others seems to
arise out of a certain internal justice, which, according to Plato, is of
power toward power (*potentiae ad potentiam*)." This first justice (of a
higher power to a lower one) is "when . . . we render the appetite obe-
dient and attribute an authority to reason which is its own."³⁹

Acciaiuoli's notion of internal justice, which he identified as Platonic,
appears as a gloss on 8.1.4/1155a, where Aristotle argues that the "highest
form of justice seems to have an element of friendly feeling in it." In
glossing the passage, Argyropoulos referred also to an "internal justice,"
and indeed the notion apparently derives from the *Nicomachean Ethics*
5.11.9/1138b, where Aristotle states that "metaphorically" and "by resem-
blance" one may speak of an internal justice, as the Platonists have spoken of a "justice" based on a relation between the rational and irrational
parts of the soul.⁴⁰

When Acciaiuoli turned to the question of friendship and the contemplative life (Books 8–10), which involved the speculative *operationes*,
he began to depart significantly from Argyropoulos. As Aristotle posed
the nature of friendship at the beginning of Book 8, he seemed to be
providing the Florentines an answer to the great problem of the 1450s,
that of disunity and political discord: lawgivers are especially concerned
about friendship, for "if men are friends, there is no need of justice between them" (8.1.4/1155a). Acciaiuoli began his commentary on this sec-

---

alii bonum, et ideo diversas producunt operationes et diversas et varias habent voluptates
et persequuntur. Cetera vero animalia aguntur et non proprie agunt. Homo autem est
liberi arbitrii et habet rationem et voluntatem, et sequendo diversa voluptaria (nam alia
alios delectant) diversas ideo persequitur voluptates."

38. Magl. XXI 137, fol. 221v (cf. ed. 1478, sig. [I]Iiv): "*In universis autem talibus* [10.5.10/
1176a]. Ostendit hac in parte philosophus quod inter omnes voluptates humanas ea est
optima que est studiosi hominis hoc pacto. Eius hominis voluptas, qui est mensura omnium operationum et voluptatum humanarum, est potissima et vera voluptas. Sed studiosus homo et virtus ipsa sunt mensura operationum et voluptatum humanarum. Ergo
eius voluptas est summa et potissima inter humanas voluptates. Patet ratio, quia in un-
oquoque genere id quod est mensura est optimum et prestabilissimum in illo genere."
The argument continues for more than a page. For the corresponding passage in Argyropoulos, see Naz. II 1 104, fols. 192v–93.

39. Magl. XXI 137, fol. 125 (cf. ed. 1478, sig. [D]D1): "[I]ustum ad alios videtur oriri ex
iustitia quadam interna, que iustitia est potentie ad potentiam secundum Platonem . . . ,
veluti cum obedientem reddimus appetitum, et tribuimus imperium rationi quod suum
est." For a later use of this concept by Pierfilippo Pandolfini, see the passage quoted below, n. 84.

40. Naz. II 1 104, fol. 139.

tion by citing the quotation from Sallust, "concordiâ parvae res crescunt, discordiâ maximae dilabuntur," that had become the political
maxim of the late 1450s. He then argued that "out of an internal friendship of oneself toward oneself seems to arise friendship toward
others."[41]

Aristotle himself does not refer to this "internal friendship" before the
ninth book of the *Ethics*, in the confusing passage (9.4.6/1166a) that begins as follows: "Whether there can be friendship toward oneself we
may omit for the present." There would "seem to be friendship (*Videbitur autem hoc amicitia esse*; δόξειε δ' ἂν ταύτῃ εἶναι φιλία) insofar as
he [or it] is two or more (*quo duo vel plura . . . habet*; ἧ ἐστὶ δύο ἢ
πλείω)." The precise meaning of the latter phrase, and whether it should
be followed by a limiting prepositional phrase (*ex iis . . . quae dicta sunt*;
ἐκ τῶν εἰρημένων: "of the aforesaid things," with the precise reference
unclear) is the difficulty.[42]

In his lectures Argyropoulos noted that some commentators say that
Aristotle wanted to resolve the controversy of "friendship toward oneself" while others deny that he made the attempt. Some argue that he
resolved the question by understanding the passage to mean that the
"friendship which is toward oneself is not properly called *friendship* because it is not between two." Others argue that Aristotle did not resolve
the question by calling friendship "two or more of the foresaid things;
that is, friendship is based on two or more of the foresaid conditions,
and because it is similar to friendship to oneself, which indeed is a certain excellence of love." Argyropoulos then concluded:

> The exposition which says that the philosopher resolved the ques-
> tion by showing how this is not properly friendship seems better:
> for friendship is not the beginning of friendship, just as virtue is
> not the beginning of virtue, and knowledge is not the beginning
> of knowledge.[43]

41.   Magl. XXI 137, fols. 124v–25.

42.   Loeb edition, with H. Rackham's translation adapted according to Argyropoulos's
Latin. The Latin quoted is taken from the Venice 1503 edition (fol. 132–132v) of Argyropoulos's translation.

43.   Naz. II 1 104, fols. 163v–64: "*Videbitur utique.* Nunc addit unum quod bifariam
intelligi potest: aut quod philosophus velit tangere solutionem aut quod nolit. Si nolit:
dicendum quod amicitia [*mg.* videbitur esse hoc pacto] est duo vel plura ex predictis,
idest quod amicitia constat in duabus vel tribus conditionibus antedictis [*superscr.* ut be-
neficentia etc.], et quod est similis amicitie ad se ipsum, que quidem est excellentia quedam amoris. Sin autem velit quoquomodo solvere, ut videtur: tum dicendum [*mg.*: Re-
linquatur nunc et ad presens quia] ex predictis colligi potest quod amicitia est duo vel
plura, idest referri ad minus potest ad duos terminos et esse inter duos vel plures. Sed
una amicitia non potest esse nisi inter duos: quando additur tertius tum fiunt due amici-

Thus Argyropoulos took the "insofar as he is two or more" as a logical contradiction disproving the original hypothesis of friendship toward oneself.

Acciaiuoli followed precisely the Platonic interpretation in rejecting Argyropoulos's gloss. Some say, he began,

> that the philosopher did not hold that there was friendship of one toward oneself through the use of the words "two or more," because friendship ought to be between two or more, and man himself is nothing unless he is unique. This exposition I do not follow at all.

Acciaiuoli then maintained that within the *genus* of friendship, one finds several grades of friendship and, negating almost the very expression of Argyropoulos, concluded that "one's friendship toward oneself is the origin and, as it were, exemplar and idea of the other friendship."[44]

tie; si addatur quartus sunt tres amicitie [amicititie *ms*] et sic successive. Ex predictis igitur colligi potest quod amicitia est inter duos aut plures, ex quo illa que est ad se ipsum non proprie dicetur amicitia, cum non sit inter duos. Preterea non est quia est excellentia quedam amoris, sed bene similis. Et dici potest quod sit amicitia sui ad se ipsum veluti iustitia ad se ipsum, idest potentiarum ad potentias. Illa autem expositio qua dicitur quod philosophus solvit ostendendo quoquomodo [quoquomo *ms.*] quod hec non est proprie amicitia videtur melior, quia amicitie amicitia principium non est, veluti virtutis virtus et scientie scientia principium non est."

44.   Magl. XXI 137, fols. 174v–75 (cf. ed. 1478, sig. [F]F8): "*Querere vero utrum ad seipsum.* Videtur hac in parte se excusare philosophus a determinatione huius questionis, scilicet utrum sit amicitia ad seipsum, quod videbatur presupposuisse superius. Queret autem aliquis utrum ad seipsum sit amicitia, et dicit quod hoc est omittendum nunc, cum antea tetigerit. Et inferius dicet nonnulla ex quibus oriri videtur solutio huius questionis, quamvis etiam hic tangat aliqua ex quibus conicere et probare possumus amicitiam esse ad seipsum. Nam dicit quod illa videtur amicitia a qua proficiscuntur duo vel plura eorum que diximus, scilicet pertinere ad amicitiam. Sed ab amicitia ad seipsum profluunt aliqua supradictorum vel omnia. Ergo illa videbitur esse amicitia. Preterea alia ratione idem videtur ostendere hoc modo: Id videtur esse amicitia cuius similitudine dicitur exsuperatio [exuperatio *ed.*] amicitie, idest amicitia perfecta que summa est amicitiarum, et ideo dicitur exuperatio [*sic*: the spelling is here inconsistent in the manuscript] . . . . Sed amicitia sui ad seipsum est huiusmodi, ut eius similitudine dicatur perfecta amicitia. Ergo amicitia sui ad seipsum est amicitia.

"Quanquam dicant nonnulli quod philosophus non vult quod sit amicitia sui ad seipsum per ea verba 'duo vel plura,' quia amicitia debet esse inter duos vel plures, et ipse homo non est nisi unus, quorum ego expositionem minime sequor. Notandum est igitur quod si amicitia constat ob hoc, et ab ea profluunt officia ea, quia vir studiosus amat seipsum et sibi tribuit ea omnia, concedere debemus dispositionem sive benivolentiam qua se quisque amat esse amicitiam, et habere gradus sicut habent iste que sunt amicorum ad amicos. Nam studiosissimus et perfectissimus se magis amabit quam minus studiosus, et sic successive, veluti amicitia ad amicum est magis et minus. Quod si quis dixerit non esse hic benivolentiam mutuam, dicendum primo quod hec amicitia sui ad seipsum est origo et quasi exemplar atque idea reliquarum. Unde amicus sumere mensuram et regulam debet ad exercenda officia erga alterum amicum, scilicet taliter qualiter studiosus erga seipsum. Deinde duo hic etiam in amicitia ad seipsum cadere videntur,

Thus with both *iustitia* and *amicitia* Acciaiuoli found the *primum* in any *genus*—the "idea" or "exemplar"—in the mind of the individual. But such "ideas" or "exemplars," as realities existing independently of their particular manifestations, were properly "separated substances" or in the domain of metaphysics. They existed either in the mind of God or in the Platonic "second god." How could they exist in the mind of man? For Acciaiuoli, they proved the divinity of man. In such an argument, as we might expect, Acciaiuoli found greater inspiration from Christian theologians and Platonists than from Aristotle. He was limited, however, by the text of the *Ethics*, and he attempted to exploit a few of the more "elevated" passages he was glossing.

Aristotle's own description of the "divinity of man" or the "divinity in man" in the tenth book of the *Ethics* (10.7.8/1177b) is parenthetical to his conception of the contemplative life. Aristotle states that the life of the mind would be "higher than the human level," for "man will achieve it not in virtue of his humanity" but because of "something within him that is divine." If the life of the mind is superior to man's life as a whole, then life according to it is "divine in comparison with human life." Some would say that we, being men, should think of human things and, being mortal, should think of mortal things. But we must, insofar as we can, "make ourselves immortal" and "do all that man may to live in accordance with the highest thing" in us. From the lecture notes we find that Argyropoulos gave this section a rather simple, straightforward gloss: the "more divine" part of man's nature is suited to contemplation.[45] Acciaiuoli's commentary, on the other hand, is quite long and covers several arguments. He first took Aristotle's notion that the life according to reason or the intellect is divine in comparison with human life as a basis for an argument that through the intellect man is similar to the separated substances and that man can live several "lives" at once (cf. *Eth. Nic.* 1.13): man who lives in perfect happiness

> does not live according to the human condition, but according as a certain divine nature exists in him, according as, namely, through the intellect he has a similitude to separated substances. It should be noted that many forces, activities, and lives are appropriate to man. For the human soul has a vegetative power, which does not seem proper to man insofar as he is man, but as he has

appetitus et ratio, que quando conveniunt et uniuntur, ita ut appetitus obtemperet rationi, tunc oriri videtur concordia et amicitia quedam potentie ad potentiam, sicut de iustitia dictum est supra. Et talis amicitia ad seipsum, cum sit origo et quasi idea aliarum, prestantissima esse videbitur, et summa cum iocunditate coniuncta."

45. Naz. II 1 104, fols. 196v–97.

something in common with plants, which do not have a more distinguished life. Thus the one living the vegetative life seems to live the life of plants. Another life is attributed to man, and this is the sensitive life, which does not seem to suit him as his ultimate activity but as he has something in common with other animals, and living such a life he seems to be like a sort of animal, like a beast. There is another life, the rational life, attributed to man, by which man is said to live not as a plant or as a beast, but with a more excellent, outstanding life.[46]

The rational life has two forms, the active and contemplative. The latter is like the life of separated substances.

Man moreover seems to be a mean between the other animals and separated substances, and to possess a similarity with both and also a dissimilarity on account of his various powers and operations. For he seems to have a similarity to the brute beasts with respect to his operation and power of sensation; he differs from them, immediately, through his active mind and life. For although he differs also on account of his contemplative life, nevertheless it is by so great a distance as not to seem an *immediate* difference. But on the other hand through the contemplative mind and life he is said to have such a similitude to the separated substances, and therefore the philosopher says that this life is more important than the human [that is, active] life. For "in the flesh," as Jerome said, if I recall correctly, "to live beyond the flesh seems divine, not human."[47]

46. Magl. XXI 137, fol. 232 (cf. ed. 1478, sig. [I]I7): Aristoteles addit "quod is qui sic vivit, scilicet vita contemplativa, non vivit secundum conditionem humanam, sed secundum quod aliquid divinum in ipso consistit, prout videlicet per intellectum habet similitudinem cum substantiis separatis. Notandum quod homini competunt plures vires et operationes et vite. Anima enim humana habet potentiam vegetandi, que non videtur competere homini ut homo est, sed ut convenit cum plantis, que plante non habent [habeat *ed.*] prestabiliorem vitam. Quare vivens vita vegetativa videtur vivere plantarum vita. Alia tribuitur homini, idest vita sensitiva, que non videtur ei ut ultima sua operatio competere, sed ut convenit cum aliis animalibus, et tali vita vivere videtur ut animal quoddam et ut brutum. Est et alia vita rationalis que tribuitur ei, qua [quia *ed.*] vivere dicitur non ut planta vel brutum, sed excellentiore et prestantiore vita."

47. Magl. XXI 137, fols. 232v–233 (cf. ed. 1478, sig. [I]I7v): "Homo autem videtur esse medius inter alia animalia et essentias separatas, et habere similitudinem cum utrisque et dissimilitudinem etiam ob varias potentias et operationes. Nam similitudinem habere videtur cum brutis sensitiva potentia et operatione, differre ab eisdem per mentem et vitam activam immediate. Nam etsi differat etiam per contemplativam, tamen est tanta distantia quod non videtur immediate differre, verum ex alia parte per mentem contemplativam et vitam talem dicitur habere similitudinem cum substantiis separatis; et ideo dicit philosophus talem vitam potiorem esse quam humanam. In carne enim (ut in-

Still glossing this same passage, Acciaiuoli moved from this "middle nature" of man toward an argument for the immortality of the soul:

> For since there is no transition from one extreme to the other without a mean, if another middle nature is assumed to be more perfect than human [nature], it would at once be separated from matter; but if more base, it would descend to the irrational and be immersed in matter itself. Thus it is fitting that the mean between the extremes be the human soul itself, since an order is given to things ordered according to their essence. This being the case a most excellent reason seems to arise for proving the immortality of the souls.[48]

Acciaiuoli's proof then followed: Souls, like separated substances, give form to matter; they do not arise from the *potentia* of matter; and whatever does not arise from the *potentia* of matter must be incorruptible and immortal.[49] By bringing in the doctrine of immortality, Acciaiuoli has turned Aristotle's argument, based wholly on the *analogy* between the intellect and the divine, into an argument for the *essence* of the human soul, which is its immortality.

In another passage (10.8.13/1179a) Aristotle argues that one pursuing intellectual activity seems dearest to the gods, for the gods delight in that which is most akin to them (*maxime . . . cognatum*; τὸ συγγενέστατον). To this notion of similitude Acciaiuoli gave the following gloss:

> It is then concluded that the philosopher Aristotle identified the final and supreme happiness of man as activity in accordance with wisdom, a wisdom whereby (he seems to have held) the wise man is connected in some way with his cause, that is with the highest god his maker. In this way he may become most beloved to him through contemplation; and through a certain friendship, if one may speak thus, he may be united to God as far as is possible.[50]

---

quit Hieronymus, si bene memini) preter carnem vivere celeste et non humanum esse videtur."

48. Magl. XXI 137, fol. 233 (cf. ed. 1478, sig. [I]I7v): "Nam cum non fiat transitio ab extremo ad extremum sine medio, si sumeretur alia natura media perfectior quam humana, statim esset separata a materia; sin ignobilior, descenderet ad inrationabilia et inmersa in ipsa materia. Quare consentaneum videtur ut sit media ipsa anima humana inter hec, cum detur ordo in essentialiter ordinatis. Hoc stante oriri videtur pulcerrima ratio ad probandam immortalitatem animorum."

49. Magl. XXI 137, fol. 233–33v (cf. ed. 1478, sig. [I]I7v–8).

50. Magl. XXI 137, fol. 241v (cf. ed. 1478, sig. [L]L2): "Concluditur autem quod ultimam et supremam felicitatem humanam collocavit philosophus Aristoteles in operatione secundum sapientiam qua virum sapientem coniungi cum causa sua quoquomodo velle videtur, idest cum summo deo auctore suo, ut ei per contemplationem eo pacto amicissi-

In Aristotle this "conjoining" was a purely abstract relationship, based
on the gods enjoying the cultivation of that part of man dearest to them:
the Stagirite did not posit any actual links between man in intellectual
activity and this loving response from the gods. Acciaiuoli established
such a connection by relying on arguments from Christian theology.
"Friendship" with God arises from the cultivation of the mind:

> Some would perhaps infer that such friendship is similar to what
> sacred writers call *charity*, and they would argue through this that
> our happiness consists no less in an act of the will, which is the
> domicile of charity, than in the activity or understanding of the
> mind. It should be noted that the highest and supreme human
> happiness, as can be gathered from what has been said by the phi-
> losopher, seems to consist more in the contemplative life, through
> which man seems in some way to be joined to God, than in the
> active. The philosopher argues this same thing, that is, that con-
> templation is our happiness, in *Metaphysics* XII where he seems to
> indicate that our human happiness consists in the contemplation
> of separated substances and especially and most significantly in the
> contemplation of God himself. For a gradation is given among
> speculative activities, and the perfection of them is assumed not
> only according to the mind and our most noble power, but also
> according to the nobility of the object (*non solum ex parte mentis et
> nobilissimae potentiae nostrae, sed etiam ex nobilitate obiecti*). On
> which account since God is the most perfect of all objects around
> which the mind considers in speculation, it is right that not any
> sort of contemplation will be in the highest rank, but that which
> will be centered on divine goodness and on the most glorious God
> himself. From this seems to arise friendship and that conjunction,
> through which the good and wise man by contemplating him is
> in some way united to his cause.[51]

mus vel acceptissimus fiat, et per quandam amicitiam, si dicere licet, ei coniungatur
quoad fieri potest." Argyropoulos's Latin is from the Venice 1503 edition, fol. 155v.

51. Magl. XXI 137, fols. 241v–42 (cf. ed. 1478, sig. [L]L2–2v) [continuing quotation
from note above]: "Ex quo forsitan nonnulli elicerent amicitiam talem esse similem ei
quam sacri scriptores apellant caritatem, et arguerent per hoc felicitatem nostram non
minus consistere in actu voluntatis, que est caritatis domicilium, quam in operatione intellectus et mentis. Notandum quod humana felicitas summa atque suprema, ut ex dictis
philosophi colligitur, in vita contemplativa videtur consistere, per quam homo coniungi
quoquomodo deo videtur, et magis quam per activam. Et hoc idem in XII.o. Methaphis-
ice tangit philosophus, idest quod contemplatio est nostra felicitas, ubi etiam indicare
videtur nostram felicitatem humanam consistere in contemplatione substantiarum sepa-
ratarum, et precipue et maxime ipsius dei. Datur enim gradus inter operationes specula-
tivas, et earum perfectio sumitur non solum ex parte mentis et nobilissime potentie
nostre, sed etiam ex nobilitate obiecti. Quare cum deus sit perfectissimum omnium

With the "nobility of the object" theme Acciaiuoli has departed considerably from the Aristotle of the *Nicomachean Ethics*. Man recognizes his divine nature and is conjoined, to some degree, to his cause: hence arises the exemplar of friendship, an internal friendship, which then becomes the basis of the external friendship with fellow man, and this forms a basis for human society far more effective than justice. Acciaiuoli took several statements of Aristotle, the more "Neoplatonic" ones, and analyzed them with considerable liberty. For other passages he recopied glosses directly from his notebook of Argyropoulos's lectures. Whether Acciaiuoli was cunning in his free interpretation of Aristotle is uncertain; in his own mind Acciaiuoli seems to have considered the more "Platonic" of Aristotle's arguments, if not the more "representative," at least the "stronger" ones. As Acciaiuoli wrote in Book 10,

> There are some who say that the philosopher said little about contemplative happiness in the books of the *Ethics*. But if we inquire diligently, we shall find that these few things contain much in their force, especially when he declares with many arguments that contemplative happiness is supreme, and the most proper of human activities, as has been clear.[52]

With the notion of the *summum in aliquo genere* Acciaiuoli argued that, through the cultivation of what was highest in him, man not only restored order to his troubled soul but found an exemplar of that true friendship on which society was based. Acciaiuoli perhaps owed the conception either directly or indirectly to Marsilio Ficino, who had formulated the notion of the *primum in aliquo genere* in his *De voluptate* of 1457, more than a half decade, that is, before Acciaiuoli's commentary.[53]

---

obiectorum circa que mens speculando versatur, merito non quecunque contemplatio erit in summo gradu, sed ea que erit circa bonitatem divinam et ipsum gloriosissimum deum. Unde oriri videtur amicitia et coniunctio illa, per quam vir bonus et sapiens quoquomodo contemplando ipsum coniungitur cause sue. Et hanc dicerent forsitan aliqui similem esse ei, quam theologi caritatem apellant, ex quo nascitur disputatio de actu voluntatis et operatione mentis, ut supra etiam diximus, cuius determinatio a sacris theologis petenda est. Patet igitur ex dictis summum bonum non simpliciter atque ex omni parte perfectum, sed tale quale vite humane competere potest, quid, et quomodo sit, sententia huius philosophi Aristotelis." Argyropoulos's brief gloss here is Naz. 11 1 104, fol. 200–200v.

52. Magl. xxi 137, fol. 240 (cf. ed. 1478, sig. [L]L1) [at 10.8.8/1178b]: "Sunt autem nonnulli qui dicunt pauca de contemplativa felicitate dixisse philosophum in libro [*sic ms.* and *ed.*: he may have wanted *libris*] ethicorum. Verum si diligenter animadvertimus reperiemus quod illa pauca vi continent multa, et presertim cum pluribus rationibus declaraverit contemplativam felicitatem esse supremam et propriissimam inter omnes operationes humanas, ut patuit."

53. Since a form of the *summum in aliquo genere* derives ultimately from Aristotle's

Yet Acciaiuoli did not take over the Ficinian notion, which described a
strict hierarchy of things within each genus deriving their essential characteristic from the greatest, the *primum*, in that *genus*; rather, he took
the *summum* in any *genus* as the basis for its lower form (for example,
the exemplar of friendship, a real thing existing in the mind as the mind
realized its divinity, as the basis for "friendship" in the ordinary sense
between two or more persons). The *primum in aliquo genere*, then, as a
notion in itself, which required some form of a strict hierarchy, Acciaiuoli did not develop. Instead, he apparently used a form of the notion
to illustrate several ethical precepts and gloss away several Aristotelian
criticisms of Plato.

The Donato Acciaiuoli who emerges from the commentary on the
Ethics is a rather different figure from the Donato Acciaiuoli of the 1450s.
Earlier he had sought individual perfection through a thorough knowledge of Latin and Greek, a devotion to an upright life and good works,
the pursuit, when of age, of public offices and embassies, and finally the
knowledge of systematic philosophical truth. But now he emphasized
unity with God through the contemplative life and, in and through this
unity, friendship and love for one's fellow man. He emphasized themes,
that is, developed by Marsilio Ficino and others of his circle. If he was
indebted directly to Ficino he concealed the debt well. Of course in this
period it would have been highly unusual for a humanist to cite another
humanist in a commentary.[54] But Acciaiuoli is also silent about Ficino
in his letters, and Ficino is likewise silent until the 1470s, when he asked
Acciaiuoli to patronize a son of Carlo Marsuppini.[55] By the time he began writing the commentary, however, Acciaiuoli was reconciled with
Cristoforo Landino, and he had always maintained close ties with many
in the Ficino circle.[56]

Due to a gap in Donato Acciaiuoli's letterbook, from the summer of
1455 to the summer of 1461, we shall need new manuscript discoveries to

---

Metaphysics and was common in medieval exegesis, any hypothesis of a debt of Acciaiuoli
to Ficino remains for now highly speculative.

54.   That is, humanist commentators in this period concealed their borrowings (except
those from some late ancient commentators) in order to appear to have approached their
subject afresh. Only toward the end of the Quattrocento, with Politian, do we detect a
new approach: skill now is weighed according to one's range of knowledge, one's philological ingenuity, *and* one's ability to subject contemporaries to a running critique. See
Grafton and Jardine, *From Humanism to the Humanities*, pp. 83-98.

55.   *Opera omnia*, p. 655 (misprinted as "Marsilius Ficinus Donato Carolo s. d." after the
common Latin form Donatus Acarolus); cf. *Letters*, I, 154. For Ficino and Acciaiuoli, see
n. 86, below.

56.   For those who were part of both the Argyropoulos and Ficino circles, see Della
Torre's summary sketch, *Storia*, p. 562.

trace Acciaiuoli's intellectual development in that period.[57] The one surviving letter (it circulated widely), a consolatory piece of November 1456 to Pandolfo Pandolfini on the death of his father, Domenico, sounds themes typical of the disciple of Giannozzo Manetti.[58] You ought not to grieve too much, Acciaiuoli wrote Pandolfo, for your father lived a full and dignified life, and you benefited greatly by his guidance and example. How different was my case, for my father was taken from me before I was born![59] The letter idealizes the competitive, individualistic striving after full intellectual and cultural development under a controlled discipleship. It has no trace of Platonic or Ficinian themes, the soul's liberation from the body and hence its greater closeness to us—or, as Ficino could boldly and cheerfully have proclaimed, our wonderful new opportunity to get to know finally Domenico Pandolfini!

In his commentary on the *Ethics*, Acciaiuoli's conception of the contemplative life as the life promoting true friendship, on which all human society ultimately depended, was a theme sounded frequently in various Florentine contexts from the early 1460s. It helped bring into ideological focus for an entire generation of better-born Florentines the "meaning" of the 1450s: the active, civic virtues, the individual seeking after political status, had brought Florence to near ruin. During the time of Argyropoulos's lectures on the *Ethics*, 1457–58, individuals in greater numbers were coming to rule irrespective of their "wisdom" and their cultivation of the "higher virtues." His lectures on the last three books of the *Ethics* would have fallen in the spring and summer of 1458, during the difficult period between the catasto of January 1458 and the Parlamento in August.[60] During the disasters of this period, when disunity was ruining Florence, could the more "intellectual" of Argyropoulos's students have heard the lectures on friendship and the contemplative life and interpreted them in terms pointing toward salvation from the failures of the 1450s? "When men are friends they have no need of justice":

57. Magl. VIII 1390.

58. Ganz, "Humanist as Citizen," lists five manuscripts. Acciaiuoli's funeral oration on Johannes Vaivoda (Hunyadi), dated 15 November 1456, is also extant in an Acciaiuoli autograph, Magl. IX 123, fols. 83–86 (inc.: Etsi non sim ignarus quam grave). Segni knew of the work (*Vita di Donato Acciaioli*, pp. 42–43), Della Torre stated that he could not find it (*Storia*, p. 364 and n.), and I have seen no mention of it in studies of Acciaiuoli since. However, Kristeller, *Iter*, I, 137, described the anonymous work and tentatively assigned it to Acciaiuoli, and, later, Black, *Benedetto Accolti*, p. 283, correctly identified it as an Acciaiuoli autograph. The oration emphasizes, naturally, Hunyadi's valor in fighting the Turks. I have seen no evidence that it was actually delivered.

59. Magl. XXXII 39, fols. 30–31v.

60. He began Book 6, that is, in January or February 1458 and finished Book 10 probably in July. See the dated inaugural oration in Müllner, ed., *Reden und Briefe*, pp. 19–30.

Acciaiuoli first inserted the Sallustian theme of *concordia*, and then, speculating on man's divine nature, attempted to give the notion numinous
and metaphysical authority.[61]

The political question was resolved by the Parlamento of 1458. Soon
thereafter Acciaiuoli dedicated to Piero de' Medici his translation of
Plutarch's life of Demetrius. In his dedication Acciaiuoli thanked Piero
for joining his father, Cosimo, in bringing it about that the city had at
last attained "that end which the wisest men wanted the best governors
of republics to have as their purpose."[62] Later, in his oration of March
1465 declaring Cosimo *pater patriae*, prepared on behalf of the Florentine government, Acciaiuoli praised Cosimo first for securing safe Florentine boundaries in the period of the great wars, second for seeing to
it that a league preserved the peace, and finally for establishing domestic
peace. In ruling the republic, he noted, the citizens themselves "have
reached a degree of harmony (*concordia*) and common feeling of minds
such as our ancestors never saw."[63] With his systematic study of Aris-

61.   For the source, see Chapter II, n. 152, above.

62.   Magl. XXIII 95, fol. 4v (autograph): "Nam repressi sunt aliorum conatus, sedate
omnes discordie, omnia bella restincta: demum hec civitas eum finem consecuta est,
quem sapientissimi viri optimis gubernatoribus rerum p. propositum esse voluerunt."
   This dedication may be a few years later than the work itself. If Vespasiano da Bisticci
is accurate, Poggio praised both this translation and the one of the life of Alcibiades,
which followed it (*Vite*, II, 26, and V. R. Giustiniani, "Sulle traduzioni latine delle 'Vite'
di Plutarco nel Quattrocento," *Rinascimento*, 2d. ser., I [1961], 19, 39). The *terminus ante
quem* for the translation, therefore, is 30 Oct. 1459, the date of Poggio's death. The passage quoted seems to refer not only to the pacification of Italy with the general peace of
1454 and 1455 but also the the optimal state of Florence with the Parlamento of 1458.
Based on this evidence alone the date would seem to be the first half of 1459.
   The life of Demetrius, however, was Acciaiuoli's first effort at translating from the
Greek, and he probably sought the opinion of several friends before publication, not
only for the translation's accuracy but also for its elegance. Poggio would be among
these. The dedication, then, could be dated to the early 1460s. A reference to *hec etas* that
"vestrâ operâ magnarum rerum copiosissima est" (fol. 4v) sounds more like an expression of the early 1460s than early 1459 (economic recovery in Florence became noticeable
only in November 1460: see Chapter II, n. 70, above).
   Moreover, the original dedication was apparently not to Piero. In the dedication, an
earlier name evoked was rigorously scratched out and replaced with *Petre* (fol. 3v)—but
the rest of the dedication, obviously biographical and addressed to a son of Cosimo,
shows no sign of change. To one other figure alone could the entire dedication have
been addressed: Cosimo's other son, Giovanni. Donato Acciaiuoli was a close friend of
Giovanni (see the letters from Poppi dated 11, 23 Aug. 1462, MAP X, 399, 412: these are
now the correct shelf marks for the letters Garin cites in "Donato Acciaiuoli cittadino,"
p. 200, n. 3). The probable dating, therefore, seems to be as follows: Late in 1460 Acciaiuoli polished the translation and, with economic recovery in Florence, prepared a dedication to Giovanni de' Medici. When Piero de' Medici's name was drawn as Gonfaloniere in late December, Donato substituted Piero's name in the dedication and published
the translation. The only other occasion for such a change would have come two years
later, with Giovanni's death (23 Sept. 1463). This, for now, cannot be ruled out.

63.   Naz. II II 10, fols. 23–24 (autograph); quotation at fol. 24: "Ipsi denique cives

totle's *Ethics* Acciaiuoli developed the ideological perspectives to give the notion of *concordia* philosophical substance. Political necessity did not dictate this optimal state for Florence; rather, man by his very nature could choose to live as a beast or in a manner approaching divinity. A Florentine following Acciaiuoli's commentary could interpret even feelings of disunity or political revolt as a sign of a troubled and corrupt soul.

On 11 August 1462, in a speech at the fourth anniversary of the Parlamento of 1458, Alamanno Rinuccini, Acciaiuoli's fellow student under John Argyropoulos, argued that the feast honoring the event served as a sign of charity and love. Through the sharing of food—"the foundation of this corporeal and fragile human life"—several pagan authors implied that man could become a god.[64] But there was a better version of the metaphor ready-made. Voluntary participation in the sharing of food as a symbol of the participation of the divine essence in us was nothing other than the Christian Eucharist. According to the Christian faith, moreover, the Eucharist contained both the symbolic and real presence of the divine.

Certain of Donato Acciaiuoli's expressions in his sermon on the Eucharist, delivered in Italian before the Compagnia de' Magi in 1468 on the Wednesday of Holy Week, are part of a Platonic metaphor.[65] At the celebration Donato constructed a delightful blend of simplicity ("let us leave behind the many subtle investigations that are made by sacred doctors . . ."[66]) and philosophical depth. The themes of friendship and the divinity of man, he emphasized, were with the sacrament at its beginning.

> As the hour of his passion approached, like a benign teacher he [Christ] wished to leave to his disciples and the Christian faithful a memorial full of all charity, full of such great delight that no intellect is sufficient to contemplate it. For if it is, and it is said that it is, the greatest sign of friendship when friends consider all

---

talem concordiam consensionemque animorum in re p. gerenda consecuti sunt, qualem nunquam maiores nostri videre potuerunt." The draft is dated, at the end, "20 Martii 1464 [s.f.]." For the circumstances of the decree of Cosimo as *pater patriae*, see Giustiniani, *Alamanno Rinuccini*, pp. 166–69.

64. *Lettere ed orazioni*, pp. 191–93.

65. *Oratione del corpo di Christo da Donato Acciaiuoli et da llui nella Compagnia de' Magi recitata die XIII aprilis 1468*, Ricc. 2204, fols. 181–84v (modern foliation). C. Trinkaus, *"In Our Image and Likeness": Humanity and Divinity in Italian Humanist Thought* (Chicago, 1970), II, 647, has noted the Platonic content of the oration, while assuming that John Argyropoulos was the source of Acciaiuoli's Platonism.

66. Ricc. 2204, fol. 181v: "[L]asceremo indrieto molte sottili investigationi che si fanno da sacri doctori circa alla sua materia, alla sua forma."

things among them to be in common, how great an expression of love and benevolence our Savior shows us in communicating to us not only his possessions but also his very own self![67]

The sacrament, he argued, is the fountain of graces:

> It is that which gives strength to our souls, that which is their life and breath, that which makes them victorious against vices and sins, that makes them peaceful and still. And if in his mortal life there is any happiness, it makes them happy and gives them a "down payment," as it were, of the strongest beatitude.[68]

The mass is called the food of the angels: "O you most happy Christians, who are made similar to the angelic hierarchy!"[69]

Here we merely have to substitute the "contemplative life" for the "mass" and "separated substances" for the "angelic hierarchy" to arrive at Acciaiuoli's earlier expression in his commentary on the *Ethics*. Philosophizing humanists were in these years delivering many such sermons, and these can be considered one part of a more "popular" philosophical movement.[70] To be sure, Donato Acciaiuoli's own sense of piety would not allow him to make so strict an analogy, nor could philosophy, for him, ever supersede the Christian sacrament.

We shall look only briefly at Donato Acciaiuoli's commentary on Aristotle's *Politics*, completed about 1472 and dedicated to Federico, duke of Urbino. That year Federico was winning many Florentine humanist dedications for his heroic sack of Volterra, a town that dared try to leave the Florentine imperium.[71] Whether, as in the *Ethics* commentary, a draft

67. Ibid.: "Ultimamente appressandosi l'ora della sua passione, come benigno maestro volle lasciare a suoi discepoli et a fedeli Cristiani uno memoriale pieno di tutta carità, pieno di tanta dilectione che non è intellecto alcuno che sufficientemente lo possa considerare. Peroché s'è, e si dice ch'egli è, grandissimo segno d'amicitia quando gli amici ogni cosa fra loro riputono essere comuni, quanta significatione d'amore et di benivolentia ci 'a mostro il salvatore in comunicarci non solamente le cose sua ma etiam se medesimo."

68. Ibid., fol. 183–83v: "Peroché lui è la fontana delle gratie, egli è quello che da vigore alle anime nostre, ch'è la vita et lo sovione, et falle victoriose contra e' vitii et peccati, che lle fa quiete et tranquille. Et se in questa mortal vita ci è foelicità alcuna, le fa essere foelici et quasi da una arra della fortissima beatitudine."

69. Ibid., fol. 183v: "Questo è quello che è detto cibo degli angioli. O felicissimi Cristiani che siate fatti simili alle angeliche ierarchie!"

70. See Kristeller, "Lay Religious Traditions and Florentine Platonism," in his *Studies*, pp. 99–122, and especially his description of Ricc. 2204 and Magl. Strozz. xxxv 211 at p. 105, n. 17, of same, as well as manuscripts in the addendum on p. 585. See also the description of ms. 0113, Principe Ginori Conti, Florence, in Kristeller's *Iter*, I, 228 (now Stanford University, ms. 308, according to a communication of Professor Kristeller).

71. For the circumstances of this commentary, see G. Zannoni, "L'impresa di Rimini

from Argyropoulos's lectures was Acciaiuoli's starting point is not known. No such draft has come to light, although, according to Vespasiano da Bisticci, Acciaiuoli heard Argyropoulos's early lectures on both the *Politics* and the (pseudo-Aristotle) *Economics*.[72] Acciaiuoli never mentioned Argyropoulos's name in the text or even the preface, nor does his rough draft of the commentary, where sources are sometimes better indicated, cite Argyropoulos in the margins. To be sure, Acciaiuoli was using Leonardo Bruni's translation of Aristotle (Argyropoulos had not made one), and Argyropoulos had already left Florence for Sixtus IV and Rome, but the silence toward the one who had been Florence's greatest contemporary Aristotelian is still striking.

Argyropoulos, as I said, was safely away at Rome, and it does not appear from extant letters, of which, in Acciaiuoli's case at least, there are many from the 1470s, that the Byzantine and Donato kept in touch.[73] Letters to Florence from Argyropoulos in the early 1470s are addressed to Lorenzo de' Medici, and they are not particularly friendly: Florence, evidently, was not only refusing to pay him his back salary but was holding on to a large part of his library.[74] Acciaiuoli's commentary on the *Politics* would seem to indicate a complete psychological break with the Byzantine—a significant break for one who had spent much of his life

---

narrata da Piero Acciaiuoli," *Rendiconti della Accademia Nazionale dei Lincei, Classe di scienze morali, storiche, critiche e filologiche*, 5th ser., 5 (1896), 198–220 at pp. 207ff., and now de la Mare, "New Research on Humanistic Scribes," p. 573. I shall be citing Acciaiuoli's autograph, Naz. II III 373. The proem is entitled (fol. 1): "Donati Acciaioli Florentini prohemium in expositionem politicorum Aristotelis [added later:] ad ill. principem F. V. D. [for 'Federicum Urbini ducem']." At the top of fol. 2 is the autograph date, "die 3.0 augusti 1472." After the *accessus* appears the title (fol. 3v): "Donati Acciaioli florentini expositio super libros politicorum Aristotelis in novam traductionem Leonardi Arretini primus liber." An elegant, polished version is Laur. S. Marco 67: for a detailed description, by L. Pinelli, see now *Catalogo di manoscritti filosofici nelle biblioteche italiane*, vol. 2, ed. D. Frioli et al. (Florence, 1981), pp. 24–26. The codex I shall cite has Acciaiuoli's autograph corrections; in the margins Acciaiuoli often indicated sources absent in the polished version.

72. Vespasiano, *Vite*, II, 13, 26.

73. In a marginal note to a draft of a consolatory letter to Lorenzo and Giuliano de' Medici, 10 Dec. 1469, on the death of their father, Piero (Magl. VIII 1390, fols. 51v–52, in a definitive version), Acciaiuoli may have indicated those whom he *now* viewed as the great Italian lights of learning and eloquence (ibid., fol. 53): "Iam ego Philelphum, Campanum, Pontanum, omnes oratores et poetas appello, ut funebribus orationibus eius obitum ornent." This might, of course, simply reinforce my earlier hypothesis that Acciaiuoli *never* considered Argyropoulos much of a Latin orator. The evidence is confusing, but when Argyropoulos attempted to return to Florence in the mid-1470s to his university position in philosophy, Francesco Filelfo wrote to Donato Acciaiuoli and Alamanno Rinuccini in support of Demetrius Chalcondylas instead, and it seems highly likely that Chalcondylas was backed by the Acciaiuoli group (see Cammelli, *Argiropolo*, pp. 149ff.).

74. Cammelli, *Argiropulo*, pp. 136ff. The MAP letter cited is now MAP xx, 609.

looking for the perfect maestro. Certainly Acciaiuoli's defense of Plato
is unrestrained, or, we might say, strained, even and especially in those
sections of the *Politics* where Aristotle criticizes Plato's community of
property and women. We must understand these passages, Acciaiuoli
explained, not as the "words" read but according to the "mind of the
philosopher." Plato's doctrine and integrity of life helped mortals
greatly: let us interpret him in the best way possible.[75]

Plato's real teaching, wrote Acciaiuoli, is not that women and wives
should be shared but that they should love one another. He never
sought turpitude in his republic. The makers of law should know that
the health of the city depends on the harmony (*concordia*) and friendship
of its citizens. Plato especially praised a city's unity: in his *Symposium*
Aristophanes shows that love forces two lovers toward one another so
that they become one.[76] And in Plato's *Phaedrus* love is described as a
divine frenzy, leading us to a remembrance of that form of love that is
beauty itself. Love is not an immoral frenzy but a divine one, spurring
us not toward the body, which in itself is not beauty, but to a recollection of God and of all the Ideas in him. It is not "beauty" proper but
that supreme beauty of God that is the cause of all things beautiful.[77]

As Acciaiuoli explained later in the commentary, the soul proceeds
through hierarchies constantly seeking God. Plato argued that we move
from things visible to things invisible: the beauty of the body leads to a
contemplation of beauty itself.[78] Existing within the soul are similitudes

75.   Naz. II III 373, fol. 33 [in *mg.* and between lines]: "Dicta igitur Platonis qui obscure
et methaphorice plerumque loquebatur, in bonam partem si licet aut libet accipiamus et
mentem summi philosophi cuius doctrina et integritas vite multis mortalibus profuit,
grato animo interpretemur." This replaced a passage crossed out: "Sic igitur solvuntur
Aristotelis argumenta qui accipiebat sententias Platonis eo modo quo vulgo sumebantur
et ut verba sonabant, que tamen non erant de mente Platonis, quia perobscure loquebatur et sensus erat interior alius quam apparebat."

76.   Ibid., fol. 25v: "[L]egum latores maxime student concordie et amicitie civium exis-
timantes in ea consistere salutem civitatis. Plato quoque idem velle videtur et unitatem
civitatis maxime laudat. Quin etiam in Symposio ubi loquitur de amore inducit Aristo-
phanem dicentem quod amor duos amatores ita compellit ad invicem ut ex duobus vel-
lent fieri unum."

77.   Ibid., fol. 31 (*mg.*): "Uxores . . . et liberos forsitan Plato hoc modo volebat esse
communes, non ut se invicem conmiscerent, sed ut se invicem diligerent ex vero caritatis
affectu, non secus quam si essent communes et a suis non differrent. . . . Hoc latissime
patet in Phedro ubi turpem amorem maxime detestatur, bonum vero extollit atque eum
apellat bonum unde oriri in nobis perfectio possit. Quin etiam amorem de quo loquebatur diffiniens dicit quod amor est furor divinus ad reminiscendum eius forme que per se
pulcritudo est. Non enim furor turpis est amor, sed furor divinus, nec simpliciter divinus
sed furor divinus compellens nos ad reminiscendum pulcritudinis non quidem corporis
que per se pulcritudo non est, sed dei et rationum omnium que sunt in illo."

78.   Ibid., fol. 132v (*mg.*): "Ait Plato in eo libro qui inscribitur Phedrus . . . ex ipsis visi-

of divine things, which exist as conceptions, or Ideas. Human souls are alike in being created by God, and they are inclined to their own perfection. Toward this perfection we must constantly strive. We first acquire the moral virtues, and we then seek the contemplation of the divine. This, Acciaiuoli stated, was the teaching of both Plato and Aristotle, "as we explained in our commentary on the *Ethics*." The active life, he argued, must yield to the contemplative. In essence Aristotle agreed with Plato: republics will be happy when wise men rule or rulers begin to philosophize.[79]

Although this Platonism of Donato Acciaiuoli has eluded modern scholars, contemporaries of Acciaiuoli—those who conversed with him and read and studied his works—knew better. I have already mentioned Landino's funeral oration. Niccolò Tignosi complained in the early 1470s that Acciaiuoli's theory of ideas, as outlined in his commentary on the *Nicomachean Ethics*, was in fact not Aristotle's position but Plato's.[80] Later in the decade, in his short dialogue *De paenitentia*, Bartolomeo Fonzio had Acciaiuoli lead the discussion and define penitence as a continuous process of the soul's improvement through love: true penitence depends on an inward judgment of the heart and mind; it is a "*gymnasium* of virtues" that leads us away from the world and toward God.[81] In the 1480s Giovanni Nesi, in his dialogue *De moribus*, has Acciaiuoli explain Aristotelian moral philosophy in terms very similar to those of his commentaries.[82] Nesi here describes Acciaiuoli as the "high-priest of Socratic philosophy."[83]

Acciaiuoli was a great personal success, and his commentaries were extremely popular. Since he was a highly respected political figure, it should come as no surprise to find his generalizations about harmony and justice echoed in the Florentine political forum. In July 1475, in a public speech introducing the new Florentine Signoria, Acciaiuoli's

---

bilibus, ut scribit Dionysius Areopagita, in contemplationem vel cognitionem invisibilium veniamus quoad fieri potest."

79. Ibid., fol. 108v: "Verum haec sunt a nobis in expositione ethicorum latius explicata. Patet igitur quod philosophus concludit contemplativam vivendi rationem supremam esse felicitatem atque eam esse vitam optimam privatim unicuique et ipsi civitati. Cui opinioni quoquomodo consentanea esse videtur sententia illa Platonis, cum inquit beatas fore res p. cum sapientes eas regerent aut qui regerentur [*sic*] sapere cepissent."

80. *De ideis*, ed. in Thorndike, *Science and Thought*, pp. 332–63; cf. pp. 308–31.

81. Printed with Fonzio, *Orationes* (Florence, 1487 + [*GW* 10171]), sig. F2–F12v. See also Laur. Ashb. 918, fols. 95–115, which has Fonzio's autograph corrections.

82. Laur. 77, 24. See R. Bonfanti, "Su un dialogo filosofico del tardo '400: Il *De moribus* del fiorentino Giovanni Nesi (1456–1522?)," *Rinascimento*, 2d ser., 11 (1971), 203–21 (the forthcoming edition she cites in the notes has not, I think, been published).

83. Laur. 77, 24, fol. 5.

friend and scholarly companion Pierfilippo Pandolfini would aver that
true justice is when "inferior and less worthy powers obey the superior
powers." This "Platonic justice," he continued, "is a true union and
peace."[84] This sort of opinion, new to the Florentine *protesto di giustizia*,
seems to be owed immediately to Acciaiuoli's commentary on the *Nicomachean Ethics*.[85]

It would be incorrect, however, to call Donato Acciaiuoli an intellectual innovator of first rank.[86] While the formal lines of influence are difficult to trace, the more important of Acciaiuoli's philosophical notions
are derivative, probably from Ficino and possibly indirectly, that is,
from the Ficino circle. His success lay in his intellectual leadership of a
group of Florentines, many of whom, for reasons that are now uncertain, felt estranged, at least for a time, from the Ficino circle. The many
attempts to define a political and ideological cause for this alienation
have been unsuccessful. For many Florentines this estrangement from
Ficino was no doubt simply a matter of taste. Many felt more comfortable with a Platonism emerging from an Aristotelian structure, outlined
by the respected and respectable young Florentine noble Donato Acciaiuoli, than with the Platonic mysteries of the presumptuous and im-
petuous Marsilio Ficino, whose curious looks and melancholic temperament evoked wonder no less than did the curiosity of his writing style.

84.   Protesto di giustizia of 13 July 1475, ed. in Santini, "La *Protestatio de iustitia*," pp.
65–74, at p. 68: "Et . . . vuole el divino Platone che, avendo le potentie rationali degnie et
nobili apartenenti all'animo et le sensitive infime et basse apartenenti al corpo, vera iustitia fussi quando le potentie inferiori et meno degnie ubidiscono alle superiori et quando
il senso ubidissi alla ragione et il corpo ubidissi all'anima; et colui nel quale la ragione
fussi soffocata et ubidissi al senso, propriamente si chiamasse iniusto. Et chi bene consi-
dera troverà che iusto mai potrà essere verso il prossimo chi in sé prima non ha questa
iustitia platonicha, la quale è una vera unione et pace, una vera tranquillità et quiete delle
potentie dell'animo nostro."

85.   The novelty of Pandolfini's Platonic conception of justice for the Florentine public
forum has been noted by A. Brown in her "Platonism in Fifteenth-Century Florence," p.
399. She does not speculate on Acciaiuoli as a possible source.

86.   I do not think, for instance, that a figure such as Ficino could have been especially
interested in Acciaiuoli's philosophical speculations, even if he had been willing to look
upon them sympathetically. Eugenio Garin has argued that the margins of a copy of the
1478 edition of Acciaiuoli's commentary on the *Nicomachean Ethics* (Florence, Bibl. Naz.
Cent., Incun. Magl. C.1.10) contain "some very interesting" annotations in Ficino's hand
(*La cultura filosofica*, p. 78 and n.). For this book, see *Marsilio Ficino e il ritorno: Mostra*,
pp. 143–44, no. III, and Kristeller, "Marsilio Ficino and His Work," pp. 96, 157. My examination of the book leaves me convinced that the marginalia are not in Ficino's hand;
they are not interesting notes in any case (mostly some index words and other verbatim
reproductions from the text itself).

IX

CRISTOFORO LANDINO
AND PLATONIC POETRY

W HEN the humanist Cristoforo Landino (1425–98) lectured on the poems of ancients and moderns (Horace, Virgil, Juvenal, Persius, Dante, and Petrarch), he often remarked on the "variety" of their style and teaching. The reader, he stated, can at times only be "stunned" (*attonitus*) by the direction a poem takes. As if following a poetic model, Landino had "variety" mark both his writing and his public career. He moved freely from Latin to Italian, from poets to orators, and from philosophical precepts to the art of writing letters. While seemingly preoccupied with composing dialogues in moral philosophy, he published an Italian translation of Pliny's *Natural History*. While arguing to his students that intellectual endeavors were best carried on apart from the affairs of state, he himself attempted to become chancellor of Florence. While polishing his *De anima* he served as secretary to the Parte Guelfa. After winning fame for an allegorical interpretation of the *Aeneid* he saw his literal or grammatical commentary of the same through the press. He lectured on philosophers as if they were poets and on poets as if they were philosophers.

As a poet and lecturer Landino helped shape the philosophical renaissance. In a way he stands in relation to Ficino as Acciaiuoli does to Argyropoulos, as a humanist, that is, who takes over and presents "humanistically" the ideas of a philosopher. The analogy is inaccurate, however, for in terms of a formal set of ideas Acciaiuoli departed significantly, as I have argued, from his mentor, while Landino did not. Furthermore, Ficino was a humanist who exploited philosophical forms of writing and who developed, through a nonhumanist methodology, several independent philosophical notions; Argyropoulos was a philosopher who now and then exploited a humanistic genre (for example, the letter and oration). On one level we could look at Landino's poetic theory, especially his notion of allegory, as the concrete application of

231

Ficino's philosophical principles to one humanist branch of literature. But poetic theory had a rich tradition, from the *prisci poetae* through the Trecento Florentines, and Landino tapped this tradition in arguing that the best poets approached "universality" in their learning, that poetry had a status above and apart from that of the other liberal arts, and that neither theories of technique nor philosophical principles alone could "explain" the work of a poet.

Before we look at Landino's conception of poetry, however, let us examine those purely personal considerations Landino may have had for wanting to argue for poetic "universality." As I stated earlier, the great challenge of Landino's early career in the Florentine Studio was his status as successor to Carlo Marsuppini, who had taught at the university all of the more humane studies and some speculative philosophy as well; as anyone in Florence who followed the Studio controversy knew, Landino was "only" a rhetorician and a poet.

Cristoforo Landino needs a modern biography: the archival material relating to his life has been only partially tapped, and the known facts of his life, particularly in the early period, are few.[1] He was born in 1425, probably in Florence, into an old but not wealthy family from Pratovecchio, a town in the mountainous Casentino southeast of Florence.[2] The muse of poetry had visited his family more than once, and Landino pointed with pride to these *studiosi*: his great uncle Francesco (il Cieco) Landini was a famous Trecento musician and composer, and his uncle Gabriele, a Camaldulensian monk under Ambrogio Traversari, had tried his hand at lyric and heroic verse.[3] In the 1430s Landino evidently studied for a time in Volterra and then took up the study of law, perhaps

---

1.   Still quite useful is A. M. Bandini, *Specimen*, 2 vols. For a clarification of some of Bandini's sources, see A. Perosa, "Una fonte secentesca dello Specimen del Bandini in un codice della Biblioteca Marucelliana," *La Bibliofilia* 42 (1940), 229–56. Some new biographical information, though largely literary, is added by recent monographs: M. Lentzen, *Studien* (1971), with lengthy bibliography, and R. Cardini, *La critica* (1973). Professor David Herlihy (Department of History, Brown University) has on computer some additional information taken from the *Tratte* of the Archivio di Stato, Florence. Special studies and some new sources will be mentioned in the notes that follow.

2.   Contemporary documentary sources usually give Landino's name as Cristoforo (or Cristofano) di Bartolomeo da Pratovecchio. In his Dante commentary of 1481 Landino mentioned that he was a Florentine, since his "body was composed there," which I suppose meant, even for a Platonist, that he was born in Florence (cited by Bandini, *Specimen*, I, 55, and by others since). Bandini accurately listed the date of birth as "1424" (ibid., p. 45), since he was writing just before Florence converted to the modern style of dating; but nearly all secondary literature has since repeated, incorrectly, the date 1424. (An exception is L. Martines, *Lawyers and Statecraft in Renaissance Florence* [Princeton, 1968], p. 504.) Landino's birth date was registered in the Florentine Tratte as 8 Feb. 1424/25 (Florence, Arch. di Stato, Tratte 443bis, fol. 72; and Tratte 40, fol. 96 [latter reference owed to Professor Herlihy]).

3.   Bandini, *Specimen*, I, 36–45.

at the University of Pavia.[4] His career then took a turn typical of that of the earliest humanists: the *studia humanitatis* competed for his attention. Consciously following Petrarch's model with Laura, he found in one Alessandra ("Xandra" in Latin) an outlet for his earliest poetic endeavors.[5] To Bernardo Nuti he composed these lines in the early 1440s:

Nos procul a nostra, dulcis Bernarde, puella
    cogimur insani discere iura fori.
Nec tantum studiis quantum invigilans lucello
    paupertas nobis imperiosa iubet;
sic heu fit postquam nostros, Bernarde, parentes
    res angusta nimis difficilisque premit.
At si quando vacat, cum turba molesta quievit,
    litibus et scissis omnia clausa silent,
protinus ad nostras avidus me confero Musas,
    quarum immortali pulsus amore feror.

(Far from our sweetheart we are compelled, gentle Bernardo, to learn the laws of the bustling Forum. Watching diligently over its little profit, more than over our studies, imperious poverty orders us about. Thus, alas, it fell out when too straitened and difficult circumstances put pressure on our parents. But whenever circumstances permit, when the bothersome crowd is at rest and all things besieged by disruptive lawsuits grow silent, straightway I eagerly turn to our Muses, by whose immortal love I am moved and borne aloft.)[6]

At the competition of Italian poetry in 1441, the famous *certame coronario*, Landino recited a composition by one of his patrons, Francesco di Altobianco Alberti.[7] Soon thereafter Landino dedicated to Leon Battista Alberti the first edition of his poems entitled *Xandra*.[8] During the 1440s he evidently supported himself as a tutor and perhaps as a scribe. He deepened his knowledge of rhetoric, poetry, and perhaps philosophy through two years of study under Carlo Marsuppini in the 1440s

4. Ibid., pp. 74–78. Notarial records of 1437 for the University of Pavia list one "Christoforus de Landinis" as a *legum scholar*: see Società Pavese di Storia Patria, *Codice diplomatico dell'Università di Pavia*, vol. 2, pt. 1: 1401–1440 (Pavia, 1913), p. 383n. (noted by Lentzen, *Studien*, p. 4n.); but this could possibly be another figure by the same name.

5. For the complexities of Landino's stylistic models, see, however, Cardini, *La critica*, pp. 1ff.

6. The passage quoted follows the older version of the *Xandra* (*Carmina*, p. 39 and n.; cf. pp. xxiii–iv); for A. Perosa's identification of this Bernardus, see ibid., p. 204.

7. Cardini, *La critica*, pp. 5, 134.

8. Ed. Perosa, in Landino, *Carmina*; for the dating, see Perosa's introduction, pp. xxxvii–viii.

and two more years in 1451–53.[9] He may have worked in the Marsuppini Chancery as a notary. At times he evidently held minor positions in the Studio, perhaps for lectures in grammar.[10] He also taught privately, probably as a teacher in his own school rather than merely as a tutor.[11]

In 1455 he competed for a chair in rhetoric and poetry in the Florentine Studio, finding among his rivals three friends, Francesco da Castiglione, Bernardo Nuti, and Bartolomeo Scala. In these years (1455–58) Landino's critics compared him to Carlo Marsuppini and found him wanting. Criteria of fame and eloquence were at stake, but critics could also point to two major lacunae in his culture: unlike Marsuppini, Landino knew neither Greek nor philosophy. One of his rivals for the Studio chair, Francesco da Castiglione, may have taught him some Greek in these years.[12] But Landino seems never to have mastered the language. To be sure, he knew enough to describe some Latin etymologies and decline Latin nouns taken from the Greek; he probably could read through some narrative, historical texts that would serve him in explicating the historical and allegorical meaning of some poetry. He may even have made a rough translation of the first five books of Diodorus Siculus.[13] For philosophical texts, he used a variety of Latin sources. He

9.   See Landino's letter to Piero de' Medici, n.d., but from the 1450s, ed. in *Carmina*, pp. 181–87 (at p. 184).

10.   Payments to him by the Studio are listed in fragmentary and damaged Monte records for 29 February 1451/52 and 31 August 1454; each is for 56 lire, 13 soldi, 4 denari (Monte Comune 1652, pp. ⟨463b⟩ [or the verso of the sixteenth folio, by count, of the volume], 678a; Monte Comune 1537, pp. ⟨28a⟩, ⟨217a⟩). (Pagination within brackets, where original pagination destroyed by fire, supplied by cross-references ["a carta," etc.] provided for each entry in the records themselves.) The first of these volumes is cited by Brown, *Bartolomeo Scala*, p. 7n., and by Park, "Readers at the Florentine Studio," p. 309. Payments were by thirds, and this would correspond to an annual salary of 35 florins (for the conversion ratios, see R. A. Goldthwaite, *The Building of Renaissance Florence* [Baltimore and London, 1980], pp. 301, 430). For the fragmentary Monte records, see my "Cristoforo Landino's First Lectures on Dante," p. 33, n. 71. Payments to Landino also appear in records of a notary of the Monte Comune, in Not. Antec. D 65 (Niccolò di Michele Dini, 1454), unfoliated, at the section dated 6 Sept. 1454 (or fol. 4v, by count). Donato Acciaiuoli mentioned in March-April 1455 that Landino "had lectured publicly for two years" (in the letter cited above, Chapter IV, n. 47), but it is not certain whether the Studio payments cited are for these lectures or for something else, such as notarial duties. Ca. 1464 Landino mentioned that he was now in his tenth year of lecturing publicly, for the first two of which he received no public salary (letter to Lorenzo de' Medici, ed. in Lentzen, *Studien*, pp. 205–10 [references at pp. 207, 209]).

11.   In the same letter of ca. 1464, Landino mentioned he was now in his tenth year of lecturing "publicly and privately" (p. 207). A *reportatio* of Landino's Juvenal lectures of 1461–62 contains a reference to "externae lectiones" (noted by E. M. Sanford, "Juvenalis," in *Catalogus translationum et commentariorum*, vol. 1 [Washington, D.C., 1960], p. 209).

12.   In these years Castiglione was teaching Greek to Donato Acciaiuoli, Pellegrino degli Agli, and probably Marsilio Ficino. Landino wrote two early poems to Francesco in his *Xandra* (*Carmina*, pp. 17, 143–44).

13.   Ricc. 138, differing from Poggio's translation, and with autograph corrections, is in

evidently pointed Marsilio Ficino toward some of these in inducing him to write out his *Institutiones ad Platonicam disciplinam*, dedicated to Landino in 1456.[14]

In the autumn of 1456, after failing to win a lectureship in rhetoric and poetry, Landino acquired a less lucrative (forty-five florins per year) and less prestigious position in the Studio, probably to lecture on Dante.[15] During this time, Landino's fame as a teacher grew, and he not only came to number the very young Lorenzo de' Medici (born 1449) among his students but also began to establish himself as a client of some of the most powerful leaders of the Medici party.[16] Early poems praise Agnolo Acciaiuoli (who had supported him in the Studio controversy of 1455), Giovanni Canigiani, Neri Capponi, and others.[17] Late in 1456 Landino attempted, unsuccessfully, to become a secretary and assistant in the Chancery of Florence as part of a desperate attempt by the Medici party to restore Poggio as chancellor. Landino blamed the failure of the attempt, and Poggio's removal from office, on a conspiracy of lawyers, whom, as a group, he began to despise (he mocked them in some lectures from the early 1460s).[18] Then in January 1458, with Medi-

---

Landino's hand: see my "Cristoforo Landino's First Lectures on Dante," pp. 28–29, n. 47, and p. 48, plate 3. For Landino's knowledge of Greek, see ibid., pp. 27–28 (and n. 47).

14.   See Kristeller, *Supplementum Ficinianum*, I, clxiii–iv, and my "Cristoforo Landino's First Lectures on Dante," pp. 34–35.

15.   See my "Cristoforo Landino's First Lectures on Dante," pp. 16–48 (p. 33, for the salary).

16.   Leon Battista Alberti mentioned Landino as Lorenzo's *praeceptor* in his *Trivia* to Lorenzo of ca. 1460: see Rochon, *La jeunesse de Laurent de Médicis*, pp. 35–36; this role is later alluded to in Landino's *Disputationes Camaldulenses* (e.g., p. 35).

17.   Landino praised Agnolo Acciaiuoli in a poem honoring the Acciaiuoli family (*Carmina*, pp. 120–22 at lines 39–61). Landino's eulogy of Neri Capponi was dedicated to Giovanni Canigiani (ibid., pp. 156–58); like Ficino, Landino dedicated an early work to Canigiani's son Antonio (ibid., pp. 86–91), who also stood as a witness for Landino's marriage contract in 1458 (Not. Antec. 616, 2 [Simone Grazzini], fol. 51–51v).

18.   *Ad Petrum Medicem de laudibus Poggi*, in *Carmina*, pp. 123–29. Note, for instance, these lines (109–14):

> Et nunc, o mores, o tempora, debitus illi—
>   ferre quis hoc poterit?—eripietur honos.
> Ah tantum vobis licuit, civilia iura,
>   Pieridum casta pellere sede chorum:
> formula quae vobis, quae competit actio summum
>   per scelus audaces inseruisse manus?

The poem continues in the same vein for twenty more lines.

In his letter to Piero accompanying this poem (ibid., pp. 187–90), Landino wrote as follows (p. 189): "Et profecto, ni ego fallor, non ita inique aut avare cum iuris consultis a rerum publicarum gubernatoribus actum est, ut suarum illos dignitatum paenitere oporteat, praesertim cum neque ingenii neque doctrinae tantum in eorum artificio eluceat, ut cum aut poetarum aut oratorum maximis ac pulcherrimis ornamentis comparandi sint." For this letter, see now R. Black, *Benedetto Accolti*, pp. 105–7, 182.

cean support, he at last won the Studio chair in rhetoric and poetry, with a salary of one hundred florins per year. In gratitude (or perhaps "in payment") he dedicated to one of the Ufficiali dello Studio, Piero de' Medici, a revised and expanded version of his *Xandra*.[19] Even more financial and political security came in 1460, when he married Lucrezia di Alberto di Adovardo degli Alberti, who brought into the marriage a handsome dowry of some five to seven hundred florins.[20]

From a variety of sources—lecture notes, inaugural orations, and contemporary references—it is now possible to reconstruct much of the sequence of lectures that Landino gave in his first decade as teacher of the humanities.[21] From 1458 he probably lectured on Cicero's *Tusculan Disputations*.[22] He then spent four years on Latin poetry: Horace's *Odes* (1459–60 or 1460–61),[23] the *Satires* of Juvenal and Persius (1461–62),[24]

These complaints were not merely *ad rem*. Juvenal's frequent references to lawyers in his *Satires* gave Landino, in his lectures on Juvenal of 1461–62, ample opportunity to discuss legal culture. In *Satire* 7 Juvenal argues that several literary groups—poets, historians, lawyers, rhetoricians, and grammarians—are rewarded far too little for their efforts. His "attacks" on these groups are satirical, imagined opinions of stingy patrons. But when Juvenal gets to the lawyers the irony vanishes, at least "in the judgment of Landino," according to the following strained gloss, recorded by the scribe (Ambros. I 26 inf., fol. 125v): "*Tunc immensa cavi spirant mendacia folles* [VII, 111]. . . . Prosequitur enim in labore ipsorum causidicorum. Sed tamen, dum haec narrat non multis laudibus illos effert, sed potius, iudicio Landini, illos deridet, nam a duabus partibus illos vituperare videtur: primo quod non diligentes sint absentibus clientibus suis, deinde quod veritatem pro nihilo habeant."

19. For the dating see Perosa's introduction to Landino, *Carmina*, p. xxxviii.

20. Bandini, *Specimen*, I, 209–10. Bandini's date, 1459, was accurate when Bandini wrote (see n. 2, above). The contract for the marriage was drawn up in 1458 (see n. 17, above).

21. For this chronology, based largely on that of R. Cardini, see my "Cristoforo Landino's First Lectures on Dante," p. 21. In the following notes, I shall merely list the extant manuscripts or editions that I shall cite, except where I can add to what has already been said in print. For additional information, and arguments on the dating, see Cardini, *La critica*, pp. 16–17, 334–41; my "A Manuscript of Cristoforo Landino's First Lectures on Virgil, 1462–63 (Codex 1368, Biblioteca Casanatense, Rome)," *Renaissance Quarterly* 31 (1978), p. 18; my "An Inaugural Oration by Cristoforo Landino in Praise of Virgil (From Codex '2,' Casa Cavalli, Ravenna)," *Rinascimento*, 2d. ser., 21 (1981), pp. 236–38; and my "Cristoforo Landino's First Lectures on Dante," pp. 21ff. and nn.

22. Inaugural oration alone extant: *Scritti*, I, 5–15. See also Brown, *Bartolomeo Scala*, pp. 264, 265 (and nn.). At least two manuscripts of the *Tusculans* were copied in Florence in 1458: Laur. 90 sup., 75 (inside back cover: "Jacobus Vespucius scrips(it) 1458"), owned by Giorgio Antonio Vespucci (ownership note on front flyleaf and inside back cover), and Laur. 90 sup., 76, copied by Alamanno Rinuccini's brother, Neri (on 18 November: see fol. 147).

23. Neither the inaugural oration nor a lecture draft is extant. The lectures are mentioned in Landino's lectures on Juvenal and Persius, Ambros. I 26 inf., as noted by Cardini, *La critica*, pp. 16n., 337n. (the correct folios, however, are 37 *verso* and 74 *verso*).

24. A lecture draft only is extant: Ambros. I 26 inf. (225 fols.), fragmentary at the beginning, and the last page may be unreadable, depending on the manuscript's current state of preservation (see my "A Manuscript," p. 18n.). Individual lectures are indicated

Virgil's *Aeneid*, Books 1-7 (1462–63),[25] and the rest of the *Aeneid* and probably more Virgil (1463–64).[26] For 1464–65 (or 1465: the Studio may have opened late because of plague) we can only be sure of the general subject, the *poeticae rhetoricaeque artis praecepta*, and that he delivered a commentary on Horace's *Ars poetica*. Lectures on Petrarch's *Canzoniere* probably date from either this year or a few years later.[27] In 1465–66 he

---

by having the lemma for the lecture's beginning circled rather than underlined: my count shows 117 lectures on Juvenal, 17 on Persius. Gatherings are of ten, and they would indicate that only one folio is missing at the beginning.

25.   A lecture draft is extant in Casanatense 1368 (280 fols.), and perhaps Laur. 52, 32 (181 fols., misnumbered 1–130, 132–182). Landino's first lecture on Book 6, copied separately in Vat. lat. 5129, fols. 69–77v, may also be taken from these lectures. In the following citations, my arguments usually derive from the Casanatense manuscript, which is more detailed than the Laurentian one (see my "Cristoforo Landino's First Lectures on Dante," pp. 17–24, 39–45, and plates 1 and 2). I shall often reproduce the corresponding passage in the Laurentian manuscript; elsewhere I shall note (with a "cf.") the pages of the latter manuscript where the corresponding passage of the *Aeneid* is discussed.
   Based on a lead provided me by Albinia de la Mare, I can now identify the scribe of the Casanatense manuscript as Florentine political figure Giovanni di Bartolomeo Guidi. This is based on a comparison between the Casanatense manuscript and plates of a manuscript of Macrobius, *Saturnalia*, signed by Guidi and dated 25 Jan. 1461/62. The latter was formerly ms. 7373 of Major J. R. Abbey (see J. J. G. Alexander and A. C. de la Mare, *The Italian Manuscripts in the Library of Major J. R. Abbey* [London, 1969], pp. 41–43 and plate 16; Miss de la Mare kindly provided me additional plates). The manuscript was sold by Sotheby's in 1978 to a private European owner (communication of Dr. Christopher de Hamel). Giovanni Guidi was the son of Bartolomeo Guidi, the notary favored by the Medici as Poggio's chief assistant in a reform proposal of 1456; both Bartolomeo and Poggio were rejected by the popular government (see Chapter II, above, and especially Black, *Benedetto Accolti*, pp. 93–97). Bartolomeo Guidi was later chosen to read the Law of the Parlamento of 1458, the proclamation of the Medici coup (see Rubinstein, *Government*, p. 104). The Johannes Bartholomaeus who sought advice from Poggio in 1455 on how to go about taking up Greek philosophy could well be Giovanni di Bartolomeo Guidi. Giovanni Guidi seems to have had a correspondence with Landino (see R. Cardini, *La critica*, pp. 44–45n), but the identification of Johannes Bartholomaeus is confusing (see, e.g., the puzzling addresses of letters in Laur. Acq. e Doni 82, as described by Kristeller, *Iter*, I, 100). Marsilio Ficino praised Guidi in 1471 as a creator, not a disputer, of law when he became a prior of the Signoria (quoted above, p. 156; see L. Martines, *Lawyers and Statecraft*, p. 69, for the date of Guidi's office). One of Ficino's disciples and closest early friends, the poet Naldo Naldi, praised Guidi in identical terms in epigrams written in his honor (Naldi, *Epigrammaton liber*, ed. A. Perosa [Budapest, 1943], pp. 56–57, no. 171; p. 61, no. 183; and probably p. 43, no. 34 [see p. 65n.]). A notary for the Florentine Chancery, Guidi became in the 1490s one of the most vicious antipopular supporters of the Medici regime, and his subsequent imprisonment and torture during the Savonarola period was no doubt welcomed by many (see Brown, *Bartolomeo Scala*, pp. 97–99, 117).

26.   Neither the inaugural oration nor a lecture draft is extant.

27.   For plague in the autumn of 1464, see de la Mare, "Vespasiano da Bisticci," I, 23n, and Brown, *Bartolomeo Scala*, p. 42.
   Landino's student Lorenzo Guidetti indicated the subject of the lectures in a letter of 18 Sept. 1465 (ed. in Cardini, *La critica*, pp. 267–69, at p. 267): "Praeceptor meus . . . cum superiori anno poeticae rhetoricaeque artis praecepta egregie exposuisset" etc. In Ricc. 646, fols. 61–84v (according to foliation in brown, upper right: fol. 67 is erroneously followed by 78), are notes on Horace, *Ars poetica*, drafted by Bartolomeo Fonzio, enti-

lectured on the art of writing letters, giving a commentary on at least
some of Cicero's *Familiares*. Whether he included *volgare* letter writing,
the subject of a quite popular treatise he wrote many years later, is not
known.[28] It is possible he lectured on Juvenal again, and then he returned to Virgil's *Aeneid*, *Eclogues*, and perhaps other Virgiliana for two
more years (ca. 1467–69).[29]

Thereafter little is known of his public lectures. Of his philosophical
dialogues, he published the *De anima* first, in 1471 or 1472, although he
had probably been working on it from the early 1460s.[30] He completed

tled (fol. 61), "Collecta sub Christophoro Landino publice legenti Florentie anno
MCCCC° supra quartum et sexagesimum. Multa sunt quae ipse non dixit, sed ego ex Tor-
tellio collegi." Other of Fonzio's notes on the same work, citing Landino, are undated in
a manuscript owned by Professor John Sparrow, Oxford University (on deposit at the
Bodleian Library as codex "2" of the Sparrow collection [at fols. 30v, 71–79v]) [see my
"Cristoforo Landino's First Lectures on Dante," p. 21, n. 20]. The dated Riccardiana
manuscript would place the lectures on Horace (or at least their beginning) before 25
Mar. 1465.

Can Landino's lectures on Petrarch also be assigned to early 1465? Cardini argues convincingly that they must be assigned to the 1460s, although he eventually arrives at ca.
1467 (*La critica*, pp. 334–41). In his undated inaugural oration before the Petrarch lectures, Landino sought to defend the study of an Italian author in the context of lectures
on the precepts of rhetoric and poetry (e.g., in *Scritti*, I, 33: "E quanto io quando nella
mente mi rivolgo quanto pochi, in sì gran turba di toscani scrittori, sieno stati quelli che
cognizione d'arte e di precetti o oratori o poetici abbino avuto" etc.). And in the Archivio di Stato, Florence, Carte Strozz., III, 291, there is a manuscript of Petrarch's *Canzoniere* (incomplete) copied by this same Lorenzo Guidetti and dated 22 Jan. 1465 (n.s.):
"Io Lorenzo di Francesco Ghuidetti scrisse questo libro anno 1464 finito a dì 22 di gien-
naio" (fol. 145v or 146v: the foliation is confusing at end). If the Studio was closed by
plague in the autumn of 1464, the delayed academic year, as in other years, would begin
on 18 Jan. 1465, or about the same time that Guidetti completed this draft. The manuscript contains some marginalia, but they are insufficiently detailed to determine if they
derive from Landino's lectures (cf. Cardini, *La critica*, p. 41n., who also mentions the
paucity of the notes). A combination of lectures on Horace and Petrarch would not have
been unusual for a disciple of *varietas* such as Landino.

Nevertheless, the dating of the Petrarch lectures must remain for now an open question. Perhaps a careful study of the script of Naz. II IV 128 (where the oration on Petrarch appears), copied by Giovanni Pigli apparently in stages during the 1460s, will lead
to firmer conclusions as to the date.

28.   Not extant. Landino's approach toward the text is known from the Massari-Gui-
detti polemics, discussed below.

29.   Inaugural oration extant, Ravenna, Casa Cavalli, s.n. (ed. and dated in my "An Inaugural Oration," pp. 235–45: for lines 23, 163, and perhaps others, the readings in the
apparatus, alas, are better than the ones I supplied; also, my identification of the scribe as
Lorenzo Guidetti is questionable). There are a few of Landino's glosses on the *Eclogues*,
1–3, copied by Bartolomeo Fonzio in 1468 (Ricc. 152, fols. 128–36v [earlier foliated 117–
25v]). The section is entitled (fol. 128): "Collecta sub Petro Cennino. Anno 1468"; but in
the left margin of the first page there is this note, "Sub Christophoro hec pagella," and in
the margins of the other pages there are glosses "secundum Christophorum."

30.   Ed. in *Annali delle università toscane*: Book 1, ed. A. Paoli, vol. 34 (1915), fasc. 1;
Book 2, ed. Paoli, n.s., vol. 1 (1916), fasc. 2; Book 3, ed. G. Gentile, n.s., vol. 2 (1917),
fasc. 3. Manfred Lentzen is currently preparing a new edition. Ricc. 417 contains an early

the *Disputationes Camaldulenses* in 1472 and published it soon there-after.[31] A third dialogue, *De vera nobilitate*, he wrote in the 1480s.[32] He enriched the Italian language and helped popularize natural philosophy with a translation of Pliny's *Natural History* in 1473.[33] He also translated Giovanni Simonetto's *Sforziad* (1489) and composed an Italian *Formulario* for writing letters (1485).[34] In the 1480s he utilized the printing press to publish his popular commentaries on Dante, Horace, and Virgil.[35] In spite of his concern for epistolary style, he did not himself exploit the genre nor attempt, as far as we know, to collect his letters, and few are extant. In public office he was less successful than he would have liked, failing in what seems to have been an attempt to become chancellor of Florence in 1465 (his close friend Bartolomeo Scala was chosen).[36] Teaching duties and laws restricting the public activity of academics, as well as his modest social standing, kept him out of ordinary public offices, but he did manage in 1465 to become chancellor of the Parte Guelfa (the position vacated by Bartolomeo Scala), and he later became a secretary in the Florence's Chancery itself.[37] He lectured in the Studio until 1497, when he retired on public pension to what had before been his summer retreat in the mountains, his native Casentino, where he died in 1498.[38]

---

form of Book I and part of Book II (mutilated at the end), with Landino's autograph corrections, additions, and prefaces. When I quote passages I shall also cite, wherever possible, the manuscript. For the dating, see my "Cristoforo Landino's First Lectures on Dante," pp. 22–23.

31. Ed. P. Lohe (Florence, 1980). For the dating, see Lohe's introduction, pp. xxx–xxxiii.

32. Ed. M. T. Liaci (Florence, 1970) and M. Lentzen (Geneva, 1970).

33. For early eds., see Lentzen, *Studien*, p. 284. The preface has a modern ed.: *Scritti*, I, 81–93. For the dating, see Lohe's introduction to Landino's *Disputationes Camaldulenses*, p. xxxi.

34. Lentzen, *Studien*, pp. 284, 286, lists early editions. The prefaces are ed. in *Scritti*, I, 181–82, 187–91.

35. Eds. listed in Lentzen, *Studien*, pp. 281–83. Prefatory material, incomplete for Horace, ed. in *Scritti*.

36. See Landino's letter of 1464, ed. in Lentzen, *Studien*, pp. 203–10; see also Brown, *Bartolomeo Scala*, pp. 42–45. Landino may have attempted to become chancellor also in 1458: see R. Black, *Benedetto Accolti*, pp. 105–7, 182.

37. Brown, *Bartolomeo Scala*, p. 45; D. Marzi, *La Cancelleria*, pp. 251ff. *passim*.

38. The date that appears in some secondary literature, 1504, is incorrect: see Verde, *Lo Studio fiorentino*, I, 366; II, 175. Landino's mummified body ("San Cristoforo," to the locals) can be viewed in the church of San Donato, in Borgo alla Collina in the Casentino.

   Some secondary literature contains references to Landino's commentary on Aristotle's *Nicomachean Ethics* (most recently C. Lohr, "Medieval Latin Aristotle Commentaries: Supplementary Authors," *Traditio* 30 [1974], 131). The source of this, I believe, is the older references to Landino's *Disputationes Camaldulenses*, where its four books are listed

As I have said, while Cristoforo Landino was competing for a Studio appointment in the mid-1450s, he was compared with Carlo Marsuppini and found wanting. In a letter to Piero de' Medici he argued that late in life Marsuppini had publicly expressed his hope that Landino would succeed him as teacher of the humanities.[39] But many from the Acciaiuoli circle seem to have viewed Francesco Filelfo as the more worthy successor, and when Poggio and the Medici blocked Filelfo's return, the Acciaiuoli group came to view John Argyropoulos as the true heir of Marsuppini, the one who would restore Greek and philosophical studies to Florence. Landino initially dealt with his lack of "universality" in two ways: first, he defended the nobility of the poetic discipline, and second, he showed how philosophy, to be efficacious, had to be presented with eloquence.

His opportunity to defend poetry seems to have come early; in the autumn of 1456, unable as yet to win the appointment in "rhetoric and poetry," he was probably chosen to lecture on the *Divine Comedy*.[40] Poetry, he said in his inaugural oration, is not *one* of the liberal arts but an art that contains in itself *all* of them. Taking up arguments that Ficino seems likely to have presented in his *Institutiones ad Platonicam disciplinam*, dedicated to Landino that very year, Landino argued that poetry's origin was God.[41] Before our souls enter our bodies, the ancient philosophers said, they inhabit heavenly seats and contemplate the harmony and beauty of the mind and Ideas of God. Led down by earthly desires, they enter mortal bodies and forget their divine nature. Through certain shadows and images, however, they have some recollection of their divine nature, and these recollections are expressed in divine frenzies: human justice recalls divine justice, and this frenzy is named "religion"; wisdom inspires the second frenzy, "prophecy"; the contemplation of beauty inspires the third, "divine love"; and the contemplation of harmonies inspires "poetry." While our souls are in heaven, they partake of that music of God's eternal mind and the measures and movements made by heaven. Then on earth the souls may comprehend these eternal

separately as the dialogues "de vita activa et contemplativa," "de summo bono," and finally two dialogues giving an allegorical explanation on the *Aeneid*. The last two then are understood to be a commentary on the *Aeneid* and the first two a commentary on ethics, or, incorrectly, on the *Ethics*. Lohr cites Bandini, *Specimen*, II, 201, who in turn cites J. Gaddius, *De scriptoribus non ecclesiasticis* . . . (Florence, 1648), I, 284. Gaddius mentions Landino, "commentaria in Ethicam," the *De anima*, Camaldulensian dialogues on the *Aeneid*, and so on.

39.   Landino, *Carmina*, p. 184.

40.   See my "Cristoforo Landino's First Lectures on Dante."

41.   See ibid., esp. pp. 34–35. The following summary is based on the ed. in Landino, *Scritti*, I, 45–55.

harmonies and be led to return upward toward the true music. The divine poets and sacred priests of the Muses, themselves inspired, are the agents of this return.

Then Landino went into a lengthy discussion of poets in antiquity: Homer, for instance, moved by divine frenzy, demonstrated a knowledge of moral and speculative philosophy and of the liberal arts well before the philosophers had developed their systems or the orators had written their histories and speeches. But who, Landino asked, can be compared with our divine poet Dante? He embraced the heavens, he embraced the earth, he embraced the underworld. He showed the eternal penalties of evil, how spirits are purified, and the nature of the highest heaven. He knew all of natural philosophy, the motions of the planets and the powers of the soul. He knew mathematics, geometry, astrology, and music. In moral philosophy he described with great cunning the moral virtues, the rewards of good conduct and the pains of evil. As the Greeks said of Homer, this our poet is similar to the ocean and its rivers, for just as the rivers rise from the ocean and return to it, so all the sciences arise from this our poet and return to him. Is there anything, Landino concluded more useful for study?

Landino may have argued that his students could learn "all of philosophy" through the poets, but many young Florentines looked elsewhere. A few months after Landino's inaugural, in early 1457, John Argyropoulos returned to Florence and took up his position in the Studio teaching philosophy. For his students, universal knowledge was to be achieved through a systematic and orderly study of Aristotle, through logic, dialectics, moral philosophy, natural philosophy, and metaphysics. Not only did his learning lack a "poetic" touch, but he dispensed with eloquence altogether. Although it is fitting, he said at the beginning of his inaugural oration, to exhort the students with the "value of the sciences" (*laudes scientiae*), I consider such things to be ostentatious and superfluous. Then, after a few words about philosophy's "usefulness," Argyropoulos went right into the definitions of philosophy and his *accessus* to the *Nicomachean Ethics*.[42] The next January (or possibly the first of February), resuming lectures on the *Ethics*, Argyropoulos again had to deliver an inaugural oration, and again he declined to give the customary, rhetorical oration in praise of science: this old, worn-out custom, he said at the beginning, is irritating to the students and boring. He went right into the divisions of philosophy.[43]

42. In Müllner, ed., *Reden und Briefe*, pp. 3ff.
43. Ibid., p. 19: "[C]um haec consuetudo inveterata iam sit ac vobis omnibus saepe percepta et cognita atque ob hanc causam sine auditorum fastidio molestiaque tractari

At this same time, January 1458, Marsuppini's "other" heir, Cristoforo Landino, won his first Studio appointment in rhetoric and poetry, and he chose to lecture also on moral philosophy, but on Cicero's *Tusculan Disputations*. In his inaugural oration, Landino alluded to his own "worthiness" to replace Carlo Marsuppini:

> Let no one think me so unaware of who I am that in so large a group of most learned men I should dare to call myself a philosopher. I am not so mad, most outstanding fathers, nor so ignorant of the facts that I would impudently arrogate to myself that which those men, so weighty and, with many years of great zeal and industry, so well experienced in the study of wisdom, can scarcely attribute honorably to themselves. When I have such difficulty protecting my own territory, would I dare launch a reckless assault on another's? For, most outstanding fathers, if I can to some degree usurp the name of *rhetorician*—and here I mean what the Latins mean by *rhetorician*, one who has the ability to teach precepts, not one who has forcefulness and richness in speaking—it will be due to your humanity, which should give pardon to one who is not well trained in its difficult teachings. The name of *philosopher*, on the other hand, neither do I require for myself nor, should it be offered by another, do I accept. Therefore I shall satisfy insofar as I am able the office publicly imposed on me: if, when I do this, some passages of philosophy occur, I shall explain these not as a professor of the faculty of philosophy but as one who has read a few things and has learned many more from my teacher, Carlo Marsuppini, who without doubt, both in Latin and in Greek letters, was the most learned and well-versed man in our age.[44]

minime possit, visum est ad ea statim accedere, quae utilitatem fructumque aliquem afferre audientibus possint." The date of the oration in the ms. is 1 Feb. 1458: but see Chapter v, n. 14, above.

44. *Scritti*, 1, 6–7: "Neque tamen sit aliquis, qui mei me adeo oblitum existimet, ut etiam in tam frequentissimo doctissimorum virorum consessu philosophum me profiteri audeam. Non sum adeo demens, praestantissimi patres, adeoque rerum omnium ignarus, ut, quod gravissimi et longa aetate, summo ardore atque industria in sapientiae studiis exercitatissimi viri vix satis honeste sibi tribuunt, tam impudenter mihi arrogem, ut cui vix suos fines tueri liceat, alienos temerario impetu irrumpere audeam. Ego enim, praestantissimi patres, si mihi rhetoris nomen—dico enim rhetorem, ut Latini appellant, qui huic praeceptorum tradendorum facultatem dant, dicendi vero vim atque copiam non dant—, si rhetoris igitur nomen mihi aliqua ex parte usurpem, erit vestrae porro humanitatis ei, qui non bene in difficili doctrina exercitatus sit, veniam dare; philosophi autem nomen neque mihi postulo neque, si ultro afferatur, accipio. Quam ob rem, cum inter legendum muneri mihi publice imposito pro viribus satisfecero, tum etiam si qui ex philosophia loci occurrent, eos non tanquam huius facultatis professor, sed ut homo qui nonnulla legerim, plurima etiam de praeceptore meo, viro omnium quos nostra saecula

Then Landino, after a lengthy praise of philosophy and an argument on the necessity of expressing philosophical truths with eloquence, spoke of an opposing approach: "One may see and daily we read quite subtle writers in this subject, who are never lacking in the deepest doctrine, the most constant systematization, and clever skill in writing." But with their thorny and subtle method of teaching they deliver a tortured doctrine, seeking rather to force the unwilling than to teach those willing to learn. How different was our Cicero, with his eloquence of speech, gravity of opinion, and richness and variety of examples![45]

This sort of critique of scholastic philosophers was commonplace among humanists. But if, as Roberto Cardini has argued, these jabs were directed more pointedly at Argyropoulos, and meant to be understood as such, we find the Byzantine's response in his inaugural oration the following October or November (1458), in which he seemed to parody the "eloquence" of the rhetorician.[46] Ostensibly a celebration of the "day" that has finally arrived to start the academic year, the oration began with an absurdly prolix statement in honor of "hic praeclarus faustusque dies," with a strained allegorical gloss on that autumn day "post hiemem idest post animi perturbationem" as the springtime of the academic discipline.[47] Argyropoulos was given, we know, to "jokes," and it may be correct that he is here satirizing Landino.[48] Certainly to a systematizer, Landino's method of philosophizing could only have been strange and unaccustomed.

No draft of Landino's lectures on either Dante or Cicero's *Tusculans* has come to light. From several references to Dante in lectures from the early 1460s, from Argyropoulos's presumed parody of Landino, and from the inaugural orations, it appears that Landino was already using an allegorical method to describe the individual's "pilgrimage" through the torments of the world toward the contemplation of God. After ask-

viderint sine controversia doctissimo et in litteris tum Graecis tum Latinis exercitatissimo, Carolo Arretino, audierim, explicabo."

45.   Ibid., p. 14: "Videre enim licet et quotidie legimus acutissimos in hac re scriptores, quibus summa doctrina, constantissimus ordo, acerrimum ingenium in scribendo nusquam defuit; sed nescio quo pacto nos id quod volunt longe antea sua exili et spinosa disserendi subtilitate, cum nullum oratorium ornatum afferant, fateri cogunt, quam nobis ita esse persuaserint: itaque multo plura ab invitis extorquent, quam a volentibus impetrent. M. autem Tullius . . . quanto . . . dicendi flumine, immortalis deus, quanta sententiarum gravitate, quanta exemplorum tum copia tum varietate iam demonstrata prosequitur!"

46.   Cardini, *La critica*, pp. 71ff. Argyropoulos's oration is in Müllner, ed., *Reden und Briefe*, pp. 31–43 (for the dating of Argyropoulos's orations, see Chap. v, n. 14, above).

47.   Müllner, ed., *Reden und Briefe*, pp. 31ff.

48.   For Argyropoulos's "difficult" and complex character, see G. Zippel, "Per la biografia dell'A." (1896), pp. 196–97.

ing myself and carefully considering, he said in his Cicero inaugural of
early 1458,

> which of the volumes of Cicero I should take for interpretation
> that would be most important for these youths who have gathered
> for our instruction, none of the so many and various works pre-
> sented itself as more fitting to the dignity of this most celebrated
> Studio, nor more appropriate to the condition of those who will
> be hearing the lectures, than that which contains the five days of
> disputations at Tusculum.[49]

With his divine arguments Cicero frees us from the fear of death, something, indeed, we find quite gratifying. But more than this, he frees us
from our exile in mortality and delivers us to our true homeland, the
senate of the Gods. "All griefs of the body and disturbances of the
soul—and there is no torment crueler in the human race—he roots out
so thoroughly that he renders our lives, afflicted by so many hardships
and oppressed by the fickle assaults of fortune, quiet and tranquil."[50] If
we follow Cicero's teaching that the highest good consists in virtue
alone, we can become "freed from the onerous rule of fortune over human affairs and directed by our own law, so that we may enjoy whatever
happens in the present and be compelled to fear nothing that the future
may hold."[51]

Then after a schematic, scholastic run-through of the divisions of philosophy—the active and contemplative, ethics, theology or metaphysics,
physics, and mathematics—Landino rejected the "systematic" conception of philosophy in favor of Cicero's: "Philosophy, my dear students,
is assuredly the 'medicine of the soul.' "[52] Landino outlined the structure
of "philosophical healing" that would be part of his allegorical, philosophical method of interpreting poets. Mortal life is a pilgrimage (*pere-*

49.   *Scritti*, I, 5: "Inquirenti mihi et diligentius mente pertractanti, praestantissimi
patres, quod potissimum ex M. Tullii voluminibus huic iuventuti, quae se in nostram
disciplinam contulisset, interpretandum assumerem, nullum ex tam varia multiplicique
copia aut huius celebratissimi gymnasii dignitati accomodatius aut eorum, qui illius au-
ditores essent futuri, rationi conducibilius occurrebat, quam id in quo quinque dierum
disputationes in Tusculano habitae continerentur."

50.   Ibid., p. 6: "Omnes autem tum corporis dolores tum animorum perturbationes,
quibus nulla apud mortale genus crudelior carnificina est, ita radicitus extirpat, ut hanc
nostram tot aerumnis afflictam, tam variis fortunae fluctibus oppressam vitam quietam
tranquillamque reddat."

51.   Ibid.: "Qua sententia id consequimur, ut gravissimo rerum humanarum fortunae
imperio liberati nostrique iuris effecti et praesentibus, qualiacunque sint, frui possimus
et ab impendentibus nihil timere cogamur."

52.   Ibid., I, 11; II, 13:" 'Est profecto,' ingenui adolescentes, 'animi medicina philosophia' [Cicero, *Tusc.* 3.3.6]."

grinatio), and philosophy grants us the provisions for our journey to the true life (*viaticum ad veram vitam*) so that we may return to our "true nature." In our stupidity we are devoted to a life of pleasure (*voluptas*), to cunning attempts to gain public office (*ambitio*), and to greed (*avaritia*). Philosophy alone frees us from human misery.[53]

As we said, the content of Landino's lectures on the *Tusculans* is now lost; we can still make a few observations about Landino's philosophizing in this period as it relates to that of Marsilio Ficino. For ideas on the general nature and function of philosophy Landino no doubt relied on Ficino. But unlike Ficino, Landino had a legal background, and he used legal terminology and sought to transcend the "legal culture" that was such an important element of earlier Florentine society. Those dedicated to *ambitio* not only "in magistratibus petendis nobis suffragantur" (a more traditional definition) but also "in forensi negocio operam praestant" (a clear reference to activities of law).[54] In 1458, in particular, that *ambitio*, uncontrolled by the higher virtues, was destroying Florentine culture and the Medici regime (in the opinion of many) with the development of illegal voting blocks (*intelligenze*) and the resurgence of power among jurists. Landino blamed Poggio's dismissal from the Chancery on the jurists, and Poggio's general critique of the legal culture surely influenced Landino as well. Philosophy, for Landino, grants us freedom from law, makes us "nostri . . . iuris," and leaves "omnia humana . . . infra nos posita." It turns forced good behavior into spontaneous good behavior.[55]

In questions that might seem purely "tactical" we can note a second difference from Ficino. To make philosophical principles "active" Ficino relied on philosophical instruction reinforced by what he called sometimes the "companionship of the teacher" (*consuetudo magistri*), sometimes "friendship," sometimes "Platonic love." Eloquence was important for him in practice but not in theory. For Landino this eloquence was essential. He saw in the *Tusculans* the perfect unity of philosophical precepts and the art of persuasion. We cannot reach the good life, he concluded his inaugural oration, "unless we both think rightly and express clearly, ornately, and impressively what we think. The one is achieved by philosophy, the other by rhetoric."[56] Indeed, one could argue that eloquence was the main theme of this oration. In a bit of bra-

53. *Scritti*, I, 11, 12.
54. Ibid., p. 11.
55. Ibid., I, 6, 11.
56. Ibid., I, 15: " . . . nisi nos et recte sentiamus et quod sentimus dilucide, ornate ac graviter explicemus, quorum alterum philosophia, alterum oratoria facultas praestat."

vura, Landino would attempt to show that he, recently appointed to
lecture as a rhetorician and poet, could elucidate philosophical principles as well as those, such as Marsuppini and Filelfo, who bore also the
title *philosophus*.

We have no evidence that Landino ever again lectured on a philosophical work in the Studio. In well over thirty years of lectures he probably did so, but the course of studies in the 1460s would seem to indicate
an exclusive interest in rhetoric and poetry. He lectured on Dante (and
perhaps repeatedly), Horace, Juvenal, Persius, Virgil, Cicero's rhetoric
and letters, and Petrarch's *Canzoniere*. Yet, inspired in part by Ficino, a
philosophical approach of great subtlety permeated these lectures, even
those dealing with a subject wholly unsuited to a philosophical gloss,
the familiar letters of Cicero. The approach, in other words, is more
complex than a theory of poetry, although in the latter the approach is
clearest.

From Landino's lectures on Juvenal and Persius (1461–62) and on
Virgil's *Aeneid*, Books 1–7 (1462–63), we have students' drafts and thus
the first good evidence of Landino's philosophical approach toward his
texts. In his inaugural oration of 1462 before the Virgil course, also extant, Landino repeated in Latin much of what he had earlier said about
Dante: poetry embraces all the liberal arts, it is one of the divine frenzies, and the poet, like the philosopher, can help us recover the Platonic
"wings" that let us fly from the world to our celestial home. Who, he
asked, has discoursed on philosophy better than the poets?[57] The liberal
arts alone "are that which can offer us a calm tranquillity of soul and
true freedom from all disturbances."[58] Landino had earlier, before lectures on Cicero's *Tusculans*, used an almost identical expression to describe philosophy: the philosopher "roots out griefs of the body and
disturbances of the soul, and renders our life quiet and tranquil."[59]

The poet (and the *studia bonarum artium*), like the philosopher (and
the *studium sapientiae*), expresses philosophical truths, but with a great
variety of forms and figments. Even Juvenal the satirist hid philosophical truths. In a lecture of 1461, Landino seized on Juvenal's statement of
his intention in his first satire:

> From the day when the rain-clouds lifted up the waters, and Deu-
> calion climbed that mountain in his ship to seek an oracle, . . . all
> the doings of mankind, their vows, their fears, their angers, and

57. Ibid., pp. 20–28.
58. Ibid., p. 28: "Bonarum . . . artium studia sola sunt, quae nobis . . . quietam animi
tranquillitatem et ab omnibus perturbationibus veram vacationem praestare possunt."
59. See n. 50, above.

their pleasures [*votum timor ira voluptas*] . . . shall form the motley subject of my page.⁶⁰

Landino found the argument similar to what he had read in Cicero:

> *Votum timor ira voluptas.* All of these things, which are carried out by men, are "disturbances" [*perturbationes*], out of which afterward vices arise. But a few things about "disturbances." Nature has given to all animated creatures, especially men, a double force, to wit, that they seek things convenient to them and shun especially things which are harmful. Each of these two things has a two-fold subdivision of its own. For there are two types of evils as there are of goods, to wit, present and future ones. If the soul exceeds the mean in either, there is then identified a "disturbance," which by philosophers is defined in this way, to wit, as "an agitation of the soul averse to right reason, contrary to nature." And there are four types of disturbances, two concerning present and two concerning future goods and evils. The parts, or subdivisions, are infinite, as Cicero says in the *Tusculans*. [Landino then summarized *laetitia*, *aegritudo*, *libido*, and *timor* (= *metus*), according to *Tusculans* 4.5–7.11–15.] . . . The poet has now put forth all these disturbances, although not with their own terms, since they speak otherwise than philosophically.⁶¹

Later, Landino again took up Juvenal as "philosopher" in that "golden satire, and one of the most weighty," the thirteenth.⁶² To console his friend Calvinus for a loss of money, Juvenal turns to the "sacred books" of wisdom. Landino explained the necessity of this endeavor:

> *At [= An] nihil in melius etc.* (18). He [Juvenal] demonstrates that he [Calvinus] is foolish, because, although wise men are rendered

---

60. *Sat.* 1.81–86 (trans. G. G. Ramsay).

61. Ambros. I 26 inf., fol. 16v: "*Votum timor ira voluptas* [*Sat.* 1.85]. Haec aguntur ab hominibus, quae omnes sunt perturbationes, ex quibus deinde vitia nascuntur. Sed pauca de perturbationibus. Dupplicem vim in omnibus animalibus presertim in homine instituit natura, scilicet ut convenientia sibi appetant, quae autem noceant vehementer repellant. Quarum duarum rerum unaqueque dupplicem spetiem seorsum habet. Nam ut malorum sic et bonorum duo genera sunt, scilicet presentia et futura, in quibus si animus modum excedit, perturbatio tunc dicitur, quae a philosophis sic distinguitur, scilicet 'aversa a recta [arrepta *cod.*] ratione contra naturam animi commotio' [*Tusc.* 4.6.11]. Et perturbationum genera quatuor sunt, duo de presentibus et duo de futuris, scilicet bonis et malis. Partes autem idest speties infinitae reperiuntur, ut apud Ciceronem in Tusculanis [cf. *Tusc.* 4.7.16]. Sed nunc de generibus . . . [etc.]. Quas omnes perturbationes nunc ponit poeta, sed non tamen his propriis vocabulis, quoniam aliter quam philosophi loquuntur. Votum nunc pro libidine" etc.

62. Ibid., fol. 170v ("aurea satira et una ex gravissimis").

prudent through long practical experience, he, however, with his practice in many matters has become no better. . . . *Abreptum crede etc.* (175). The poet now answers, and incites him with more weighty and philosophical reasons, and he does this with great prudence. For he first pacified him with examples and familiar expressions, which for a man greatly disturbed have more influence than the most weighty and grave reasons of philosophers. . . . *Chrisippus non dicet idem* (184). Now with the speeches and authorities of philosophers he arouses him, as we said earlier.[63]

For Landino, the latter, direct method of Juvenal, used in advising Calvinus, was not a typical poetic technique, nor in most cases was such a technique more effective than the other, where philosophical truth is expressed without philosophical arguments. The commentator can discover the indirect method through an allegorical interpretation, although in a satire such an interpretation must remain fragmentary, because satires simply are not susceptible to a general allegorical approach. Irony is not the same as poetic figments, and although the latter color each satire, a single general projection of "philosophical" truth cannot be traced through sixteen satires.

In the first six books of Virgil's *Aeneid*, however, Aeneas starts out in the *vita voluptuosa* of Troy and arrives at the *vita contemplativa* in Italy. Here a general, allegorical, philosophical interpretation was possible.

Through the wanderings of Aeneas, Landino explained in 1462–63, Virgil portrays the four ages of man. In Troy Aeneas was in "childhood," or that first age where, bound to Helen, he was addicted to the *vita voluptuosa*. Then, with Troy captured, he set out for Italy and the contemplative life. But in the sea, or the "*perturbationes*," he was deflected from his course and went to Thrace, or *avaritia*, and then to Africa, or *ambitio*. These two are parts of the active life. Finally, counseled by the gods, he made his way into a port in Italy, which means the "tranquility of mind" and the contemplative or speculative life. Virgil conceals other, particular philosophical truths at various stages of Aeneas's journey. First, man has a double appetite: one obeys reason

63.   Ibid., fol. 171: "*At nihil in melius etc.* Demostrat hunc esse stultum, quod cum homines ex longa rerum experientia prudentes reddantur, ipse vero usu multarum rerum nihilo melior fiat."

Fol. 176: "*Abreptum crede etc.* Respondet nunc poeta et urget ipsum gravioribus rationibus et philosophicis, neque sine summa prudentia, cum illum mansuefecerit prius et exemplis et consuetudine, quae in homine multum perturbato plus momenti habent quam gravissim(a)e et severissimae philosophorum rationes."

Fol. 176v: "*Chrisippus non dicet idem.* Nunc vocibus et auctoritatibus philosophorum ipsum urget, ut superius diximus."

and one does not. These Plato had expressed as the black and white horses of the chariot. Reason is like a charioteer, and it alone can steer man toward the contemplative life. Second, Venus, who is divine love, leads Aeneas along the way: this means that one cannot reach the contemplative life without divine aid.[64]

Several forms of allegorizing could lead to such a scheme, and Landino was employing only one of them. How, we may ask, did Landino think such an interpretation is derived? Is the poet aware of the allegorical meaning the commentator discovers? When the poet "colors" a great philosophical truth with poetic figments, is he cunning in this effort? Christian exegesis allowed the commentator to discover an allegorical truth of which the writer, pagan or Hebrew, was unaware, although in the case of the Hebrews, as well as perhaps Virgil, the Holy Spirit did not merely guide the commentator in the interpretation but secretly planted the deeper truth in the mind of the prophet or poet. Yet for most pagan writings the commentator could take great liberties, finding, as had Augustine, a "good" meaning quite apart from what the mind of the poet held. Hence, several levels of interpretation were possible.

For the humanists new problems arose, both because of their emphasis on "original sources" and through their discovery of a "middle age" of intellectual activity between themselves and antiquity. Traditional Christian exegesis in many ways was unappealing, but particularly in the case of Virgil it could not be shaken off altogether. Petrarch allegorized Virgil, although in his *Secretum* he has "Augustine" at one point temper this effort:

> I cannot but applaud that meaning which I understand you find hidden in the poet's story [*Aeneid* 1. 52 ff.], familiar as it is to you; for whether Virgil had this in mind when writing or whether without any such idea he only meant to depict a storm at sea and nothing else, what you have said about the rush of anger and the authority of reason seems to me expressed with equal wit and truth.[65]

Petrarch carried the question of the poet's intention no further. Coluccio Salutati, whose allegorical *De laboribus Herculis* Landino closely fol-

---

64. This paraphrase is based on the lengthy allegorical summary from the lectures, at the beginning of Book 6 (see my "Cristoforo Landino's First Lectures on Dante," pp. 39–40n.): Casanatense 1368, fols. 203v–4v; Laur. 52, 32, fol. 135–135v; Vat. lat. 5129, fols. 69–77v.

65. From trans. W. H. Draper, *Petrarch's Secret* (London, 1911), p. 102. For the Latin, see Petrarch, *Prose*, ed. G. Martellotti et al. (Milan, 1955), pp. 124–26.

lowed, raised the question more explicitly when he argued that the expositor should impose on the poets' "proper names," that is, the names of gods, meanings not considered by the authors themselves:

> All of the poets' fables should either be reduced, with a proper exposition, to God, to the things created, or to something pertaining to them. And when the mystical interpreter opens up the hidden things of the poet and has changed them by referring individual things to God, to nature, or to customs, although he has found what the author could not have known or said, no doubt he should consider himself to have lit upon a permissible meaning. For if the interpreter can adapt the system of proper names to what can be believed, I would boldly assert that he no doubt has elicited the true meaning of the author, or if perchance it was not the true teaching and the names do not correspond to what the author intended, he will have found a meaning far more suitable than what the author had purposed.[66]

On one level Salutati looked backward and on another he looked forward. His threefold division of a divine, natural, and human law allowed, through the natural law, a "meaning" to be imposed on human activity above and apart from what humans experience. The meaning, then, was not accidental. It did not depend on the ingenuity of the commentator. The natural law "bends" all human expression in a certain way, dependent ultimately on the law of God. This operated equally on pagans as it does on Christians. The commentator could discern the forms and regularities of human experience and hence demonstrate the usefulness of pagan writings.[67]

For his conception of allegory Landino probably owed a great deal to Salutati.[68] Specifically, he refused to allow the commentator to impose

---

66. *De laboribus Herculis*, ed. B. L. Ullman (Zurich, 1951), I, 86: "[O]mnia . . . que apud poetas fabulosa videntur, oportet vel ad deum vel ad creaturas aut ad aliquid ad hos pertinens debita expositione reduci. Cumque poetarum abdita misticus interpres aperiet, et ad deum, naturam, vel mores singula referens adaptaverit, sine dubitatione reputet se, quamvis incogitatum ab autore dici queat id quod invenerit, in sententiam tolerabilem incidisse. Quod si ad illa que senserit adaptare poterit propriorum nominum rationem, audacter affirmem ipsum sine controversia veram autoris elicuisse sententiam, aut si forsitan illa non fuerit, et ad id quod autor intendisset nomina non accedant, longe commodiorem sensum quam autor cogitaverit invenisse."

67. See Krantz, "Legal Thought," esp. pp. 81–82n.

68. See Lentzen, *Studien*, pp. 149–50; Cardini's notes to Landino, *Scritti*; and especially Lohe's notes to Landino's *Disputationes Camaldulenses*. For an overview of Landino and humanist criticism of Virgil, see now C. Kallendorf, "Cristoforo Landino's *Aeneid* and the Humanist Critical Tradition," *Renaissance Quarterly* 36 (1983), 519–46. Unfortunately we cannot now speculate on the degree of Landino's debt to his teacher, Carlo Marsup-

any allegorical sense on a work that the work itself did not contain.[69] Yet Landino detested the legal science and had no use for any "natural inclination" in the legalistic sense. At times he spoke of pagan poets "concealing" truths in order to hide them from the masses, although for Landino this "allegorizing" was parenthetical and not a major part of his exegesis.[70] For Landino two (or more) levels of interpretation were fundamental. Is the poet aware of both? In his lectures Landino did not seem to raise the question in express terms. He finally did when he reworked his Virgil lectures of 1462–63 into a publishable commentary on *Aeneid* 1–6, which were Books 3 and 4 of his *Disputationes Camaldulenses* of 1472. When I undertook to write out these figments, Landino stated at the beginning of his preface to Book 3,

> in which Virgil hid that most profound knowledge, by which he described in a divine way the highest good of man and expressed in a wonderful way the path by which we set out toward it, I feared that I would fall under the reprehension of some men, who, measuring all things by the feebleness of their own intellect,

pini, since almost nothing of the latter's instruction is known. In a manuscript of Landino's lectures on Virgil, 1462–63 (cod. Casanatense 1368), there is an opinion in the margin attributed to a "Ka. Ar.," which I suspect is Karolus Aretinus or Marsuppini (fol. 53v); in another margin "Carolus" is a conspicuous reference word (fol. 151v). But Laur. Aedil. 202, a copy of Virgil containing glosses perhaps by Carlo Marsuppini (see A. M. Bandini, *Bibliotheca Leopoldina Laurentiana seu catalogus manuscriptorum qui . . . in Laurentianam translati sunt*, vol. 1 [Florence, 1791], col. 508), throws no light on either passage, nor are the notes elsewhere philosophically interesting.

69.   Landino referred to Christian "allegorizing" in his Juvenal lectures, when he glossed a particularly obscene passage (6.33ff.) where the satirist says young boys are preferable to women (Ambros. I 26 inf., fol. 97, cited by Cardini, *La critica*, pp. 30–31n): "Sunt qui vituperent poetam adeo in matrimonium rem quidem sanctissimam invehi. Quod respondetur illis: non in matrimonium sed in adultera ita acerrimum esse. . . . Quid? Non illi summum artificium in his verbis esse comprehendunt? . . . Nonne hoc etiam, nedum Virgilius reliquique huiusmodi poetae, sed et Yeronimus et Augustinus sanctissimi quidem viri, cum ab aliquo scelere homines deterrere voluerint, factitarunt? Itaque poeta noster non ut approbet libidinem pueri (nam eam maxime detestatur), sed ut ab impudicis mulieribus homines avocet et hoc officio utatur, ideo rem habere cum puero satius esse dixit. Quam ob rem taceant qui non satis artificium optimi oratoris calluerint." This passage merely justifies extreme forms of poetic rhetorical "color." In his Virgil lectures Landino cited Augustine in support of his own attempt to get at the "hidden" meaning of the *Aeneid*. This, incidentally, falls on the same passage (1.52ff.) where "Augustine" questions Petrarch's allegorizing in the *Secretum*. This is one of Landino's first lectures on the *Aeneid*, and he appears defensive about the approach he soon will take more boldly (Casanatense 1368, fol. 9v): "Animadvertatis tamen quod omnia quae hic ponuntur non sunt ad phisicam referendam, ut in theologia nostra, ut recte ait Augustinus: Ponunt enim quedam quae subserviunt illis quae exprimunt." Cf. Laur. 52, 32, fol. 12: "Et hec sint satis de physica, ad quam non omnia tamen referenda sunt, ut Augustinus dicit de prophetis: Nam multa adhibentur quae subserviunt illis quae rem exprimunt."

70.   E.g., *Disputationes Camaldulenses*, p. 113.

would believe that Virgil himself contrived nothing beyond fables
to delight the lazy ears of his listeners and would reckon that I had
made up all the things I say according to my own free choice.[71]

Landino's answer seems at first unsatisfactory: these critics know neither
what poetry is nor where its origin lies. He then surveyed the categories
identical to those in his earlier inaugural orations: poetry embraces all
the liberal arts; just when it seems to be dealing with fables it expresses
things from the fount of divinity; one of the divine frenzies of Plato
applies also to poetry. Landino then referred again to his critics: "If they
wish to slander me, let them speak of my rashness, since I have approached things greater than my powers, rather than think that I have
seen something which Virgil did not see."[72]

The task of the interpreter was not merely to show how Virgil understood the divinity of man as he brought Aeneas through the active to
the contemplative life. Rather, the interpreter must understand the divinity of Virgil himself. The interpreter must—and this expression Landino used many times—open up the mind of the poet. In doing this the
interpreter understands the "true nature" of poetry. Hence, there are
two levels of interpretation, each dealing with objective reality. On one
level are analyzed the poet's words, on the other the poet's mind. The
former deals with considered opinions and express teachings; the latter
deals with the poet's deeper intention, perhaps not always fully and consciously understood by the poet himself. The poet must have some appreciation of either his own divinity or the divinity of his inspiration;
otherwise he could not write a poem "worthy" of an allegorical interpretation. But he need not have grasped wholly the Platonic doctrine of
the immortality of the soul. Indeed the *prisci poetae* who preceded Plato
could not have.

Yet Virgil was "clearly a good man and dedicated to the Platonic
teachings," and his intention in the *Aeneid* was to portray a virtuous
man for us to imitate.[73] In various places, to be sure, Virgil presents

71. Ibid., p. 110: "Cum statuissem eum sermonem . . . litteris mandare quem Leo Bap-
tista Albertus . . . de iis figmentis habuisset, in quibus P. Virgilius profundissimam illam
scientiam occultat, qua summum hominis bonum divinitus describit et qua via ad id prof-
iciscamur mirifice exprimit, verebar, ne in nonnullorum reprehensionem inciderem, qui
cuncta ex sui ingenii imbecillitate metientes et Maronem ipsum nihil praeter fabellas quibus otiosas auditorum aures delectaret commentum esse credant et nos pro arbitrio nostro quae dicimus omnia finxisse existiment."

72. Ibid., p. 115: "[Q]ui tamen, si nos carpere voluerint, potius temeritatis arguant,
quoniam ea quae supra nostras vires sunt aggressi fuerimus, quam aliquid quod Maro
non viderit nos vidisse putent."

73. That Virgil was a "vir plane bonus et Platonicis dogmatibus deditus" appears in

opinions according to various philosophical sects; but the poet was still a thorough Platonist. In some cases Landino's commentary on a particular passage must become rather strained. On Dido's death, Virgil says that her life "in ventos . . . recessit" (4.705). In his lectures Landino presented first two opinions of Servius, each of which gave the passage an Epicurean meaning; the death is portrayed

> according to those who say the soul is airy, that is, it returns into its own matter. Or [it is portrayed] according to those who say that the soul perishes with the body, as we say "it has died," "it has vanished to the winds." But I believe that Virgil was concerned with no such thing, but that he said *in ventos* on account of the velocity with which the soul left the body.[74]

At other times, where the more profound philosophical issues are at stake, Landino considered a nonphilosophical gloss as perfectly legitimate. Landino defined four possible meanings for any passage: (1) the historical (*ad historiam*), where the text follows what Virgil knew from historical annals; (2) the mythical (*ad fabulam*), where gods behave according to myths about them; (3) the natural-scientific or astrological (*ad physicam*), where gods represent natural forces or astrological influences; and (4) the philosophical or allegorical (*ad allegoriam*). No one category in itself can "explain" Virgil. On Venus's lament to Neptune, in Book 5 (779 ff.), Landino noted the following: "These words are referred to allegory quite well, and to history and to myths. But individual words are not referred to allegory; individual words are referred to history and to myth. Hence I shall take them up now one by one."[75]

Landino's personal preference was for the allegorical interpretation, an interpretation he called "nostra allegoria."[76] Such an interpretation

---

Landino's *accessus* to the lectures on the *Aeneid*, discussing the *intentio poetae* (Casanatense 1368, fol. 2v); cf. Laur. 52, 32, fol. 2v.

74. Casanatense 1368, fol. 177: "Atque *in ventos*, secundum illos qui animam aerem dicunt, hoc est 'rediit in materiam suam,' aut secundum eos qui dicunt animam cum corpore perire, ut intelligamus 'evanuit,' 'in ventos recessit.' Sed ego credo nihil tale Virgilium curasse, sed *in ventos* dixisse propter velocitatem qua anima corpus relinquit." From the other manuscript, the entire gloss reads as follows (Laur. 52, 32, fol. 119v): "*At in ventos*: vel secundum opinionem illorum qui in aere vitam esse vel secundum illos qui mortalem animum censerent vel neutrum sensit ex mea sententia." Cf. Servius's commentary, ed. Stocker et al. (Oxford, 1965).

75. Casanatense 1368, fol. 200: "Et haec ad allegoriam optime referuntur, et ad historiam et fabulam. Sed non singula verba ad allegoriam: singula tamen ad historiam et fabulam referuntur. Unde illa attingam modo unum modo alterum." Cf. Laur. 52, 32, fol. 133v.

76. For example, Casanatense 1368, fol. 154v: "*Melioris famae* [*Aen.* 4.221]. Ad hoc scilicet oculos torsit, ut ad meliorem cultum eos reducant [reducent *cod.*]. Optime autem

could not explain the entire *Aeneid*, as he knew. In his *Camaldulensian Disputations* (ca. 1472), which contain in Books 3 and 4 an allegorical interpretation of *Aeneid* 1–6, Landino would deliberately exclude those passages not subject to an allegorical interpretation. In his lectures Landino seemed to want to find a preferred interpretation for any passage, one that was not always allegorical. Hence, some passages are "better" explained by *historia*, although an allegorical meaning is concealed. The latter must become parenthetical yet somehow be intended by the poet. A few of Landino's glosses therefore appear curious. On *Aeneid* 2. 621–22, when Venus speaks to Aeneas and then disappears, and "dread shapes and mighty gods inimical to Troy come to view," Landino gave this gloss:

> *Apparent*. Servius says—and this is a good interpretation—he says that with Venus gone, that is, with pleasure gone, it is right for Aeneas to see the gods. This, as I said, is a good interpretation and perhaps the best. But it fits quite poorly with our principal theme. Let us say therefore that "they come to view" because a man, dedicated to virtue, recognizes the life he has previously led; hence Aeneas, filled with true love, sees "dread shapes."[77]

Here Landino has probed quite deeply into the *penetralia* of the text and indeed quite deeply into the poet's mind, *if* a philosophical interpretation, "our principal theme," lay beneath the interpretation the poet himself intended.

Iuppiter oculos illuc detorsit, ut Aeneam ad optimam vitam reducant [reducent *cod.*], secundum allegoriam nostram." Cf. Laur. 52, 32, fol. 111 (at *Aen.* 4.222): " . . . non discrepant a nostro incepto." Since Landino was giving lectures he had to follow Virgil's text "literally"—that is, he had to follow the passages in order. He could not rearrange them, as he did in his *Disputationes Camaldulenses*, so that the allegorical picture would stand out more clearly. Even so, at the beginning of Book 6, he resumed a lemmatic commentary (in the manuscripts even passages are underlined) of a section of Book 1 (the description of the Libyan port, 1.159ff.), to reinterpret the passages allegorically (Casanatense 1368, fol. 204–204v [lemmata underlined]; Laur. 52, 32, fol. 135v [only a few lemmata, one of which underlined, but then underlining canceled]; Vat. lat. 5129, fol. 70–70v [many lemmata, none underlined]). In this light, Craig Kallendorf's contention that Landino in his lectures approached the *Aeneid* as a "*grammaticus* and *rhetor*," unlike his approach in the *Disputationes Camaldulenses*, seems rather strained ("Cristoforo Landino's *Aeneid*," p. 524).

77.   Casanatense 1368, fol. 100: "*Apparent* [*Aen.* 2.622]. Dicit Servius, et bene: dicit remota Venere, idest voluptate, fuisse illi fas deos videre. Hoc, ut dixi, bene et fortasse optime dictum est. Sed nostro proposito minime convenit. Dicamus ergo 'apparent,' quod homo deditus virtuti suam anteactam vitam recognoscit, unde Aeneas vero amore repletus 'facies diras' vidit." Cf. Laur. 52, 32, fol. 78: "*Et spissus [sic] noctis se etc.* [2.621]. Hic Servius multa, et Venerem pro lascivo amore capit, quae possent procedere, sed impedirent hanc nostram interpretationem. Capimus enim Venerem pro vero amore, et Troyam incensam pro voluptate."

The very structure of the humanist lecture facilitated "two levels" of interpretation. When Guarino of Verona told his students how to read the classics, he suggested that they read each section twice. One chooses a section, he wrote, and reads through it in its entirety, attempting to grasp the sense as a whole. Then one reads through it again, word by word, analyzing each word and phrase in its particularity.[78] Landino seemed to have followed this practice in his lectures. He read to his students a section, perhaps the entire section for that day's lecture, and explained the "meaning" of the whole.[79] Landino often, but not always, gave the entire section a "higher," Platonic meaning. But when he analyzed each word, he explained the historical, mythical, or natural-scientific meaning of the passage.

When Landino explained the "meaning" of the *Aeneid*, he interpreted the "innermost meanings" (*intimi sensus*) of the poet's mind, which he found to be wholly Platonic and directed toward the contemplative life.

---

78.   Guarino, letter to Martino Rizzoni, ca. 1425 (in *Epistolario*, ed. R. Sabbadini, vol. 1 (1915; rept. Turin, 1967), pp. 498–99: "Te quoque ipsum cuipiam lectioni destines velim, ut non solum doceas, sed et discas. Aliquem tibi desume novum auctorem, quem non visum antea perlegas, vel Ovidium Metamorphoseon vel Valerium vel utrumque . . . . Est autem pernecessaria studiis litterarum et historiae et fabularum lectio; non expavescas, si primis congressibus intellectui non respondent; tu tantum pulsa et iterum voca, sic tibi aperietur et iterum respondebitur. Non improbarim, ut incipiens partem aliquam vel librum primum in transcursu perlegas, quod cum feceris, accurate ac diligenter incohans repete et omnia discute, ut et ne verbum quidem indiscussum abire sinas." This also was the plan, elaborated somewhat, followed much later in the century by Politian, as he noted in his commentary on Statius, *Commento inedito alle Selve di Stazio* (1480–81), ed. L. Cesarini Martinelli (Florence, 1968), p. 61: "Sed ut distinctius agamus utque vos facilius singula percipiatis, talem rationem inivimus, ut sententiam primo ipsam explicemus, tum ordinem lectionis aperiamus, mox singula ipsa verba diligentissime exponamus, deinde quae ad artificium pertinerent exequamur ac, siqua interim adnotatione digna elici sententia possit, eam ex abdito erutam afferamus in medium." (For these references I am indebted to Anthony Grafton.)

79.   For Landino's lectures on Juvenal and Persius, the scribe marked each new lecture by circling, rather than underlining, the lemma (these new lectures are often also signaled by such phrases as "ut pridie diximus" and "in hesterna lectione"). Here we can see quite clearly that Landino gave his texts "two readings," even when, as usually in the case of Juvenal, a "philosophical" interpretation was irrelevant. At *Sat.* 6.610, e.g., the scribe circled the lemma "Hic magicos affert cantus, hic Thessala vendit" and then reproduced a gloss explaining how that day's lesson fitted into the satire as a whole (Ambros. I 26 inf., fol. 120): "Quod ab omni egregio oratore factitatum est, nunc in poeta nostro plane dilucideque cernitur. Ita enim in hac satira argumenta disposuit, ut nihil deesse ad summam prudentiam videatur. Primo igitur summa libidine mulieres percitas esse demonstravit, quod apud viros omnino validissimum fuit. Deinde quaedam non minima tamen de superstitione et vaticiniis in medium coniecit, quae sunt coacervata multum momenti habebant. Postremo vero quod locus facilius in memoria residet, ea narrat quae ipsos coniuges ab illis multum alienare possint, nempe quae ad salutem suam, idest ad vitam, pertineant, cum et veneno et ferro suos maritos aggrediantur. Hec ad argumentorum dispositionem: quae vero ad presentem lectionem attineant facilius in textu cognoscentur."

In his lectures on the *Aeneid*, rather than plucking out the kernel of
"philosophical truth" he found there—an approach he later took, and
self-consciously so, in his *Disputationes Camaldulenses*—Landino sought
to explain the work as a whole. For the passages that did not contain
the "deeper Platonic meaning" (*altior sensus Platonicus*), Landino
seemed to depend on the richest traditions of the humanist movement,
particularly the tradition represented by the two humanists he admired
so greatly, Poggio Bracciolini and Leon Battista Alberti. In their works
they took to its highest level a theme dear to many humanists: human
affairs are marked by diversity, and this *varietas* is a good thing.

Landino praised especially the variety of the poet's style. He described
for his students the *flosculi* and *lepores*, the "flowers" and "pleasantries"
in the poem.[80] These were an integral part of the poem and hence an
integral part of the poet's mind. Each stylistic change in the poem must
be deliberate and must fit the content of the particular passage. The
commentator must explain when and how these changes take place, so
that the reader (or hearer) will understand the true meaning, both in
form and content, of a passage and hence be able to appreciate fully the
intention of the poet. When Landino confronted the mind of the poet
he literally stood in awe, as if he saw something mysterious and not
wholly penetrable. At no time could the poet's mind be reduced to one
or another category. Possibly as early as the 1450s, and almost certainly
by the early 1460s, Landino began to plan or write a dialogue outlining
philosophical teaching on the human mind. This work, entitled *De anima*, was drafted perhaps in the early 1460s, revised during that decade,
and then published in 1471 or 1472.[81]

The dialogue, in three books, is staged as if it took place in the early
1450s, with the interlocutors Carlo Marsuppini, Paolo Toscanelli, and
Landino himself. Formally the dialogue is instruction by Marsuppini for
the young Landino (now in his late twenties), and a reference in the
work to the promising young Marsilio Ficino (now not yet twenty)
makes the dialogue an idealized portrayal of the beginnings of the philosophical renaissance. It also allowed Landino to answer the old charge
that he was impious toward his former teacher, Marsuppini. The stated
purpose of the work, which was dedicated to Ercole d'Este, was modest
and traditional: I am bringing together ancient teachings on the soul,

80. For Landino's rhetorical "color," see Cardini, *La critica*, pp. 34ff. In his lectures on
Virgil, 1462–63, Landino contrasted Homer's construction of a *catalogus*, narrated "simpliciter," with that of Virgil, decorated with *flosculi* et *lepores* (on *Aen.* 7.647ff., Casanatense 1368, fol. 274v; cf. Laur. 52, 32, fol. 179v). Cf. also Guidetti's defense of Landino's
use of *flosculi*, below.

81. For the dating, see my "Cristoforo Landino's First Lectures on Dante," pp. 22–23.

explained elsewhere "in many and diverse volumes" more "acutely and artfully" than "clearly and plainly," so that those readers who are unable to pore through those volumes can have a clearer and more ready grasp of ancient teachings.[82] The work is, indeed, chiefly a survey: ancient philosophical opinion on the soul is presented, and the preferred doctrine, the Platonic and of course Christian teaching, is treated in depth.

In the first dialogue, Landino praised the *prisci philosophi* for the progress they made in coming to a true understanding of the nature of the soul; he conceded, however, that according to truth later writers—and here he meant medieval philosophers and contemporary academics— were superior.[83] In his preface to the second dialogue, Landino pointed to two things necessary for philosophers: right thinking and eloquence. These, he said, which "the *prisci scriptores* treated as united, were later, either because of the difficulty of the subject matter or because of human negligence, treated separately, so that those practiced in philosophy and those in the *ars dicendi* are each allured by their own pursuit and will not even touch the other."[84] The argument is traditional: humanists had always criticized the separation of professional studies in rhetoric from professional concerns in the other disciplines. But with Landino, does the concern for the unity of philosophy and eloquence differ?

When the *prisci poetae* united philosophy and eloquence, was the focus of their considered efforts the attempt to make philosophical truths "active" through the art of persuasion? Humanists traditionally emphasized this concern, and, as in his preface to his lectures on Cicero's *Tusculans*, Landino appreciated this also. But this was not the basis of his praise of poetic eloquence. Rather, Landino attempted to establish a philosophical basis for that eloquence itself. How did the *prisci* unite philosophical truths under poetic fictions? Here, for Landino, one must look to the mind itself. The human mind, he argued in *De anima*, takes things perceived by the senses and only assimilates them in accordance with what already exists in the mind. From the ancient and scholastic

---

82. Book 1, ed. cit. (n. 30, above), p. 2. For this theme as a genre, see Kristeller, *Medieval Aspects of Renaissance Learning*, p. 6.

83. Landino spoke quite harshly of the arrogance of "nostrae aetatis homines," who too quickly sniffed at, and treated "quadam insuper commiseratione," the efforts of the *prisci philosophi*: Book 1, Ricc. 417, fol. 11; ed. cit., p. 17. The arguments may have been commonplace, but one would like to know more about what "scholastic grudges" Landino was here harboring—or were these barbs directed toward Argyropoulos, who in appreciating the ancients yet still treated them with "quaedam commiseratio"?

84. Book 2, Ricc. 417, fol. 44v; ed. cit., p. 5: "Nam quae prisci scriptores coniunctim tradiderunt, deinceps vero sive rei difficultate, sive hominum negligentia seorsum tractata sunt, ut et qui in philosophia et qui in arte dicendi exercerentur, ita quisque suo studio delectatus sit, ut alterum ne attigerit quidem."

sources he knew that the mind had internal senses: the *sensus communis*, *imaginatio, existimatio, memoria,* and *phantasia.* The *sensus communis,* he argued, is a sense that unites the others, so that, for instance, when one perceives honey by the eye, one at once tastes honey on the tongue. *Imaginatio* is like a treasury of the mind that holds forms or images drawn from the senses, such as benevolence or friendship. *Existimatio* requires a force of judgment: one sees a person and judges him to have that benevolence or friendship. Judgments proceeding from this reckoning are called *intentiones,* and these are held in the mind by *memoria.* *Phantasia* uses both *memoria,* or *intentiones* stored in the mind, and *imaginatio,* or forms derived from sense, and composes and divides them, and compares the *intentiones* with themselves. Poetic figments are in part explained by the internal senses, culminating in *phantasia.*[85] How did Hesiod create the Chimera?

> Although no animal such as the Chimera conceived by Hesiod has been seen, once we have seen the head of the serpent, the lion, and the goat, it is easy to conceive of that figure in that *sensus* [that is, *phantasia*]. . . . For this *sensus* has an unlimited power for these images, for it not only uses things received by the senses but ponders and fashions things similar to them.[86]

With man, the fantastic images are not accidental but are assimilated and expressed according to some mind-directed goal:

> But this power is greatest when it is conjoined to reason: instructed by reason it diversifies actions in wonderful ways. This, certainly, cannot happen with beasts, for they are moved by nature, not by reason. Since nature reveals herself as the same thing to all things which are of the same species, for all of them things are observed in the same way. Thus you see for each genus of birds standard practices both in constructing nests and in training the young, so that a turtle-dove never differs from a turtle-dove, nor an eagle from an eagle. By the same reason bees produce honey and ants gather food, and . . . even if you run through all forms of all animals, you shall see standard haunts for them, standard types of food, and finally, standard paths in all duties of life. In man, on

---

85. Book 2, ed. cit., pp. 100–107.

86. Book 2, Ricc. 417, fol. 130v; cf. ed. cit., pp. 107–8: "Nam, quamvis nullum usquam tale animal visum sit, qualis ab Hesiodo Chimera fingitur, tamen, cum draconis, cum leonis, cum denique caprae caput viderimus, facile fuit eam effigiem sensu concipere, in qua haec tria simul connecterentur. Est autem innumera quaedam horum simulacrorum vis, quia non solum utitur receptis a sensibus, sed etiam iis similia comentatur [*sic*] atque fingit."

the contrary, there are diverse customs, diverse habits of dress, diverse forms of building. Thus who would doubt that all these powers are acted out in beasts by nature, rather than they themselves acting? But in man they wholly act, since, by using the protection of reason, they can preserve their own liberty.[87]

The mind perceives in various ways, through various forces: it perceives material objects; it perceives in the absence of immediate material objects, when it simply forms an image in the mind; it perceives through *intentiones* (when, for instance, having identified the image of Cicero with friendship, one sees a stranger and immediately judges him a friend or foe according to similar attributes); and it perceives without any matter or other condition present. This latter, Landino argued, is the most excellent and is inwardly divine: "This perception is of the mind alone, which we call the intellect (*intellectus*), by which we know what the soul is, what God is, and what the other incorporeal things are."[88]

When Virgil described Aeneas being led from the active to the contemplative life, he was describing the progress of a mind, and nothing more. Landino sometimes expressed this as "taking oneself from the active to the contemplative life," but he followed Plato (and Ficino) in identifying man's true nature with his mind, and the body as either a vestment or a prison. Yet even the phrase *mentes ad vitam* appears in the Virgil lectures of 1462–63, as, for instance, in this gloss early in Book 5:

It is most difficult to direct our minds to the speculative and sublime life (*Difficillimum enim est mentes nostras dirigere ad vitam speculativam et sublimem*). For always, when we are set up to head in that direction, disturbances arise which try to trouble and interrupt us. Thus Aeneas, setting out from the Trojan harbor, that is,

87. Book 2, Ricc. 417, fols. 130v–31; cf. ed. cit., p. 108: "Sed maxima eius vis est cum rationi coniungitur. Nam ab ea instructa miris modis actiones variat.

"Quod quidem brutis accidere non potest: natura enim moventur non ratione. Verum, cum natura omnibus quae eadem spetie sunt eandem se prebeat, visa quoque omnibus illis similia occurrent. Ita videbis singula volucrum genera singula habere et in nidis construendis et in pullis educandis instituta, ita ut nunquam turtur a turture atque ab aquila aquila differat. Pari ratione mellificant apes, pari ratione cibaria congerunt formicae, et, ne longior in re apertissima sim, discurras licet per omnes omnium animantium formas, eadem in illis latibula, idem escae genus, eandem postremo in omnibus vitae officiis viam annotabis. In homine vero contra diversi mores, diversi vestium habitus, diversae aedificationum figurae. Quapropter quis dubitet vires has omnes in brutis agi potius a natura quam ipsae agant, in homine vero agere omnino, quippe quae rationis patrocinio usae suam libertatem tutari possint?"

88. Book II, Ricc. 417, fol. 95; cf. ed. cit., p. 59: "Quae perceptio solius mentis est, quem intellectum vocamus, quo et quid anima sit, quid deus et reliqua quae incorporea sunt nostra ratione, nullis etiam earum rerum quae in sensum cadunt intentionibus adiuvantibus, consequimur."

from pleasure, that he might come to Italy, that is, to the contemplative life, falls into storms at sea, that is, disturbances. When, likewise, he sets sail from Africa, now he falls into others. For always, while we are in this present life, we are afflicted by them unless we have acquired the virtues of the purified soul.[89]

Aeneas's progress, then, is a progress of mind or soul. The virtues through which he traveled, Landino explained in an earlier lecture, were formalized by Plotinus out of Plato's teaching. These are the moral and political virtues (*virtutes morales et politicae*), where virtuous activity is difficult for us; the purifying virtues (*virtutes purgatoriae*), where we enjoy virtuous activity; the virtues of the purified soul (*virtutes animi iam purgati*), where we welcome adversity as a means of putting virtues into practice; and the exemplary virtues (*virtutes exemplares*), which, in God alone, are images or forms of all the others.[90]

The contemplative life, therefore, was a status of soul: it had nothing to do with the renunciation of worldly life in any literal sense. Indeed, it implied the opposite, for the perfected human soul, with the *virtutes animi iam purgati*, welcomes activity in the world as a means of exercising its virtues. When Aeneas sets out to explore the coast of Carthage (1. 305ff.), he conceals his ships and takes with him two hunting spears.

> These things can be reduced to allegory. . . . True wise men ought not to dedicate themselves to the speculative life that they might forsake the active. Hence Aeneas is such a man: first he disposes of his affairs and takes care for his comrades, which pertain to the active life, . . . and he sets out with two hunting spears, that is, with the two virtues, speculative, to wit, and moral.[91]

89.   Casanatense 1368, fols. 177v–78 (at *Aen.* 6.9): "Difficillimum enim est mentes nostras dirigere ad vitam speculativam et sublimem. Unde semper cum illuc tendere dirigimur, perturbationes exoriuntur quae vexare conentur et nos interrumpere. Unde Eneas solvens a Troiano portu, idest a voluptate, ut Italiam perveniret, idest ad vitam contemplativam, incidit [incidicit *cod.*] in marinas tempestates, idest in perturbationes. Cum item ex Africa solveret, nunc in alias incidit. Semper enim dum in hoc vita presenti sumus illis afficimur, nisi iam adepti sumus virtutes illas animi iam purgati." Cf. Laur. 52, 32, fol. 120: "[D]ifficillime cum simus in purgatoriis virtutibus constituti mens nostra ad speculationem doctrinarumque excellentiam erigitur."

90.   When discussing the *virtutes* Landino first cited Seneca (who indeed mentions the first three virtues in *Epistulae morales*, 64) and then, citing Plotinus, took care to indicate an intermediate source, Macrobius, "qui id ex Plotino se hausisse [haurisse *cod.*] affirmat" (Casanatense 1368, fol. 151, at *Aen.* 4.159). In the other manuscript (Laur. 52, 32, fol. 109v), Seneca's opinion is described as "ex sententia Plotini" (!). For the *virtutes*, see p. 192, above.

91.   Casanatense 1368, fol. 32 (at *Aen.* 1.320, after a literal gloss on *nuda genu*): "Quae vero ad allegoriam reduci possunt haec sunt. . . . Veri sapientes non debent ita se dare vitae speculativae ut activam deserant. Unde Aeneas vir talis primo disponit sua et suo-

In his own life, of course, Landino himself followed the double ideal, both in giving public lectures and in seeking public office.[92] He knew full well that the "traditional" image of the contemplative "wise man" was of one who was removed entirely from the world. He addressed the question in *De anima*:

> There are those who deny that there are virtues in anyone except the wise man. Moreover, they define this wise man as one who, disdaining all mortal and perishable things, knowing divine things only, establishes his life, as far as human weakness allows, by the exemplar of these divine things. And there is indeed in these matters alone perfect and absolute virtue. But if we agree with those (who so define virtue), rarely—dare I say never—have virtues been found or will they be found in man. Therefore let us treat the human race with more indulgence and embrace those also who are able to care for, if not the morally upright duties, at least the morally indifferent ones, as people who are zealous and furnished with virtue. I even think divine Plato shared this opinion. . . . For, since man is neither a lone wanderer nor alien to association with other men, but is born for meeting together and holding counsel, man thinks it to be among the first of his duties that he dwell in cities, look out for the republic, safeguard his fellow citizens, protect friends, and finally, keeping the hand and heart from all unjust conduct, with the forces of the mind and body look out for the common good.[93]

---

rum sociorum curam gerit, quae ad vitam activam pertinent, . . . et proficiscitur cum duobus hastilibus, idest cum duabus virtutibus, speculativa scilicet et morali." Cf. Laur. 52, 32, fol. 34–34v: "Allegoria vero sic se habet, meo iudicio, quod vir sapiens non debet ita se vite speculative tradere ut penitus active rationem amittat. Ideo Eneas non prius exire voluit quam omnia componere(t) et suis provideret. . . . [D]uo hastilia idest duplicem virtutem secum fert, scilicet moralem et speculativam."

92.   Neither Landino's theory nor his practice supports Garin's assertion that, in comparison with Donato Acciaiuoli, "al Landino, rispettabile maestro di scuola, la scuola bastava" ("Donato Acciaiuoli cittadino," p. 200). Here, too, it may be mentioned that Landino lacked the social standing to win the sort of offices held by Acciaiuoli.

93.   Book 3, ed. cit., pp. 51–52: "Sunt autem qui negent in quenquam nisi in sapientem cadere virtutes. Sapientem autem eum diffiniunt, qui, caducis mortalibusque omnibus contemptis, sola divina sapiat, et ad eorum exemplar, quoad imbecillitatis humanae facultas patiatur, vitam instituat. Et est profecto in iis solis perfecta absolutaque virtus; verum si illis assentiamur, raro, ne dicam nunquam, in homine aut repertae sunt aut reperientur virtutes. Itaque clementius agamus cum genere humano; atque eos quoque, qui, si non recta, saltem media officia tueri possunt, veluti studiosos et virtutibus praeditos, amplectamur; qua quidem in sententia et divinum illum Platonem fuisse crediderim. . . . Nam, cum homo neque solivagus neque a reliquorum hominum consortio alienus sit, sed ad coetus conciliaque celebranda natus, id in primis ad suum officium pertinere existimat, ut urbes incolat, ut reipublice consulat, ut suorum civium salutem tutetur, ut

Even in the *Disputationes Camaldulenses*, where in Book 1 ("De vita activa et contemplativa") Landino placed a higher value on the philosophical works of Cicero, works written when Cicero was retired from public life, Landino stressed the importance of public duties. Landino underscored the particular circumstances that led Cicero to abandon the public life. It was a precept even of Plato, Landino argued, that if fools govern, the wise man should attempt to replace them or attempt to make them better. *Only* if neither is possible should the wise man "close in upon himself and benefit man in some other manner." In fact (he has Alberti conclude the first dialogue), when I speak of some dedicated to contemplation and others to action, I do not mean by this two different types of man. Mary and Martha (representing the contemplative and active life) are sisters who "live under the same roof."[94]

A decade earlier, lecturing on Virgil, Landino was less poetic but even more explicit: while one can divide "by reason" the active and contemplative life, they are not truly separate.

> Reason is twofold, just as life is also, speculative, to wit, and active; but not because they are inwardly divided. They are intermixed one with the other. For the speculative life tends toward truth, the active life toward goodness. These two are not distinct by their essence, but by a rational process they can be divided by our mind. For the true is "knowable" by reason, but the good "seekable" by reason: each life, therefore, has need of the other life.[95]

Landino went so far as to convince his students that the "mind" of Cicero, with its great *varietas*, was the proper subject for study even when one considered Cicero during the period of his active life. In 1465–66, after four years of lectures on Latin poets, Landino decided to teach his students the precepts of writing letters by delivering a commentary on Cicero's *Familiar Letters*. By now famous for concentrating on the

---

socios protegat, ac denique ab omni iniuria manus animumque continens et animi et corporis viribus in commune consulat."

94.   Ed. cit., pp. 42–47. For a different interpretation of this section, see E. Garin, *L'Umanesimo italiano*, pp. 100–105.

95.   Casanatense 1368, fol. 214 (at *Aen.* 6.119): "Ratio . . . bipartita est, sicut etiam duplex est vita, speculativa scilicet et activa. Non quod penitus sint divisae: sunt enim invicem commixtae. Nam speculativa tendit ad veritatem, activa vero ad bonitatem: quae duo non sunt distincta essentia sui, sed ratione quadam nostra mente distingui possunt. Nam verum est ratione cognoscibile, bonum vero ratione appetibile: indiget itaque altera vita alterius auxilio." Cf. Laur. 52, 32, fol. 140v: "Ratio . . . dupliciter consideratur, aut in vita activa aut in speculativa. Quarum [?] altera ad bonum, altera ad veritatem refertur. Quae quamvis essentia coniuncta sint, tamen vocabulis distinguuntur."

flosculi and *lepores* of poetry, Landino was challenged by the philologists.[96]

The challenge came from Buonaccorso Massari of Lucca to one of Landino's most loyal students, Lorenzo Guidetti.[97] Cicero's letter to Lentulus (*ad Familiares* 1.1), Massari wrote Guidetti, is difficult because of its subject matter (*propter historiam*): Would you explain to me how your Landino intends to expound this letter? Guidetti answered: People are too anxious about the *historia* of the letter. Landino teaches that the most important things to understand are what *genus dicendi* the author uses, what composition of words, with what *flosculi* and *sobrietas* the letters are constructed. Even though letters should not be treated like orations, the letters yet contain a sublime style in sublime matters, a subdued style in subdued matters. Those primarily concerned with *historia* waste their time in trifles (*in minutiis*). A true Vallian, Massari then challenged Guidetti to produce from his teacher Cicero's true meaning of the word *religio* in the letter; he also objected to Landino's term *flosculi* to describe the *floridum genus dicendi*. Guidetti defended *flosculi* as a proper metaphor and suggested to his rival that his arguments were becoming trivial indeed.[98]

While the debate was in many ways a replay among students of the Valla-Poggio polemics of more than a decade earlier, it also demonstrates Landino's great appreciation of the depth and variety of the author's mind as the true basis for exegesis. The marvelous complexity of the human mind, appreciated and expressed by the poets, formed the basis of Landino's theory of poetic philosophy. Surely the universality of a Leon Battista Alberti, who spoke in the *Disputationes Camaldulenses* often the very words that Landino had used in his lectures, could never be reduced to a simple formula about man's contemplative nature; nor could the Poggian theme of *res hominum variantur* permit any simple solution to the problem of the good life. Perhaps even better than Ficino, Landino realized that the mind, which moved from the active to the contemplative life, was a complex mechanism indeed. He explained the complexity in part in his *De anima* but more effectively in his emphasis on poetic universality and variety of expression. Virgil had

---

96.   See Cardini's insightful analysis of the Guidetti-Massari polemics and their "philological" implications (*La critica*, pp. 39–65). Once again in these debates we see the survival of Poggian humanism in the philosophical renaissance.

97.   For Guidetti, see Cardini, *La critica*, pp. 39–41nn. See also Iacopo Ammannati, *Epistolae et commentarii* (Milan: Minutianus, 1506), sigs. A7v, J4, and now A. C. de la Mare, "New Research on Humanistic Scribes," pp. 510–11, no. 41. See also nn. 27, 29, above. This Lorenzo di Francesco Guidetti is surely the "Lorenzo di Francesco di Guidetto Guidetti" born 16 March 1438/39 (Tratte 443bis, fol. 33).

98.   Ed. in Cardini, *La critica*, pp. 267–86.

Aeneas be led by divine love to the contemplative life, but the many difficulties Aeneas faced on the way could only stand for the many directions the human mind could take.

The poetic philosopher, such as Dante or Virgil, secretly probes each reader's mind, searching for its own special tenor, and then, finding it, captures the soul and leads it to the good life. The poet is the master of deception, alluring the soul with but another form of what it had hitherto enjoyed: thus the soul, deceived by mixed poetic styles, is carried along, until suddenly that which it thought it was enjoying is found to be something else entirely, something higher and better, and the soul discovers that the previous "life" it was enjoying is inadequate. "Whatever men have done and whatever they have known," Landino explained before his lectures on Dante and Virgil, "the poetic discipline adorns with wonderful figments and carries over into another species." The poets "mix together the greatest seriousness with the greatest delight, and leave the hearers in a stupor."[99] This is eloquence, to be sure, but an eloquence especially suited to the nature of the soul: this poetic, allegorical eloquence thus served philosophy not by taking obscure philosophical tenets and making them clear but by taking clear philosophical tenets and making them obscure.

The poetic was not the only route to the good life: this Landino knew. He himself relied heavily on the more systematic philosophizing of Ficino, just as Virgil had need of his Plato and the Platonists. But the young Florentines, who had to be cajoled and prodded, against their will, to the good life, needed the poetic discipline and the lectures of Landino. One cannot enjoy the life of pleasure or public ambition and be convinced at once that the speculative life is better simply because *summa philosophia* dictates that this life is in accordance with man's true nature. Virgil realized this when he led Aeneas (and the reader) from the "very great disturbances of (sensual) love" in Book 4 to the highest philosophical teaching of Book 6. Book 5, Landino explained, is "fitting and, as it were, necessary": here, with "trifles, games, and a certain delectable variety" the souls of the readers are "restored and revived," made ready to accept the serious doctrine of the sixth book.[100] Likewise Juvenal, in his thirteenth satire, used the "deeper philosophical reasons" to console a youth; but he first used examples and familiar expressions, which, for the troubled soul, have more impact than the "very weighty and grave reasons of philosophers."[101]

99. *Scritti*, 1, 20, 21. Landino used similar expressions many times: see my "Cristoforo Landino's First Lectures on Dante," pp. 29–30.

100.   Casanatense 1368, fol. 177; cf. Laur. 52, 32, fol. 120.

101. See p. 248, above.

With his poetic allegory, Landino made a unique contribution to the revival of Plato. His approach was in harmony with that of Marsilio Ficino, whose central philosophical notions he wholly accepted and expounded. While Landino, unlike Donato Acciaiuoli, can be called part of the Ficino circle, like Acciaiuoli he expounded Platonic truths for a particular Florentine audience. By bringing Acciaiuoli and Marsilio Ficino into his dialogue, the *Disputationes Camaldulenses*, Landino showed how the different forms of philosophizing were in themselves valuable and important. By having Leon Battista Alberti lead the discussions, he demonstrated the harmony of the philosophical approaches with the best traditions of humanism. After all, when Virgil had Aeneas, in Book 6, approach the Sibyl at the Euboean rock in order to discover what the future would bring, he found a hundred tunnels leading to her cave and an answer in "a hundred rushing streams of sound." This means, Landino told his students in 1463, "that we make our approach toward wisdom not by one path alone but by many. For there is not the same path for all. For there are many things which lead us to it. . . . Hence the passage from the Evangelist: 'In my father's house are many mansions.' "[102]

The more general, cultural significance of Landino's ideas I have in part already alluded to. In leading the young Florentines from the political virtues (*virtutes politicae*) to the virtues of the purified soul (*virtutes animi iam purgati*) he was creating, through philosophy, ideological structures that would unify Florentines and prevent any recurrence of the events of the 1450s—or so he hoped. Florence itself seems to have moved from *voluptas* (the Trecento), through *avaritia* (the early Quattrocento) and *ambitio* (the late 1450s), to *contemplatio* (the 1460s)—although humanists preferred more general terms to express the transition. If Ficino was Florence's Socrates (or Venus!) then Cosimo was her Aeneas. Landino's lectures were immensely popular, as both his salary and contemporary sources attest, and his published works were diffused widely.[103]

That he emphasized Dante and Virgil is itself significant, for each had a great hold on the popular imagination apart from whatever "meaning"

102.   Casanatense 1368, fol. 208v (on *Aen.* 6.43): "Et bene . . . 'centum'. Non enim una sola via ad sapientiam [spatientiam *cod.*] accedimus, sed pluribus. Non omnibus enim eadem est via. Plures enim sunt res quae nos ad illam ducunt. Omnis enim via optima est ad ipsam foelicitatem, dummodo honeste [honestae *cod.*] recteque vivamus. Unde est illud in Evangelio: 'In domo patris mei mansiones multae sunt' [Joh. 14:2]." Cf. Laur. 52, 32, fol. 138 (on 6.42): "Habet preterea hoc antrum diversos aditus, idest variae sunt disciplinae per quas ad sapientiam accedimus, ut illud in sacra scriptura: 'Domus mea habet multas mansiones.' "

103.   For Landino's increasing salary, see Chapter IV, nn. 42, 79, above. For the diffusion of his published works, see Lentzen, *Studien*, pp. 280–87.

they contained. The only thing comparable were certain books of sacred literature. Landino had Lorenzo de' Medici say as much in the *Disputationes Camaldulenses*, when Lorenzo described his early training in Dante:

> From my early childhood, according to the plan of both parents, I became so familiar with the entire work of the Florentine poet that there were indeed few passages in it which I could not easily recite when they required entertainment. But what could I, a youth, perceive from such a divine poet beyond mere words? But now when I run through in my mind the whole theme of the work, I can admire greatly the genius of the man.[104]

Lorenzo, that is, at one time knew only the "literal" Dante. But now, as he recalled the words and enjoyed the poetic *varietas*, he found he was being secretly led to the contemplative life.

While Lorenzo's own genius may have been exceptional, Landino took especial care that the principles he was expounding made their way into the Italian language, so that they could affect those who knew little or no Latin. He found in Dante themes identical to those of Virgil, and he lectured early, and apparently often, on the *Divine Comedy*. We have no draft of those lectures and little early evidence of his theory of the Italian language; but I shall close this chapter by looking briefly at one of his inaugural orations, delivered in Italian ca. 1465–67, before lectures on Petrarch's *Canzoniere*.[105]

Adapting a theme developed by Poggio in his brilliant critique of Valla, Landino argued that the "Italian language" question was less theoretical than practical. The philosophical shortcomings of Italian, he stated, are not the fault of the "nature of the language" but of the "one who uses it."[106] To enrich the Tuscan language, one must first have a true and perfect understanding of Latin and then, "every day, bring Latin words into our idiom."[107] The content of every language is words and meanings (*parole e sentenzie*). Hence one must indeed study ele-

---

104. Ed. cit., p. 254: "Ego a prima paene pueritia ex utriusque parentis instituto adeo familiare universum opus Florentini poetae mihi reddidi, ut pauci omnino sint in eo loci, quos ego, si quando illi huiuscemodi oblectamenti genus requirerent, non facile ad verbum exprimerem. Sed quid poteram puer ex tam divino vate praeter mera verba percipere? Nunc autem, cum universum rei argumentum mente percurro, summa admiratione eius viri ingenium prosequor."

105. Ed. in *Scritti*, I, 33–40. For the dating, see n. 27, above.

106. *Scritti*, I, 33: " . . . non la natura d'essa lingua ma la negligenzia di chi l'usa [è] in colpa." For Poggio and the *ratio* versus the *usus* of the Latin language, see his first invective against Lorenzo Valla, in his *Opera omnia*, I, esp. p. 203.

107. *Scritti*, I, 38. Landino warned, however, that such efforts should not be forced.

gance of expression; but to keep the "meanings" (*sentenzie*) from being "frivolous," lacking depth, spirit, and strength (*gravità, buon suco,* and *nervi*), one must at least to some extent be introduced to philosophy.[108] Eloquence of this sort is accompanied by true virtue and the highest good, and it is essential to the free republic:

> This can lead the good citizens to hate the wickedness and crimes of the evil citizens, and to punish them; it can free the innocence of the powerless from the penalty of false judgments; it can incite the *popolo*, who are by nature lethargic, toward those things in which public honesty consists, or it can call them back from errors, or inflame them against destructive citizens or calm them down when they are incited against the good ones. All of the turbulent and boisterous agitations of the soul this [eloquence] can excite or repress according to need.[109]

Landino here paraphrases and nearly translates a passage in the first book of Cicero's *De oratore* (1.202).[110] But with Cicero the peroration was the capstone of a long argument on the importance of public law: the *domus iurisconsulti*, he had just stated, was the "totius oraculum civitatis" (1.200). The efficacious eloquence he describes was one grounded in a thorough knowledge of the *publica iura* (1.201). Such arguments would have been warmly welcomed in the legal culture of late Trecento and early Quattrocento Florence, that culture so viciously attacked by Poggio Bracciolini and ridiculed, too, by Cristoforo Landino.

Instead of knitting eloquence and law, Landino is here, in the mid-1460s, uniting eloquence and philosophy, and, more particularly, describing the dangers of an unphilosophical language and an unphilosophical way of thinking. A decade earlier, when the hegemony of the Medicean party in Florence was unraveling, Landino had evidently begun to remedy the defect through popular lectures on Dante, using

108. Ibid., p. 37: "Le sentenzie, le quali non saranno tratte da veri studi d'umanità, sempre fieno [*sic*] e frivoli e leggieri, né mai potrà avere lo scrittore gravità o buon suco o nervi nello stile quando non fia [*sic*], se non al tutto dotto, almanco alquanto introdotto in filosofia."

109. Ibid., p. 38: "Né cosa alcuna si troverrà che in una libera e ben governata repubblica più utilità e ornamento seco arrechi che la eloquenzia, purché da vera virtù e somma bontà accompagnata sia. Questa può la sceleratezza e fraude de' cattivi mettere in odio de' buoni cittadini e condurgli al supplicio; questa può la innocenzia degl'impotenti liberare dalla pena de' falsi giudicii; questa può el populo, per sé medesimo lento e tardo, o incitar a quelle cose dove consiste l'onore publico, o rivocarlo dagl'errori, o infiammarlo contra a' pestilenti cittadini, o mitigarlo quando contro a' buoni incitato fussi; questa può facilmente tutti e' concitati e turbulenti movimenti dell'animo secondo el bisogno eccitare e reprimere."

110. As noted by R. Cardini, ibid.

themes taken from Marsilio Ficino's Platonic philosophy. But before
that great Platonic movement that led to the founding of the Platonic
Academy in 1462 and 1463 had begun, even the notion was lacking, at
least in lay circles, that it was dangerous to have the Florentines remain
so philosophically illiterate.

CONCLUSION

REGARDLESS of the particular vicissitudes of politics and society in the mid-Quattrocento, Florence's expanding culture necessitated a speculative philosophical revival. The Greek world was being absorbed almost as readily as the Latin, and had not Cosimo de' Medici happened to commission Ficino alone, another translator or expositor would have taken his place, or the Platonic dialogues would have been meted out among the Florentine and other humanists just as Plutarch's lives were shared by their translators. Moreover, Ficino's genius was not required to overcome natural impediments to a Platonic revival. When Plato's Socrates pursued boys too avidly, others, like Ficino, could have understood that two millennia after the fact a Latin audience was not penalized by having a sentence here and there left untranslated. As for things perhaps even more distasteful to the better-born Florentines—Plato's community of women and property—citizens of the new Athens were perfectly happy to let metals of this sort be refined by the allegorical fire into the pure gold of love and harmony.

Ficino's genius, furthermore, could not set the bounds for speculative philosophical interests in mid-Quattrocento Florence. The range of a philosophical, or a potentially philosophical, culture among educated laymen was wide indeed. Perhaps the clearest signal that a new intellectual world was looming comes from an unlikely source, Poggio Bracciolini. When a young, better-born scholar expressed to him an interest in philosophical studies, Poggio replied that he, for his part, had never taken up philosophy. But he urged the other to go ahead—as long as he would take up the Greek sources first-hand. Poggio never attempted otherwise to circumscribe the pursuits or methods of the rising philosophical stars.

269

The circle of aristocratic intellectuals led by Donato Acciaiuoli and Alamanno Rinuccini had clearer goals for their philosophizing. Above all else, they sought cultural refinement and sure marks of their aristocracy. They knew how to dress, ride, and behave. Their speeches and letters, adorned with Latin eloquence, set them far above the rabble. Their pursuit of Greek, understood by few even among the learned, set them apart further as they began to embellish their letters with the culture of Hellas and as they worried about which life of Plutarch they would try their hand at translating.

As better-born Florentines, they, in their majority, took up the offices of the active life also—those for which wealth and status made them eligible. But they began to sigh a bit as they assumed these coveted prizes, and they pretended that these were burdens they had taken up only for the sake of the weaker brethren. Was it not better, Donato Acciaiuoli asked Marco Parenti in 1455, to pursue the contemplative rather than the active life? More than twenty years later, in his funeral speech for Acciaiuoli, Cristoforo Landino maintained the fiction: Acciaiuoli fulfilled the duties of the active life, but as he did so he really aspired to be a philosopher-ruler, and the happier life for him was that of the mind.

For the Acciaiuoli circle the aristocrat was, first and foremost, a complete, even universal, man. He required a superior level of culture, the better pursuits of the active life, and the better pursuits of the mind. Giannozzo Manetti, with his style, culture, and learning, epitomized this ideal and became the model for a whole generation of Florentines. Alamanno Rinuccini would later praise Manetti for being the only Florentine, in the generation before his own, willing to master those speculative philosophical studies normally reserved for doctors and theologians. Clinging to a culture based on models and exemplars, the younger followers of Manetti believed that true intellectual enrichment required a systematic program of training, and for this they wanted the best teacher available. They turned first, it seems, to one of Italy's finest and most renowned humanists, Francesco Filelfo. But there was strong opposition in Florence to this old Medici foe, and the younger scholars instead had to take up studies in Greek literature and philosophy under a different teacher, the immigrant from Byzantium John Argyropoulos.

At least at first, John Argyropoulos's teaching struck a responsive chord. It was Aristotle's teaching, Argyropoulos told his students in 1457, that man was born imperfect but that he was made perfect through knowledge. Argyropoulos then claimed that perfection would be reached through an understanding of all areas of active and speculative philosophy and that this understanding was gained by a systematic study of Aristotle. He outlined for his students the books he would teach, a program of studies that covered Aristotle's moral philosophy, natural philosophy, and metaphysics, and in the 1450s and 1460s he lectured on these texts one after the other.

The impact of this teaching in Florence is difficult to assess. It is certainly incorrect to conclude that Argyropoulos and his students were a coterie of civic humanists opposed to a Medici tyranny. Nor is it correct to label Argyropoulos a great Platonist. While Argyropoulos recognized Plato's contribution to the development of early philosophy, he never considered Plato much more than an unsystematic Aristotle. As for the trendier forms of Neoplatonism, Argyropoulos shunned any attempt to resurrect Hermetic truths and the philosophical lore of the ancient theology.

While some of Argyropoulos's students, at least initially, attended his lectures with a great deal of enthusiasm, it seems likely that Alamanno Rinuccini was right when he noted that they lost interest fairly quickly. Even Donato Acciaiuoli, who started the lecture series by taking down the Byzantine's lectures verbatim, began at last to be distracted, and he finally showed a remarkable degree of independence when he wrote out the Aristotle commentaries, based in part on these lectures, which he published under his own name.

While John Argyropoulos from early 1457 was teaching individual perfection through systematic knowledge, Marsilio Ficino and those of his circle were emphasizing themes of love, harmony, and friendship. Why did he become popular? The answer is difficult. Perhaps if whole series of Florentine intellectuals and patricians had written detailed letters describing their feelings and emotions in the 1450s, we could understand the psychological transformations that led to the revival of Plato. But we should not hope to find such sources in the Quattrocento, where autobiographical statements, when they occur, tend to be formalized and lacking in introspection.

But if we imagine ourselves in the crowded classroom of Cristoforo Landino in the academic year 1456–57, where, it now appears, he lectured in Italian on Dante's *Commedia* and used in part themes developed by Marsilio Ficino in his first great exposition of Plato, the *Institutiones ad Platonicam disciplinam*, we may well arrive at some understanding of why Neoplatonic opinions so quickly took hold of the imaginations of many Florentines. The earliest philosophers affirm, Landino told his students, that our souls originally participated in the beauty and harmony of the divine; here on earth, sunk in mortal contagion, they can scarcely remember their real nature. Such philosophers as Plato and such philosophical poets as Dante can assist us in turning away from the vulgar appeals of the world and can lead us toward the eternal beauty

and harmony of our souls. Some fifteen months later, before lectures on
Cicero's *Tusculans*, Landino would present similar themes, as he explained to his students that excessive physical desires, greed, and seeking
public office—an excessive attachment, that is, to the things of this
world—would deflect them from their true happiness in contemplation
and harmony,

If Landino's students, and their fathers who heard the inaugural lectures outlining the goals of the course, recognized in these teachings a
form of the solution to the political problems of the 1450s and a resolution of the crisis of the Medici party, then we find here the true origins
of the Platonic Academy of Florence. In the 1450s the perennial danger
to the Medici reached a critical point. Turning from the Medici party,
many of the better-born began to look after their individual material
interests apart from the interests of their class, they sought individual
political power, and they made alliances with members of the lower
classes. What they began to lack, that is, was a close attachment to one
another.

Most of his central philosophical precepts Landino probably owed to
Ficino, who, after all, had dedicated to Landino his first great work of
Platonic philosophy, the *Institutiones ad Platonicam disciplinam*. During
the same years of Landino's first lectures on Dante and Cicero, Marsilio
Ficino was intellectually challenging the Florentine ruling class. Like
Landino, he emphasized the themes of philosophical contemplation and
the spiritual union of souls through divine harmony. By the summer of
1458, when the Medici held their coup, Ficino was corresponding with
members of the Agli, Canigiani, and Capponi families. To reach a wider
audience, he wrote many early works in Italian, and several of his Latin
works were translated and disseminated by others.

By the time of the Platonic Academy's founding in 1462 (or perhaps
1463), Ficino's ideas were fashionable. His intellectual influence now
clearly eclipsed that of Florence's other leading philosopher, John Argyropoulos. Many who were studying Aristotle now heard Ficino's lectures on Plato as well. And when Donato Acciaiuoli decided to publish
a commentary on Aristotle based on Argyropoulos's lectures, he freely
departed here and there from his Byzantine teacher to embrace a Platonic opinion. More and more the better born, as they were seeking the
individual perfection promised by Argyropoulos's lectures on Aristotle,
were willing to make this endeavor only in the context of the harmony
and friendship demanded by Marsilio Ficino and his Academy.

The sources for the Platonic revival, however, cannot be found simply
in the social conflicts and political crises of Quattrocento Florence. One
cannot describe humanist thought and ignore the humanities. Besides

the classical authors, Landino owed a great deal also to the more recent poets and allegorizers. Ficino took much from scholastic thought, and the forms of many of his ideas appear especially in religious and monastic settings. One of his great accomplishments was to take the themes of harmony, friendship, and love, then flourishing among the learned clerics, and communicate them to the Florentines at large. He served the Florentine public as a priest helping to lead his flock toward the one true good, and so likewise his Platonic philosophy became a Platonic theology.

I have attempted to show in this study, therefore, how the Platonic humanists were anything but idle contemplatives speculating on the eternal verities in a splendid isolation. The students of Argyropoulos, as thinkers seeking individual perfection and indifferent to the world, were far better suited for such a role. Their commitment to the "active life" meant only that they were well-to-do enough to hold public office. The Platonic humanists, on the other hand, taught and preached in the heart of Florence, made certain that their ideas made their way into the Italian language, and, in their philosophical conception of friendship, created a new ideology for the Medici party.

To be sure, if we wish to consider Neoplatonism as an ideology and to describe its role in the social history of ideas, we would have to describe it as an antipopular ideology created for a political and economic elite. Yet if I appear to have treated the creators of this ideology with too great sympathy, I should like to stress that their patrons were no group solidly in power seeking to be entertained. Nor did threats to Medici hegemony come from an emerging social and political class. If the popular revolt of the 1450s had been successful, possible results would have been a regime not unlike that of the Savonarolan period, or even a neocorporatist *retranchement* of "medieval" guilds. As appealing as a Ciompi victory in the late Trecento may be, it is difficult even to conceive of a progressive form of popular revolution in the Quattrocento, and an industrial revolution with a progressive working class was centuries away. Even if the Medici regime had been completely toppled in the 1450s, Medici foes from the *upper* classes would very likely have finally won the day, and they offered a Venetian factionalism or a Milanese signorialism, and among plausible alternatives to the regime of the Medici party was the type of oligarchy characteristic of the early modern era, in which a frozen aristocracy was allied with the church.

The literary and artistic products of the philosophical renaissance have been and can be widely admired, and no less estimable are the products of the humanists and philosophers. The ideal of beauty was as surely described and praised by the intellectuals as it was sung by the lyricists and drawn by the painters. The Neoplatonists stressed the immortality of the soul. They fell far short of the modern conception of individuality, to be sure, but they contributed to this conception, and in the Neoplatonists, at least in our period, the contemplative ideology bore no trace of a program for imitating either the ideal prince or the ideal saint. The intellectuals at least counseled neither submissiveness nor any sort of unity based purely on class or political status. Many scholars have assumed a necessary relationship between philosophical humanism and what has been viewed as Lorenzo de' Medici's growing status as a prince. No one has yet clarified, however, how a conception of individuality or a doctrine of the immortality of the soul become necessary niches in a new princely ideology.

The efficacy of the Neoplatonic teachings of "harmony" is difficult to assess. Whether the Florentines could really embrace, and embrace for long, any set of ideas that demanded that they love God and one another before their own wealth, political status, or self, remains a question. The Neoplatonic intellectuals sought out and took over forms of thinking, particularly religious ideas, that humanists of an earlier age had been unable to control. Rather than being the subject of the moderns' scorn, for having failed to protest a Medici regime, perhaps we should honor them as the intellectuals of an emerging political and social class. Whether we study these thinkers for their contribution to the history of ideas, as others have skillfully done, or take the approach used here and look at their role as intellectuals, we still can quite cheerfully greet the slogan of the Academy, *a bono in bonum omnia diriguntur*—"from the good to the good all things are directed"—both as a moment in the Florentine Platonists' contribution to our culture and as a banner for those intellectuals unwilling to remain indifferent to their own.

ONE OR TWO
LORENZO PISANOS?

B EARING the name "Lorenzo Pisano" is, apparently, a member of the noble Gambacorta family of Pisa, a Florentine gold- and silver-smith, a canon of San Lorenzo in Florence, a lecturer on Dante in the Florentine Studio, an occasional holder of ecclesiastical offices in Rome, an object of Marsilio Ficino's praise, and a "humble priest." In his *Codici latini* (1938), Cardinal Mercati advanced the thesis of two "Lorenzo di Giovanni Pisano" 's principally because: (1) in many Lo-renzo Pisano manuscripts the Lorenzo bears the less prestigious title *presbyter* rather than *canonicus*, and (2) in a dedication to Eugenius IV, Lorenzo complained of his poverty, hardly appropriate to a nobleman holding the canonry at San Lorenzo. Mercati noted, however, that the works he described (the *Enchiridion*, the *De Iesu temptatione hortisque conflictu* [Vat. lat. 3706], the *Dialogi humilitatis*), and some other works he mentioned from printed catalogs, all seemed to be written by the same figure and that this was the person praised by Marsilio Ficino; but this figure, he argued, was not the Lorenzo di Giovanni Pisano who held the canonry of San Lorenzo and who died in 1465. The question is not crucial for this study, since I look at works that Mercati conceded belong to the person praised by Ficino. Yet it seems clear that the figure here described held the canonry of San Lorenzo and died in 1465. When Mercati first proposed the two "Lorenzo Pisano" 's he had not seen A. Mancini's study of 1932 on Lorenzo ("Laurentius canonicus pi-sanus"), which discusses the biography of Lorenzo Pisano written by Lorenzo's nephew, Teofilo (Pisa, Bibl. Univ., cod. 688). In an appendix to his survey Mercati took up Mancini's arguments (pp. 274–86) and suggested that Teofilo may have been gathering information at random and confusing the two Lorenzo Pisanos himself. (Teofilo, in fact, copied into the Pisan manuscript a letter from Lorenzo [fol. 28–28v] to which he affixed the date 1468!)

But for a single Lorenzo Pisano the following arguments can be made.

First, Teofilo, the son of Lorenzo Pisano's brother Gherardo, is not so far removed from Lorenzo Pisano as Mercati assumed. To be sure, the biography was written many years after Lorenzo's death. Teofilo calls himself "artium et medicinae doctor" (fols. 95v, 114v), a title that he evidently had only in 1476 (see A. Verde, *Lo Studio fiorentino*, III, 903, no. 1235). But this Teofilo was Lorenzo Pisano's heir. For the testament, see Florence, Archivio de Stato, Notarile Antecosimiano, M 270 (1464–65, Lotto di Francesco Masi), unfoliated, under 18 Sept. (1465). Among the witnesses was Francesco da Castiglione. The testament is summarized also in an account book of the Archivio di San Lorenzo (on deposit at the Bibl. Laurenziana), vol. 2413, fol. 39v. Moreover, Teofilo appears as a witness in a legal matter dated 17 Nov. 1464 concerning Lorenzo Pisano and the church of San Lorenzo (Not. Antec., M 270 [1464–65], unfoliated), and, among many other documents relating to his presence in San Lorenzo, he is described as *trahens moram in dicta ecclesia* (ibid.).

Second, in his *De misericordia* dedicated to Cosimo de' Medici (a manuscript cited but not examined by Mercati), Lorenzo Pisano mentioned his past career as a silversmith and how Giovanni di Bicci de' Medici rescued him, giving him, that is, the canonry at San Lorenzo created by the Medici (Munich, Bayer. Staatsbibl., Clm 109; fol. 1v): "Quando cum multis aliis ego quoque munificentia partis tui ex vilissima fabri argentarii arte ad litterarum dulce otium translatus sim . . . . "

As for the confusion over Lorenzo Pisano's title (sometimes *presbyter* when the more prestigious *canonicus* would seem more appropriate), I would suggest that Lorenzo affixed the label *presbyter* to some of his works simply as an expression of modesty. The title could have varied according to whether he or an admiring scribe affixed it. In the Pisan manuscript, copied wholly or in part by his nephew Teofilo, the title *canonicus* abounds. In Lorenzo's oration to Pius II, for instance, the following title is given: "Oratio Laurentii canonici Pisani ad Pium secundum hec est" (fol. 115v). In this oration he mentions his *Dialogi quinque*, where his name in the title is Laurentius presbyter Pisanus, and he describes himself in the oration as "ego humilis presbyter" (fol. 116).

To be sure, here I touch on only one aspect of Cardinal Mercati's discussion: his is the first real analysis of Lorenzo Pisano's manuscripts, and he had the good sense to oppose Mancini's notion that this Lorenzo was not worth much study!

LORENZO PISANO'S
DE AMORE

THE *De amore*, composed of four dialogues, was apparently placed with the *De misericordia* in the library of San Marco by Cosimo de' Medici in the early 1460s: see Ullman and Stadter, *The Public Library*, p. 238, no. 966. The two works there listed together are copied, evidently as a unit, in Munich, Bayer. Staatsbibl., Clm 109, fols. 1–49 and 50–324. The copy was apparently made in 1551 (but see the description of *De misericordia*, Appendix C, below). For this manuscript see Mercati, *Codici latini*, p. 101, and Kristeller, *Iter Italicum*, III, 612.

The *De amore* has been studied from Magl. XXI 115 (inc.: Quando omnipotenti deo placuit), fragmentary at the end, containing, that is, the first three dialogues and part of the fourth.

Another fragmentary manuscript is Barcelona, Bibl. Central, cod. 668, 75 fols. (seen on microfilm). It contains the first two dialogues and part of the third. It ends abruptly in the middle of fol. 75v (des.: hominem ad conformia sibi), which corresponds to Magl. XXI 115, fol. 135bis *recto*, line 6 from the end.

One complete manuscript is Budapest, Szechenyi Library (Bibl. Musei Nationalis), Clmae 185 (seen on microfilm; for a description, see E. Bartoniek, *Codices latini medii aevi* [Catalogi Bibl. Musei Nationalis Hungarici, 12; Budapest, 1940], pp. 148–49). The Budapest manuscript, 228 folios in a fifteenth-century hand, has, on fol. 1, both a miniature, apparently portraying Lorenzo himself, and an unidentified coat of arms. The last line of fol. 199 in the Budapest manuscript corresponds to the *desinit* of the fragmentary Florentine one.

Another complete manuscript is Paris, Bibl. Nat., cod. lat. 6451A, 182 fols. The Paris manuscript has not been noted before in studies of Lorenzo Pisano; nor is it mentioned in Kristeller's *Supplementum Ficinianum* or *Iter*. I was led to it by the good summary description in *Catalogus codicum manuscriptorum Bibliothecae Regiae*, vol. 4 (Paris, 1744), p. 526. The manuscript's arrangement is identical to Magl. XXI 115. Its des., "inde in sua abierunt omnes" (fol. 182), is followed by a colophon: "Silvester Pisanus generoso sanguine Palmierorum natus, divino flante amore hos dialogos scripsit. In XX.o II.o anno suae florentis aetatis. In domo Andreae Lottoringi de Stufa sub D.a L.a [Domina Lena?]." (For some codicological data on this manuscript see now A. Derolez, *Codicologie des manuscrits en écriture humanistique sur parchemin. II: Catalogue*, Bibliologia, 6 [Turnhout, 1984], p. 100, no. 660. For this and eight other Silvestro Palmieri manuscripts, see now also de la Mare, "New Research on Humanistic Scribes," pp. 536, 598, no. 67.) Silvestro's date of birth should then date the manuscript. But I have found no direct evidence for the date. This Silvestro was the son of Giovanni di Michele Palmieri, who had married Bartolomea, the sister of Lorenzo Pisano. She is aged thirty-six in the Pisan catasto of 1428: Silvestro is not numbered among her children and is probably the product of a later marriage of Giovanni Palmieri (see the source cited above, Chapter VI, n. 119). Silvestro commissioned a funeral plaque for his illustrious brother, or half-brother, Mattia, in the church of Santa Maria Maggiore, Rome; he is also mentioned in Mattia's will of 1483 (see the sketch of Mattia in *Memorie istoriche di più uomini illustri pisani*, III [1792; rept. Bologna, 1972], 225–52, and in L. Lanzani, "L'umanista Mattia Palmieri e la sua storia 'De bello italico,' " *Studi Storici* 14 (1905), 365ff.

Silvestro Palmieri's name does not seem to turn up among Pisan baptismal records (according to a communication of Professor Michele Luzzati, Scuola Normale Superiore, Pisa, who is now studying the records). However, we do know that Silvestro was chosen prior in the Pisan government in 1469, 1470, and 1471 (*Memorie istoriche*, p. 240) and that one was eligible for such an office from the age of thirty (F. Bonaini, ed., *Statuti inediti della città di Pisa dal XII al XIV secolo*, vol. 2 (Florence, 1870), Breve del Popolo, chap. 69, p. 505, and chap. 145, p. 607). We may assume that Silvestro, from a better family, would have been chosen prior soon after becoming eligible, which would point toward a birthdate of about 1438 or 1439. This would date the Paris manuscript to about 1460.

This would also seem to be about the year when Lorenzo wrote the work. Teofilo's *Vita* mentions that Lorenzo (d. 1465) composed it in his old age ("tandem senio confectus"), Pisa, Bibl. Univ., cod. 688, fol. 95v; cf. fol. 114. The title of the third dialogue, "Iacobus," in the Budapest manuscript (fol. 99: Presbyteri Laurentii Pisani dialogus tertius de

amore qui dicitur Iacobus a singulari litterarum sacrarum magistro et
preceptore suo et ordinis fratrum mìnorum patre generali incipit) could
only refer to Iacobus de Sarzuela, who was Father General of the Friars
Minor from 1458 to 1464 (Marianus de Florentia, "Compendium
Chronicarum Fratrum Minorum," *Archivum Franciscanum Historicum* 4
[1911], 136 and n., 318).

The Andrea di Lotteringo della Stufa, mentioned in the Paris colophon, was a prominent Florentine banker and Medici partisan. He had
close ties with San Lorenzo: according to documents cited below, he
seems to have endowed a chapel and canonry. He is mentioned in the
records of the San Lorenzo notary, Lotto di Francesco Masi: 10 Sept.
1448 (Notarile Antecosimiano, M 271 [1383–1499], fol. 23); 25 May 1451
(N. A., M 273 [1398–1480], fol. 444); 22 June 1461 (N. A., M 268 [1461–
98], fol. 1); and 10 Sept. 1467 (N.A., M 273, fol. 227v). The document of
1461 also mentions Giovanni Spinellini, who was cited as a fellow priest
of Lorenzo Pisano in Ambrogio Traversari's letter to Niccolò Niccoli,
August 1430, discussed by Mercati, *Ultimi contributi*, p. 69.

APPENDIX C

SOME NOTES
ON MINOR WORKS OF
LORENZO PISANO

Sermo de temptatione Iesu to Eugenius IV, Vat. lat. 3706, 22 fols., with folios misnumbered at end (pref. inc., fol. 1: Duas nuper edidi orationes; text inc., fol. 3: "Ductus est Iesus in desertum . . . ." Non me fugit, beatissime pater). This may be compared with the *De natura daemonum et tentatione libri 3* to Cardinal Giordano Orsini (El Escorial, Biblioteca Real, cod. L.III.16 [seen on microfilm], described in G. Antolín, *Catálogo de los códices latinos de la Real Biblioteca del Escorial*, vol. 3 [Madrid, 1913], 39), and which may have later been revised into part of the *Dialogi quinque*. See G. Mercati, *Codici latini*, pp. 98–99, and Teofilo, *Vita*, Pisa, Bibl. Univ., cod. 688, fols. 95v, 114.

De gradibus virginitatis to Castor presbyter (inc. Sepenumero viri sapientia et ingenio clari), Vat. Ottob. lat. 368, fols. 66v–79; cf. Teofilo, *Vita*, fols. 95v, 114.

De pace, Lucca, Bibl. Statale (formerly Bibl. Governativa), cod. 366, fols. 1–39 (modern foliation), fragmentary, containing end of Book 1 and beginning of Book 2. Book 1 des. (fol. 15): "labuntur properare monuerunt. Presbyteri Laurentii canonici Pisani liber secundus de pace incipit. [fol. 15v] Quanta laetitia superiori sermone delibuti fuissemus." Described by Teofilo, *Vita*, as two dialogues *De pace et infinita bonitate dei* (fols. 95v, 114).

De misericordia to Cosimo de' Medici, Munich, Bayer. Staatsbibl., Clm 109, fols. 1–49 (pref. inc., fol. 1: Quoniam multi me longe praeclariores; text inc., fol. 2v: Cum consumata fuissent). These dialogues are named "Ciprianus" (for Cipriano Rucellai? see Chapter VI, n. 148), "Leonardus" (for Leonardo Dati), and "Laurentius" (for Lorenzo Pisano himself). See Kristeller, *Iter*, III, 612, and Ullman and Stadter, *Pub-*

lic Library, p. 238, no. 966. The work is mentioned in Teofilo, *Vita*, fols. 95v, 114. There is a reference to this dialogue in Lorenzo Pisano's *De amore* (Magl. XXI 115, fols. 5v–6), with which the *De misericordia* was transcribed in the Munich manuscript, in Florence apparently in 1551 (but this should be examined: the script, seen by me only on microfilm, seems somewhat older).

In Psalmum "Dixit Dominus etc." (Laur. Conv. Soppr. 256, fols. 9–20); fragmentary at beginning; title and attribution in later hand; script elegant, humanistic. It is a commentary on Ps. 109, and is addressed to "A." (as on fol. 17, 17v). By style and subject matter the work seems to be Lorenzo's, but this should be studied. Teofilo mentioned no such work but did state that Lorenzo lectured on the *Psalter* (*Vita*, fols. 95v, 113v). For the manuscript (formerly SS. Annunziata 1382.6), see the handwritten inventory entitled *Supplementum alterum ad catalogum codd. Graecorum, Latinorum, Italicorum, etc. Biblioth. Med. Laurentianae* . . . . II, 149–50 (kept in the manuscript reading room of the library).

The Pisan manuscript copied by Teofilo also contains a *De vita monastica* to Arsenius grecus, fols. 30–54 and 96–104 (latter an abbreviated version) [pref. inc., fol. 30: Saepenumero et diu cogitanti mihi optime virorum; text inc., fol. 31v: Qui secum habitat monachus est]; *De pascha et resurrectione* to Card. Angelotto Fosco, fols. 55–95 (pref. inc.: Cum nocturnos algores; text inc., fol. 57: Heri huius celebrationis desiderio fatigatus); an oration to Pius II, fols. 115v–16v (inc. Postquam, beatissime papa Pie, spiritus); a letter to Card. Columpnensis familiaris suus, fols. 28v–29 (inc. Per adolescentem Cornelium famulum); and a letter to Paul II, fol. 28–28v (inc. Post obscula [*sic*] beatorum pedum).

Teofilo also mentions (fols. 95v, 114) a commentary on the *Nicomachean Ethics*, a *libellus De honore parentum*, an *opusculum De invidia* to Calixtus III (mentioned also by Lorenzo Pisano in his *Dialogi quinque* [see Chapter VI, n. 130]), and a few other works.

The work containing meditations on God and the soul by a Laurentius sacerdos, in Laur. 76, 55, and New Haven, Yale University Library, ms. 540 (latter not seen: described in Kristeller, *Iter Italicum*, vol. 5, forthcoming), is not, I believe, by Lorenzo Pisano.

SELECT BIBLIOGRAPHY

Note: This bibliography includes only works cited more than once and in abbreviated form in the notes.

Acciaiuoli, Donato. *Donati Acciaioli Florentini expositio super libros Ethicorum Aristotelis in novam traductionem Argiropyli Bisantii.* Florence: San Jacopo di Ripoli, 1478 (= *GW* 140).

Adam, R. G. "Francesco Filelfo at the Court of Milan." Ph.D. diss., Oxford University, 1974: copy at Warburg Institute, London. Now being edited for publication by the Deutsches Historisches Institut, Rome.

Alberti, Leon Battista. *Della famiglia.* Vol. 1 of *Opere volgari.* Ed. C. Grayson. Bari, 1960.

Allen, M. J. B. See Ficino, *Philebus Commentary.*

Argyropoulos, John. *Argyropouleia.* See Lampros.

Bandini, A. M. *Specimen literaturae Florentinae saeculi XV* . . . 2 vols. Florence, 1747–51.

Bec, C. *Les livres des Florentins (1413–1608).* Florence, 1984.

Benadduci, G. "Prose e poesie volgari di Francesco Filelfo." *Atti e memorie della R. Deputazione di storia patria per le province delle Marche* 5 (1901), xli–xlviii, 1–261.

Bisticci, Vespasiano da. See Vespasiano da Bisticci.

Black, R. *Benedetto Accolti and the Florentine Renaissance.* Cambridge, 1985.

Bracciolini, Poggio. Ep. (Epistulae), listed by book and letter number, according to the arrangement in T. Tonelli's edition (Florence, 1832), which is cited in parentheses by volume and page: all rept. in *Opera omnia*, vol. 3.

———. *Opera omnia*. Ed. R. Fubini. Turin, 1963–69. Volume 1 reprints the Basel, 1538, edition of Poggio's works; vols. 2 and 4 contain miscellaneous reprints and new editions; vol. 3 is the Epistulae (as above).

Brown, A. M. *Bartolomeo Scala, 1430–1497, Chancellor of Florence: The Humanist as Bureaucrat*. Princeton, 1979.

———. "The Humanist Portrait of Cosimo de' Medici, Pater Patriae." *Journal of the Warburg and Courtauld Institutes* 24 (1961), 186–221.

———. "Platonism in Fifteenth-Century Florence and Its Contribution to Early Modern Political Thought." *Journal of Modern History* 58 (1986), 383–413.

Brown, V. "Giovanni Argiropulo on the Agent Intellect: An Edition of Ms. Magliabecchi V 42 (ff. 224–228v)." In *Essays in Honour of Anton Charles Pegis*, 160–75. Ed. J. R. O'Donnell. Toronto, 1974.

Brucker, G. "A Civic Debate on Florentine Higher Education (1460)." *Renaissance Quarterly* 34 (1981), 517–33.

Burckhardt, J. *The Civilization of the Renaissance in Italy*. Trans. S. G. C. Middlemore. Rev. and ed. I. Gordon. New York, 1960.

Cammelli, G. *Giovanni Argiropulo*. Vol. 2 of *I dotti bizantini e le origini dell'Umanesimo*. Florence, 1941.

Cardini, R. *La critica del Landino*. Florence, 1973.

———, ed. *Scritti*. See Landino, Cristoforo.

Caroti, S., and Zamponi, S. *Lo scrittoio di Bartolomeo Fonzio, umanista fiorentino*. Milan, 1974.

Cohn, S. K., Jr. "The Character of Protest in Mid-Quattrocento." In *Il tumulto dei Ciompi: Un momento di storia fiorentina e europea*, 199–220. Ed. Istituto Nazionale di Studi sul Rinascimento. Florence, 1981.

Cristiani, E. "Una inedita invettiva giovanile di Marsilio Ficino." *Rinascimento*, 2d. ser., 6 (1966 [1967]), 209–22.

De la Mare, A. C. "New Research on Humanistic Scribes in Florence." In *Miniatura fiorentina del Rinascimento, 1440–1525: Un primo censimento*, 393–600. Ed. A. Garzelli. Scandicci (Florence), 1985.

———. "Vespasiano da Bisticci, Historian and Bookseller." Ph.D. diss., University of London, 1965: copy at Warburg Institute, London.

Della Torre, A. *Storia dell' Accademia platonica di Firenze*. 1902; rept. Turin, 1968.

Dizionario biografico degli italiani. Ed. Istituto della Enciclopedia Italiana. Rome, 1960–.

Ficino, Marsilio. *Commentaire sur le Banquet de Platon*. Ed. R. Marcel. Paris, 1956. Cited in text as *De amore*.

———. *The Letters of Marsilio Ficino*. Trans. Language Department, School of Economic Science, London. 3 vols. London, 1975–81.

———. *Opera omnia*. 2 vols. Basel, 1576; rept. Turin, 1959.

———. *The Philebus Commentary*. Ed. M. J. B. Allen. Berkeley, 1975.

Field, A. "Cristoforo Landino's First Lectures on Dante." *Renaissance Quarterly* 39 (1986), 16–48.

———. "An Inaugural Oration by Cristoforo Landino in Praise of Virgil (From Codex '2', Casa Cavalli, Ravenna)." *Rinascimento*, 2d. ser., 21 (1981), 235–45.

———. "John Argyropoulos and the 'Secret Teachings' of Plato." In J. Hankins, J. Monfasani, and F. Purnell, Jr., eds., *Supplementum Festivum: Studies in Honor of Paul Oskar Kristeller*, 299–326. Binghamton, N.Y., 1987.

———. "A Manuscript of Cristoforo Landino's First Lectures on Virgil, 1462–63 (Codex 1368, Biblioteca Casanatense, Rome)." *Renaissance Quarterly* 31 (1978), 17–20.

———. "The *Studium Florentinum* Controversy, 1455." *History of Universities* 3 (1983), 31–59.

Filelfo, Francesco. *Cent-dix lettres grecques de François Filelfe publiées intégralement pour la première fois d'après le* Codex Trivulzianus 873, *avec traduction, notes et commentaires*. Ed. E. Legrand. Paris, 1892.

———. *Epistolae familiares*. Venice, 1502.

———. "Prose e poesie volgari." See Benadduci.

Fossi, F. *Monumenta ad Alamanni Rinuccini vitam contexendam*. Florence, 1791.

Fubini, R. "Ficino e i Medici all'avvento di Lorenzo il Magnifico." *Rinascimento*, 2d. ser., 24 (1984), 3–52.

Ganz, M. "The Humanist as Citizen: Donato di Neri Acciaiuoli, 1428–1478." Ph.D. diss. Syracuse University, 1979.

Garin, E. *La cultura filosofica del Rinascimento italiano*. Florence, 1961.

Garin, E. "Donato Acciaiuoli cittadino fiorentino." In *Medioevo e Rinascimento*, 199–267. 4th ed. Bari, 1973.

———. "Platonici bizantini e platonici italiani: 1. Nuove indagini sul Pletone." In *Studi sul Platonismo medievale*, 155–90. Florence, 1958.

———. "La rinascita di Plotino." In *Rinascite e rivoluzioni: Movimenti culturali dal XIV al XVIII secolo*, 89–129. Bari, 1976.

———. *L'Umanesimo italiano*. 8th ed. Bari, 1975.

———, ed. *La disputa delle Arti nel Quattrocento*. Florence, 1947.

Gentile, G. "In margine all'epistola 'De divino furore.'" *Rinascimento*, 2d ser., 23 (1983 [1984]), 33–77.

George of Trebizond. *Comparationes phylosophorum Aristotelis et Platonis*. Venice, 1523; rept. Frankfurt, 1965.

Gherardi, A., ed. *Statuti della Università e Studio fiorentino dell'anno 1387, seguiti da un'appendice di documenti dal 1320 al 1472*. 1881; rept. Bologna, 1973.

Giustiniani, V. R. *Alamanno Rinuccini, 1426–1499: Materialien und Forschungen zur Geschichte des florentinischen Humanismus*. Cologne, 1965.

Goldthwaite, R. *Private Wealth in Renaissance Florence*. Princeton, 1968.

Grafton, A. *Joseph Scaliger: A Study in the History of Classical Scholarship*. Vol. 1. Oxford, 1983.

Grafton, A., and L. Jardine. *From Humanism to the Humanities: Education and the Liberal Arts in Fifteenth- and Sixteenth-Century Europe*. Cambridge, Mass., 1986.

Gutkind, C. S. *Cosimo de' Medici, Pater Patriae, 1389–1464*. Oxford, 1938.

Henderson, J. "Piety and Charity in Late Medieval Florence: Religious Confraternities from the Middle of the Thirteenth Century to the Late Fifteenth Century." Ph.D. diss., University of London, 1983.

Iusim, M. A. "Neopublikovannyi traktat Lorentso Pizano." *Srednie veka* 42 (1978), 122–44.

Kallendorf, C. "Cristoforo Landino's *Aeneid* and the Humanist Critical Tradition." *Renaissance Quarterly* 36 (1983), 519–46.

Kent, D. *The Rise of the Medici: Faction in Florence, 1426–1434*. Oxford, 1978.

Krantz, F. "Florentine Humanist Legal Thought, 1375–1450." Ph.D. diss., Cornell University, 1971.

———. "Between Bruni and Machiavelli: History, Law and Historicism in Poggio Bracciolini." In *Politics and Culture in Early Modern Eu-*

rope: Essays in Honor of H. G. Koenigsberger, 119–51. Ed. P. Mack and M. C. Jacob. Cambridge, 1987. Cited in text as "Poggio."

Kristeller, P. O. "L'état présent des études sur Marsile Ficin." In XVIe Colloque International de Tours. *Platon et Aristote à la Renaissance*, 59–77. Paris, 1976.

————. *Iter Italicum*. 3 vols. London and Leiden, 1963–83.

————. "Marsilio Ficino and His Work after Five Hundred Years." In *Marsilio Ficino e il ritorno: Studi*, I, 15–196 and plates.

————. "Marsilio Ficino as a Beginning Student of Plato." *Scriptorium* 20 (1966), 41–54.

————. "Marsilio Ficino as a Man of Letters and the Glosses Attributed to Him in the Caetani Codex of Dante." *Renaissance Quarterly* 36 (1983), 1–47.

————. *Medieval Aspects of Renaissance Learning*. Ed. and trans. E. P. Mahoney. Durham, N.C., 1974.

————. *Il pensiero filosofico di Marsilio Ficino*. Florence, 1953.

————. *The Philosophy of Marsilio Ficino*. Trans. V. Conant. 1943; rept. Gloucester, Mass., 1964.

————. *Renaissance Thought and Its Sources*. New York, 1979.

————. *Studies in Renaissance Thought and Letters*. 1956; rept. Rome, 1969.

————. *Supplementum Ficinianum*. 1937; rept. Florence, 1973.

Lampros, S. P. *Argyropouleia*. Athens, 1910.

Landino, Cristoforo. *Carmina omnia*. Ed. A. Perosa. Florence, 1939.

————. *De anima*. Book 1, ed. A. Paoli in *Annali delle università toscane*, vol. 34 (1915), fasc. 1; Book 2, ed. A. Paoli, n.s., vol. 1 (1916), fasc. 2; Book 3, ed. G. Gentile, n.s., vol. 2 (1917), fasc. 3.

————. *Disputationes Camaldulenses*. Ed. P. Lohe. Florence, 1980.

————. *Reden Cristoforo Landinos*. Ed. M. Lentzen. Munich, 1974.

————. *Scritti critici e teorici*. Ed. R. Cardini. Rome, 1974.

Legrand, E. *Cent-dix lettres*. See Filelfo, Francesco.

Lentzen, M. *Studien zur Dante-Exegese Cristoforo Landinos, mit einem Anhang bisher unveröffentlichter Briefe und Reden*. Cologne and Vienna, 1971.

Lentzen, ed. *Reden*. See Landino, Cristoforo.

Machiavelli, Niccolò. *The Chief Works and Others*. Vol. 3. Trans. A. Gilbert. Durham, N.C., 1965.

Mancini, A. "Laurentius canonicus pisanus." *Bollettino storico pisano* 1, no. 1 (1932), 33–47.

Manetti, Giannozzo. *De dignitate et excellentia hominis.* Ed. E. R. Leonard. Padua, 1975.

———. *Dialogus consolatorius.* Ed. A. de Petris. Rome, 1983.

Marcel, R. *Marsile Ficin (1433–1499).* Paris, 1958.

Marchesi, C. *Scritti minori di filologia e di letteratura.* Florence, 1978.

Marsilio Ficino e il ritorno di Platone: Mostra di manoscritti, stampe e documenti, 17 maggio–16 giugno 1984. Catalog ed. S. Gentile, S. Niccoli, and P. Viti. Florence, 1984.

Marsilio Ficino e il ritorno di Platone: Studi e documenti. Ed. G. C. Garfagnini. 2 vols. Florence, 1986.

Martines, L. *Lawyers and Statecraft in Renaissance Florence.* Princeton, 1968.

———. *The Social World of the Florentine Humanists, 1390–1460.* London, 1963.

Marzi, D. *La Cancelleria della Repubblica fiorentina.* Rocca S. Casciano, 1910.

Mercati, G. *Codici latini Pico Grimani Pio . . . esistenti nell'Ottoboniana.* Vatican City, 1938.

———. *Ultimi contributi alla storia degli umanisti.* Vatican City, 1939.

Mohler, L. *Kardinal Bessarion als Theologe, Humanist und Staatsmann.* 3 vols. 1923–42; rept. Aalen, 1967.

Molho, A. "Cosimo de' Medici: *Pater Patriae* or *Padrino?*" *Stanford Italian Review* 1 (1979), 5–33.

Monfasani, J. *George of Trebizond, a Biography and Study of His Rhetoric and Logic.* Leiden, 1976.

Moreni, D. *Continuazione delle memorie istoriche dell'Ambrosiana Imperial Basilica di S. Lorenzo di Firenze.* 2 vols. Florence, 1816–17.

Müllner, K., ed. *Reden und Briefe italienischer Humanisten.* 1899; rept. Munich, 1970, with indexes and bibliographical addenda by B. Gerl.

Palmieri, Matteo. *Vita civile.* Ed. G. Belloni. Florence, 1982. Cited in text as *Della vita civile.*

Park, K. "Readers at the Florentine Studio According to Communal Fiscal Records (1357–1380, 1413–1446)." *Rinascimento,* 2d. ser., 20 (1980 [1981]), 249–310.

Phillips, M. *The Memoir of Marco Parenti: A Life in Medici Florence.* Princeton, 1987.

Poggio Bracciolini. See Bracciolini, Poggio.

Poliziano, Angelo. *Detti piacevoli.* Ed. T. Zanato. Rome, 1983.

———. *Angelo Polizianos Tagebuch (1477–1479).* Ed. A. Wesselski. Jena, 1929.

Rabb, T. K., and J. E. Seigel, eds. *Action and Conviction in Early Modern Europe: Essays in Memory of E. H. Harbison.* Princeton, 1969.

Rinuccini, Alamanno. *Lettere ed orazioni.* Ed. V. R. Giustiniani. Florence, 1953.

Rochon, A. *La jeunesse de Laurent de Médicis (1449–1478).* Paris, 1963.

Rotondò, A. "Nicolò Tignosi da Foligno (Polemiche aristoteliche di un maestro del Ficino)." *Rinascimento* 9 (1958), 217–55.

Rubinstein, N. *The Government of Florence under the Medici (1434 to 1494).* Oxford, 1966.

———. "Poggio Bracciolini cancelliere e storico di Firenze." *Atti e memorie della Accademia Petrarca di Lettere, Arti e Scienze.* n.s., 37 (1958–64 [1965]), 215–39.

Sabbadini, R. *Storia del Ciceronianismo e di altre questioni letterarie nell'età della Rinascenza.* Turin, 1885.

Segni, A. *Vita di Donato Acciaioli.* Ed. T. Tonelli. Florence, 1841.

Seigel, J. E. "The Teaching of Argyropulos and the Rhetoric of the First Humanists." In T. K. Rabb and J. E. Seigel, eds. *Action and Conviction*, pp. 237–60.

Sensi, M. "Niccolò Tignosi da Foligno: L'opera e il pensiero." *Annali della Facoltà di Lettere e Filosofia* (Università degli Studi di Perugia) 9 (1971–72 [1973]), 359–495.

Sillano, M. T., ed. *Le ricordanze di Giovanni Chellini da San Miniato, medico, mercante e umanista (1425–1457).* Milan, 1984.

Stinger, C. L. *Humanism and the Church Fathers: Ambrogio Traversari (1386–1439) and Christian Antiquity in the Italian Renaissance.* Albany, 1977.

Thorndike, L. *Science and Thought in the Fifteenth Century.* 1929; rept. New York, 1963.

Torre, Arnaldo della. See Della Torre, Arnaldo.

Trebizond, George of. See George of Trebizond.

Ullman, B. L., and P. A. Stadter. *The Public Library of Renaissance Florence: Niccolò Niccoli, Cosimo de' Medici and the Library of San Marco.* Padua, 1972.

Verde, A. *Lo Studio fiorentino, 1473–1503.* 4 vols. Florence, 1973; Pistoia, 1977; Florence, 1986.

————. "Giovanni Argiropolo e Lorenzo Buonincontri professori nello Studio fiorentino." *Rinascimento,* 2d ser., 14 (1974), 279–87.

Vespasiano da Bisticci. *Le vite.* Ed. A. Greco. 2 vols. Florence, 1970–76.

Viti, P. "Documenti ignoti per la biografia di Marsilio Ficino." In *Marsilio Ficino e il ritorno: Studi,* 1, 251–83.

Walser, E. *Poggius Florentinus, Leben und Werke.* Leipzig, 1914. Pp. 325–560 rept. in Poggio Bracciolini, *Opera omnia,* vol. 4.

Weintraub, K. J. *The Value of the Individual; Self and Circumstance in Autobiography.* Chicago, 1978.

Weissman, R. F. E. *Ritual Brotherhood in Renaissance Florence.* New York, 1982.

Zambelli, P. "Platone, Ficino e la magia." In *Studia humanitatis: Ernesto Grassi zum 70. Geburtstag,* 121–42. Ed. E. Hora and E. Kessler. Munich, 1973.

Zippel, G. "Carlo Marsuppini" (1897). In his *Storia e cultura,* pp. 198–213.

————. "Per la biografia dell'Argiropulo" (1896). In his *Storia e cultura,* pp. 179–97.

————. *Storia e cultura del Rinascimento.* Padua, 1979.

INDEX OF MANUSCRIPTS

GENERAL INDEX

A., 281
academy. *See* Platonic Academy of Florence
Acciaiuoli, Agnolo, 21n, 22, 35, 68, 70, 73, 86, 89–90, 207, 235
Acciaiuoli, Alessandro, 209n
Acciaiuoli, Donato di Iacopo, 60
Acciaiuoli, Donato di Neri, x, 5, 27n, 43, 57, 58, 59, 64, 68, 69, 70, 71–72, 104–105, 107–108, 109, 111–12, 115n, 122, 124, 130n, 132–33, 141, 173, 202–230, 234n, 261n, 265, 270, 271, 272; career, 35–37, 59–61, 72–76, 80–82, 86, 115n, 202–207; and Studio controversy, 78n, 82–83, 86–91, 97, 99, 100–101, 103–104, 105, 125n; notes on Argyropoulos's lectures, 4, 76, 110n, 111, 114, 115n, 126, 205, 207–208, 208n, 208–211, 214–217; commentary on Aristotle, *Nicomachean Ethics*, 4, 15, 37, 46, 50, 99n, 126, 203, 204, 205–206, 209–222, 224–25, 229, 230n; commentary on Aristotle, *Politics*, 204, 226–29; letterbook, 37, 86n, 101n, 222–23; oration before the Compagnia de' Magi, 133, 135–36, 225–26; funeral orations and consolatory works, 37, 223, 224, 227n; translations of Plutarch, 37, 43, 63, 224
Acciaiuoli, Maddalena (Strozzi), 68
Acciaiuoli, Piero, 59–60, 61, 72
Acciaiuoli, Zenobi, 136, 181
Acciaiuoli circle. *See* Florentine Lyceum
Acciaiuoli family, 235n
Accolti, Benedetto, 40n, 102n, 140, 145, 148
Aegidius Romanus. *See* Giles of Rome

Agli, Antonio degli, 160, 173n, 177n, 181; and Lorenzo Pisano, 161, 168, 170; *De mystica statera*, 136, 136–37, 173–74, 180–81, 184–85, 200
Agli, Pellegrino degli, 16, 176, 181–82, 183, 183n, 194, 197, 234n
Agli family, 16, 44, 272
Agnolo da Lecco, 74n, 74–75, 88, 99, 206
Alamanni, Andrea, 78n, 84–85, 88n, 90–92, 96n, 97, 100, 101–102, 104, 132
Alberti, Francesco di Altobianco, 233
Alberti, Leon Battista, ix, 13, 25, 26n, 27, 45–46, 66, 131, 157–58; and Cristoforo Landino, 8, 205, 233, 235n, 252n, 256, 263, 265
Alberti, Lucrezia di Alberto di Adovardo degli, 236
Albertus Magnus, 206
Albizzi faction. *See under* conspiracies and tumults
Alessandra, 233
Alessandri, Alessandro degli, 27n, 29, 42n
Alfonso V of Aragon, 67
Alfonso de Palencia, 5n, 58n, 107–108
Ammannati, Iacopo, 36n, 72, 73, 74n, 75, 80n, 81n, 86, 98n, 109n, 206n, 263n
Anacharsis, 26
Anaxagoras, 119
Antoninus, Saint, 133n, 136, 177, 181
Antonio Battista, 30
Antonio di Mariano. *See* Muzi, Antonio di Mariano
Antonio Serafico da San Miniato. *See* Morali, Antonio
appetitus naturalis, 146, 147

women (*cont.*)
   marriage; sexuality and conjugal relations

Xanthus Viriatus (*or* Viretus). *See* Viriatus, Xanthus

Xenocrates (ps.-). *See under* Ficino, Marsilio
Xenophon, 72, 85

Zanobi, Iacopo, 103n
Zoroaster, 119